lonely planet

Atlantic Canada

Newfoundland & Labrador p165

New Brunswick p105

Prince Edward Island p138

Nova Scotia p50

Darcy Rhyno, Jennifer Bain, Cathy Donaldson, Carolyn Heller

Crab traps, Victoria-by-the-Sea (p146), Prince Edward Island

CONTENTS

Plan Your Trip

The Guide

Land Acknowledgement

Lonely Planet respectfully acknowledges that Canada is the traditional territory of more than 630 First Nations communities as well as Inuit and Métis communities. We offer gratitude to the Indigenous Peoples for their care for, and teachings about, this land.

Gros Morne National Park (p196), Newfoundland

Toolkit

Storybook

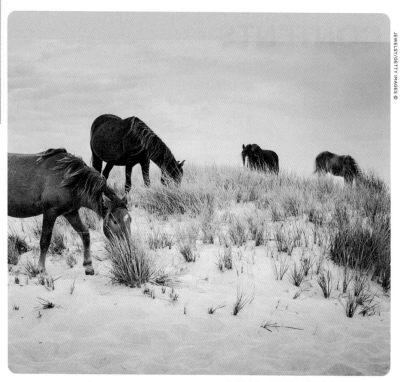

Sable Island National Park Reserve (p62)

ATLANTIC CANADA

THE JOURNEY BEGINS HERE

Atlantic Canada is my backyard, my playground, my home. The connection is more than family, more than familiarity. It has as much to do with the sheer variety of landscape, heritage and experience around me. One morning I might be eye to eye with the world's largest mammals on a whale-watching tour, and in the afternoon I can be on a petroglyph tour with an Indigenous guide. That evening I might be sipping the world's best sparkling wine in the vineyard that grew the grapes. The thread that ties such disparate experiences together is the reliable affability of the people. Sure, every destination claims its people are the friendliest, but in Atlantic Canada, hospitality and friendliness are a way of life. I know because warmly welcoming visitors is in my blood, and it's what I'm hoping to achieve in these pages.

Darcy Rhyno

darcyrhyno.com

Darcy started as a fiction writer, so his travel work is founded in storytelling.

My favorite experience is a day trip to Sable Island reserve (p62), the 40km sandbar inhabited only by 500 wild horses, 400,000 seals and a scientist or two – it's like a mid-Atlantic safari.

WHO GOES WHERE

Our writers choose the places that, for them, define Atlantic Canada.

SUMMIT ART CREATIONS/SHUTTERSTOCK ©

My summer place on **Fogo Island** is on an island off an island. Newfoundland and Labrador are home to three of my favorite things: puffins (pictured), icebergs and whales. But what stands out is just how much people love to chat. You really do have to factor that into your plans for the day.

Jennifer Bain

@thesaucylady

Jennifer is a journalist and author who travels the world in search of quirk. *Read more about Fogo Island on p186.*

WENDYCOTIE/SHUTTERSTOCKK ©

It's a lovely summer day in **Moncton**. After a short drive, we arrive at a favorite beach – Parlee (pictured) or Aboiteau – for a picnic dinner and sunset stroll. Chairs unfolded beneath a pink-tinged sky, we settle in and crack open the cooler. Life is good.

Cathy Donaldson

@cathykdonaldson

Cathy has been exploring the world as a travel writer based in New Brunswick for more than two decades. *Read more about Moncton on p113.*

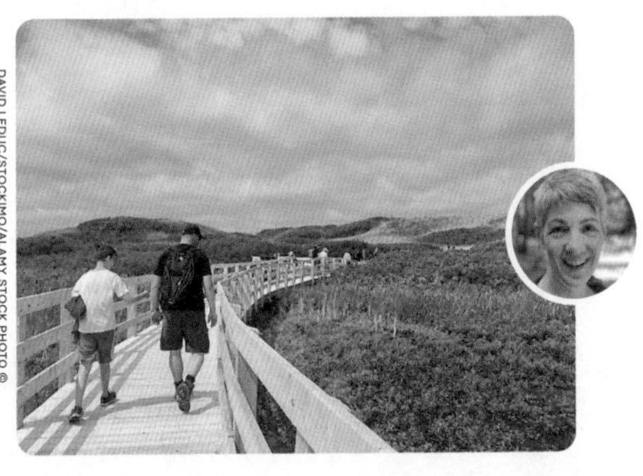

DAVID LEDUC/STOCKIMO/ALAMY STOCK PHOTO ©

I fell in love with Prince Edward Island when I spent five days on the **Island Walk**. While I walked only 120km of the 700km route, my wanderings took me along sandy beaches, above red cliffs and through fields of wildflowers, with plenty of seafood chowder, mussels and locally caught lobster to fuel my days.

Carolyn Heller

@CarolynBHeller

Based in Vancouver, Carolyn writes about culture, food and offbeat adventures. *Read more about the Island Walk on p145.*

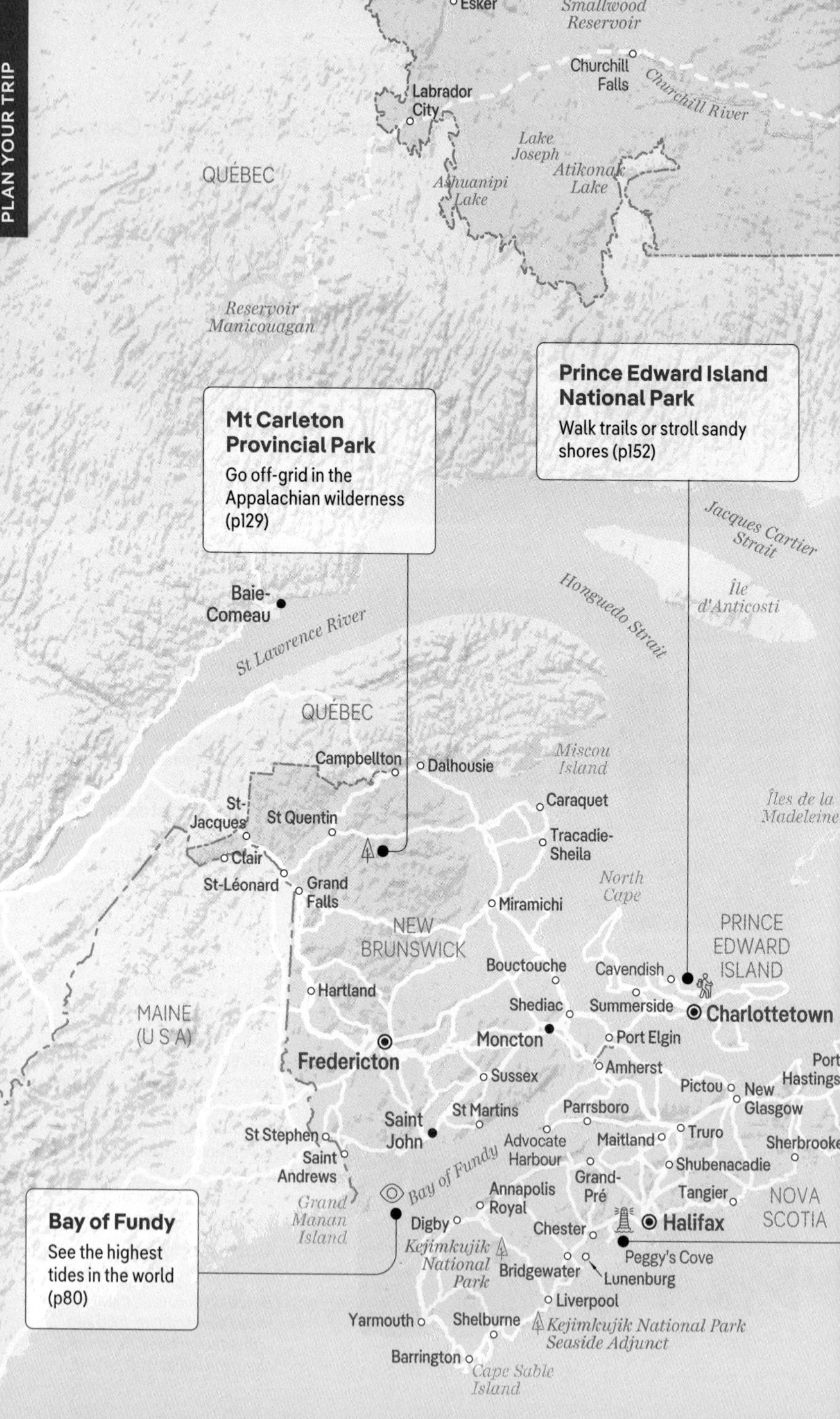

Esker
Smallwood Reservoir
Churchill Falls
Churchill River
Labrador City
Lake Joseph
Atikonak Lake
Ashuanipi Lake
QUÉBEC
Reservoir Manicouagan
Prince Edward Island National Park
Walk trails or stroll sandy shores (p152)
Mt Carleton Provincial Park
Go off-grid in the Appalachian wilderness (p129)
Jacques Cartier Strait
Île d'Anticosti
Honguedo Strait
Baie-Comeau
St Lawrence River
QUÉBEC
Miscou Island
Campbellton
Dalhousie
Caraquet
Îles de la Madeleine
St-Jacques
St Quentin
Tracadie-Sheila
Clair
St-Léonard
Grand Falls
North Cape
Miramichi
NEW BRUNSWICK
PRINCE EDWARD ISLAND
Bouctouche
Cavendish
Hartland
Shediac
Summerside
Charlottetown
MAINE (U S A)
Moncton
Port Elgin
Fredericton
Amherst
Port Hastings
Sussex
Pictou
New Glasgow
Saint John
St Martins
Parrsboro
St Stephen
Advocate Harbour
Maitland
Truro
Sherbrooke
Saint Andrews
Shubenacadie
Bay of Fundy
Grand-Pré
Grand Manan Island
Annapolis Royal
Tangier
NOVA SCOTIA
Bay of Fundy
See the highest tides in the world (p80)
Digby
Chester
Halifax
Kejimkujik National Park
Bridgewater
Peggy's Cove
Lunenburg
Liverpool
Yarmouth
Shelburne
Kejimkujik National Park Seaside Adjunct
Barrington
Cape Sable Island

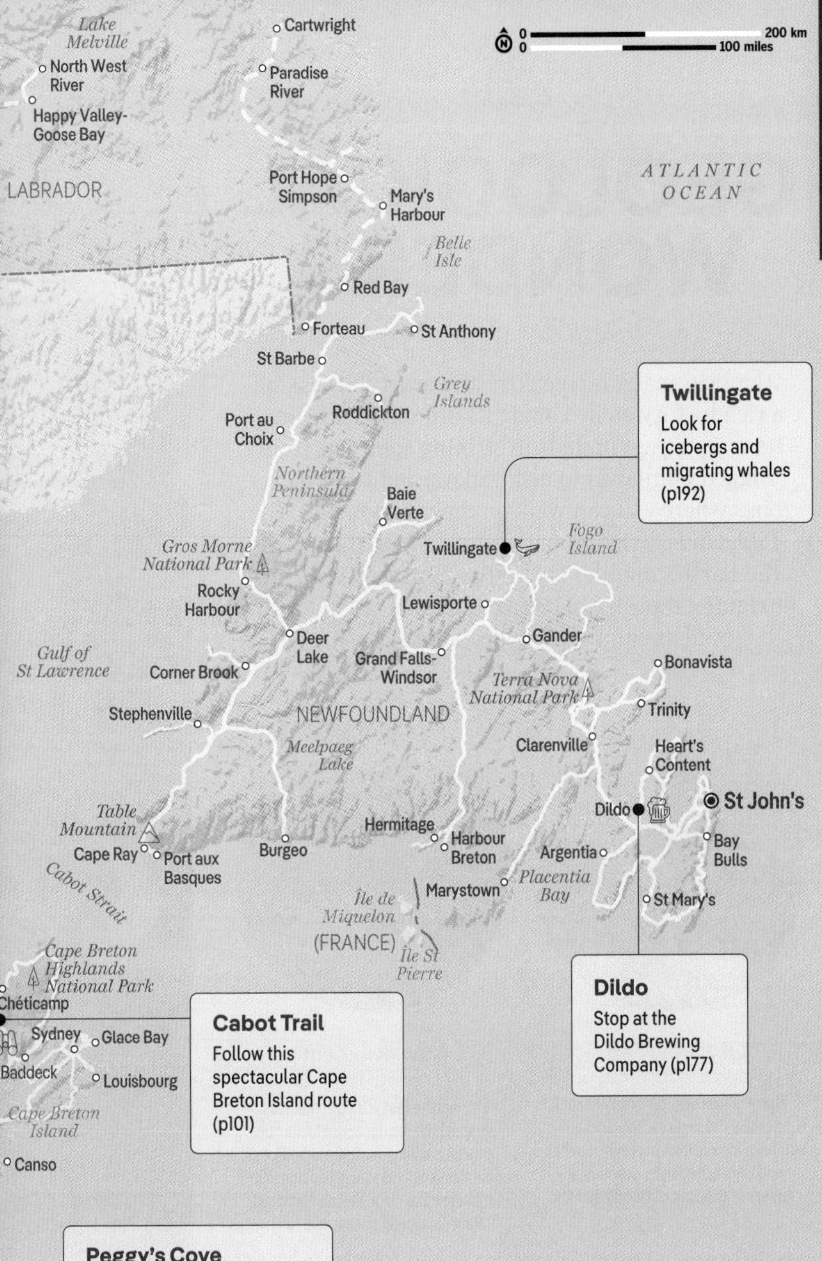

0 200 km
0 100 miles
Lake Melville
Cartwright
North West River
Happy Valley-Goose Bay
Paradise River
LABRADOR
Port Hope Simpson
Mary's Harbour
ATLANTIC OCEAN
Belle Isle
Red Bay
Forteau
St Anthony
St Barbe
Grey Islands
Roddickton
Port au Choix
Northern Peninsula
Baie Verte
Twillingate
Fogo Island
Gros Morne National Park
Rocky Harbour
Lewisporte
Gander
Deer Lake
Gulf of St Lawrence
Corner Brook
Grand Falls-Windsor
Bonavista
Terra Nova National Park
Trinity
Stephenville
NEWFOUNDLAND
Clarenville
Meelpaeg Lake
Heart's Content
Dildo
St John's
Table Mountain
Hermitage
Harbour Breton
Cape Ray
Port aux Basques
Burgeo
Argentia
Bay Bulls
Placentia Bay
Marystown
Cabot Strait
Île de Miquelon
(FRANCE)
Île St Pierre
St Mary's
Cape Breton Highlands National Park
Chéticamp
Sydney
Glace Bay
Baddeck
Louisbourg
Cape Breton Island
Canso
ATLANTIC OCEAN
Twillingate
Look for icebergs and migrating whales (p192)
Cabot Trail
Follow this spectacular Cape Breton Island route (p101)
Dildo
Stop at the Dildo Brewing Company (p177)
Peggy's Cove
Visit Nova Scotia's best-known lighthouse (p65)

GEOLOGICAL WONDERS

Atlantic Canada is a geological marvel showcasing a rich history etched along its dramatic coastline. Its unique past unfolds in striking contrasts from rugged highlands to lush valleys, and from tidal zones where you can walk on the ocean floor to the Tablelands, where you can stroll exposed parts of the Earth's mantle. The region is packed with an intriguing tapestry of rock and terrain to explore as well as significant collections of fossils.

Rock Medley

There's amazing diversity in rock across the region. See ancient volcanic formations in Newfoundland and Labrador, and sedimentary layers in the Bay of Fundy's cliffs.

Glacial Impact

During the last ice age, glaciers shaped the landscape of Atlantic Canada, carving its distinctive fjords and valleys and shaping the coastline in places like Gros Morne National Park (pictured above and left).

Canadian Appalachians

Much of Atlantic Canada is within the Canadian Appalachian Region, a continuation of the Appalachian Mountains that stretch through the eastern United States.

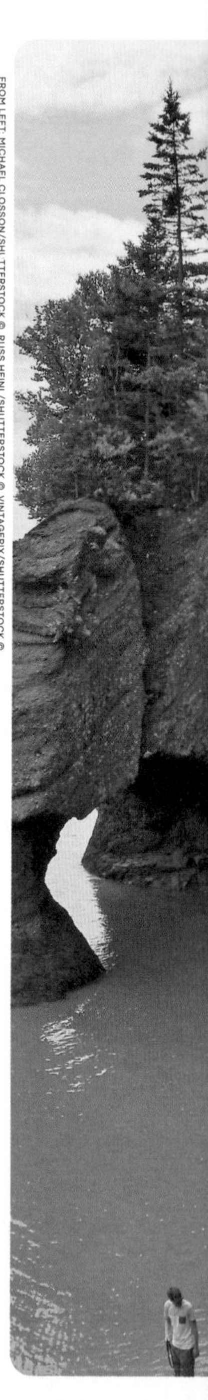

Hopewell Rocks Provincial Park (p119), Bay of Fundy

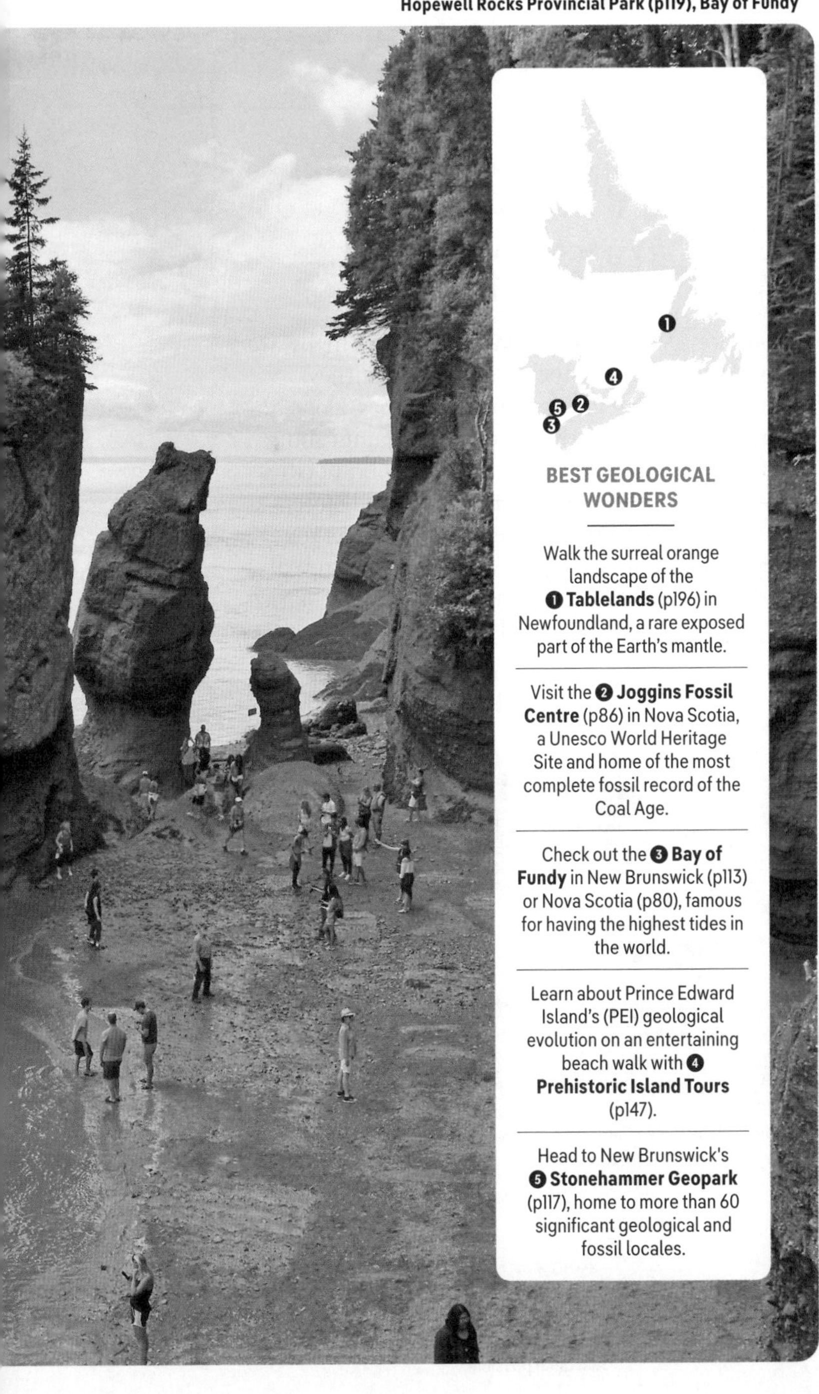

BEST GEOLOGICAL WONDERS

Walk the surreal orange landscape of the ❶ **Tablelands** (p196) in Newfoundland, a rare exposed part of the Earth's mantle.

Visit the ❷ **Joggins Fossil Centre** (p86) in Nova Scotia, a Unesco World Heritage Site and home of the most complete fossil record of the Coal Age.

Check out the ❸ **Bay of Fundy** in New Brunswick (p113) or Nova Scotia (p80), famous for having the highest tides in the world.

Learn about Prince Edward Island's (PEI) geological evolution on an entertaining beach walk with ❹ **Prehistoric Island Tours** (p147).

Head to New Brunswick's ❺ **Stonehammer Geopark** (p117), home to more than 60 significant geological and fossil locales.

SCENIC ROADS & HIGHWAYS

Prepare for a visual feast. Atlantic Canada's highways and roads lead visitors on inspiring journeys, rolling through picturesque landscapes, along coastal cliffs and sandy shores, past quaint fishing villages, through lush valleys and into vibrant cities and towns. Even if you've traveled here before, you'll find your breath taken away again as you ascend mountains and stop at lookoffs that reveal panoramic vistas of the expansive Atlantic. Memories will be etched forever.

Catch a Whale

While driving in the region, you might spot whales breaching in the Bay of Fundy, or whales, dolphins or porpoises at the Canso Causeway.

Farm-to-road Flavors

Carry cash for roadside stands offering produce such as berries and veggies. No staff? Follow the honor system: choose your product, leave payment in the jar.

Animal Alert

Drive with care, as this region is home to moose, deer, bears and other critters. Wear a seat belt. Avoid driving at night if possible.

Cabot Trail (p101)

BEST DRIVING EXPERIENCES

Drive Newfoundland's ❶ **Viking Trail** (p204) for Norse history, icebergs, geological and natural wonders, and World Heritage Sites.

Follow Nova Scotia's spectacular ❷ **Cabot Trail** (p101) along undulating coastline, up mountains and into communities rich in history and culture.

Discover 11,000 years of human history and 300 million years of natural history in Nova Scotia's ❸ **Cliffs of Fundy Unesco Geopark** (p84).

Meander along the ❹ **Fundy Trail Parkway** (p113) in New Brunswick, a stunning 30km route that hugs the Bay of Fundy.

Sample PEI potatoes, listen to the wind and sleep in a lighthouse along the ❺ **North Cape Coastal Drive** (p163).

SEASIDE TOWNS

Visitors can find a bounty of charming seaside towns and villages across the Atlantic region. Each holds stories of seafaring pasts and offers a warm welcome. Accommodations in these coastal gems range from quiet inns to luxe hotels bursting with amenities. Dining options can also vary from homey diners to upscale restaurants. Take a walk in the salty air, explore local history, crack open a lobster, decompress. Embrace the soothing rhythm of coastal life.

Shoot the Breeze

Many seaside towns and villages have wharves where fishers may be found. Don't hesitate to ask them about their trade. They're generally happy to chat.

Attend a Festival

When planning your visit to a town, check local calendars for upcoming festivals – a fun way to glimpse local life, music, heritage and food.

Embrace the Weather

Pack layers for unpredictable weather in coastal towns and villages. Even in summer, it can be breezy and cool. Bring decent footwear for exploring.

Lunenburg (p64)

BEST SEASIDE-TOWN EXPERIENCES

Take in ❶ **Twillingate** (p192), at the heart of Iceberg Alley in Newfoundland, for the chance to see glacial giants and migrating whales.

Venture to Nova Scotia's Unesco-listed ❷ **Lunenburg** (p64), renowned for its colorful architecture, shipbuilding heritage and vibrant seafaring culture.

Set course for ❸ **Saint Andrews** (p121), a charming New Brunswick town with a rich history, lush gardens and whale-watching tours.

Eat your way through PEI's ❹ **Victoria-by-the-Sea** (p146), sampling freshly shucked oysters and warm lobster rolls.

Make ❺ **Fundy-St Martins** (p120) your New Brunswick base for seaside rejuvenation or a launchpad to sea-cave adventures or scenic motoring on the Fundy Trail Parkway.

GO OFF-GRID

You can truly make the great escape in Atlantic Canada. Find peace off-grid amid pristine landscapes. Unplug along rugged coastlines, hike ancient forests and paddle tranquil waters. Swap your computer screen for a star-filled sky. Discover hidden coves, picnic on secluded shores, do yoga on the beach. Whatever path or activity your choose, look forward to restoring your spirit, mind and body. And if you want to connect with others, local hospitality is never far away.

Sustainable Stays

Consider backcountry camping or staying at eco-friendly lodges that prioritize sustainable practices. Immerse yourself in nature, with minimal impact. Leave no trace.

Responsible Hiking

Particularly in protected areas, stay on marked paths to minimize your impact on fragile ecosystems. Straying off trails can lead to erosion and disrupt habitats.

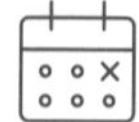

When to Go

The best time for off-grid camping or hiking is May to September. The weather is warmer and there are longer daylight hours.

Nature Space Resort & Retreat Centre (p156)

BEST OFF-GRID EXPERIENCES

Take a ferry to ❶ **Miquelon** (p184), the less-traveled island that's part of St-Pierre and Miquelon, off Newfoundland, for a day's hiking.

Visit Nova Scotia's ❷ **Cape Chignecto Provincial Park** (p86), a premier wilderness experience with backcountry camping and Bay of Fundy views.

Hike and camp in the Appalachians, and do some stargazing, at New Brunswick's ❸ **Mt Carleton Provincial Park** (p129), a designated dark-sky preserve.

Make tracks for ❹ **Kouchibouguac** (p114) or ❹ **Fundy National Park** (p114) in New Brunswick, where you'll find backcountry campsites and great hikes.

Paddle an ocean lagoon and snuggle into a yurt at PEI's ❺ **Nature Space Resort** (p156).

JUST BEACHY

You're never too far from an ocean, large lake, bay or strait in Atlantic Canada. That's good news for many, especially those who love the beach. Some locals take a bracing stroll midwinter or a spring jaunt to build a sandcastle in anticipation of the upcoming season. Visitors and locals alike treasure summer beach days most, to bask in the sun, splash in the waves or take a dip in some of the country's warmest waters.

FROM LEFT: MATHEW SHAWN TURNER/SHUTTERSTOCK ©, JAMES MARSHALL/GETTY IMAGES ©, DOUG MCLEAN/SHUTTERSTOCK ©

Beach Season

The summer beach season runs from about late June to early September. Lifeguard supervision at some beaches begins around July 1 and ends late August.

Accessible Beaches

Many beaches in Atlantic Canada have accessibility features, such as mats to allow those with mobility issues safe access to the beach and water.

Water Quality

Check beach signage or local water-quality advisories before swimming. While many beaches are pristine, occasional advisories may be issued due to rainfall or bacterial levels.

New River Beach (p124)

BEST BEACH EXPERIENCES

Join the crowds on ❶ **St Vincent's Beach** (p246) in Newfoundland when humpback whales gorge on capelin close to shore.

Go for a dip or enjoy the views at one of New Brunswick's top beaches, such as ❷ **Parlee** or ❷ **Aboiteau** (p114).

Hike across rugged terrain to the observation deck at Nova Scotia's ❸ **Kejimkujik National Park Seaside** (p69), overlooking vast silver beaches with plentiful seals and seabirds.

Wander trails between the dunes or stroll sandy shores in ❹ **Prince Edward Island National Park** (p152).

Visit New Brunswick's breathtaking ❺ **New River Beach** (p124), great for swimming, building sand sculptures and hiking nearby trails.

FROM LEFT: LESPALENIK/SHUTTERSTOCK ©, JIAQING/SHUTTERSTOCK ©, KNIPSDESIGN/SHUTTERSTOCK ©

FOR THE LOVE OF LIGHTHOUSES

Traditional red-and-white lighthouses are an iconic part of Atlantic Canada's landscape. These sentinels that guided ships through treacherous waters may no longer be operating or open to the public, but they remain popular among tourists and locals. They're often excellent destinations for hikes, picnics and photography. The federal government has designated many lighthouses under the Heritage Lighthouse Protection Act and transferred them to new owners across Canada. The status recognizes their beauty and historical importance.

Still Working

While many beacons have been replaced by automated units, 23 staffed lighthouses still operate in Newfoundland and Labrador, and one on New Brunswick's Machias Seal Island.

Easternmost Beacon

Cape Spear Lighthouse (pictured above), the oldest surviving lighthouse in Newfoundland and Labrador, is perched on a cliff overlooking the Atlantic at North America's easternmost point.

Oldest Light

In 1758, the oldest existing lighthouse in North America was built on Sambro Island at the entrance to Halifax harbor.

Peggy's Cove (p65)

BEST LIGHTHOUSE EXPERIENCES

Climb the stone tower of Newfoundland's ❶ **Cape Bonavista Lighthouse** (p180) to see a light that was fueled with seal oil in the 1800s.

Admire the red-capped lighthouse at ❷ **Peggy's Cove** (p65), Nova Scotia's best-known beacon, now with an accessible viewing platform.

Check out the whale skeleton, climb the lighthouse tower and walk the coastal trail at ❸ **Cape Forchu** (p74) in Nova Scotia.

Take the short trail to ❹ **Swallowtail Lighthouse** (p123), perched at the northern end of New Brunswick's Grand Manan Island and ideal for sunsets.

Clamber to the lookout atop PEI's oldest lightstation, ❺ **Point Prim Lighthouse** (p147), built in 1845.

ON TAP

While the industry may not be new, craft breweries continue to be extremely popular in Atlantic Canada. Small, independent operations are popping up everywhere, so there's an almost dizzying array of options to try. Sample wheat beers, pale ales, ambers, stouts and many more, some flavored with locally sourced ingredients such as blueberries, spruce and lobster (yes, really). And that packaging! Many canned products in the region feature striking, innovative designs. Cheers!

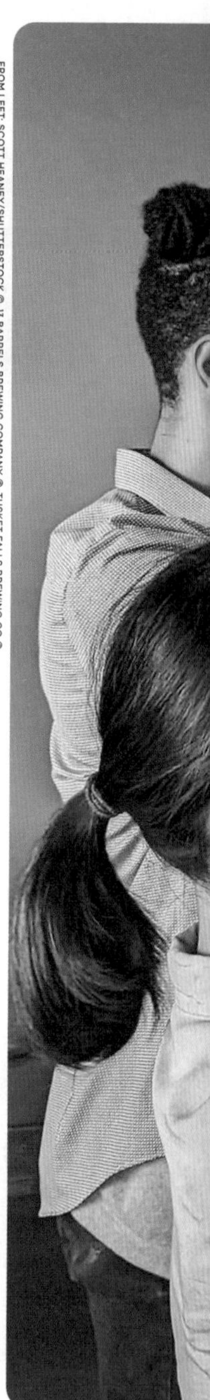

A Beer for All Tastes

Options range from Tatamagouche's Two Rivers Baltic Porter to Trailway's Pretty Please Sour Ale and everything in between.

Social Hubs

Craft-beer taprooms are often the gathering places of small towns, villages and even some cities. Their relaxed, friendly vibe is a huge draw.

Enjoy Responsibly

Indulge in Atlantic Canada's craft-beer scene safely. Designate a driver who will be sticking to non-alcoholic drinks or use other transportation to get you around.

Tusket Falls Brewing Co (p72), Yarmouth

BEST BREWERY EXPERIENCES

Stop at Newfoundland's **1 Dildo Brewing Co** (pictured far left; p177), in a tiny seaside town that boasts a Hollywood-style sign for its attention-grabbing name.

Relax on the patio at **2 Tusket Falls Brewing Co** (p72) in Nova Scotia with a pint of crisp Slow by Nature lager.

See why Nova Scotia's **3 Tatamagouche Brewing** (p83) is a favorite for its ales and IPAs while excelling at session beers and barrel-aged brews.

Enjoy magnificent views at friendly **4 13 Barrels** (pictured left; p131) in Bathurst, New Brunswick, home of the award-winning Gnarly Light Lager and Tall Tales IPA.

Drink beer and benefit the community at **5 Upstreet** (p144), PEI's first B-Corp certified company.

REGIONS & CITIES

Find the places that tick all your boxes.

Newfoundland & Labrador

ICEBERGS, PUFFINS AND GEOLOGICAL WONDERS

This province is two in one: Newfoundland's island and Labrador's mainland. From downtown St John's to the smallest outport, you'll be greeted by friendly locals, great music and good times. After a cod moratorium wiped out fishing for many, the resilient folks here now celebrate other treasures, including icebergs, puffins and whales.

p165

New Brunswick

NATURAL WONDERS AND CULTURAL PRIDE

New Brunswick offers family fun, outdoor adventure, historical and cultural attractions, and fantastic seafood. In dynamic cities, quaint towns and charming seaside villages, find outstanding restaurants and galleries, cute shops and festivals galore. Walk on the ocean floor, hike national parks, go whale watching and make memories on dreamy coastal shores.

p105

Nova Scotia

OCEAN PLAYGROUND AND CULTURAL HOMELAND

Nova Scotia's varied landscape includes ocean shores, lakes, highlands, forests and tidal wonders. Its cultural fabric is equally diverse, as Mi'kmaw, Acadian, Celtic, British and African legacies weave a rich tapestry with more recent immigration. Traditions including lobster suppers and fiddle music thrive from urban Halifax to the province's tiniest villages.

p50

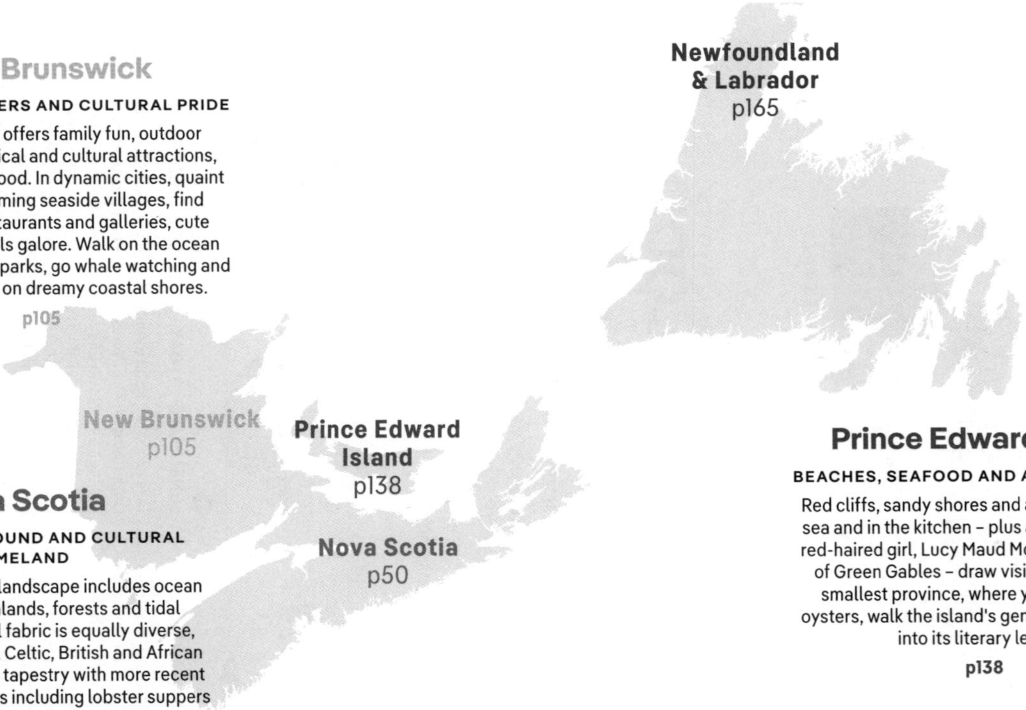

Prince Edward Island

BEACHES, SEAFOOD AND A BELOVED ANNE

Red cliffs, sandy shores and adventures on the sea and in the kitchen – plus a famous fictional red-haired girl, Lucy Maud Montgomery's Anne of Green Gables – draw visitors to Canada's smallest province, where you can tong for oysters, walk the island's gentle terrain and dig into its literary legacy.

p138

METALPRINTS/SHUTTERSTOCK ©

Peggy's Cove (p65)

ITINERARIES

Nova Scotia Loop

Allow: 7 days **Distance**: 880km

This itinerary showcases historical and natural diversity within easy reach of Halifax. Explore beautiful Peggy's Cove and the Unesco-listed old town of Lunenburg, wander the picturesque streets of Liverpool, savor the vineyards of Wolfville and end your journey in Joggins, where the relentless tides have carved magnificent cliffs and exposed fascinating fossils.

1 HALIFAX 2 DAYS

Soak up some culture and history on the **Halifax** (p56) waterfront. Visit the **Halifax Citadel National Historic Site** (p56) for panoramic views and more background on the city. Head to a local pub or a fine-dining restaurant before settling in for the night. Venture to **Peggy's Cove** (p65) the next day to see its famed lighthouse. Plan to spend the night in Lunenburg.

2 LUNENBURG 1 DAY

Take a morning stroll through **Lunenburg** (p64), a World Heritage Site known for its colorful buildings. Historic tall ship the **Bluenose** (p64) was built in Lunenburg, and you can still see a replica vessel here. Travel to **Kejimkujik National Park Seaside Unit** (p69) for a spectacular hike. The popular Harbour Rocks trail and Port Joli Head trail both feature coastal terrain and impressive views.

3 LIVERPOOL 1 DAY

Enjoy a sunset dinner at **White Point Beach Resort** (p68) just south of **Liverpool** (p68), and stay the night at the resort. Wake up to panoramic views of the Atlantic Ocean. After a snack stop in Liverpool, journey to pretty **Annapolis Royal** (p76), visiting **Port Royal** (p77), the first permanent settlement in what would become Canada, and **Fort Anne National Historic Site** (p78).

FROM LEFT: DANNY KRONSTROM/SHUTTERSTOCK ©, LAZYLLAMA/SHUTTERSTOCK ©, REGINE POIRIER/SHUTTERSTOCK ©

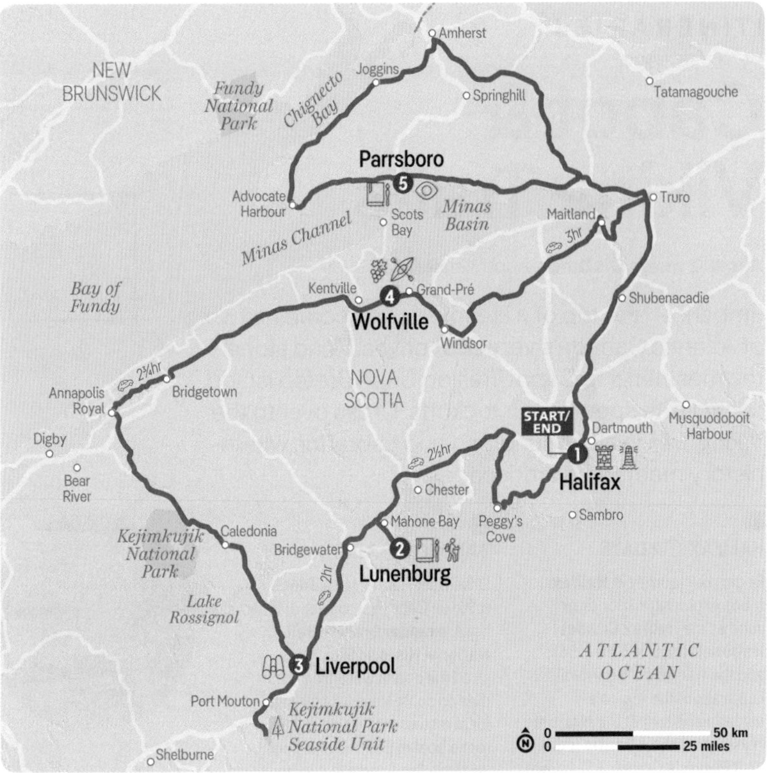

4 WOLFVILLE 2 DAYS

After staying overnight in **Wolfville** (p80), visit the nearby wineries and end the day with a meal at a fine vineyard restaurant. The next day, tour **Grand-Pré National Historic Site** (p81), a poignant symbol of Acadian heritage that commemorates the forced deportation of Acadian settlers in 1755. Continue to Maitland for a **tidal-bore adventure** (p85) on the Shubenacadie River. End the day in Parrsboro.

5 PARRSBORO 1 DAY

Check out the Cliffs of Fundy Geopark by first exploring the **Fundy Geological Museum** (p85). Drive through charming **Advocate Harbour** (p84) en route to the **Joggins fossil cliffs** (p86), a Unesco World Heritage Site and home to the most complete fossil record of the Coal Age. From here you can easily return to Halifax, or continue to Prince Edward Island (PEI) or other destinations.

ITINERARIES

Cabot & Viking Trails

Allow: 2 weeks **Distance**: approximately 1500km

Embark on the trip of a lifetime as you combine two of Atlantic Canada's very best drives. Wind along the mesmerizing Cabot Trail on Cape Breton Island, taking in its spectacular lookoffs. Cross over to the Viking Trail in Newfoundland and Labrador, where history meets wild landscapes.

1 HALIFAX 2 DAYS

Begin your journey in **Halifax** (p56), exploring visitor draws such as the **Halifax Citadel National Historic Site** (p56) and the waterfront boardwalk. Learn about the region's seafaring history at the **Maritime Museum of the Atlantic** (p63). Visit **Peggy's Cove** (p65), known for its iconic lighthouse. Enjoy local cuisine at one of the many outstanding restaurants in the area.

2 BADDECK 2 DAYS

Drive from Halifax to **Baddeck** (p96) on Cape Breton Island. Visit the **Alexander Graham Bell National Historic Site** (p99), stroll the quaint waterfront and dine on some fresh lobster at a local restaurant. The next day, rent a boat in Baddeck Harbour and view landmarks including Kidston Island Lighthouse from the water. For golfers, there's 18-hole Bell Bay, with views of stunning Bras d'Or Lake.

3 INGONISH 2 DAYS

Continue on the Cabot Trail to **Ingonish**. Hike trails with ocean views in **Cape Breton Highlands National Park** (p99). Splash in the waves at Ingonish Beach and soak in nature's beauty. The next day, hike along the Middle Head trail, play a round of golf at Keltic Lodge – Stanley Thompson's famous 'mountains and oceans' course – or sign up for a **whale-watching** adventure.

4 MARGAREE HARBOUR 2 DAYS

From Ingonish, head to the western side of Cape Breton Island and the **Skyline Trail** (p100), one of the top hikes on the island. Stop in **Chéticamp** (p99) to learn about the community's rich Acadian culture. Stay in **Margaree Harbour** (p99), then visit Inverness Beach, golf at Cabot Cape Breton, go tubing on the Margaree River or sample single-malt whiskey at the Glenora Distillery.

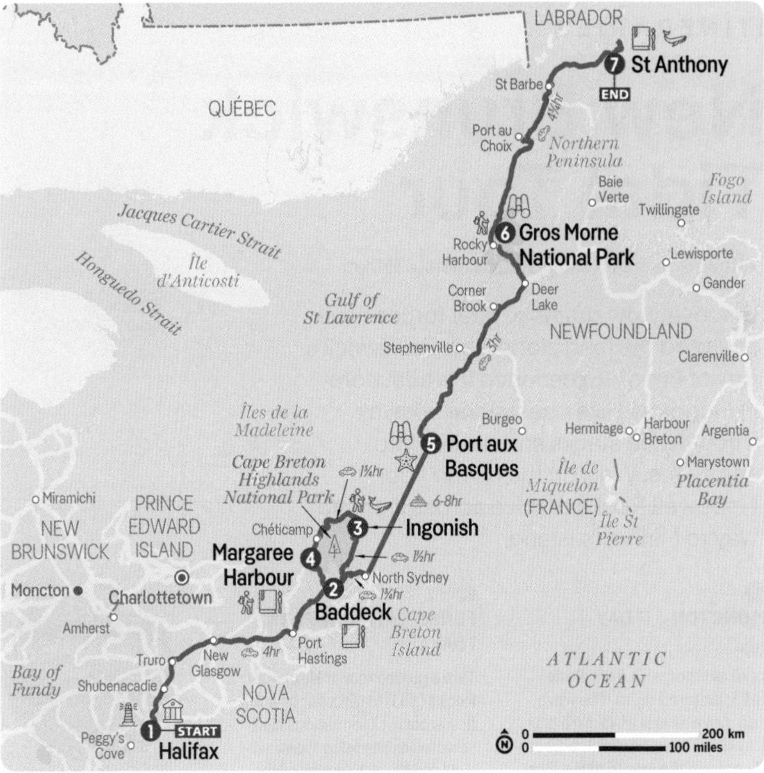

LABRADOR
QUÉBEC
7 St Anthony
END
St Barbe
4¾hr
Port au Choix
Northern Peninsula
Baie Verte
Fogo Island
Twillingate
6 Gros Morne National Park
Rocky Harbour
Lewisporte
Jacques Cartier Strait
Île d'Anticosti
Honguedo Strait
Gulf of St Lawrence
Corner Brook
Deer Lake
Gander
NEWFOUNDLAND
Stephenville
3hr
Clarenville
Îles de la Madeleine
Burgeo
Hermitage
Harbour Breton
Argentia
5 Port aux Basques
Cape Breton Highlands National Park
1¼hr
Marystown
Île de Miquelon (FRANCE)
Placentia Bay
6-8hr
Miramichi
PRINCE EDWARD ISLAND
NEW BRUNSWICK
Chéticamp
3 Ingonish
Île St Pierre
4 Margaree Harbour
½hr
North Sydney
Moncton
Charlottetown
2 Baddeck
1¼hr
Cape Breton Island
Amherst
Port Hastings
New Glasgow
4hr
Truro
ATLANTIC OCEAN
Bay of Fundy
Shubenacadie
NOVA SCOTIA
1 START Halifax
Peggy's Cove
0 200 km
0 100 miles

5 PORT AUX BASQUES ⏱1 DAY

The traditional **Cabot Trail** (p101) route takes visitors from Margaree Forks through Middle River and back to the Trans-Canada Hwy at Baddeck. Continue to North Sydney for the scenic six- to eight-hour ferry crossing to **Port aux Basques** in Newfoundland. On the way, enjoy onboard amenities and watch for marine wildlife. Reserve for this trip, and check Marine Atlantic for up-to-date information.

6 GROS MORNE NATIONAL PARK ⏱3 DAYS

From Port aux Basques, drive to Deer Lake and the start of the Viking Trail. Continue to **Gros Morne National Park** (p196), where you can explore fjords, hike Gros Morne Mountain, and walk on the Earth's mantle at the **Tablelands** (p196). Take a guided hike to better understand the area's geological significance. In Rocky Harbour, visit **Lobster Cove Lighthouse** (p198) and savor local seafood.

7 ST ANTHONY ⏱2 DAYS

From Gros Morne, head to **Port au Choix National Historic Site** (p203) for in-depth information about Indigenous cultures present in the region for thousands of years. Continue to Unesco-listed **L' Anse aux Meadows National Historic Site** (p204) to learn about the Vikings, the first Europeans to explore the area. Stay in St Anthony, where colossal icebergs and majestic whales grace the seascape.

ITINERARIES

New Brunswick Tidal Tour

Allow: 6 days **Distance**: approximately 350km

Discover how dramatic tidal forces have sculpted the land along New Brunswick's Bay of Fundy. Experience the tidal bore in Moncton. Hike coastal trails, kayak through sea stacks and paddle into sea caves. Walk on the ocean floor at Hopewell Rocks or drive across it on the way to Ministers Island.

1 MONCTON 1 DAY

Witness the intriguing tidal bore at Moncton's **Bore Park** (p113; pictured right). The wave can move as fast as 13km/h and travel 30km up the Petitcodiac River from the mouth of the Bay of Fundy. **Parlee Beach** (p114) in Shediac also showcases the tidal range: at low tide, expansive sandy shores are revealed that are entirely covered during higher tides. Spend the night in Moncton.

2 FUNDY NATIONAL PARK 1 DAY

Take a guided tour at **Hopewell Rocks** (p113) to discover how the flowerpot rock formations were sculpted by the tides. Consider a guided kayak tour around the sea stacks. Join a beach walk led by **Fundy National Park** (p114) naturalists and slosh through the mudflats where tiny sea creatures make their home. Spend the night in Fundy National Park or Alma.

3 FUNDY TRAIL PARKWAY 1 DAY

Drive along the **Fundy Trail Parkway** (p120), which hugs the Bay of Fundy. Get a map at the parkway entrance and be sure to park at P15 to take the **Walton Glen Gorge Trail** (p120), with breathtaking views of the 'Grand Canyon of New Brunswick'. Make other stops to explore, such as at **Long Beach**. Spend the night in Fundy-St Martins.

4 FUNDY-ST MARTINS 1 DAY

Explore tidal wonders in the fishing village of **Fundy-St Martins** (p120). Wander through captivating sea caves or go on a kayaking adventure into and around the caves. Witness the surreal spectacle of boats sitting on the ocean floor during low tide (pictured right), only to float again with the rising waters. Spend another night in Fundy-St Martins or in Saint John.

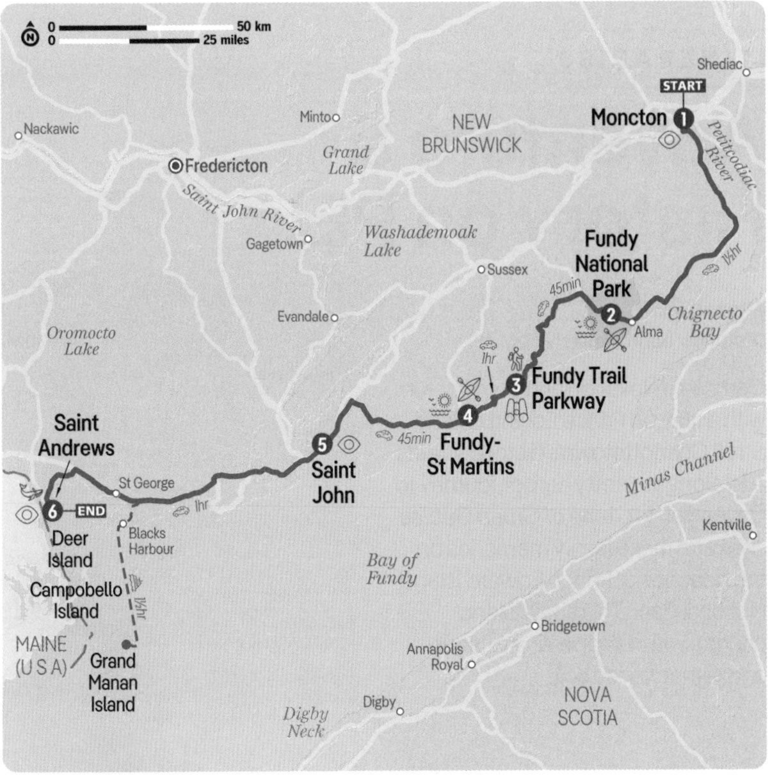

5

SAINT JOHN 1 DAY

Begin your stay in **Saint John** (p117) by learning about the surrounding **Stonehammer Geopark** (p119), whose geologic history goes back a billion years. Witness the **Reversing Falls rapids** (p119), created when the Bay of Fundy's powerful tides collide with the Saint John River's currents. Fuel up at one of uptown's many great restaurants. Spend the night in Saint Andrews.

6

SAINT ANDREWS 1 DAY

Saint Andrews (p121) is located between the mouth of the Saint-Croix River and Passamaquoddy Bay. Since the river is an inlet of the Bay of Fundy, it experiences the bay's huge tidal variations. At low tide, you can cross the ocean floor to **Ministers Island** (p123). During your stay, take a **whale-watching excursion**, and learn about tides and ecosystems at the **Fundy Discovery Aquarium** (p124).

Detour: *If time permits, extend your visit by a few days and venture to three islands in the Charlotte Coastal Region: Deer Island, Campobello and Grand Manan, nicknamed the 'Queen of the Fundy Isles.'*

ITINERARIES

Adventure & History on PEI

Allow: 1 week
Distance: approximately 500km

Combine relaxation and outdoor fun with a stay on Prince Edward Island. Stroll Charlottetown's historic streets and along its pretty harbor, journey to Cavendish for *Anne of Green Gables* sites and make family memories on the beaches of Prince Edward Island National Park. This small island charms with its appealing villages and signature red soil.

❶
CHARLOTTETOWN ⏱1 DAY

Head to provincial capital **Charlottetown** (p142). Take a tour or meander through the downtown, including the waterfront, with a stop at the **Confederation Centre of the Arts** (p142). Enjoy a seafood dinner at one of the city's upscale eateries or a friendly pub. If you're visiting the area during the summer Charlottetown Festival of theater and music, take in a show. Stay overnight in Charlottetown.

❷
VICTORIA-BY-THE-SEA ⏱1 DAY

Drive to historic **Victoria-by-the-Sea** (p146) to watch chocolate makers ply their trade at **Island Chocolate**. Stroll Water St or explore the coastline by kayak and fuel up with lunch at **Landmark Oyster House** (p146). Wander through the area's charming shops before a seafood feast at **Lobster Barn** (p146). Return to Charlottetown for the night.

Detour: *Travel west towards Summerside to check out the* ***Acadian Museum*** *(p162) in Miscouche. Stay in Summerside for the night.*

❸
CAVENDISH ⏱2 DAYS

Drive to **Cavendish** (p148). Explore Green Gables Heritage Place to see sites made famous in LM Montgomery's classic novel. Make tracks for the gorgeous beaches of **Prince Edward Island National Park** (p152). The next day, visit **North Rustico** (p149). Rent a kayak or bike, then recharge with fresh seafood at **New Glasgow Lobster Suppers** (p150). Spend a second night in Cavendish.

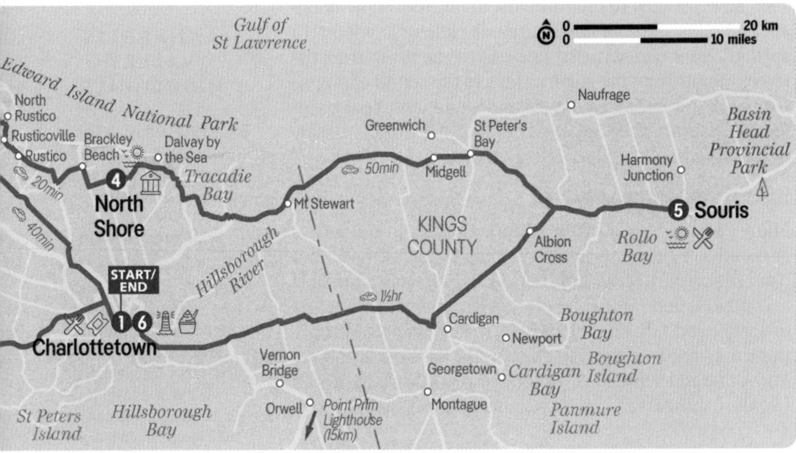

4

NORTH SHORE ⏱1 DAY

Drive east to **Brackley Beach** (p152). Discover local art and exceptional gardens at Dunes Studio Gallery & Café, and stay for lunch. Stop in at National Historic Site **Dalvay by the Sea**, set within Prince Edward Island National Park. Next, visit the park's heavenly **Greenwich section** (p153). Stay in atmospheric accommodations, such as **Mysa Nordic Spa & Resort** (p154) on St Peters Bay.

5

SOURIS ⏱1 DAY

The next day, head to **Basin Head Provincial Park** (p156) for lovely beaches and 'singing sands.' In **Souris** (p155), take a Lobster Lovers cruise with **The Fiddling Fisherman** (p155), then sample potato fudge at **Oh Fudge!** (p144). Experience the FireWorks Feast at chef Michael Smith's **Inn at Bay Fortune** (p158), then sleep in a floating wine barrel at **Nellie's Landing** (p157).

6

CHARLOTTETOWN ⏱1 DAY

In the morning, return to **Charlottetown**, stopping en route at **Point Prim Lighthouse** (p147). Have chowder by the water at **Point Prim Chowder House** (p146). In Charlottetown, wander to Victoria Row for live music or go on an **Experience PEI walking tour** (p144). Visit the flagship **COWS Creamery** shop (p147) for a delicious ice cream in a freshly made waffle cone before you leave.

WHEN TO GO

If you love snowy adventures, come in winter. Spring, summer and fall are generally the prime seasons.

While the sun, warm temperatures and sandy beaches are big draws for Atlantic Canada in summer, the other seasons have goodies to offer in most areas, too. Snowmobilers and other outdoor adventurers flock here in winter. In spring, visitors can witness the region come to life, from the sweet aroma of maple-sugar camps to the sound of migratory birds returning to forests and shorelines. Leaf peepers enjoy seeing the landscape burst into a vibrant display of red, orange and gold in fall.

Shoulder Seasons

Many people enjoy visiting Atlantic Canada in the warmer months of July and August, but you'll pay the most for a place to stay during this high season. Expect more affordable accommodations and fewer crowds in the shoulder seasons of spring and fall. Some lodgings, restaurants and attractions may not be open, but there's still lots to see and do. May–June and September–October give you the best of both worlds in most areas: decent weather and reasonable prices.

I LIVE HERE

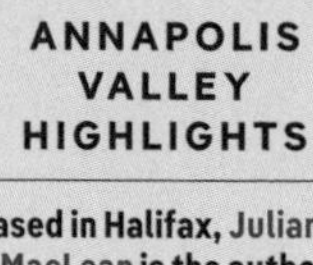

ANNAPOLIS VALLEY HIGHLIGHTS

Based in Halifax, Julianne MacLean is the author of more than 40 novels, several set in Atlantic Canada. @JulianneMacLean

I was the Annapolis Valley Apple Blossom Queen in 1986 and had the honor of touring all the charming historic towns in the valley. The festival is held every year in late May when the orchards are in full bloom. Whenever we have guests who come from afar, the dramatic lookoff at Blomidon is a top destination to show off our beautiful province.

Peggy's Cove (p65)

THE NOR'EASTER

This region is susceptible to intense nor'easter storms, so named because of the strong northeasterly winds that herald their arrival. These storms – more common in winter – may bring heavy snowfall and cause coastal flooding or other destruction.

Weather through the year (Halifax)

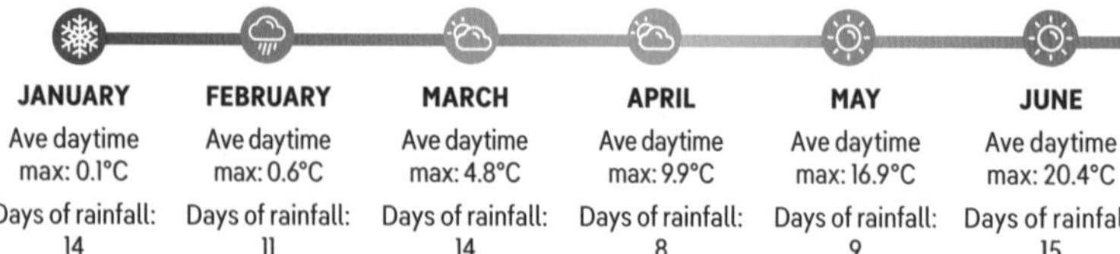

JANUARY
Ave daytime max: 0.1°C
Days of rainfall: 14

FEBRUARY
Ave daytime max: 0.6°C
Days of rainfall: 11

MARCH
Ave daytime max: 4.8°C
Days of rainfall: 14

APRIL
Ave daytime max: 9.9°C
Days of rainfall: 8

MAY
Ave daytime max: 16.9°C
Days of rainfall: 9

JUNE
Ave daytime max: 20.4°C
Days of rainfall: 15

SEA EFFECTS

If you come in summer or a shoulder season, keep in mind that Atlantic Canada is so named because of its location along the Atlantic Ocean, which distributes heat and moisture while driving weather systems. Expect occasional fog, showers or a downpour.

Festival Mania

Cavendish Beach Music Festival (p243) Multiday, all-ages outdoor spectacular in July that draws thousands to hear a lineup of top country artists perform in the seaside town of Cavendish, PEI. **July**

Atlantic Nationals Automotive Extravaganza (p114) Five-day July event in Moncton, New Brunswick, that revs up the area with the best of classic, vintage and custom automobiles. Car lovers from near and far take part. **July**

Writers at Woody Point (p196) August festival that attracts renowned authors, poets and storytellers from around the world. Attendees enjoy discussions, readings and workshops surrounded by Newfoundland's Gros Morne National Park. **August**

Celtic Colours International Festival (p97) Performers flock to this October festival, which showcases the rich heritage of Celtic music and culture through concerts and events held across Cape Breton Island, Nova Scotia. **October**

Fun & Fab

Annapolis Valley Apple Blossom Festival (p75) Nova Scotia's orchards in full bloom create a stunning backdrop for parades, concerts and family-friendly activities in May. **May**

Iceberg Festival (p204) Held in June, this event offers a unique opportunity to witness massive icebergs as they float past the Newfoundland coast from points north. Enjoy boat tours with licenced operators and cultural events during the festivities. **June**

Tyne Valley Oyster Festival (p162) In July and August, this celebration showcases PEI's famed oysters, offering delectable dishes and entertainment. The festival also hosts shucking competitions and other oyster-related contests. **July & August**

Balloon Fiesta (p114) Witness a dazzling display of colorful hot air balloons each September in Sussex, New Brunswick. Visitors can watch balloon competitions, take tethered rides and experience the magic of a balloon glow after dusk. **September**

I LIVE HERE

AN ALL-SEASON DELIGHT

James Mullinger is an award-winning comedian, bestselling author and co-founder of *The Maritime Edit* magazine. @themaritimeedit

Saint John, New Brunswick, is truly a city for all seasons. Lily Lake at Rockwood Park is home to the city's best lobster roll, trails and views. In summer I love swimming and sunning here, and during winter, joining the hordes of skilful skaters on the lake's frozen surface. Come fall you're too busy marveling at the vivid, bright trees to even notice the lake! Paradise.

Saint John (p117)

REGIONAL DIVERSITY

Average temperatures across the Atlantic provinces vary dramatically by region. While St John's, Newfoundland, hovers around freezing due to oceanic moderation in winter, northern New Brunswick faces -20°C. Meanwhile, July sees average highs around 23°C in Charlottetown, PEI, while Gander, Newfoundland, struggles to reach 15°C.

  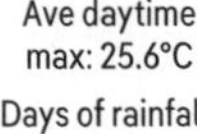 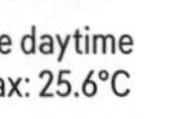 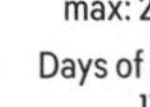 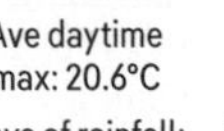

JULY	AUGUST	SEPTEMBER	OCTOBER	NOVEMBER	DECEMBER
Ave daytime max: 25.4°C	Ave daytime max: 25.6°C	Ave daytime max: 20.6°C	Ave daytime max: 16.7°C	Ave daytime max: 10.4°C	Ave daytime max: 4°C
Days of rainfall: 8	Days of rainfall: 10	Days of rainfall: 11	Days of rainfall: 12	Days of rainfall: 14	Days of rainfall: 14

SETH K. HUGHES/GETTY IMAGES ©

Gros Morne National Park (p196)

GET PREPARED FOR ATLANTIC CANADA

Useful things to load in your bag, your ears and your brain.

Clothes

Layers Pack versatile clothing for varying weather. Layering is key to staying comfortable, as the weather can be unpredictable. Bring a mix of lightweight shirts, long-sleeved tops and sweaters. A waterproof, windproof jacket is a good idea to protect against sudden rain or gusty winds.

Boots and shoes Diverse terrain calls for a mix of footwear. A sturdy pair of waterproof hiking boots will keep your feet dry while exploring rocky shores or hiking trails. Comfortable walking shoes are ideal for urban adventures. Pack a pair of sandals for warmer days. Insulated, waterproof footwear is a must in winter.

Manners

Greetings Atlantic Canadians are known for their warmth and friendliness. A smile and a simple 'hello' or 'good morning' go a long way in creating a positive impression.

Make an effort People here love to chat. Discussing the weather or recent events is a great way to connect with locals.

Courtesy Use 'please' and 'thank you' in daily interactions. Politeness is highly valued.

Hats Try to bring a hat. A wide-brimmed model offers sun protection on clear days, while a waterproof hat or a cap with a brim will keep you dry in showers.

READ

Barometer Rising (Hugh MacLennan; 1941) Historical drama set during the Halifax Explosion of 1917.

The Shipping News (Annie Proulx; 1993) Poignant Newfoundland tale of personal and cultural transformation.

The Acadian Saga (Dean Jobb; 2004) Engaging historical account of Acadian heritage and survival.

Anne of Green Gables (LM Montgomery; 1908) Beloved coming-of-age classic set in Prince Edward Island.

Words

While English is widely spoken across the region, using a few French words may aid communication and reflect your appreciation for Atlantic Canada's cultural diversity.

Hello (Bonjour) This friendly greeting is a great first step to connecting with locals.

Thank you (Merci) Use to show appreciation for hospitality and services, or even for someone holding the door for you.

Please (S'il vous plaît) When you're making requests, using this term adds a layer of politeness.

Excuse me (Excusez-moi) If you need to get someone's attention or navigate a crowd, saying 'excuse me' or *'excusez-moi'* is a respectful way to go about it.

Yes (Oui)/No (Non) Basic affirmative and negative.

How are you? (Comment ça va?) It's common courtesy to ask this when chatting with someone you've met.

Sorry (Désolé) Canadians are known for using (and maybe even overusing) this term, even if they've accidentally brushed by you.

Where is...? (Où est...?) Essential term when seeking directions.

Help (Aidez-moi) What to say in an emergency.

Hospital (Hôpital) What to ask for when seeking serious medical help.

I'm lost (Je suis perdu) Locals will generally help travelers find their way when they hear this.

Restroom/bathroom (Toilettes) What to ask for when nature calls.

Beach (Plage) To help you reach sandy shores.

Goodbye (Au revoir) Bid a polite farewell.

See you later (À plus tard) Say goodbye more casually.

WATCH

The Grand Seduction (Don McKellar; 2013) Residents of a small fishing community in Newfoundland charm a doctor into becoming the town's full-time physician.

Shattered City: The Halifax Explosion (Bruce Pittman; 2003) Gripping portrayal of the catastrophic explosion and fire.

Anne of Green Gables (Kevin Sullivan; 1985; pictured) Captivating miniseries adaptation of the classic novel set in picturesque Prince Edward Island.

Maudie (Aisling Walsh; 2016) Touching portrayal of Nova Scotian artist Maud Lewis and her inspiring journey.

LISTEN

North Country (The Rankin Family; 1993) Blend of folk and Celtic music reflecting Nova Scotia's heritage and landscapes.

Up (Great Big Sea; 1996) Classic album by Newfoundland's own Great Big Sea, featuring energetic folk tunes.

Atlantic Voice (CBC Radio) Podcast covering a wide range of topics related to Atlantic Canada's culture, history and current affairs.

East Coast Music Hour (CBC Radio) Radio program showcasing artists and bands from Atlantic Canada.

SHAUNL/GETTY IMAGES ©

Mi'kmaw dancers at Mawio'mi Powwow, Halifax

TRIP PLANNER

INDIGENOUS CULTURAL EXPERIENCES

A growing number of Indigenous communities across Atlantic Canada offer experiences introducing visitors to their cultures. The traditional territory of the Mi'kmaq people encompasses present-day Nova Scotia, New Brunswick, Prince Edward Island and parts of Newfoundland. Labrador is also home to two other Indigenous groups – the Inuit and the Innu.

Mi'kmaw Experiences in the Maritimes

NOVA SCOTIA

Book an interpretive tour with a Mi'kmaw guide at **Kejimkujik National Park** (p71), which has been designated a National Historic Site for its more than 500 Mi'kmaw petroglyphs.

Learn more about Mi'kmaw history, culture and art with a workshop at **Millbrook Cultural & Heritage Centre** (p84). Nearby, **Alan Syliboy Art Studio** (p84) has works by the renowned Mi'kmaw visual artist.

Eskasoni Cultural Journeys (p101) combines walking experiences on Goat Island with basketry, dancing, smudging, traditional games and cooking sessions.

NEW BRUNSWICK

The Elsipogtog First Nation's **Heritage Path Tour** (p115) includes a smudging ceremony and insight into Mi'kmaw beliefs and traditions.

At Fredericton's Odell Park you can go on an illuminating walk with **Wabanaki Tree Spirit Tours** (p110). St Mary's First Nation elder Cecilia Brooks and her son,

HOW TO BE A BETTER GUEST

Learn Whose Land You're On Sites including Native Land (native-land.ca) can help you identify which Indigenous nations' territories you're visiting.

Target Your Dollar Support businesses that directly benefit Indigenous communities. Seek out companies and experiences that are Indigenous owned, or led by Indigenous guides or staff.

Educate Yourself Before any experience, ask if there are cultural practices or customs that you should be aware of.

Request Permission Ask before taking photos, audio recordings or videos.

Listen Don't hesitate to ask questions, but be respectful. If your guide or host prefers not to discuss an issue, don't press it.

Anthony, will teach you about traditional uses of local plants for food or medicine.

On the Meteenagiag (Red Bank) First Nation, **A Taste of Metepenagiag 'Ookdotaan'** (p136) immerses visitors in Mi'kmaw history, shares Metepenagiag stories as you walk local trails and includes a traditional meal.

PRINCE EDWARD ISLAND

Join members of the **Lennox Island First Nation** (p160) for cooking, craft and culture workshops. **Lennox Island Cultural Centre** has exhibits detailing the nation's legends, heritage and cultural practices.

Indigenous Cultures in Newfoundland & Labrador

In Gros Morne National Park, the short interpretive **Mattie Mitchell Trail** (p198) recounts the story of a noted Mi'kmaw hunter, guide and prospector. On the **Discover Mekapisk** experience (p199), with the support of an Indigenous guide, you'll try your hand at the skills the region's First Peoples used to survive centuries ago.

Arrange a farmstay and Indigenous cultural experience at **Upper Humber Settlement** (p202). Among other activities, co-owner Lauralee Ledrew of the Qalipu First Nation leads a medicine wheel and fire wheel circle meditation.

The **Beothuk Interpretation Centre** (p230) details the complicated relationship between Newfoundland's First Peoples and European settlers.

In Labrador, visit Caribou Place, the gallery-cafe of Southern Inuit multimedia artist Charlene Rumbolt, who specializes in big wall hangings, prints, traditional beadwork, caribou-hair sculptures and more.

WHO WERE THE BEOTHUK?

Newfoundland's original inhabitants were known as the Beothuk, a term meaning 'the people' or 'true people' in their own language. An Algonquian people, the Beothuk lived primarily along the island's southern and northeastern coasts. When Europeans arrived in the region in the early 1500s, they reportedly called the Beothuk 'Red Indians' for the red ochre that they used to paint their bodies, and their canoes and other belongings. This may have contributed to the term that settlers applied to other Indigenous peoples.

To avoid the Europeans, the Beothuk left their coastal territories and relocated to the inland regions. By the mid-1700s, as a growing number of Europeans began to arrive in Newfoundland, the Beothuk were further displaced. Adding to the Indigenous people's distress, conflict between them and the settlers increased, and European-brought diseases killed more and more of the Beothuk.

While some scholars consider the Beothuk an extinct people from the time a Beothuk woman named Shanawdithit died of tuberculosis in 1829, Mi'kmaw oral history disputes this belief. These histories say that after European settlers forced the Beothuk from their coastal lands, some who moved inland may have intermarried with other Indigenous nations, continuing their genetic heritage if not their traditional ways of life.

Mussels

THE FOOD SCENE

Plentiful local seafood makes Atlantic Canada a delicious destination for fish fans. You'll find unique culinary experiences here, too.

Anywhere you go in Atlantic Canada, it's all about the seafood. Lobster, oysters, mussels, clams, cod and more are all fished around the region and turn up on restaurant tables, on food-truck menus and in local kitchens. If you're a seafood lover, set aside a chunk of your travel budget for dining.

The food scene is about more than just the bounty of the sea, though. Look for fresh greens, berries, potatoes or whatever is in season during your travels. The region's Indigenous peoples and Acadian communities have both contributed many distinctive dishes, and Newfoundland and Labrador have a unique local cuisine as well; sample dishes such as *toutons* and Jiggs dinner as you explore that province.

Try to schedule your visit around a local food festival, perhaps combining music, film and things to eat. Or book a cooking class or other culinary experience to dive deeper into the region's dining culture. With all the excellent eating, you might barely have time for the beach.

Acadian Cuisine

Acadians (French-speaking settlers) arrived in Atlantic Canada in the 1600s, and their traditional foods are found throughout the region.

Popular Acadian dishes include *fricot* (a comforting stew of chicken, potatoes and carrots), meat pie (savory pastry often filled with a mix of ground pork and chicken, and served with molasses and pickled

Best Atlantic Canadian Dishes

LOBSTER ROLL
Bun filled with lobster meat, plus mayonnaise or melted butter

SEAFOOD CHOWDER
Creamy soup made with fish, clams or other shellfish

FRIED CLAMS
Breaded with a crispy batter, usually served with French fries

HODGE PODGE
Rich vegetable chowder made with seasonal vegetables and cream

vegetables) and *rapûre* ('rappie pie,' a casserole made from shredded potatoes, onions and often pork or chicken).

While in the rest of Canada *poutine* means French fries drenched in brown gravy and topped with squeaky fresh cheese curds, Acadians have other *'poutines.' Poutine râpée* is a savory boiled potato dumpling stuffed with ground pork, while *poutine à trou* is a sweet treat: apples, raisins and cranberries are baked into a pastry ball and topped with a brown-sugar syrup.

Like many other Atlantic residents, Acadians rely on the sea for many ingredients. Frying clams or smelts is a common preparation, locally caught fish are often smoked, and cod is frequently shredded and fried into fish cakes. In southwestern Nova Scotia, you'll see creamed lobster – lobster meat in a cream sauce served on toast – everywhere along the coast, even on many breakfast menus.

Vegetarian Options

Seek out vegetarian cafes, such as Halifax's **enVie A Vegan Kitchen** (p62) or Charlottetown's **Farmacy + Fermentary** (p143); Farmacy's owners use vegetables from their own farm whenever they can. The Mediterranean menus at **Daryâ** (p61) in Halifax aren't exclusively vegetarian, but they have ample veg-only options, from chickpeas with tahini to avocado fattoush salad.

At the **PEI Potato Country Kitchen** (p163), vegetarians can sample oversized baked potatoes loaded with cheese – with a side of homemade potato chips.

Farmers' Markets of Nova Scotia (farmersmarketsnovascotia.ca) lists markets around that province. In New Brunswick, Saint John, Fredericton, Moncton and Dieppe all have farmers markets, and in Newfoundland the **St John's Farmers' Market** operates all year. With more than 60 stalls, the year-round **Charlottetown Farmers Market** (p144) is PEI's largest.

FOODIO/SHUTTERSTOCK ©

Hodge podge

ISLAND IMAGES/ALAMY STOCK PHOTO ©, VERENA MATTHEW/ALAMY LIVE NEWS ©

FOOD FESTIVALS

Nova Scotia Lobster Crawl (February) Throughout February you'll find lobster-focused events across the province's South Shore.

Shediac Lobster Festival (July) This crustacean celebration takes place every summer on New Brunswick's Acadian coast.

PEI International Shellfish Festival (September) Sample local seafood, cheer on the oyster-shucking and chowder-making contests, and enjoy live music at this island fish fest.

Roots, Rants & Roars (September) Newfoundland and Labrador's chefs face off in the 'cod wars' at this annual food and culture festival.

PEI Fall Flavours Festival (October) Two weeks of events across PEI, highlighting everything local and delicious across 'Canada's Food Island.'

PEI Fall Flavours Festival

DONAIR
Halifax's pita-wrapped spiced beef slathered with sweet creamy sauce

JIGGS DINNER
Newfoundland boiled dinner, usually with beef, cabbage, carrots and potatoes

TOUTONS
Fried dough served with molasses in Newfoundland

FISH AND BREWIS
A traditional Newfoundland dish of salt cod and hard bread

Favorite Fish

Lobster Try it everywhere in Atlantic Canada, but don't miss a traditional PEI lobster supper (p150), where mussels, chowder, salads and pies keep company with your crustaceans.

Oysters A PEI specialty, these bivalves are served raw, grilled, fried or baked.

Cod Newfoundland's most popular fish, often served as fish and chips (fried and served with French fried potatoes), as cod *au gratin* (baked with cheese and cream sauce) or pan-fried with scrunchions (crispy bits of pork fat).

Sweet Treats

Pets de soeurs Similar to a cinnamon roll or pinwheel, these Acadian pastries have an unusual name: 'nuns' farts.'

Bakeapple jam A Newfoundland jam made with these small berries, often called cloudberries.

Blueberry grunt A classic Nova Scotian sweet, this cobbler-like dessert features wild blueberries topped with biscuit dough.

Fish and chips

Thirst Quenchers

Iceberg beer Beer made with iceberg water? Look for it at Newfoundland's Quidi Vidi Brewing Company.

Nova Scotia's wines Nova Scotia is Atlantic Canada's main wine-producing region, so seek out local labels or plan a wine-tasting tour.

Beer without the buzz Try non-alcoholic Libra, which PEI's Upstart Brewing crafts in pale ale, IPA and pilsner varieties.

Screech Newfoundland's local rum, an ingredient in the infamous 'screech-in ceremony' that makes visitors honorary Newfoundlanders.

MEALS OF A LIFETIME

Inn at Bay Fortune (p158) Chef-owner Michael Smith is known for the lavish FireWorks Feasts he creates at this PEI inn.

Ballet by the Ocean (p116) Accompanied by a tasting menu featuring New Brunswick ingredients, the Atlantic Ballet performs in a spectacular outdoor setting in Grande-Digue.

Woodroad (p100) Fine dining overlooking the sea in Cape Breton, Nova Scotia.

Chanterelle Restaurant (101) Also in Cape Breton, this inn-restaurant sources its ingredients from fishers and farms within 100km of the property.

Wild Caraway (p85) This dining destination in Nova Scotia's Advocate Harbour highlights the region's wild and local products.

THE YEAR IN FOOD

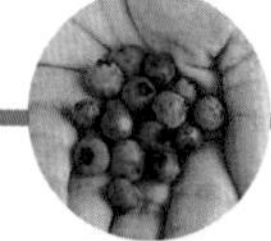

SPRING

It's not only Québec and Ontario that tap sugar maples in early spring; you'll find maple syrup in the Maritimes, too. Other spring delicacies in the region include snow crab and fresh fiddlehead greens.

SUMMER

Summer brings many fresh fruits and vegetables, including wild blueberries and chanterelle mushrooms. Scallops are in season in PEI, and summer is lobster season in Newfoundland and Labrador.

FALL

Fruit and vegetable harvests continue through the autumn, with apples, cranberries and potatoes all in season. In Newfoundland and Labrador, you'll find moose on restaurant menus, often as burgers or sausages.

WINTER

Nova Scotia's lobster season begins in late November and continues into May. While some say PEI oysters are best in winter, the island's wild oysters are harvested May through mid-July and mid-September through November.

Lobster, Doyle Sansome & Sons (p195), Twillingate

KHANH NGO PHOTOGRAPHY/GETTY IMAGES ©

Lobster roll

HOW TO... Lobster 101

Nearly everywhere you go across Atlantic Canada you can sample one of the region's favorite shellfish – lobster. But if you've never eaten a lobster, tackling this crustacean can feel somewhat daunting. Here's how to get started.

Let's Roll

The simplest way for a newbie to sample this seafood is in a lobster roll (shredded lobster meat served in a long, toasted bun). It can be prepared cold, where the meat is tossed with mayonnaise, or warm, with melted butter dressing the lobster meat.

Tackling a Whole Lobster

For the full lobster experience, order a whole steamed or boiled lobster, available at restaurants throughout the region. To protect your clothing, tie on your lobster bib before digging in. (The spectacle of you in your plastic bib makes a classic photo op.)

Your lobster will come with two critical utensils: a cracker (a tool similar to a nutcracker that you use to break open the shell) and a small seafood fork or pick, which helps you pull the meat from the legs and other small spaces.

Next Steps

Lobsters are meatiest in their tails and claws. Use the cracker to crack the claws, then remove the meat. You can often break off the tail with your hands, employing the cracker on the tail shell if the meat doesn't come out easily. Many consider the bright reddish roe (eggs) that you'll find in the body of a female lobster to be a delicacy. There are bits of meat in the narrow legs that you can pull or suck out.

Lobster is typically served with melted butter and a lemon wedge. Dip the meat in the butter, add a squeeze of lemon and enjoy!

DIY

You can buy cooked, ready-to-eat lobsters from seafood markets or fish cooperatives by the water, too. Take them back to your accommodations if you have a place to eat – and the necessary utensils – or set up your lobster picnic by the shore.

MORE LOBSTER DISHES

While purists insist that the only way to cook a lobster is simply steaming or boiling it, you'll find the seafood in numerous other preparations.

Made from a stock of lobster shells, lobster bisque is a creamy soup with shredded lobster. Lobster *poutine* amps up the classic Canadian creation of French fries, gravy and cheese by tossing cooked lobster meat into the mix. You might also try lobster mac 'n' cheese (baked cheesy elbow-shaped pasta made richer with lobster meat) as well as other pastas topped with lobster.

Lobster pizza? Lobster poke? Lobster congee? If you love lobster, why not?

PT HAMILTON/SHUTTERSTOCK ©

Lobster traps, Peggy's Cove (p65)

HOW TO... Catch Your Dinner

Of course, you can enjoy Atlantic shellfish at restaurants, seafood shacks and other eateries across the region. But wouldn't it be more memorable to learn to catch and prepare your own?

First, Catch Your Crustacean

You can go lobster fishing or at least learn how the crustaceans are caught with several companies in Nova Scotia, including **Peggy's Cove Boat Tours**, **Tusket Island Tours** and **Sober Island Boat Tour**.

In New Brunswick, **Shediac Bay Cruises** offers LobsterTales cruises, where you're introduced to lobster fishing before you enjoy a lobster meal. For pre-adventure inspiration, ogle the **world's largest lobster**, a 90-ton sculpture near the Shediac waterfront.

On Prince Edward Island (PEI), **The Fiddling Fisherman** takes you out on the Chaisson family's fishing boat, *Chaisson a Dream,* where you'll learn how lobster fishers trap their catch. The owner's fiddle music accompanies your on-board lobster dinner.

Tong & Shuck

Prefer oysters? Learn to tong for them with PEI's **Along the Edge Experiences**, where you'll gather the mollusks using long tongs, learn to shuck them, then dig into your harvest. Alternatively, go to 'oyster school' at **Cascumpec Bay Oyster Company**, another place to try tonging, shucking and tasting.

For a more active adventure, contact **Nature Space Resort & Retreat Centre** on PEI. It works with an oyster farm to combine a kayaking adventure with an introduction to oyster farming – and, naturally, there are samples.

Clams, Cod & More

Also on PEI, **Tranquility Cove Adventures** will teach you to dig for clams, which you'll steam and eat. The same company can take you fishing for mackerel.

In Newfoundland and Labrador, cod is the king of fish. At Labrador's **Battle Harbour National Historic Site** you can head out on a cod-fishing adventure to learn how the fish is caught.

Les Zigotos, a nonprofit association on the island of St-Pierre, off Newfoundland, hosts summertime tours in traditional wooden dories that often include fishing for cod.

CHANNEL YOUR INNER CHEF

Want to learn more about how to use Atlantic ingredients and products from around the region? Book a cooking workshop at the **Culinary Institute of Canada**, a professional culinary school in Charlottetown, PEI.

Although many future chefs study here before going on to work in restaurants across the country and beyond, you don't have to be a pro to take its classes. The institute offers regular 'Culinary Boot Camps:' hands-on half- or full-day courses for home cooks that introduce you to regional dishes and how to prepare them. You'll enjoy the results in the harbor-view dining room, and go home with recipes and new culinary skills.

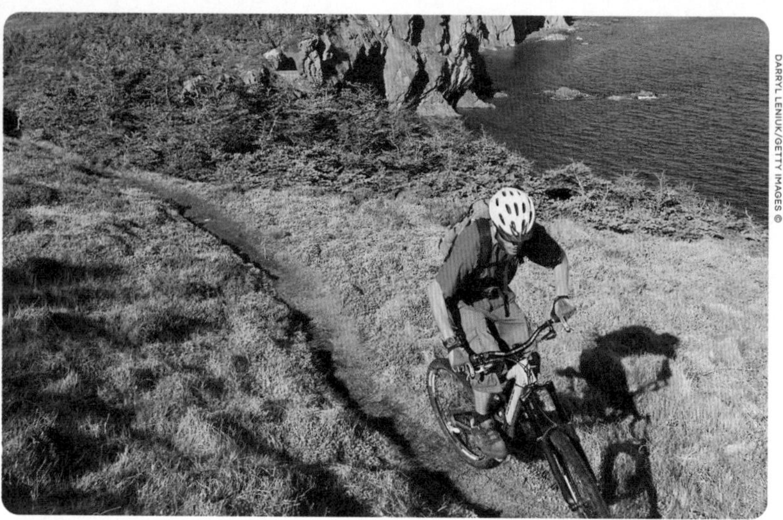
DARRYL LENIUK/GETTY IMAGES ©

Bonavista Peninsula (p178)

THE OUTDOORS

Bring your outdoor toys to Atlantic Canada. This is big-ocean country with equally vast tracts of inland wilderness for endless exploration.

Kayaks, mountain bikes, camping gear and hiking shoes – this is the gear that will make an already enjoyable East Coast holiday into an epic one. For self-styled fun there are trails, waterways, parks, front-country campgrounds and backcountry cabins and campsites. Or let an expert lead the way: go hot-air ballooning, learn to surf, or practice tricks at a mountain-bike skills park. And there's always the low-key option: spend a day at one of the hundreds of beaches, some busy and serviced, others wild and remote.

Hiking, Walking & Cycling

Major new hiking and walking routes mean self-propelled adventure is part of the year-round enjoyment of the outdoors in Atlantic Canada. Inspired by Spain's Camino de Santiago, Prince Edward Island's 700km, 32-section Island Walk (p145) circumnavigates PEI. Some walkers complete a section a day, while others cycle the distance in a week. However you choose to tackle it, the route leads down red dirt roads, parallels long strands of sandy beach, and cuts through busy villages and towns where seafood and craft beer are the rewards.

The hiking story is repeated in the other provinces, but with wilder alternatives. Cape Breton's Skyline Trail (p100) is perhaps the best known for its commanding view of the Cabot Trail far below. Hikes to the top of Gros Morne Mountain (p196) in Newfoundland and Mt Carleton (p130) in

Offbeat Outdoor Fun

RIVER RAFTING
Go mud sliding and brown-water river rafting in the crazy tidal bore on Nova Scotia's **Shubenacadie River** (p85).

HARVESTING MUSSELS
Gather wild mussels on a boat tour from **Murphy's Campground** in Nova Scotia for an evening campfire feast (p93).

HOT-AIR BALLOONING
Ride in a hot-air balloon at the **Balloon Fiesta** held every September in New Brunswick (p114).

FAMILY ADVENTURES

Spend the night in a tent, a guardhouse or even a prison in Nova Scotia's **Fortress of Louisbourg** (p102).

Sleep in a caboose or the station master's house and eat in a dining car at the **Train Station Inn** in Nova Scotia (p84).

Stand in the infinity room at New Brunswick's **Science East**, a converted jail that still has barred doors and windows (p111).

Learn to spin wool, cook at the hearth, forge a horseshoe or feed the cows at **Kings Landing**, New Brunswick (p111).

Find fossils on the beach with a guide from **Prehistoric Island Tours** on PEI (p147).

Meet Vikings at L'Anse aux Meadows (p204), Newfoundland, and see a **replica Viking ship** at nearby Norstead (p205).

New Brunswick end, respectively, in views of a sprawling coastline and a forest said to consist of 10 million trees. Home to caribou and polar bears, the 9700-sq-km Torngat Mountains National Park in Labrador is so wild and remote that hiking there is only possible with an Indigenous guide.

Many trails in the region are open to cyclists, and some such as those in New Brunswick's Fundy National Park (p113) are made for all-season mountain biking.

Boating

Much of Atlantic Canada's history and culture is founded in the people's relationship with the sea. From the Indigenous invention of the canoe through centuries of shipbuilding to today's busy fisheries, East Coast folk have always felt at home on the water. The coastline of Canada's four Atlantic provinces stretches 30,000km. Inland, the region's 488,000 sq km are dotted with lakes, crisscrossed by rivers and punctuated with waterfalls. With so much water, it's almost compulsory to get out in a boat. Kayak among Nova Scotia's '100 Wild Islands' (p94; there are actually 282) or 'flowerpot' sea stacks at New Brunswick's Hopewell Rocks (p113). Chug aboard a converted fishing boat to spot icebergs off Newfoundland (p170). Bob in a fishing boat off PEI to catch mackerel for your onboard supper (p155). Canoe ancient Indigenous waterways or just sleep in a houseboat.

Bonavista Peninsula (p178)

Guided Tours

Friendliness and outdoor adventure – two of Atlantic Canada's strengths – become one on guided outdoor tours. Take a forest walk with Indigenous guides who turn plants into medicine. Forage ingredients for supper. Zip in a Zodiac to whale feeding grounds in the Bay of Fundy (p122) or off Newfoundland (p193), where guides call the giants by name as they surface. On land or sea, guides are as knowledgeable as they are hospitable.

CLAM-DIGGING
Dig for clams and fish for mackerel aboard a real fishing boat with **Tranquility Cove Adventures** on PEI (p155).

WALKING ON ANCIENT ROCKS
Hike on rocks from the Earth's mantle in Newfoundland's **Gros Morne National Park** (p196).

PADDLEBOARDING WITH GOATS
Become one of the herd at **Beach Goats** in PEI. Hop on a paddleboard with a goat, try goat yoga or just take a walk on the beach with them (p163).

TUBING DOWN THE RIVER
Spend a lazy summer afternoon floating on an inner tube along New Brunswick's **Miramichi River**, drink by your side (p134).

ACTION AREAS

Where to find Atlantic Canada's best outdoor activities.

Boating

1. Shubenacadie River (p85)
2. 100 Wild Islands (p94)
3. Digby Neck (p78)
4. Saint Andrews (p122)
5. Miramichi River (p134)
6. Nashwaak River (p110)
7. North Rustico (p151)

Beach

1. Clam Harbour Beach (p93)
2. Lawrencetown Beach (p92)
3. Crescent Beach (p69)
4. Kouchibouguac National Park (p114)
5. Prince Edward Island National Park (p152)
6. Basin Head Provincial Park (p156)
7. Cabot Beach Provincial Park (p151)

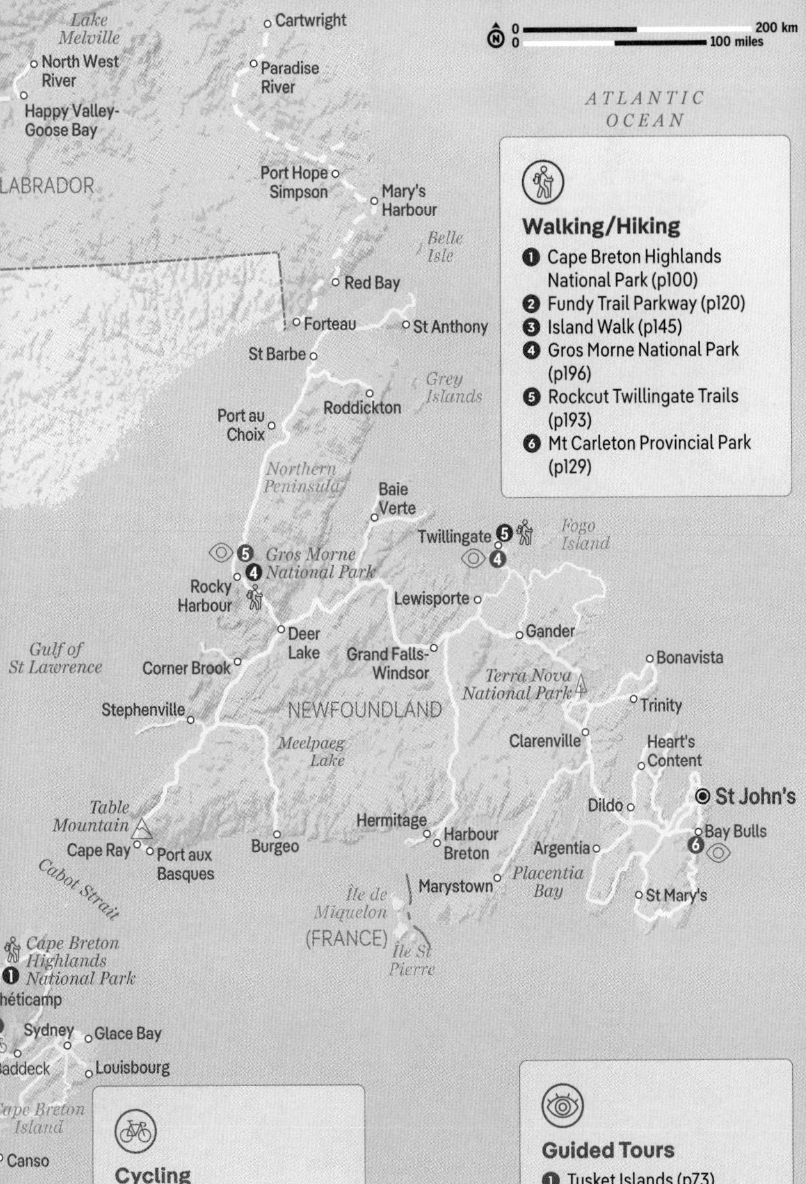

Walking/Hiking

1. Cape Breton Highlands National Park (p100)
2. Fundy Trail Parkway (p120)
3. Island Walk (p145)
4. Gros Morne National Park (p196)
5. Rockcut Twillingate Trails (p193)
6. Mt Carleton Provincial Park (p129)

Cycling

1. Cabot Trail (p101)
2. Keppoch Mountain (p89)
3. LaHave River to Petite Riviere (p70)
4. Kouchibouguac National Park (p114)
5. Mt Carleton Provincial Park (p129)
6. Confederation Trail (p158)

Guided Tours

1. Tusket Islands (p73)
2. Kejimkujik National Park (p71)
3. Souris Harbour (p155)
4. Twillingate (p192)
5. Western Brook Pond (p198)
6. Witless Bay (p177)

ATLANTIC CANADA

THE GUIDE

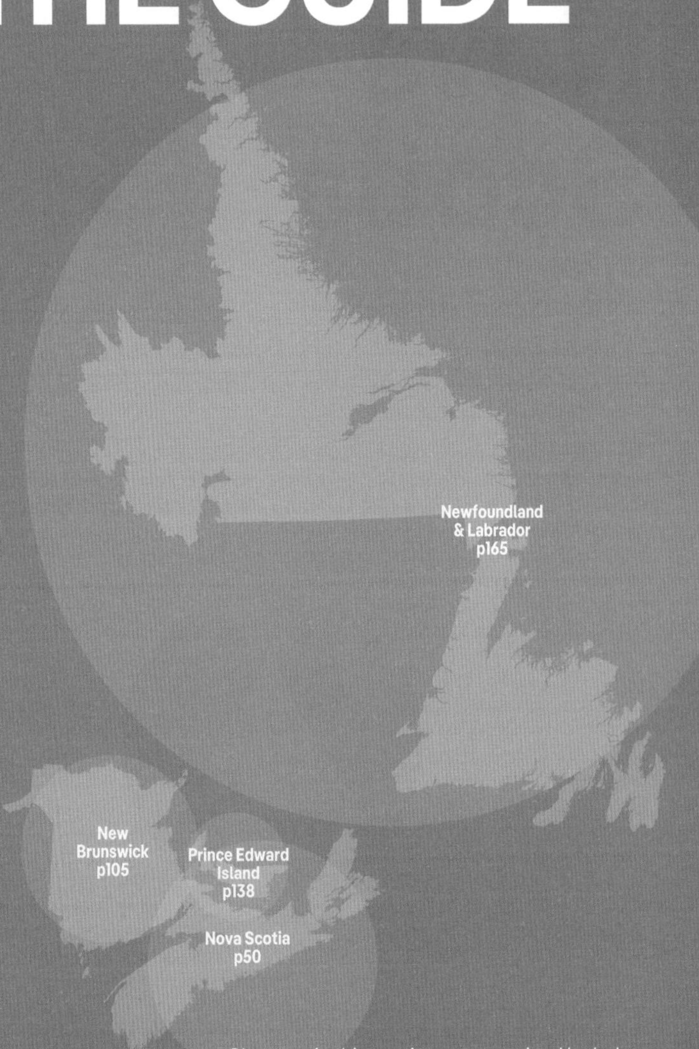

Chapters in this section are organised by hubs and their surrounding areas. We see the hub as your base in the destination, where you'll find unique experiences, local insights, insider tips and expert recommendations. It's also your gateway to the surrounding area, where you'll see what and how much you can do from there.

Hopewell Rocks Provincial Park (p113)

J DUQUETTE/SHUTTERSTOCK ©

Nova Scotia

OCEAN PLAYGROUND AND CULTURAL HOMELAND

Mi'kmaw, French Acadian, Celtic, British and African heritage shaped by the sea and the ways of life forged from it define Nova Scotia.

When Scottish settlers came to build a fortification in Annapolis Royal in 1629, they arrived with a flag, a coat of arms and the name of the province that would become Nova Scotia. Scottish King James I had bestowed the territory – actually Indigenous Mi'kmaw lands called M'kma'ki – on courtier Sir William Alexander eight years earlier. Indigenous history in the region goes millennia deep. Without the help of the Mi'kmaq and their 10,000 years of experience living on these lands, the earliest Europeans would not have survived. Settler history now stretches across 400 years, with pockets of British, French Acadian, Celtic and African heritage.

In Halifax, Nova Scotia's capital, these cultural threads have interwoven with more recent Chinese, Arab, Indian and Middle Eastern immigration to form a complex tapestry. Beyond urban Halifax, those early influences remain prominent. That lobster you order might be from a 10th-generation fishing family. The fiddle music you dance to in a Cape Breton pub might have been written by a Scottish farmer who was a self-taught virtuoso. Mi'kmaw artist Alan Syliboy's latest painted drum could have been inspired by petroglyphs carved into rocks along an ancient Indigenous canoe route.

Nova Scotia's landscape is as diverse as its cultural fabric. Bold ocean shorelines are interspersed with stretches of soft sand, marshy coves and tiny islands. The world's highest tides erode tall cliffs and expose vast sea floors.

THE MAIN AREAS

HALIFAX
Historic, hip capital. p56

LUNENBURG & THE SOUTH SHORE
Seafaring heritage. p64

ANNAPOLIS ROYAL & THE FRENCH SHORE
Verdant lands and the world's highest tides. p75

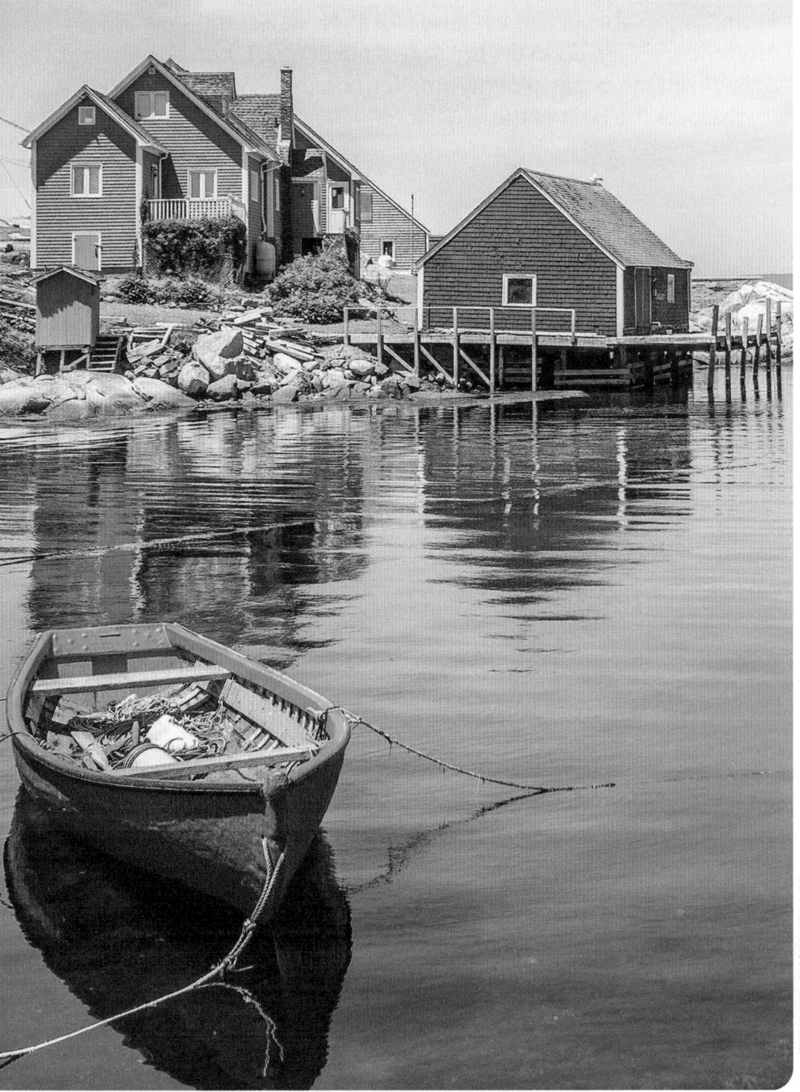

SAM AND BRIAN/SHUTTERSTOCK ©

Left: Tipi, Port-Royal National Historic Site (p77); Above: Peggy's Cove (p65)

Find Your Way

From Cape Sable Island to Cape North, Nova Scotia stretches 580km tip to tip, but you're never more than 65km from the ocean. Follow smaller, coastal roads to discover the best of the province.

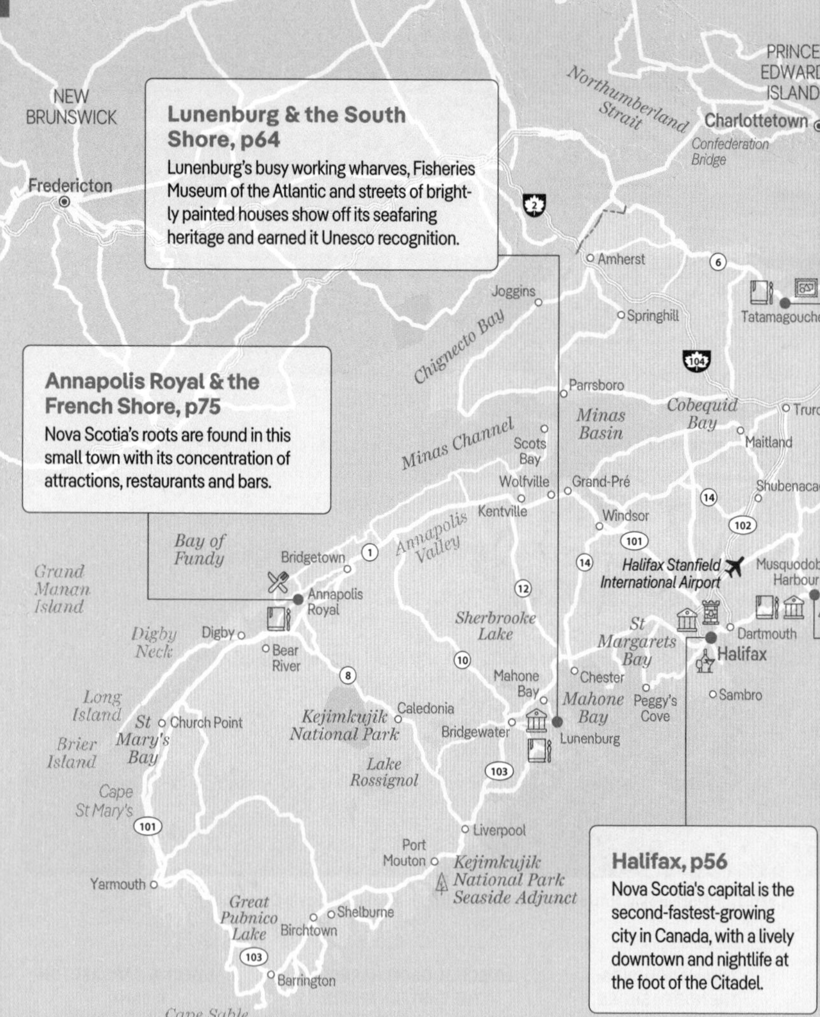

N
0 100 km
0 50 miles

Tatamagouche & the North Shore, p83

Community spirit and independence define this town and the surrounding region, home to Nobel Prize winners and important geological sites.

Baddeck & Cape Breton Island, p96

Cape Breton's geographic center has attracted visitors for generations, both for its natural beauty and for its Alexander Graham Bell connection.

Musquodoboit Harbour & the Eastern Shore, p90

This seaside village with a craft brewery and train museum makes a perfect stopover during explorations of the wild Eastern Shore.

CAR

The province has limited public transit, so the best way to reach each rewarding corner of Nova Scotia is by car. For premium views and to make unexpected discoveries, stick to the designated visitor driving routes.

BICYCLE

In a relatively small province with quiet rural roads, lots of accommodations and a great variety of landscapes and cultural hubs, cycling is popular and a recommended transportation option.

BUS

In Halifax, Metro Transit operates a reliable, affordable fleet of buses, as well as two ferries across the harbor. Public transit is limited or nonexistent in other regions.

Plan Your Days

With a capital city that's always improving, endless coastline, meandering scenic drives and dozens of small towns, Nova Scotia is ideal for a quick, intense visit or a deeper dive into its varied culture and landscape.

ADRIEN LE TOUX/SHUTTERSTOCK ©

Halifax Public Gardens (p62)

One Day in Halifax

- If you're limited to a quick trip, spend your time in Halifax. After a guided tour of the **Citadel** (p56), walk the streets around this steep, fortified hill that dominates the downtown, where there are plenty of restaurants, after-dark spots, and attractions such as the **Art Gallery of Nova Scotia** (p60) and **Halifax Public Gardens** (p62). A walk along the waterfront leads past intriguing stops such as the **Maritime Museum of the Atlantic** (p63) and the **Museum of Immigration at Pier 21** (p59).

- At the ferry terminal, take a quick, scenic hop across the harbor and walk around downtown **Dartmouth** (p63).

Seasonal Highlights

There's rarely a Nova Scotia day that's too hot or too cold: the Atlantic moderates temperatures year-round. The warmest days are best spent at the beach, the coldest on the slopes.

FEBRUARY

Music festivals liven up winter in Halifax. Ski hills in Cape Breton, the North Shore and the Annapolis Valley are open.

MAY

Against the green shoots and leaves of spring is set the colorful, fragrant **Apple Blossom Festival** in the Annapolis Valley.

JULY

Summer kicks off with province-wide **Canada Day** celebrations and whale-watching tours in the Bay of Fundy and around Cape Breton.

EB ADVENTURE PHOTOGRAPHY/SHUTTERSTOCK ©, GREENSEAS/SHUTTERSTOCK ©, CL-MEDIEN/SHUTTERSTOCK ©

A Long Weekender

- Make the best of a long weekend trip to Nova Scotia by turning south from Halifax. Drive the scenic Lighthouse Rte down the South Shore to Unesco-listed Lunenburg to see the **Bluenose II** (p64) and the **Fisheries Museum of the Atlantic** (p64). Continue to the **Kejimkujik National Park Seaside** (p69) for a hike to a protected beach with seals.

- Cut across the province to explore Nova Scotia's roots in Annapolis Royal and at the **Port-Royal National Historic Site** (p77). Join a whale-watching cruise from **Brier Island** (p78) before continuing on to the **Grand-Pré National Historic Site** (p81).

More Time to Meander

- With 10 days at your disposal, extend the long-weekend itinerary by continuing to the **Black Loyalist Heritage Centre** (p71), Yarmouth's **Cape Forchu Light** (p74) and Clare's ***tintamarre*** celebrations (p75). Spend a day driving the Parrsboro Shore, from the newly designated **Cliffs of Fundy Unesco Geopark** (p84) to **Joggins fossil cliffs** (p86). Pause in Advocate for a locavore lunch at **Wild Caraway** (p85).

- Continue along the North Shore to Cape Breton for two days on the **Cabot Trail** (p99) and a day at the **Fortress of Louisbourg** (p102). Return via the Eastern Shore, stopping at living museums at **Sherbrooke Village** (p91) and **Memory Lane Heritage Village** (p91).

AUGUST

The noisy Acadian *tintamarre* celebrations contrast with long, lazy days at any of Nova Scotia's dozens of beaches.

SEPTEMBER

Labour Day brings thousands of bikers to **Digby's Wharf Rat Rally** (p78) and hikers taking advantage of cooler temperatures.

OCTOBER

Cape Breton lights up with fall foliage and comes alive to the sounds of the **Celtic Colours International Festival** (p97).

NOVEMBER

Special pre-Christmas dinners at Fortress Louisbourg, Sherbrooke Village and other living museums kick off the holiday season.

Halifax

GETTING AROUND

Halifax is a walkable city, in spite of the steep streets downtown. It's known to be pedestrian friendly – if you look as though you might want to cross a street, the traffic stops. In recent years, many bike lanes have been added, too. Metro Transit runs frequent, reliable buses around the city and ferries across the harbor. From Halifax Stanfield International Airport, you can rent a car, hop a bus or hail a cab to the city.

TOP TIP

Orient yourself using the twin green suspension bridges that span the harbor. The city core is built on a peninsula, most of it walkable, although driving and public transit are more practical beyond the downtown. The steep streets below the Citadel are best explored on foot, as are the streets and green spaces surrounding it.

As it's the largest city in eastern Canada, all roads and flight paths lead to Halifax, Nova Scotia's capital and effectively the capital of the entire Atlantic region. Writer Thomas H. Raddall's catchy phrase for Halifax, 'Warden of the North,' captures its history as a military bastion. The city is arranged first around its dominant landmark, Citadel Hill, a grassy, glacial drumlin (hill of debris) crowned with a fortress, and also around the excellent harbor, home of mighty navies, container piers and cruise-ship docks. The city's waterfront, streetscapes and architectural heritage are born of its military history and anchor much of what makes Halifax worth visiting. Other influences, such as Indigenous, Black and French Acadian cultural heritage, ripple across the city's history, popping up in the arts, sports, community spaces and local place names. Five universities, including the Nova Scotia College of Art and Design, lend Halifax a youthful, creative vibe.

Ascend Halifax Citadel

From glaciers to ghosts

Just 11,000 years ago, glaciers retreated from Nova Scotia, leaving a scoured landscape and drumlins, one of which dominates the Halifax skyline. For thousands of years the Mi'kmaq lived in permanent villages around the drumlins looming over Kjipuktuk (The Great Harbour). On June 21, 1749, some 2000 settlers led by Edward Cornwallis, Governor of Nova Scotia, arrived in Kjipuktuk, renamed it Halifax and began construction of a city and fortifications on the slopes of the largest drumlin. Cornwallis proved to be a brutal British leader, paying a bounty for Mi'kmaw scalps and hatching a plan to expel all French settlers from Nova Scotia. Despite its violent beginnings, Halifax grew, becoming the provincial capital. Fortifications were rebuilt four times until the star-shaped Fort George was completed in 1856. It still crowns that drumlin known today as the **Halifax Citadel National Historic Site**.

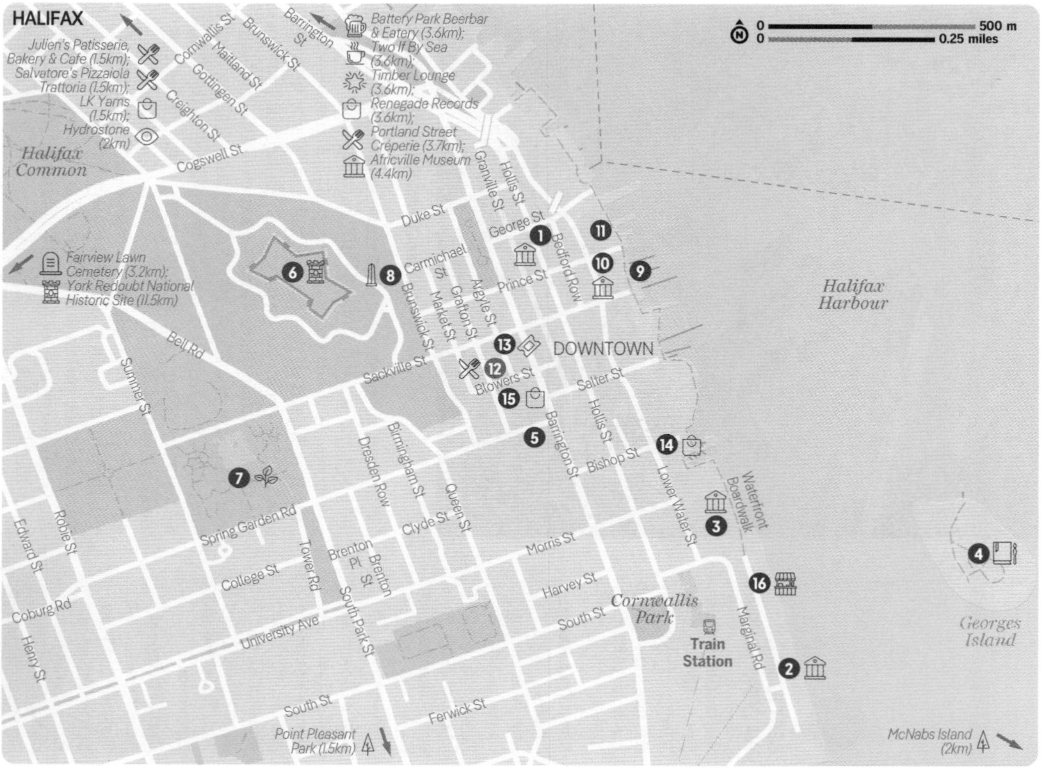

HALIFAX

Julien's Patisserie, Bakery & Cafe (1.5km); Salvatore's Pizzaiola Trattoria (1.5km); LK Yarns (1.5km); Hydrostone (2km)

Battery Park Beerbar & Eatery (3.6km); Two If By Sea (3.6km); Timber Lounge (3.6km); Renegade Records (3.6km); Portland Street Créperie (3.7km); Africville Museum (4.4km)

Fairview Lawn Cemetery (3.2km); York Redoubt National Historic Site (11.5km)

Point Pleasant Park (1.5km)

McNabs Island (2km)

Halifax Common · DOWNTOWN · Halifax Harbour · Georges Island · Cornwallis Park · Train Station · Waterfront Boardwalk

Cornwallis St · Maitland St · Brunswick St · Barrington St · Gottingen St · Creighton St · Cogswell St · Granville St · Hollis St · Duke St · George St · Bedford Row · Carmichael St · Prince St · Argyle St · Grafton St · Market St · Sackville St · Blowers St · Salter St · Bishop St · Lower Water St · Marginal Rd · Bell Rd · Summer St · Spring Garden Rd · Dresden Row · Birmingham St · Queen St · Clyde St · Morris St · Harvey St · South St · Brenton Pl · Brenton St · Tower Rd · College St · University Ave · South Park St · Robie St · Edward St · Coburg Rd · Henry St · Fenwick St

0 – 500 m
0 – 0.25 miles

SIGHTS
1 Art Gallery of Nova Scotia
2 Canadian Museum of Immigration at Pier 21
3 Discovery Centre
4 Georges Island
5 Halifax Central Library
6 Halifax Citadel National Historic Site
7 Halifax Public Gardens
8 Halifax Town Clock
9 HMCS Sackville
10 Maritime Museum of the Atlantic
11 Queen's Marque

EATING
12 Pizza Corner

ENTERTAINMENT
13 Neptune Theatre

SHOPPING
14 Bishop's Landing
15 Black Market Boutique
16 Seaport Farmers Market

Costumed 78th Highlander soldier, Halifax Citadel

BEST HALIFAX WALKING TOURS

Halifax Ghost Walk
Setting off from the Town Clock on Citadel Hill, take a spooky two-hour tour through Halifax.

Ghost Tour, Halifax Citadel
After dark, tour the Citadel grounds by lantern and hear the legend of the gray lady. Follow the guide into the very walls of the fortress.

Best of Downtown Halifax Tour
Sample lobster *bao* and smoked scallops with a full-sized cocktail on Curated Food Tours' downtown exploration.

Best of Quinpool Road Area
Curated Food Tours' best neighborhood tour includes fusion dishes such as Japanese crispy fried chicken, plus three craft beverages.

SHAUNL/GETTY IMAGES ©

Halifax Citadel National Historic Site

Visitors might be startled by a reminder of this history when the noon gun is fired from the hill, rattling windows in the downtown, as it has every day since 1857. An extensive new exhibit designed in partnership with Mi'kmaw historians tells Halifax's complex history, as do guided daytime tours and the nighttime Ghost Tour. A costumed 78th Highlander soldier curates the Raise Your Spirits! tour, linking each of three Compass Distillery spirits, barrel aged in the Citadel, with stories of early life within its walls and in the city on the slopes below the hill.

Standing like a four-tiered wedding cake on the side of the hill, the **Town Clock** is perhaps the city's best-known landmark. Atop the rectangular, clapboard-clad base stands an octagonal tower supported by 12 columns. The center tier holds the blue clockface, which has kept time since 1803. The rest of the building is a faithful reconstruction of the original, which was an excellent example of Palladian architecture, a style popularized in Venice.

WHERE TO STAY

Stardust Motel
Basic, but here's the best deal in Halifax, with free parking and wi-fi. No breakfast. $

Halliburton House Inn
This elegant, downtown boutique hotel with fine dining occupies a historic 1823 property. $$

Courtyard Marriott Halifax Downtown
This is an affordable stay with great harbor and waterfront views, plus fine dining. $$

A Day on Georges Island

Dark tunnels and sunny picnics

The Halifax Citadel is part of the five-site **Halifax Defense Complex**. **York Redoubt National Historic Site** sits on a bluff overlooking the mouth of Halifax Harbour. Walk the grassy park, exploring the remains of fortifications built in 1793 to guard the city from seaward attack. Admission is free. Just a 20-minute drive from downtown, it's a pleasant place to spend an hour. A Halifax Transit bus line reaches the site.

The tree-lined trails of Point Pleasant Park are situated at the tip of peninsular Halifax within walking distance of downtown. At the park's highest point stands the **Prince of Wales Tower**, a solid stone Martello tower that dates from the 1790s. It was the first of its kind in North America. Across the harbor on uninhabited McNabs Island – a provincial park – stand the remnants of **Fort McNab**, built in the 1880s to balance the harbor defenses. Not much remains but a large gun and some concrete bunkers, but walking the island is a significant wilderness experience sandwiched between two urban areas. Private ferries carry passengers to the island.

Opened to visitors in 2020 for the first time in over 50 years, **Georges Island** is a drumlin set in the middle of the harbor. You can reach the island by ferry from Cable Wharf on the Halifax waterfront. Interpretive panels detail the island's importance to the Indigenous Mi'kmaq and to the French Acadians, hundreds of whom were held here before the British deported them in the mid-18th century. The island's lighthouse was the first in Canada to be automated. Parks Canada is still building the visitor experience, but the current highlight is a guided tour through the dark tunnels of **Fort Charlotte**, at the center of the island, to see huge cannons and underground munitions vaults. Bundle a 'Perfect Picnic' with your ferry ticket to enjoy a lobster-roll lunch on the island's grassy slopes, which offer grand views of downtown Halifax and Dartmouth.

Land at Pier 21

Immigration museum and buzzing waterfront

Known as the gateway to Canada, Pier 21 served as a major entry point for 1.5 million immigrants from 1928 to 1971. It's now home to the Canadian **Museum of Immigration at Pier 21**. Waves of immigrants landed here, then headed west by train to settle elsewhere in the country, but left behind traces of Irish, Italian, Greek and other ethnicities. As Canada's last remaining immigration terminal, the pier was named

BEST SEAFOOD IN HALIFAX

McKelvies
Set in a historic fire station, now with a beer garden. Seafood dominates the menu. **$$**

Shuck Seafood & Oyster Bar
Finally, Halifax has a serious oyster bar, and one with sustainably sourced seafood. **$$**

Bar Kismet
A broad bar menu complements dressed-up dishes such as local scallops with black sesame. **$$**

Five Fishermen
Long a downtown landmark, Five serves divine seafood. **$$$**

Sea Smoke
This new Canadian, Asian fusion restaurant serves everything from chowder to shrimp tempura. **$$**

Press Gang Restaurant & Oyster Bar
Compare oysters from a dozen Maritime growers, then tuck into a full seafood dinner. **$$$**

WHERE TO STAY

Westin Nova Scotian
This stylish Halifax waterfront classic shares space with the city's railway station. **$$$**

Sutton Place Hotel Halifax
Centrally located, this hotel complex in the new convention-center footprint is itself a destination. **$$$**

Muir Halifax
Simply the finest Halifax hotel, with handmade furnishings and harbor views from nearly every room. **$$$**

BEST PUBLIC ART

The Wave
Halifax's first whimsical waterfront artwork, *The Wave* still attracts the curious.

Sail
Sails emerge and merge in Edoardo Tresoldi's 6.4m-tall wire-mesh sculpture at Queen's Marque.

Drunken Lamp Posts
Three streetlight poles slump like drunken sailors, one leaking water to suggest the waterfront's seedy past.

Freak Lunchbox Mural
On Barrington St, Jason Botkin's wild, ocean-themed mural brightens Halifax like an Audubon illustration.

John Dunsworth Mural
On Quinpool Rd, see two faces of the late, beloved actor, aka Mr Lahey of television's *Trailer Park Boys*.

North Is Freedom
On Gottingen, two figures scale a 6m steel monolith inscribed with poetry by George Elliott Clarke.

a National Historic Site in 1997 and opened in 2011 as one of just two national museums outside Canada's capital, Ottawa. Permanent and temporary exhibits are well designed to engage visitors of all ages. The most insightful and moving exhibits make use of oral history and artifacts donated by Pier 21 immigrants.

The weekend **Seaport Farmers Market** recently moved to Pavilion 23 and marks the endpoint of the waterfront walk. Dozens of vendors sell local produce, hot bites, crafts, pet treats and craft beverages. The Halifax waterfront stretches from here to the twin Purdy's Wharf towers. You can almost hear the creaking of tall ships at their moorings and the whistles of freight trains from a time not long past. In the 1970s Halifax got serious about transforming its waterfront of crumbling piers and decaying warehouses into a safe, welcoming miracle mile, and now a vibrant mix of excellent restaurants, buzzing bars, cozy pubs, chic hotels, intriguing museums and boutique shops thrives within steps of the water. Works of nautically themed public art, both whimsical and profound, are scattered along this pedestrian zone. Shop for wines at **Bishop's Landing**, see the **Titanic exhibit** at the Maritime Museum of the Atlantic (p63), step aboard the WWII-era corvette **HMCS Sackville**, take the kids to the science **Discovery Centre** and planetarium, catch the **ferry to Dartmouth**, rest in a hammock on a pier, or just soak your feet in the ocean at the new **Queen's Marque** development, where broad steps leading into the water have become the latest attraction.

Check Out the Library

Downtown community hub

The **Halifax Central Library** is more than just a place to read. The award-winning 2014 building that resembles a loose stack of books is the pride of the city and a popular hangout. The building's airy, bright interior with its crisscrossing staircases, comfortable nooks, and quiet cafes on the bottom and top floors attracted two million visitors in its first year.

An Artist's House

Visit the provincial gallery

Inside the **Art Gallery of Nova Scotia**, the star of the show is the entire tiny house belonging to Maud Lewis, part of a permanent exhibition on her life and work: small paintings of snowy vistas, summer days, oxen at work and cats at rest. The famous folk artist painted the walls of her little home, where she produced thousands of rural scenes and sold them

BEST WATERFRONT RESTAURANTS

Drift
Has unexpected takes on Atlantic seafood, such as tuna crudo with sea buckthorn. **$$$**

Bicycle Thief
Halifax darling serving up dockside seafood dining with Italian flair. **$$**

Black Sheep
Set in the old Keith's Brewery; savor the umami flavors in dishes such as Bulgogi poutine. **$$**

Halifax Central Library

to tourists for $5 apiece. Today, some fetch hundreds of thousands of dollars.

Wander Downtown

Shop and snack near pizza corner

Downtown Halifax wraps around the northern and western slopes of the Citadel. Be sure to explore the side streets above and below the main arteries, Spring Garden Rd and Barrington St, where you'll find the city's highest concentration of shops, bars and restaurants. At Blowers and Grafton Sts, the late-night snacking spot known as **pizza corner**, try Halifax's official food since 2015: the donair, a Greek gyro with a locally developed sweet sauce. Pizza and donair joints across the city serve them. A door away from pizza corner is **Black Market Boutique**, a decades-old landmark shop known for its colorful batik-style facade, post-hippie feel, and stock of natural-fiber clothing, African masks, incense and gemstone jewelry.

Steps away, on Argyle St, the **Neptune Theatre** is the largest professional theater in Atlantic Canada.

THE AFRICVILLE STORY

From 1840 to 1970, a tight-knit Black community known as Africville lived at the northern end of urban Halifax. In the 1960s the city hatched a plan to remove its residents and demolish the entire neighborhood. The city said it needed the land to make way for the MacKay Bridge, which now spans the harbor, but many called the move racist. The city relocated residents to the far side of Dartmouth, miles away from their waterfront home. Today, one building, a reconstruction of the church that the city demolished – along with houses, a school, a post office and shops – stands on the site. Inside the church, exhibits in the **Africville Museum** tell the story of this lost neighborhood.

Salt + Ash
Everything from pizza to whole fish to cocktail garnishes is cooked over an open flame. $$

Daryâ
The name Daryâ – Persian for sea – suggests Mediterranean fusion; try the Bifteki burger with feta and harissa. $

Peacock Wine Bar
Local seafood is elevated in dishes such as seared scallops, popcorn grits and mushrooms. $$

SABLE ISLAND

Only about 500 people are permitted to visit **Sable Island National Park Reserve** each year. Like a white thread on blue fabric, this 40km-long sandbar lies 300km off the coast in the Atlantic Ocean. It's a truly wild place where 2500 pairs of terns nest, and 400,000 grey seals breed and birth their pups in the world's largest colony. A herd of 500 wild horses has survived on the island's grasses for 250 years. The only consistent human presence is scientist Zoe Lucas. She has conducted island research for 50 years and is a highlight of a Kattuk Expeditions guided tour, usually with owner Fred Stillman. Flights leave from Halifax's airport.

Hydrostone

A Green Space Apart

Halifax's city garden

On Spring Garden Rd, stroll the **Halifax Public Gardens** founded in 1837. It spans just one city block, but it's an oasis of trees and traditional gardens around a duck pond, with grassy spaces, fountains and monuments. Music is sometimes performed from the ornate gazebo.

The Hydrostone

A little taste of Europe

Fronted by a street of small shops and eateries, this enclave at the northern end of peninsular Halifax has a European feel. Planned and built according to a single architectural theme, the whole neighborhood rose from the ashes of the 1917 Halifax explosion that razed this end of the city. **Salvatore's Pizzaiola Trattoria** makes the best thin-crust pizza in the city – the sesame-seed crust of the Pomodoro is topped with olives, feta, garlic and sun-dried tomatoes. Pop into **Julien's Patisserie, Bakery and Cafe** for fresh, rustic breads and stay for a cappuccino and pastry. If you're a fan of the fabric arts, don't miss **LK Yarns**, which stocks local, hand-dyed and exotic yarns.

MUST-TRY RESTAURANTS

Fawn
Exciting new fine-dining option with French and Italian influences. $$

Stubborn Goat
This gastropub is a city landmark for its casual atmosphere, craft beer and elevated pub food. $$

enVIE a Vegan Kitchen
Flavorful dishes, such as lion's mane mushroom schnitzel, please vegans and omnivores. $

The Titanic

Halifax's connection to the doomed ship

If you're fascinated by the story of the 'unsinkable' *Titanic*, which famously sank on its maiden voyage in 1912, you'll be intrigued by Halifax's connection to the tragedy. At the **Maritime Museum of the Atlantic** a permanent exhibit outlines the ship's construction and includes a reproduction deck chair and more than 50 objects of interest, including pieces of wreckage.

As the *Titanic* sank, nearby ships rushed to the scene to rescue survivors and retrieve victims. Of the 337 individual remains to be recovered, 150 are interred in Halifax, most of them at Fairview Lawn Cemetery, which has 121 simple headstones arranged in three curved rows. The headstone to an unknown child was erected for an unidentified baby who is now known to have been an English citizen. Another headstone is marked J. Dawson. Your initial thoughts may turn to Jack Dawson, the character played by Leonardo DiCaprio in the 1997 film *Titanic*, but the grave actually belongs to ship employee Joseph Dawson.

BEST NIGHTLIFE HANGOUTS

The Carlton
Known for singer-songwriters, traditional music and an excellent menu. Try the pork belly and scallops.

Obladee
Cape Breton music sensation and sommelier Heather Rankin converted this former bookstore into Halifax's best wine bar.

Lower Deck Downtown
Timber ceilings and wooden benches are hallmarks of this original, after-hours party pub.

Bearlys
Gritty pub hosting Halifax's blues scene and an unexpected Filipino-Mexican-Canadian fusion menu.

Hangouts Across the Harbor

A jaunt to Dartmouth

Throwing a double-bladed axe at a wooden bullseye isn't a typical urban experience, but it's bringing people to downtown **Dartmouth**. Founded by real-life lumberjack and seven-time world log-rolling champion Darren Hudson, the **Timber Lounge** is within steps of the Dartmouth ferry terminal. While there you can sample a few craft beers by **New Scotland Brewing**, which shares the space. These and other hangouts where plaid is de rigueur make for a fun neighborhood that still has a small-town feel, even as condos rise at its edges on land reclaimed from the harbor. Within these dozen small city blocks you can sip lattes at **Two If By Sea** and brunch at **Portland Street Créperie**, stop in at shops like **Kept Gifts & Housewares**, poke through stacks of vintage music at **Renegade Records** and **Taz Records**...and then head out to chuck some axes. If lumberjacking isn't your style, **Lake City Cider**, the **Dear Friend Bar** and **Battery Park Beerbar & Eatery** make great places to spend an evening.

BITTEN BY THE LUMBERJACKING BUG?
Wild Axe Park (p73) in Barrington extends Darren Hudson's Lumberjack AXEperience beyond axe throwing to log rolling, sawing, pole climbing and more.

2 Doors Down
Halifax chef Craig Flinn presents East Coast–inspired creations such as shellfish-crusted haddock. $$

Brooklyn Warehouse
A New York–style, bare-bones bistro serving 'smalls' such as oysters motoyaki and 'bigs' such as lamb ragù. $$

Field Guide
A north-end Halifax gathering place; the open kitchen assembles locavore tacos, *bao*, gnocchi and salads. $

Lunenburg & the South Shore

GETTING AROUND

Unless you're cycling, the only way to get around the South Shore is by car. Follow signs for the Lighthouse Rte and Yarmouth & Acadian Shores. There's no public transit, but towns are walkable. Some towns have parking meters in the core, but generally parking is free. The ferry to Maine departs from Yarmouth.

From Halifax to Yarmouth, Nova Scotia's jagged coastline runs roughly northeast to southwest, but it's known as the South Shore. Characterized by quiet stretches of silver sand, long inlets, peaceful coves and dramatic headlands, this coastline is also home to the region's busiest fishing communities. Don't be shy. Get out on those wharves where the lobster fleet docks, and you'll meet friendly fishers eager to show off their boats and spin a seafaring yarn or two. As you'd expect, you'll also find lots of that fresh seafood at local restaurants.

For two centuries after its founding in 1753, the town of Lunenburg served as the headquarters for Atlantic Canada's shipbuilding industry. It earned Unesco World Heritage status in 1995 for its intact original layout. Walking Lunenburg's waterfront and steep streets lined with colorful wooden buildings is the closest you can get to immersing yourself in Nova Scotia's fishing heritage.

TOP TIP

Stick to the South Shore's coastal roads. Follow the Lighthouse Rte, aka Trunk 3, when possible. It meanders from Halifax to Yarmouth through villages and past beaches, wharves and historical sites. Avoid Hwy 103: Nova Scotia's 100-series highways are constructed away from the coast and are anything but scenic.

Get to Know Lunenburg

Take in the town's historic sights

Lunenburg is often photographed from the water to show off both its signature fire-engine-red fisheries buildings that line the waterfront and its steep streetscape, scaffolding up the hill as if built from random, brightly colored LEGO blocks. Getting to know Lunenburg starts aboard the fishing schooner **Theresa E. Connor**, permanently docked as part of the adjacent **Fisheries Museum of the Atlantic**. It's housed in a former fish-processing plant and loaded with exhibits about the history of the fishery and the town. In 2021 the museum expanded to include the **Big Boat Shed**, a working boatbuilding shop where hundreds of ships, including the original *Bluenose*, was constructed. If the **Bluenose II**, Canada's best-known tall ship, is in port, don't miss a chance to poke around or, if you're lucky, take a short sail.

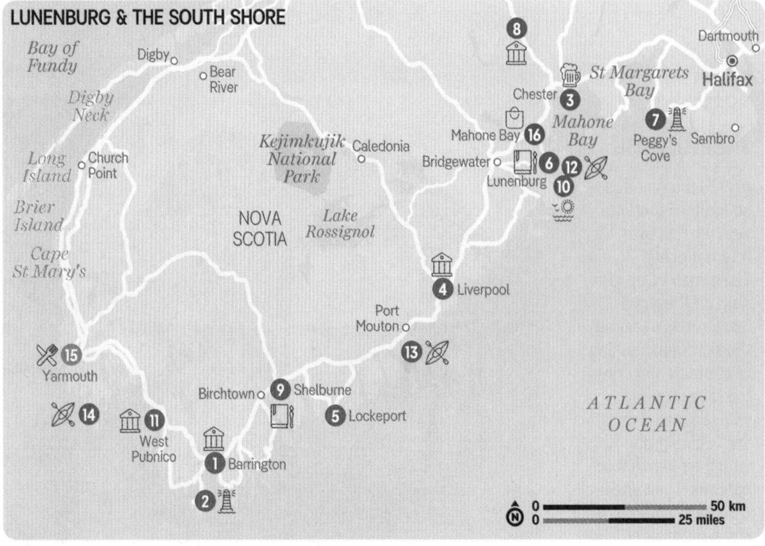

Linger on the low streets where **Ironworks Distillery** crafts Rum Boat Rum, Heart Iron Whisky and other spirits befitting its setting in a former and partially intact 1893 foundry where ship's anchors and chains were once fashioned. Continue on, browsing nautically themed shops, choosing a seafood restaurant for dinner and meeting the artist-owner of the **Laurie Swim Gallery**, a legendary Canadian quilt maker who has captured historical and personal moments in her fine work. Crowning Nova Scotia's colonial model town is the three-storey **Lunenburg Academy**, a former elementary school built in 1894. A National Historic Site, the building is now home to a music academy. If you prefer guided tours, sign up with **Lunenburg Walking Tours** for its daytime Essential Lunenburg, a one-hour walk to see the town's historic highlights, or the 90-minute Haunted Lunenburg nighttime tour by lantern light.

SIGHTS
1 Barrington
2 Cape Sable Island
3 Chester
4 Liverpool
5 Lockeport
6 Lunenburg
7 Peggy's Cove
8 Ross Farm Museum
9 Shelburne
10 Ovens
11 West Pubnico

ACTIVITIES, COURSES & TOURS
12 Blue Rocks
13 Kejimkujik National Park Seaside
14 Tusket Islands

EATING
15 Yarmouth

SHOPPING
16 Mahone Bay

Visit an Iconic Fishing Village

Rugged, romantic Peggy's Cove

Nova Scotia's South Shore begins in **Peggy's Cove**, where the red-capped lighthouse is Nova Scotia's best-known landmark. Propped on bare granite rocks worn smooth by pounding surf, the famous feature built in 1915 at the mouth of the

WHERE TO EAT FROM LIVERPOOL TO BARRINGTON

Quarterdeck
Seafood dining on a deck perched over the ocean next to Summerville Beach. $$

Charlotte Lane Cafe
New owners have continued the award-winning service at this top Nova Scotian restaurant. $$

Capt. Kat's Lobster Shack
It's lobster galore on a menu designed for the 'lobster capital of the world.' $$

THE BLUENOSE

In 1920 the American schooner *Esperanto* won the first ever International Fisherman's Cup race, held off the Nova Scotia coast. Testing the skills and stamina of captains and crew, the race required ships to rush from the fishing grounds with their perishable catches. Their pride wounded, Lunenburg shipwrights got to work, building a fishing schooner that would prove the fastest in the world. The following year, the *Bluenose* took back the trophy and never gave it up. After the original *Bluenose* was lost at sea, the replica *Bluenose II* came to life in the same Lunenburg shipyard. An image of the *Bluenose* under full sail has adorned the back of the Canadian dime since 1937.

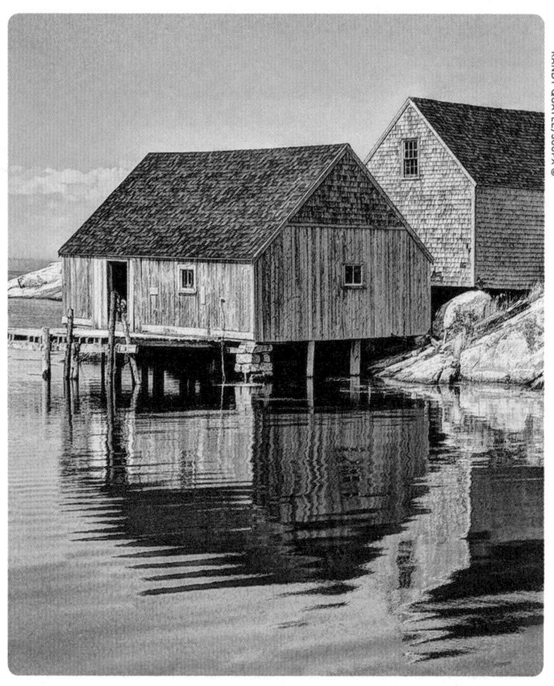

RANDY QUAYLE/500PX ©

Peggy's Cove

tiny harbor, really no more than a gap in the granite coastline, once led fishermen to safe haven and even housed a post office. In 2022 a broad viewing deck opened to keep the curious safe from unpredictable waves.

Explore the village, which hasn't changed much since it was first settled in 1811. Colorful wooden homes balance atop rocky outcrops and fishing shacks lean over the clear water. Stop at folksy gift shops such as **Hags on the Hill**. **The William deGarthe Art Gallery** exhibits works by the artist who carved into the adjacent bare bedrock the **Fishermen's Monument**, depicting 32 sou'westered men toiling on the sea.

Head out on the bay for a couple of hours with **Peggy's Cove Boat Tours**. Aboard the 18-passenger craft equipped with an underwater video camera, learn how lobster is fished before tucking into an onboard lobster dinner. You might spot puffins, and there's always the chance of whale, seal or dolphin sightings. Landlubbers can remain ashore for a seafood lunch at **Tom's Lobster Shack** or the **Sou'Wester**.

SOUTHWESTERN NOVA SCOTIA STAYS

White Point Beach Resort
This beachside inn with a swimming pool and golf course rents cottages and glamping domes. $$

Quarterdeck
Management just added modern, condo-style units to complement the beachfront rooms. $$

Seaside Cottages
Stay in a scene that once graced Canada's $50 bill. $$

Unwind in Chester

Sailing destination for 200 years

Summer sailing home for generations of Americans, the tiny town of Chester is known for fun on the water and for its streets of fine heritage homes. Chester sits at the tip of a small peninsula that juts into Mahone Bay. According to local lore, 365 islands are scattered across the bay, but the actual number is likely lower. Still, these protected waters, islands and inlets have sheltered ships under sail for at least 300 years. Every year in mid-August, the town hosts **Chester Sail Week**, a great time to watch boats rigged in colorful jibs and mainsails ply the waves. As a port for visiting sailors, it's not surprising that Chester claims Nova Scotia's oldest pub, the historic **Fo'c'sle Tavern**, nicknamed Chester's living room. However, there's more to Chester than its nautical side. The **SENSEA Nordic Spa** wasn't an instant hit when it opened in 2020, but as the pandemic waned it quickly developed a happy clientele. A day pass is the best option, so you can enjoy the lakeside pools, saunas and showers at a leisurely pace.

THE FERRY TO TANCOOK

Two of Mahone Bay's many islands stand out: Big Tancook and Little Tancook. A ferry makes several daily round trips to them from Chester. For under $10, you can enjoy a 50-minute adventure on the sea and a day wandering one of the islands. Most people go to the largest, Big Tancook, where there's still a one-room school. You'll find seasonal restaurants and gift shops with roads reaching to the far side of the island. A new car ferry will soon replace the passenger ferry, but it's better to walk on or take a bicycle anyway. The island is only 1.5km wide and 4km long, so getting around is relatively easy.

Pretty as a Picture

Browse scenic Mahone Bay

Three churches stand shoulder to shoulder on the waterfront in the town of **Mahone Bay**, 11km west of Lunenburg. This mini streetscape rivals Peggy's Cove as Nova Scotia's most recognized postcard-worthy scene, but it's the shopping that keeps visitors in town. Just north of town on Trunk 3, Heidi Wulfraat's **HW WoolWorks** studio is a little piece of heaven for fabric fans who knit, quilt, spin or weave. The pink twin peaks at the **Teaser** beckon with clothing, jewelry and cosmetics, much of it made locally. Pick up some Nova Scotian blends at the **Tea Brewery**, then choose some baked goodies to go with your cuppa at **Jo-Ann's Deli Market & Bake Shop**. Walk east on Main St to find restaurants and more specialist shops: **Amos Pewter**, **The Cozy Quilt**, **Encompassing Design Rug Hooking Studio** and **Suttles & Seawind**, a clothing designer so distinctive for its country chic that its products were featured in Bloomingdale's and Saks Fifth Avenue. Quench the thirst you've worked up with all that walking at Mahone Bay's craft-beer storefront and taproom, **Saltbox Brewery**, where that South Shore nautical theme continues with Storm Surge Maritime Ale, Holy Mackerel Pale Ale and Crustacean Elation Lobster Ale. There's no mackerel in the mackerel beer, of course, but there's actual lobster in the lobster ale.

Coopers Inn
A quiet garden and generous breakfast make the harbor view all the more enjoyable. $$

Islands Provincial Park
Camp in this pretty, harbor-edge park with sites among granite boulders and mature pines. $

Ye Olde Argyler Lodge
Cookouts on the shore overlooking a bay of islands lend the lodge loads of atmosphere. $$

THE MYSTERY OF OAK ISLAND

Did Captain Kidd bury treasure on Oak Island near Mahone Bay? The question obsessed Dan Blankenship and brothers Rick and Marty Lagina, generating 10 seasons of *The Curse of Oak Island*, the popular History Channel series. The mystery and the curse started in the late 1700s, when kids discovered an expertly constructed 130m shaft. Now nicknamed the money pit – as much for the fortune spent searching it as for the phantom treasure said to be buried there – the hole in Oak Island has attracted worldwide attention. The island is temporarily closed to visitors for the construction of an interpretive center, but you can book a tour from the water with **Salty Dog Sea Tours**.

Blue Rocks & Stone Ovens

Rugged coastline east and west of Lunenburg

On either side of Lunenburg Bay are two defining South Shore places, their coastal features captured in their names: to the north, Blue Rocks and to the south, the Ovens. Fishing shanties and brightly painted homes line the narrow road to **Blue Rocks**, whose shale shoreline shines blue against the sea and sky. If you didn't bring your own kayak, get out on the water with **Pleasant Paddling** to explore the many inlets and islands created by the jagged geology.

Ovens Natural Park is a seaside campground owned by the Chapin family – relatives of musician Harry Chapin, who sometimes performed here – and it's best known for its sea caves. When the waves are big enough, they boom against the caves' stone walls. There's also a history of gold mining here, and some campers pan for gold on the gravel beach.

Pirates, Country Music & Beaches

Seaside Liverpool and Lockeport

History is a spectrum in **Liverpool** on the Mersey River, both named for their counterparts in England when European settlers arrived in the 1750s. During Privateer Days in June, you can learn about the privateers (government-sanctioned pirates) who attacked British colonial Nova Scotia. The **Perkins House Museum** was the historic 1766 home of Simeon Perkins, who defended Liverpool against American privateers and did some of his own pirating. At **Fort Point Lighthouse Park** you can crank the foghorn inside the museum lighthouse. The engaging **Hank Snow Museum**, set in a former railway station, displays the famous country singer's costumes, 140 records and two Cadillacs. The composer of some 85 singles, including 'I've Been Everywhere,' grew up nearby. Sculptor Ivan Higgins is quickly turning his **Cosby's Garden Centre** into a new attraction with his Concrete Creations: dozens of life-size, whimsical statues and fictional characters, such as a giant tortoise, acrobats, dragons, Peter Pan–like figures, and forest animals. The Creations populate the private park of tall trees and boulders behind the garden center.

The seaside golf course at **White Point Beach Resort** is underrated, probably because the resort is known for so much more, such as the lodge and cabins overlooking the beach, the pool, and the many special events. There's good swimming at **Summerville Beach Provincial Park** where Broad River cuts through the beach and warms the cold Atlantic waters. Both White Point and the **Quarterdeck** in Summerville

WHERE TO EAT FROM PEGGY'S COVE TO LUNENBURG

Rhubarb Restaurant
Serves a mix of local seafood and classics such as steak frites. Many travel for the Sunday brunch. $$

The Fo'c'sle
Nova Scotia's oldest tavern, aka Chester's living room, is known for its good food and atmosphere. $

Kiwi Cafe
Signature dishes such as the lobster Benny make Kiwi the best breakfast and lunch spot around. $

Blue Rocks

PIONEER LIFE ON ROSS FARM

Experience life as a pioneer farmer on a day trip to **Ross Farm Museum**, about 30.5km from Chester on Rte 12. In the summer of 1816, Captain Ross and his family led dozens of disbanded British soldiers into Nova Scotia's interior to establish a settlement and build farms. The following year, Ross built Rosebank, a wood-frame house constructed of hand-hewed lumber. Today, interpreters in 19th-century regalia work in the house and on the farm for real, demonstrating their woodworking, blacksmithing, barrel-making and ox-shoeing skills. You can help plant the crops, dip some candles and take a wagon ride around the farm.

have built new accommodations and excellent restaurants for extended beachside stays. Don't miss the **Kejimkujik National Park Seaside**, a 1.5km hike across a barren headland to a remote beach where seals and shorebirds feed and rest.

The town of **Lockeport** is linked to the mainland by a short causeway across **Crescent Beach**, which graced the Canadian $50 bill issued in 1954. Ask at the **Beach Centre** for a guide to this hardworking fishing community with its old-fashioned **Town Market**.

Loyalists & Freed Slaves

Walk Shelburne's 10 heritage blocks

The strange thing about historic **Shelburne**, the town's 10-block waterfront **heritage district**, is that it was shaped almost as much by Hollywood as by its colonial beginnings. When films such as *The Scarlet Letter* were shot here, electrical lines were buried, buildings were constructed and others were altered to fit the period, making for unobstructed views.

Much of the town dates from just after its founding in 1783 by settlers loyal to the British crown who were seeking refuge after the American Revolution. Some 10,000

MORE BLACK HISTORY

The **Black Cultural Centre** (p90) in Cherrybrook at the edge of Dartmouth explores more of the urban Black experience and celebrates African-Nova Scotian accomplishments.

Lamprai & Spice Cafe
In a town stuffed with restaurants, this hole-in-the-wall stands out for homemade Sri Lankan dishes. $

Beach Pea Kitchen & Bar
The relatively new Beach Pea serves local and imported seafood dishes with a Mediterranean twist. $$

South Shore Fish Shack
The Shack perfected classic fish-and-chips, then added lobster, scallops and burgers. $

THE RIVER TO RIVER RIDE

The 13km coastal cycling route from the LaHave River to Petite Rivière makes a leisurely outing with plenty of stops. Begin at 1 **LaHave Bakery**, whose yellow Adirondack chairs invite you inside for takeaway picnic items. Walk the neighborhood, starting with the 2 **LaHave Craft Co-op** and LaHave River Books in the bakery building. Next, step inside the whimsical world of 3 **Child at Heart Wooden Models**, where Paul Kelley crafts miniature planes, boats and animals. You'll spot pottery displays to lure you inside 4 **Westcote Bell Pottery**, a former country store, to browse more works, this time by artists Vaughan Smith and Jacqueline Cohen. Across the street, in the 5 **Heart to Hand Studio** and showroom, Monica O'Halloran-Schut and Dave Schut fashion fine contemporary jewelry. Take a short detour to 6 **Fort Point Museum & Lighthouse**, then continue 6.4km southwest along the Dublin Shore, enjoying the seaside scenery, to 7 **Ploughmans Lunch** for pastries and espresso. If you'd prefer to picnic, head to 8 **Crescent Beach**, a silver strand stretching to the LaHave Islands. Half a kilometre beyond is 9 **Rissers Beach Provincial Park**, where you can camp, swim, hike and paddle. Immediately after is the village of Petite Rivière. If you're hungry, try the dish of local mussels, sausage and baguette at 10 **Osprey's Nest Public House**. Follow the river on Italy Cross Rd to 11 **Maritime Painted Saltbox**, a gallery of lively local scenes by Tom Alway and Peter Blais. Extend your ride 2.7km upstream to sample wine at 12 **Petite Rivière Vineyards** before doubling back or looping around on Mt Pleasant Rd. Extend your ride at the northern end by boarding the 13 **LaHave River ferry** across the river and back.

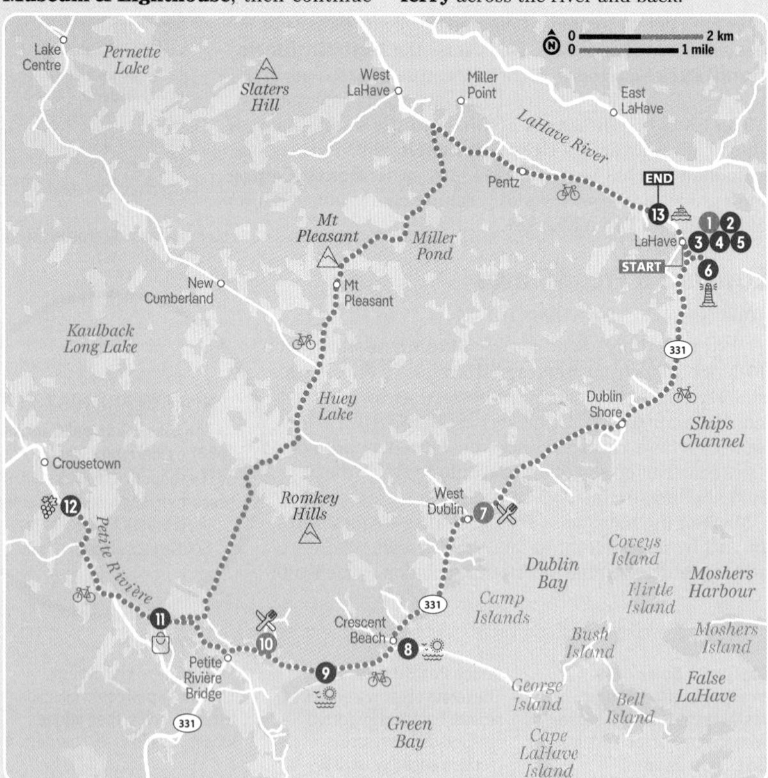

Black Loyalist Heritage Centre

settled here, among them hundreds of Black Loyalists who had been freed or had escaped from slavery and were given refuge by the British. In Shelburne, the Black Loyalists again faced racism and violence, and were pushed to nearby **Birchtown**. Even there, they were poorly treated and eventually attacked in the meager shelters they'd managed to construct. Subsequently, many of them followed leaders such as Boston King, who negotiated with the British the founding of Freetown in Sierra Leone. Novelist Lawrence Hill immortalized this migration in his novel *The Book of Negroes*, later made into a miniseries and partially shot here. Today, the excellent **Black Loyalist Heritage Centre** in Birchtown tells the story in multimedia exhibits and a reconstructed pit house, a log-covered hole in the ground where those early Black settlers survived their first few years.

Shelburne took shape and thrived in the Age of Sail, when the waterfront bustled with shipbuilding, trade and fishing activity. At **Museums by the Sea** – half a dozen historic buildings filled with artifacts – costumed guides lead interpretive programs. Kids can dress in 18th-century clothing,

CANOE KEJI

Kejimkujik National Park, known locally as Keji, covers 404 sq km of forest, lakes and rivers in southern Nova Scotia. Together with the provincial **Tobeatic Wilderness Area**, it provides a wealth of opportunities for paddling, hiking and camping. Keji is Canada's only national park with National Historic Site status, granted for its important Mi'kmaw heritage, including more than 500 petroglyphs – book a Mi'kmaw guide for an interpretive tour. Camp at one of 344 front-country campsites (154 with electricity) or rough it at one of 47 backcountry sites. Many can only be reached by canoe, which you can rent from **Whynot Adventures** outfitters in the park. Mountain bikers will enjoy the technical challenges on the new Ukme'k Trail that hugs the Mersey River.

BEST STAYS FROM PEGGY'S COVE TO LUNENBURG

Oceanstone Seaside Resort
This inn with big seaside cottages and a spa is best known for its Rhubarb Restaurant. $$

Mecklenburgh Inn
Chester's only accommodations, this century-old property has upper- and lower-deck views of the bay. $$

Ovens Natural Park
Camp or choose a rustic cabin on bluffs overlooking the ocean, steps away from sea caves. $

DORY RIVALRY

In the 1870s Nova Scotian shipwrights and fishermen designed the double dory (a small flat-bottomed boat) to fish for cod, Atlantic Canada's most valuable species for five centuries. Schooners sailed to the fishing grounds and lowered dories, each carrying two fishermen, over the side. When the dory was full, the fishermen would row back to the mother ship and unload.

At the **Dory Shop Museum** in Shelburne you can see a dory under construction and learn about master builder Sidney Mahaney, who assembled 10,000 dories in his lifetime. Debate continues whether the Shelburne dory or the slightly different Lunenburg dory is the better design. In another friendly competition, Lunenburg and its sister town, Gloucester in Massachusetts, occasionally host the International Dory Races.

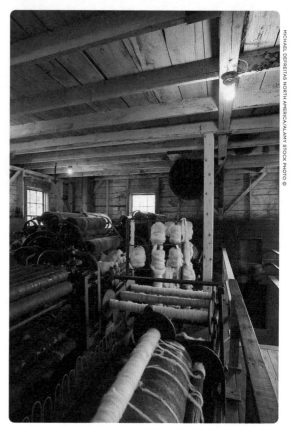

Barrington Woolen Mill Museum

try candle dipping and sample a strange drink called switchel at the 1785 **Ross-Thomson House**. You can also visit the **Shelburne Barrel Factory** in a building from the movie set, and stick around for the Saturday-morning farmers market.

Woolen Mill & Lumberjack Skills

Oceanside Barrington and Cape Sable Island

An eclectic quartet of museums and a lumberjack park make **Barrington** worth a stop on the Lighthouse Rte. A waterwheel still powers the old workings at the red **Barrington Woolen Mill Museum**, where wool was processed into cloth-

WHERE TO EAT IN YARMOUTH

Tusket Falls Brewing Co.
The smoked pub grub from the giant homemade barbecue complements excellent craft beer. $

Mr Gonzalez Mexican Cuisine
Your favorite Mexican dishes from tacos to burritos, all with vegetarian alternatives. $

Honey Bees
What started as a hundred-flavor ice-cream shop now serves unexpectedly delicious sushi. $$

ing. A short walk away, climb to the top of the red-and-white-striped **Seal Island Light Museum** to see the massive lighthouse lens. Between these two, the **Old Court House** is home to a local military museum and other exhibits, while the **Old Meeting House** hosted religious and municipal events from its construction in 1765 by the New England settlers who built this community. Behind the woolen mill, seven-time world log-rolling champion Darren Hudson runs **Wild Axe Park**, where he teaches visitors to throw axes and chop, saw and roll logs like a pro. Book ahead on his website to reserve your Lumberjack AXEperience.

Drive on to **Cape Sable Island** via the short causeway and explore any of the very busy wharves where fishers are happy to chat. Continue on to the **Hawk**, a beach at the far end of the island. When the fog lifts, the great 30m **Cape Sable Lighthouse** rises from the mist above its sandy island home.

Explore the Pubnicos

Acadian communities and remote islands

The Pubnicos are a series of French Acadian communities that hug the shores of Pubnico Harbour. Follow the Lighthouse Rte along East Pubnico around to **West Pubnico**. There, you'll find the **Musée des Acadiens des Pubnicos** and 7-hectare **Village Historique Acadien de la Nouvelle Ecosse**. Both interpret the history of this Acadian enclave. The 19th-century replica village stands in a community that's been inhabited by French settlers since 1653. Meet costumed guides in two traditional houses, a blacksmith shop, a boat shop and other period buildings. In the interpretation center there's a cafe serving local dishes and a gift shop stocked with the work of local artisans. Later, hang out at **Boatskeg Distilling**, where two fishers craft spirits in a former boat-building shop with views of the harbor over lush marshes.

Continuing on to Argyle, you'll find the **Argyle Township Court House & Gaol**, a National Historic Site. Built in 1805, the jail in the basement is Canada's oldest. Take a guided tour to hear stories of 150 years of small-town criminals.

The **Tusket Islands** should be better known for their fog-wrapped beauty and unique culture. The waters around the islands and headlands, some linked by roads, are frequented by seabirds, seals and whales, and the region is populated by a few fishing families. For a look around the shredded shoreline, take a boat tour with **Tusket Island Tours** or paddle with **Candlebox Kayaking**.

KAYAK THE SOUTH SHORE

Matt DeLong, owner of Candlebox Kayaking, recommends three top sea-kayaking locations. facebook.com/candleboxkayaking

Port Mouton
White-sand beaches – the most notable is Carters – provide opportunities to view seals, porpoises, bald eagles and even minke whales. Hire a guide the first time, then return with friends.

Tusket Islands
Tall wharves and fishing shanties decorate these rarely visited islands. The tidal range results in strong currents best navigated by intermediate to advanced paddlers or with a guide.

Kejimkujik National Park Seaside
Launch from St Catherine's River wharf to see seals, porpoises and even black bears from your kayak. Pause at St Catherine's River Beach – a long, protected white-sand beach – before paddling to Little Port Joli Beach.

WHERE TO STAY IN YARMOUTH

Gothik Guest House
An 1877 Gothic-revival home, this is one of Yarmouth's prettiest buildings and an affordable stay. $

MacKinnon-Cann Historic Inn
Rooms in this Victorian inn are furnished to honor each of the 20th century's first six decades. $$

Rodd Grand
The largest in the region, this basic but comfortable hotel has 132 rooms. $$

BEST LIGHTHOUSES IN NOVA SCOTIA

Fort Point, Liverpool
On a grassy point at the harbor mouth; browse the museum and crank the antique foghorn.

Sandy Point, Shelburne
At low tide you can walk across a sandbar to the lighthouse – great for sunset photos.

Cape Forchu, Yarmouth
It's so atmospheric that creepy 2018 film *The Lighthouse* was shot here. You can climb the lighthouse tower.

Cape d'Or, Advocate Harbour
Dine and sleep at this cliffside beacon overlooking powerful Bay of Fundy tides.

Cape George Point, Antigonish County
Watch fishing boats far below, and see Prince Edward Island and Cape Breton from the hilltop perch.

PATRICK HATT/SHUTTERSTOCK ©

Firefighters Museum

Explore Revitalized Yarmouth

Fun attractions and plenty to eat

Many Americans find their way to Yarmouth via **The CAT** high-speed car ferry from Bar Harbor in Maine. Other US visitors end their Atlantic Canadian explorations here and take a return trip home. If you're in either category, pause to take a look around Yarmouth, a town that has recently improved its visitor experiences. The Main St improvement program won a 2022 National Urban Design Award for its creative shelters, benches and sidewalk gardens. New murals blaze with color, and older attractions have modernized their activities. At the **Cape Forchu Light**, you can climb the tall, narrow lighthouse tower, check out the 15m humpback-whale skeleton named Foggy, walk the coastal trail in **Leif Erikson Park** and visit the free **Cape Forchu Museum** in the 1912 lighthouse-keeper's house. Don't miss the surprisingly engaging **Firefighters Museum**, with early hand pumpers and an 1863 horse-drawn steam engine that's Canada's oldest. Woven through the historic town with its heritage captains' homes, colorful main street, chain restaurants, taprooms and local diners is a mix of international restaurants, including Vietnamese, Mexican, Caribbean and Japanese options. On Saturday mornings, visit the busy **Yarmouth Farmers Community Market** in a handsome stone building for hot treats and fresh produce.

Annapolis Royal & the French Shore

Much of western Nova Scotia is divided into two distinct sub-regions: the French Shore to the south and the Annapolis Valley to the north. One of Atlantic Canada's prettiest towns, Annapolis Royal sits at the divide between these regions. The town overlooks the mouth of the Annapolis River at the western end of the fertile Annapolis Valley. Across the river, in 1605, Samuel de Champlain built the small fortification of Port-Royal – the first permanent settlement in what would become Canada. In present-day Annapolis Royal, you can visit the Fort Anne National Historic Site, where 70 Scottish settlers built the first fortifications in 1629. From their short-lived settlement would come Nova Scotia's name, flag and coat of arms. In the 18th century New Englanders loyal to the British settled here. The face of Annapolis Royal is mostly Victorian – it was an era when shipbuilders, fishing captains and merchants built big, ornate homes.

GETTING AROUND

Unless you're cycling, the only way to get around the Annapolis Valley is by car. Follow signs for Yarmouth & Acadian Shores, then for the Evangeline Trail. There's no public transit, but towns are walkable. Some towns have parking meters in the core, but generally parking is free. The ferry to Saint John, New Brunswick, departs from Digby.

Make Some Noise!

Acadian tintamarre festivities

Every August 15 on National Acadian Day, French-speaking communities across the Maritime provinces pull pots and pans from their kitchens, paint their faces in the tricolor red, white and blue, and then parade in the streets, making as much noise as possible with those kitchen utensils and any other noisemaker they can find. In the Clare region of Nova Scotia, also known as the French Shore and Baie Ste-Marie, hundreds of vehicles draped in streamers, balloons and Acadian flags wind through communities along the 35km coastal parade route. Onlookers wave flags, cheer and make noise as the parade passes. This *tintamarre* (Acadian celebration in the Maritimes) is in celebration of the Acadian people's perseverance 250 years after the British deported the entire French-speaking population in *le grand dérangement* (great

TOP TIP

The Annapolis Valley is known for its apple orchards and, increasingly, its vineyards. Visit in May, when the scent of flowers fills the air during the Apple Blossom Festival, or in fall, when apples are abundant at farm stands.

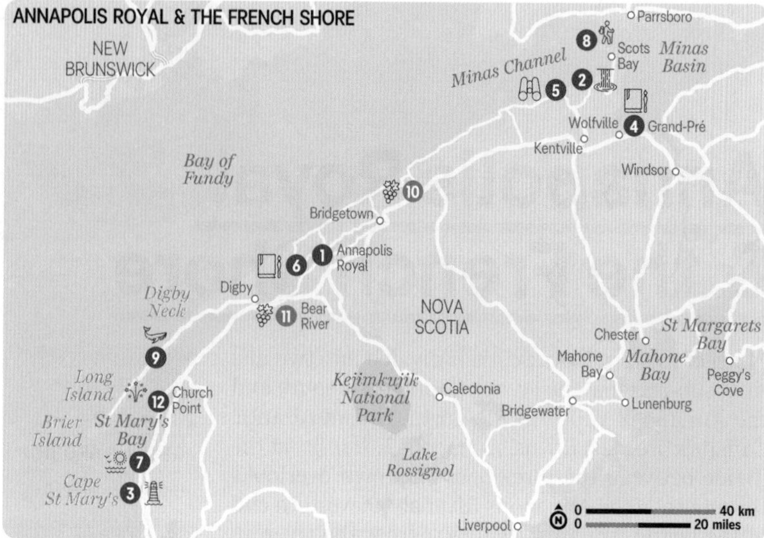

SIGHTS
1 Annapolis Royal
2 Baxters Harbour
3 Cape St Mary Lighthouse Park
4 Grand-Pré National Historic Site
5 Hall's Harbour
see 3 Mavillette Beach Provincial Park
6 Port-Royal National Historic Site
7 Smuggler's Cove Provincial Park

ACTIVITIES, COURSES & TOURS
8 Cape Split
9 Digby Neck

DRINKING & NIGHTLIFE
10 Annapolis Valley
11 Bear River

SHOPPING
12 Church Point

expulsion). In the 1950s Acadian communities began these *tintamarre* parades to proclaim their presence.

The *tintamarre* ends at the Université Ste-Anne in **Church Point**, where the **Rendez-Vous de la Baie** has a museum that tells the full Acadian story. Beside the university stands the 56m-high Gothic **Église Ste-Marie**. Shrinking congregations have put this, the largest wooden church in North America, in peril and closed the magnificent interior to visitors, at least for now, but it's still worth a look from the outside.

Stroll Broad Beaches & Explore Jagged Headlands

A dramatic coastline made for smuggling

Annapolis Royal enjoys a gorgeous natural setting. At **Smuggler's Cove Provincial Park** you can descend steep steps to a cobblestone beach and a sea cave where rum runners hid illegal hooch during Prohibition. **Mavillette Beach Provincial Park** is ideal for a beach day, especially when huge tides expose vast sand flats. Looking northwest, you'll see the village, wharf and fishing boats at Cape St Mary's. On a dramatic bluff overlooking the village is **Cape St Mary Lighthouse Park**. The obvious attraction is the red-capped lighthouse, but the granite **monument** featuring a fisherman at a ship's

CLARE TO ANNAPOLIS ROYAL STAYS

L'Auberge au Havre du Capitaine
Small and simple, this Meteghan River hotel is known for its friendliness. $

Digby Pines Golf Resort & Spa
This newly renovated château-style hotel has winter swimming in the outdoor heated pool. $$

Fundy Complex Dockside Suites
Mid-town suites, steps from bars and restaurants, overlook the harbor. $$

Port-Royal National Historic Site

wheel is a moving sight: it's dedicated to the many local Acadian fishers lost at sea over the past 250 years. Try spotting boats and seabirds on the bay using the viewing scope. Beyond the nautical rope fence jut short, jagged cliffs, below which seals sometimes sunbathe.

Meet the Governor at Port-Royal

Role-play a French settler

In 1605, after just one winter during which he lost almost half of the 79 colonists in his company, Samuel de Champlain abandoned a small island in the St Croix River on the border between what is now Canada and the US. The survivors crossed the Bay of Fundy and built Port-Royal, a timber fort on the Annapolis River. With the help of the Mi'kmaq, whose people had lived there for over 10,000 years, the company was able to survive the next winter and, within a few years, thrive. The following year Governor de Poutrincourt arrived with 50 men to help the settlers. Today, a costumed interpreter playing de Poutrincourt greets you at the **Port-Royal National Historic Site**, immediately presses you into work and escorts you inside the fortifications to your station. It's an entertaining way to learn how early settlers lived.

SHOP AT FRENCHY'S

When Edwin Theriault, aka Frenchy, imported a single bale of secondhand clothing from the US in 1971 to sell at his store in Little Brook, he started a phenomenon and a chain. Shoppers flock to these bare-bones stores to sift through bins for everyday clothes and brand-name bargains. Prices are ridiculously cheap, regardless of the retail value. Etiquette has developed around the precise way to rifle through the bins: everything is shoved to one end, then piled item by item at the other until a particular shopper is finished. Frenchy's has outlets across Nova Scotia and a worthy impersonator called Guy's Frenchy's.

Bread & Roses Inn
Gorgeous interiors match the lush garden setting of this rare brick Queen Anne Revival inn. **$$**

Queen Anne Inn
In its park-like setting, this 1865 Victorian mansion is ornate inside and out. **$$**

Dunromin Campground
Across the river from Annapolis Royal, camp with a tent or RV, or rent a waterfront cabin. **$**

Eye to Eye with Giants

Whale-watching at Digby Neck

The 40km-long, 5km-wide peninsula of **Digby Neck** and the two islands beyond point into the mouth of the Bay of Fundy. Here the world's highest tides create a top whale-watching destination where the world's largest mammals feed in the nutrient-rich waters. Fast Zodiacs and leisurely converted fishing boats depart from small ports for short runs to the feeding grounds of 12 whale species, as well as porpoises and seabirds. All the crews have decades of experience. **Petit Passage Whale Watch** departs from East Ferry on the mainland side of the short ferry crossing at the Petit Passage Cafe, though it's best not to indulge in its Acadian dishes and seafood until after the tour. The boat has padded seating and a washroom. **Adventure Bay Whale Watch** departs from Tiverton, a very short ferry ride across Petit Passage on Long Island. The *Casie and Boys*, a real lobster-fishing boat built in Cape Island, is equipped with a washroom. **Freeport Whale & Seabird Cruises** departs from Freeport at the far southern tip of Long Island from Tiverton and hosts passengers aboard another former fishing boat, the *Georgie Porgie*, equipped with a protective roof, padded seats and a washroom. On the last scrap of land, Brier Island, **Mariner Cruises** departs from Westport aboard a converted fishing boat. Its protective roof has railings so passengers can view whales from above. Also departing from Westport, **Brier Island Whale & Seabird Cruises** operates three vessels (two Zodiacs and a former Cape Islander fishing boat). If you're one of the 12 passengers aboard a Zodiac, you'll be dressed in a buoyant orange survival suit. Don't be alarmed, though: these boats are the fastest way to reach the whales and zip from pod to pod, but they're also very stable and safe. The whales are also kept safe: all Nova Scotia whale-watching operators follow a strict code of conduct when viewing any marine life. See p246 for more detail.

WHARF RAT RALLY

The little town of Digby, also known as the scallop capital of the world, is always worth a stop, but when the Labor Day long weekend rolls around (incorporating the first Monday in September), you'll have to make a choice: either you're into motorcycles or you're not. The resident population of 2000 swells to 50,000 when bikers from across the continent descend on the town, filling the streets with food vendors, pop-up shops, music and leather-clad riders on Harleys. Be warned that, during the event, there's usually not a spare room within an hour's drive.

A Royal Green Town

A walk around Annapolis Royal

Annapolis Royal is the greenest town in Nova Scotia. Easily walkable, it's built along an L-shaped main street with the Annapolis River and a waterfront boardwalk on one side and a lush wetland on the other. The wetland borders the 7-hectare **Annapolis Royal Historic Gardens** and the 15 hectares of grassy, rolling lawns at the **Fort Anne National Historic Site**. Best known for its 2000 roses, the gardens were named

CLARE TO WINDSOR RESTAURANTS

La Cuisine Robicheau
Acadian food such as rappie pie (a potato dish with meat) is sometimes accompanied by traditional music. $

La Vieille École
In a handsome old schoolhouse, Acadian seafood dishes are served at tables overlooking the Bay of Fundy. $$

Sydney Street Pub & Cafe
Digby's craft-beer pub prepares local dishes such as fried fish and international favorites such as souvlaki. $

DANITA DELIMONT/SHUTTERSTOCK ©

Bear River Vineyards

the 2015 Canadian Garden of the Year. The Saturday-morning **Farmers & Traders Market** is one of the busiest and best in the region, attracting many local organic farmers. Still, there's far more to Annapolis than history and greenery. Choose from many excellent restaurants and cafes, sample refreshments at the **Annapolis Brewing** taproom and the **Mad Hatter Wine Bar**, browse shops such as **Far-Fetched Antiques** and **ARTsPLACE** gallery, visit the **Sinclair Inn Museum** (in Canada's second-oldest wooden building) and see live entertainment at **King's Theatre**.

Wine, Coffee & Art

A detour to Bear River

The nearby community of Bear River makes a worthwhile short detour from Annapolis Royal. Stop by the new **Bear River Vineyards** to sample wines made from grapes grown in the Annapolis Valley's most westerly vineyards. Pull over at **Sissiboo Coffee Roaster** for a dark, rich brew from its cafe. Coffee in hand, stroll to the bridge over the river for a peek into **Flight of Fancy Arts** to see original sculptures and paintings.

THE FARMERS' ROUTE

Follow Rte 1 for 68km through the Annapolis Valley to discover small towns and farms. Near Aylesford, turn onto Rte 221 to find **Dempsey Corner Orchards**, where there's a season for every fruit, including 57 apple varieties. Near Berwick, take Rte 360 to **Meadowbrook Meat Market**, where handmade sausages are sold in its shop overflowing with locally sourced foods. Between New Minas and Wolfville, **Noggins Corner Farm Market** offers a cornucopia of crops, a U-pick and a corn maze. The Saturday **Wolfville Farmers' Market** is tops in the region. Its store is open every day except Monday. **The Tangled Garden** on Rte 1 creates preserves such as gooseberry-lemon balm jelly from its herb and berry garden.

Churchill's
Under new management with a new chef, Churchill's at Digby Pines Resort is once again the area's fine-dining go-to. **$$$**

Roof Hound Brewing
Kingston's craft brewery pairs brews with burgers, tacos and salads. **$**

Hole in the Wall Restaurant
The menu at Windsor's bistro ranges from Italian-style pizza to lobster croissants and burrito bowls. **$$**

GOOD CHEER IN ANNAPOLIS ROYAL

Samuel de Champlain created L'Ordre de Bon Temps (the Order of Good Cheer) dining club to get the French settlers through the harsh winters. You'll find the same hospitable vibe here today.

Whiskey Teller
Elevated pub food fired over an open grill in an 1884 brick building. **$**

Restaurant Composé
European-inspired dining room with fine riverside views. **$$**

Bistro East
Salads, pastas and pizzas; dinner only. **$$**

1 Fish 2 Fish and Chips
Reliable fish-and-chips takeout. **$**

German Bakery, Sachsen Cafe & Restaurant
Hearty breakfasts, lunches and early dinners. **$**

Brown Dog Kitchen
Generous breakfast sandwiches, curries and savory pies. **$**

DAVE REEDE/DESIGN PICS/GETTY IMAGES ©

Cape Split

Walk on the Ocean Floor

Tidal resonance at the Bay of Fundy

The tidal range in the **Bay of Fundy** is the world's greatest, in places swinging 16m in six hours. Traditional Mi'kmaw and Western origin stories for this world wonder both involve bathtubs. After the Mi'kmaw god Glooscap created the world, he asked Beaver to dam the bay so he could take a bath. When Whale complained that his feeding ground was blocked, Glooscap ordered Beaver to smash the dam. Science says that 100 billion tons of water squeezes in and out of the funnel-shaped bay. For comparison, all the world's rivers combined move only half that much. This massive motion, called tidal resonance, is like water sloshing back and forth in a bathtub. Head to **Hall's Harbour** and **Baxters Harbour**, where a 15m waterfall drops into the bay, to see boats resting on the ocean floor where they floated just hours before.

Up, Up & Away

Float over the valley

For an experience that rises above the ordinary, **East Coast Balloon Adventures** takes a few lucky passengers on daily hot-air-balloon flights over the Annapolis Valley. Professional

WHERE TO STAY NEAR WOLFVILLE

Grand-Pré oTENTiks
New oTENTiks (yurt-tent hybrids) set in a meadow overlooking the Unesco site. **$**

Evangeline
Rooms are available in the historic home and updated motel. **$$**

Inn at Grand-Pré Winery
The winery's founder turned his historic vineyard home into a six-unit luxury inn. **$$**

pilot Seth Bailey has been ballooning all his life. His wife, Katherine, is crew chief, specializing in tracking their balloon as it drifts over the landscapes until Seth eventually sets it down in a field. The friendly couple are walking encyclopedias of ballooning history, science and adventure.

Hike Cape Split

Picnic in high meadows

Possibly the most spectacular view at the end of any Nova Scotian trail awaits those who make the two-hour, moderately challenging hike through mature forest to the end of **Cape Split**, a 450-hectare provincial park since 2019. From grassy bluffs, you can look 60m straight down to five stone sea stacks and a fat wedge of rock sheered from the cliffs by tides that roar past the cape. The view beyond is over Minas Basin. Count on four to six hours to make the return trip. Avoid the cliff edges and instead enjoy a picnic in the headland meadows. For the more adventurous and fit, a path leads down to the shore at the foot of the cliffs, but it requires rappeling down an eroding bank and sure-footedness on the slippery rocks at low tide. The reward is a few hours of wandering through a dramatic coastline right out to those sea stacks.

Taste a World-Class Brut

Tour the valley's wineries

It took barely two decades for the **Annapolis Valley** to earn a place among Canada's great wine-growing regions. The moderate climate and rich, rocky soils are ideal for growing crisp whites such as Nova Scotia's signature l'Acadie Blanc. The varietal is blended with other wines to create Tidal Bay, Nova Scotia's only appellation wine. Because growing conditions are similar to those in Champagne, France, the Annapolis Valley is ideal for small-batch sparkling wines that represent a distinctive East Coast terroir. Benjamin Bridge Brut is considered one of Canada's finest. The 2017 Prestige Brut Estate from l'Acadie Vineyards won gold at the 2023 Decanter World Wine Awards, a first for a Nova Scotian wine.

Remember Those Cast Out

The Unesco site of Grand-Pré

The region's epicenter of French Acadian history is the **Grand-Pré National Historic Site**, World Heritage listed by Unesco for its farmland cleverly dyked off from the sea in the 17th century. A well-designed visitor center tells the story of

BEST WINERIES TO VISIT

Benjamin Bridge
Glass in hand, tour the hillside vineyards set on a slope down to the Gaspereau River.

Gaspereau Vineyards
This boutique winery makes one of Nova Scotia's favorite reds, Lucie Kuhlmann.

L'Acadie Vineyards
Named for the region's signature varietal, L'Acadie handcrafts bright, refreshing sparkling wines. Try the rosé.

Luckett Winery
Reds and whites are served with the best winery lunches and sweeping vineyard views.

Domaine de Grand Pré
Come for the excellent shop, tasting room and restaurant. Stay in the historic inn.

Lightfoot & Wolfville
The newest big winery, restaurant and shop; its wine is made following strict biodynamic growing techniques.

WOLFVILLE'S GRAND VICTORIAN INNS

Blomidon Inn
This 33-room Victorian wonder has the feel of an English manor. Experience a meal in the dining room. **$$**

Tattingstone Inn
Ornate furniture, a garden setting, and gourmet dinner and breakfast make Tattingstone stand out. **$$**

Gingerbread House B&B
In spite of its name and the ornate facade, some rooms here are more contemporary than Victorian. **$$**

DEVOUR FOOD & FILM

Since 2009, when Slow Food Nova Scotia founded **Devour! The Food Film Fest**, up to 15,000 movie buffs have descended annually upon Wolfville at the head of the Annapolis Valley, the breadbasket of the region. Devour! is the world's largest festival of its kind, with more than 100 events including cooking demonstrations, film workshops, the great Chowder Smackdown and the Street Food Rally. The highlight of the festival, which takes place in the last week of October, is the collection of shorts, docs and dramatic films from around the world. Most are shown in the Al Whittle Theatre. Of the many chefs and filmmakers who have attended, perhaps the most notable was Anthony Bourdain.

ART BABYCH/SHUTTERSTOCK ©

Memorial church, Grand-Pré National Historic Site

early French settlement and of *le grand dérangement* by the British beginning in 1755. Knowledgeable guides lead visitors through the center to a diorama of the region, artifacts and a small movie theater that help tell the story of these early French settlers, their cooperative relationship with the Mi'kmaq, the tragic expulsion and their return to settlements across the Maritime provinces. The tour extends to the park-like grounds around the center.

After refusing to sign oaths of allegiance to the British crown, nearly 14,000 Acadians were deported from across the region – 98 families consisting of 600 people from Grand-Pré alone – and their homesteads were burned behind them. The Cajuns of the American South are among their descendants. Amid weeping willows, the grassy grounds stretch to a 1922 **memorial church** on the site of the original Acadian church. At the entrance to a garden walkway leading to the church stands a statue of Evangeline, the character created by American poet Henry Wadsworth Longfellow, casting a longing look over her shoulder toward her lost homeland. Published in 1847, Longfellow's lengthy poem *Evangeline: A Tale of Acadie* went through 270 editions and 130 translations, becoming compulsory reading material in American schools. Its popularity kickstarted tourism in Nova Scotia, and shipping routes and train lines were built or improved to transport the many tourists making their way to Grand-Pré. Monuments to Longfellow and to John Frederic Herbin, who first envisioned this memorial site, stand on these grounds.

Tatamagouche & the North Shore

To some, Nova Scotia on a map resembles a duck or a lobster. The North Shore looks like the leg of either creature. Its varied geography is the connective tissue between the province and the continent, between Halifax and Cape Breton Island. The world's highest tides shape the Parrsboro Shore, exposing 350 million years of natural history, while the gentle waters of the Northumberland Strait lap at Tatamagouche. The communities' cultural heritage is just as varied, ranging from lumbering or coal-mining centers to university and industrial towns. Unesco sites and Nobel Prizes are woven into the fabric of the North Shore's story.

The village of Tatamagouche exemplifies the proud heritage and contemporary spirit of northern Nova Scotia. Its name likely derives from a Mi'kmaw term meaning 'where the waters meet.' Indigenous people and settlers alike valued it as the meeting place of the Waugh and French Rivers where they empty into the Northumberland Strait.

GETTING AROUND

Unless you're cycling, the only way to get around the North Shore is by car. Follow signs for the Evangeline Trail and the Sunrise Trail. There's no public transit, but towns are walkable. Some towns have parking meters in the core, but generally parking is free. Car ferries from the terminal at Caribou, near Pictou, link Nova Scotia and Prince Edward Island.

Meeting of Waters, Meeting of Minds

Community life in Tatamagouche

Tatamagouche has always been strong in community spirit, undertaking projects such as **Creamery Square**, a former dairy that's become a marketplace, heritage center and performance venue. The community built and operates its own wind turbines that generate most of the village's electricity. Nearby, **Jost Winery** pioneered winemaking in the region in 1986. Since a Jost family member opened **Tatamagouche Brewing** in 2014, it's become a regional favorite and a cornerstone of local life.

TOP TIP

You can follow the Parrsboro Shore from Truro around the Northumberland Strait to the Canso Causeway, but don't forget to look inland. Communities such as Springhill, Oxford and Wentworth are skipped all too often, as are engaging attractions such as the Springhill Miners' Museum and Ski Wentworth, where summertime mountain biking and hiking replaces winter skiing.

Stops Before the Road Ends

Wildlife, mastodons and Mi'kmaw culture

Roads from the Annapolis Valley and Halifax merge into Hwy 102, which ends at the Trans Canada Hwy. A few stops are worth making before the highway ends. **Shubenacadie**

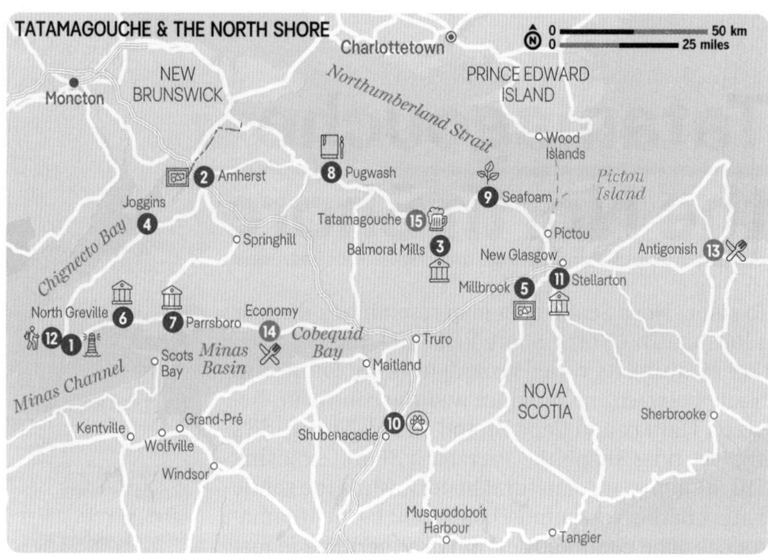

SIGHTS
1 Advocate Harbour
2 Amherst
3 Balmoral Mills
4 Joggins
5 Millbrook
6 North Greville
7 Parrsboro
8 Pugwash
9 Seafoam
10 Shubenacadie Wildlife Park
11 Stellarton

ACTIVITIES, COURSES & TOURS
12 Cape Chignecto Provincial Park

EATING
13 Antagonish
14 Economy

DRINKING & NIGHTLIFE
15 Tatamagouche

Wildlife Park is a 40-hectare zoo for mostly North American animals born in captivity or rescued. At the Stewiacke rest stop (aka **Mastodon Ridge**) – exactly halfway between the equator and the North Pole – kids will go gaga over the life-size mastodon sculpture commemorating the discovery nearby of real bones in 1991. Among the fast-food options is an outlet of **Coldstream Clear** craft distillery. At **Millbrook** are two unmissable stops. The new **Alan Syliboy Art Studio** exhibits works by the renowned Mi'kmaw visual artist, and nearby the **Millbrook Cultural & Heritage Centre** makes this a great place to learn more about Mi'kmaw history, culture and art. Next to the highway, a 12m statue of the Mi'kmaw god Glooscap towers over the site.

Nova Scotia's Fundy Geopark

Explore the Parrsboro Shore

The Glooscap Trail that begins in the Annapolis Valley continues along the Parrsboro Shore, but it feels more a part of northern Nova Scotia, where the scenic drive is called the Sunrise Trail. From Truro, take Rte 4, which becomes Rte 2 through Bass River, Economy and Five Islands to Parrsboro. From there, Rte 9 leads to **Advocate Harbour** and Apple River. The entire way is part of the new **Cliffs of Fundy Geopark**,

WHERE TO STAY NEAR PUGWASH

Train Station Inn
Owner 'Boxcar' Jimmy LeFresne saved Pugwash's train station and train cars, converting them to an inn and restaurant. $$

Fox Harb'r Resort
Fox has its own golf course and airport, and offers a range of activities and rooms. $$$

Customs House Inn
Rooms in this 1873 customs office are spacious, vintage and grand. $$

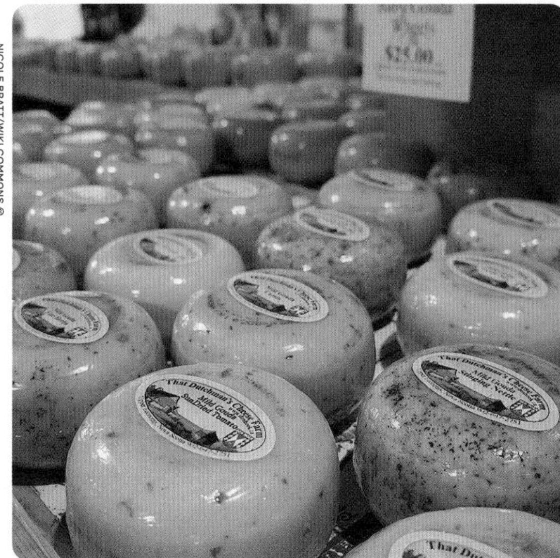

NICOLE BRATT/WIKI COMMONS ©

That Dutchman's Cheese Farm

Unesco designated for the depth and importance of its natural and human history. The best place to learn about the designation and the dozens of worthwhile stops is a site with two names: the **Cobequid Interpretation Centre/Cliffs of Fundy Welcome Centre** in Economy.

Leaving Truro, the first stop is the **Joy Laking Gallery**, the studio for one of Nova Scotia's foremost watercolor artists. In **Economy**, second-generation **That Dutchman's Cheese Farm** makes excellent Gouda and a renowned sharp blue cheese, Dragon's Breath. Kids will enjoy its animal and nature park. A relatively leisurely hike, the 5km **Economy River Falls Trail** loop, leads through mature forest to a small waterfall. The coastal **Five Islands Provincial Park** is named for a cluster of tiny near-shore islands with a colorful creation story. In this story, the Mi'kmaw god Glooscap threw great clods of mud at Beaver onto the vast tidal flats after the animal dammed the god's medicine garden.

Signs of Ancient Life

Parrsboro's geological treasures

Parrsboro is the epicenter of the Cliffs of Fundy Geopark. Start exploring at the **Fundy Geological Museum**, where

SHOOT THE SHUBIE

Tidal-bore rafting is like splashing around in a river of chocolate milk. Zodiacs carrying half a dozen adventurers cruise the **Shubenacadie River** just before it turns into a milkshake. The world's highest tides from the Bay of Fundy collide with the muddy river current, churning the river into standing waves. After this natural phenomenon subsides, boats pull into the shore, where the river banks become slick, mucky slides and adults turn into playful children. Wear clothes you don't mind tossing afterwards. Local tour companies such as **Tidal Bore Rafting Resort** rent riverside cottage accommodations and run activities such as lunch on the river floor at low tide and a lobster boil with tastings of regional rum around the campfire.

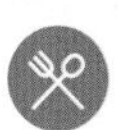

PARRSBORO SHORE RESTAURANTS

Briny Bay
One of several fish-and-chip shops in Economy, this homey one hosts live music. $

Black Rock Bistro
Healthy salads, bowls and seafood are paired with local craft beer and cocktails. $$

Wild Caraway
A culinary destination; chef Aitken works with ingredients foraged and harvested from sea and garden. $$

EVOLUTION ETCHED IN STONE

Naturalist Charles Darwin cited **Joggins** as a place where the fossil record can best teach us about evolution. Some 200 fossilized species that lived 300 million years ago have eroded from these cliffs. This is the world's most complete fossil record of the Coal Age, qualifying it as a Unesco World Heritage Site. Fossils of whole trees that grew in steamy forests well before the dinosaurs can still be seen in the cliff strata, and visitors are practically tripping over fossils as they walk among the rocky debris. Exhibits, displays and fossils inside the **Joggins Fossil Centre** tell the whole story of the site. Brown-bag-lunch guided tours depart from the center.

CURTIS WATSON/SHUTTERSTOCK ©

Cape Chignecto Provincial Park

dioramas and life-size models of pre-dinosaur habitats, animals and giant insects based on local fossil discoveries depict early life on Earth. Geology shop **Tysons' Fine Minerals** sells and displays semiprecious stones and fossils from here and around the world. Comb the gravel spit that is the start of the **Partridge Island Lookoff & Hiking Trail** for your own geological treasures.

A reminder of more recent history, the **Ship's Company Theatre** is built around the *Kipawo*, the last local ferry, and presents live theater and music.

Dining & Hiking on the Edge

History and wilderness from Parrsboro to Advocate

Halfway between Parrsboro and Advocate, the **Age of Sail Heritage Museum** in **North Greville** is one of Nova Scotia's better small museums. Set on the banks of the tidal Greville River, the museum tells the story of this hamlet when it was a thriving lumbering and shipbuilding center. Just before reaching Advocate Harbour, follow signs for the short walk to the **Cap d'Or Lighthouse**, perched on an arrowhead of cliffs jutting into the Bay of Fundy. The lightkeeper's house is now an inn and restaurant. Hiking and camping in **Cape Chignecto Provincial Park** is one of Nova Scotia's premier wilderness

PARRSBORO SHORE ACCOMMODATIONS

Five Islands Provincial Park
Open-field and wooded campsites overlook islands and dramatic tide changes. $

Riverview Cottages
Parrsboro's cute, rustic cabins sit on a quiet side street next to the mouth of a small river. $

Parrsboro Mansion Inn
One of several inns, this 1880 beauty set on wide lawns started life as a mansion. $

experiences, with 40km of trails, lots of backcountry camping and views from 180m cliffs overlooking the Bay of Fundy.

The Artisans of Amherst

Learn rug hooking

As the geographical center of the Maritime provinces, Amherst has long been a manufacturing and transportation hub. It's also the western starting point of both the Sunrise and Glooscap tourism routes. Recently, the town has upped its tourism game with beautification projects, such as a mural depicting local history. The town center is dominated by Victoria Sq, which is surrounded by 19th-century red stone buildings and includes a war monument and a gazebo. The most dramatic of these landmarks is the **First Baptist Church of Amherst**, with round red turrets and tall windows.

Participants travel from across the continent for workshops at the renowned **Deanne Fitzpatrick Rug Hooking Studio**. Fitzpatrick creates original designs, dyes her own fabrics and builds rug-hooking starter kits. At **Maritime Mosaic**, an arts-and-craft market in what was the Two Barkers, the largest department store east of Montréal, more than 60 vendors create and sell original works.

Go Deep

Salt, peace and pewter in Pugwash

Pugwash's endearing name comes from the Mi'kmaw word *pagweak* (deep waters). It's the perfect moniker for a town that's deep literally and figuratively: here you'll find a salt mine that descends to 300m and **Thinkers Lodge**, a National Historic Site for deep thinking about world peace. There's a little waterfront park named for Thinkers Lodge founder Cyrus Eaton, and a lighthouse on a point at the harbor entrance. The tiny port accommodates small freighters for salt exports.

Pugwash is also known as the home of the factory and principal retail shop of **Seagull Pewter**, Canada's largest pewter manufacturer. When **Basic Spirit** opened its pewter studio and shop in 2003, Pugwash became a national pewter hub.

Stop & Smell the Lavender

Fragrant fields in Seafoam

The 50-hectare **Seafoam Lavender Farm**, an award-winning Nova Scotian export success story, could be mistaken for a field in France. Walk down the aromatic rows, then wander over to the shop. Owners Dave and Suzy Belt might be

NORTH-SHORE CAFES & RESTAURANTS

Train Station Inn
Have lunch at Tatamagouche's railway-station cafe or eat dinner in a real railway dining car. **$$**

Sugar Moon Farm
On weekends, head inland from Tatamagouche for hearty sugar-shack grub best enjoyed with maple syrup. **$**

Sea Grape Cafe
Enjoy a charcuterie lunch on the patio overlooking Jost Winery. **$$**

Stone Soup Cafe & Catering
On the Pictou waterfront; dishes vary from African peanut soup to smoked-meat sandwiches. **$**

Mezza Lebanese Kitchen
Popular among Antigonish college students for its shawarmas and falafels. **$**

Tall & Small Cafe
Bistro sandwiches, salads, soups and baked goodies in Antigonish. **$**

WHERE TO STAY NEAR ANTIGONISH

Birchwood Campground & Cottages
Three cottages, plus tent- and RV-site options; also has family activities, a pool and restaurant. **$**

Summer Hotel, St Francis Xavier University
In summer, no-frills dorm rooms and two-bedroom suites are open to budget travelers. **$**

Antigonish Victorian Inn
Stay in grand furnished rooms in this 1904 midtown inn with a huge backyard garden. **$$**

demonstrating soap making, serving samples of lavender honey and tea or offering a tour back into the fields to show off their many lavender varieties.

CANADA'S MAYFLOWER

In 1773 the ship nicknamed Canada's *Mayflower* left Scotland bound for Pictou with 189 Highland Scots. During the 11-week journey, 18 passengers died of disease. Since 2000 a replica of the original ship – which was actually called the *Hector* – has been moored next to the **Northumberland Fisheries Museum & Lobster Hatchery** at the Hector Heritage Quay. Out of the water at research time, the ship was undergoing a major rebuild using timber from 2022's destructive Hurricane Fiona. Updated interpretive narratives will tell the story of the ship's arrival 250 years ago from the perspective of the Indigenous Mi'kmaq, who have lived on these shores for thousands of years.

Grist to the Mill

Industry in Balmoral Mills and Stellarton

The water-powered **Balmoral Grist Mill** is a museum, but a woodland stream powers the creaking workings as it has since 1874. Oat cakes made from oats ground by the giant stone are sold in the shop. Nearby, just north of Denmark, the **Sutherland Steam Mill** hews its lumber with heritage machinery.

Beside the Trans Canada Hwy in **Stellarton**, the **Museum of Industry** is filled with animated exhibits and important artifacts, including two massive steam-train engines. The *Samson* is Canada's oldest and one of the world's first. The *Albion* is possibly Canada's second oldest. Here, you can watch an interpreter operate a mini lumber mill and see expert quilt makers hand-sew traditional quilts. Entering the **Coal and Grit gallery** is like ducking into a mine shaft. If you're lucky, Paul Laland, the grandson of a miner, will be on duty. He tells gripping stories of hardscrabble towns, terrifying coal-mining disasters and heroic rescues.

Peace by Chocolate

An inspiring success story

The uplifting story of **Peace by Chocolate** went global after Canadian prime minister Justin Trudeau made a speech to the United Nations to highlight the little Antigonish company as an example of how refugees can contribute to their new countries. In their native Syria, the Hadhad family ran a successful chocolate company. After their factory was bombed, the family sought refuge in Canada. They settled in **Antigonish** with the help of local sponsors. The family was soon selling a few chocolates at the local farmers market. From those humble beginnings in 2016, Peace by Chocolate employs nearly 100 people, including refugees from Syria and Ukraine. There's now a feature documentary about its story. The company sells products across the country and at its outlets in Antigonish and Halifax. Its chocolate bars are labelled with the word 'peace' in dozens of languages or sold in wrappers stamped with Nova Scotian sayings such as 'give'r' (short for 'give her', which means 'step on it') and that familiar Canadian sentence ender, 'eh?'

WHERE TO EAT NEAR ANTIGONISH

East Avenue
Authentic, tasty Middle Eastern dishes by the Almethyb family, recently arrived from Syria. **$**

Maple Cedar Syrian Kitchen
East meets West at northern Nova Scotia's best urbanesque restaurant. Try the blackened-fish tacos. **$$**

Gabrieau's Bistro
A landmark fine-dining restaurant, Gabrieau's now has a tempting sushi menu. **$$$**

REGINE POIRIER/SHUTTERSTOCK ©

Balmoral Grist Mill

Explore the Cape George Loop

From gypsum to gin

Together, Rtes 337 and 245 between Antigonish and New Glasgow follow 56km of shoreline around Cape George. Studded with panoramic lookouts and plenty of stops, the route makes a rewarding day trip. Begin at **Crystal Cliffs**, a quiet beach off Crystal Cliffs Farm Rd where soft gypsum outcrops have been eroded by the waves into pink and white sculptures. For a challenging hike, hit the **Cape George Hiking Trail** through ravines and onto plateaus. Pause at Ballantyne's Cove for its bucolic beauty, and visit the **Tuna Interpretive Centre** for a history of world-class bluefin-tuna fishing and to connect with local charters. The best views are from the **Cape George Point Lighthouse**, the site of a light since 1861. Another lighthouse stands at the wharf in Arisaig next to the beach and **Arisaig Provincial Park**, so designated for the nearly half-billion-year-old fossils of crinoids and trilobites – early ocean life-forms – that emerge as the cliff erodes. Overlooking this scene is **Steinhart Distillery**, where Thomas Steinhart makes Nova Scotia's best gin and serves German food. At **Knoydart Farm**, where the organic milk flows as freely as the humor and good cheer, you can sample cheddar cheeses from the milk of happy, grass-fed cows. Finally, stroll and swim at **Big Island Beach**, the long spit of sand that links the island to the mainland.

KEPPOCH

By most standards, Keppoch Mountain near Antigonish isn't much more than a broad hill, but recent developments have transformed its former downhill ski runs into a year-round destination for outdoor enthusiasts. The downhill runs are now trails for cross-country skiing, fat-tire biking and snowshoeing, but in summer these same 30 trails make great hiking and mountain-biking routes, all well marked. Those former ski runs make for some exciting cycling. Kids will enjoy testing their Frisbee skills on the 18-hole disc-golf course and monkeying around on the rope-climbing playground. There's even a lake and dock for swimming. Fat-tire bikes and cross-country skis are available for rent.

Musquodoboit Harbour & the Eastern Shore

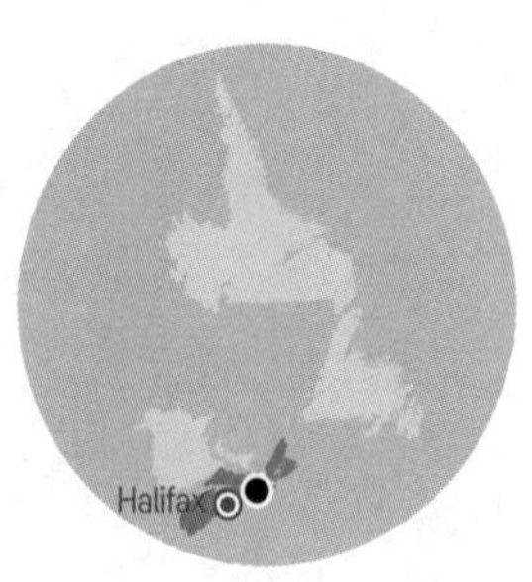

GETTING AROUND

Unless you're cycling, the only way to get around the Eastern Shore is by car. Follow signs for Marine Dr. There's no public transit. Parking is free.

Underrated for too long, this 320km stretch of coastline is the wildest in Nova Scotia. Stretching from the fringes of Halifax to the Canso Causeway, this coast (promoted by local tourism initiatives as Marine Drive) is a frayed fabric of long, narrow coves, finger peninsulas and rocky islands. Hike miles of rugged seaside trails, learn to surf, enter a sandcastle-building contest, gather your own mussels, do a little fishing, and camp beside the ocean. In this outdoor playground, spotting a family of fluffy red foxes, a colony of seals or a raft of eiders is just another day at the shore. Come in from the surf and sun for craft beer, seafood, folk art and heritage experiences. At the same time, the Eastern Shore is unusually rich in living history – the line between museums and contemporary life is sometimes blurred. Of the few coastal villages, Musquodoboit Harbour offers the most in services and attractions.

TOP TIP

A car is the only practical way to get around quickly in this remote area, but cycling is possible. Accommodations are limited, so camping and bed-and-breakfasts are recommended, as is packing for outdoor activities such as kayaking, hiking, cycling and spending long days at the beach.

Settlers to the Shore

Explore Black and Acadian heritage

To dig into the settler history of the Eastern Shore, begin at the **Black Cultural Centre** in **Cherry Brook**, at the edge of urban Halifax. Black history goes back centuries in Nova Scotia. Since 1983 the center has told the story of the first Africans to call Nova Scotia home, their arrival in numbers after the American Revolution, their upheaval from the downtown Halifax neighborhood of Africville in 1970 (see p61), and the significant accomplishments of community members.

The little-known story of French-speaking Acadians on the Eastern Shore is told at the **Acadian House Museum** in West **Chezzetcook**, where interpreters, musicians and crafters bring Acadian culture to life in a farmhouse built in 1850. At the far end of the region, at Parc de nos Ancêtres (Ancestors' Park; p94) in **Larrys River**, stands a semicircle of interpretive panels and boulders painted with scenes from Acadian history. On a nearby roadside hilltop overlooking **Tor Bay** and the Sugar Islands, a platform resembles the deck of an early

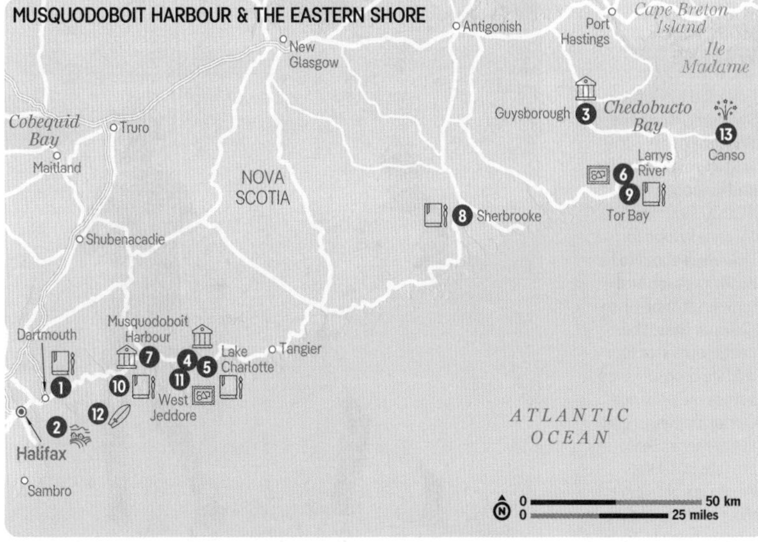

French sailing ship. This is **Place Savalette**, a National Historic Site that marks the meeting between early-17th-century French explorer Samuel de Champlain and Captain Savalette, who sailed with summer fishing crews across the Atlantic to these waters from 1565 to 1607.

Fishing, Forestry & Shipbuilding Heritage

Three living-history settler museums

The smallest of the Eastern Shore's three living-history villages is **Fisherman's Life Museum** in **Jeddore Oyster Ponds**, where the Myers family home, barn and fishing dock have been restored to their early-20th-century selves. Second-generation resident Ervin Myers raised 12 daughters in the little cottage, scratching a living from the sea.

Six kilometers east at **Lake Charlotte**, **Memory Lane Heritage Village** recreates Nova Scotian rural life in the 1940s. From the entrance through the general store, visitors time-warp back to the WWII period. Memory Lane is a complete village with houses, barns, farm animals, a one-room school, a church, a gold miner's shack and a rustic cookhouse restaurant.

Sherbrooke Village blurs the line between past and present 85km east. Until recently, residents lived and worked in parts of this late-19th-century living-history museum made

SIGHTS
1 Cherry Brook
2 Fisherman's Cove
3 Guysborough
4 Jeddore Oyster Ponds
5 Lake Charlotte
6 Larrys River
7 Musquodoboit Harbour
8 Sherbrooke Village
9 Tor Bay
10 West Chezzetcook
11 West Jeddore

ACTIVITIES, COURSES & TOURS
12 Lawrencetown Beach

ENTERTAINMENT
13 Canso

SHOPPING
see 12 East Lawrencetown

MARINE DRIVE EAST ACCOMMODATIONS

Marmalade Motel
All eight rooms, with names like 'No Drama Lama,' sing with personality and come with ocean views. $$

SeaWind Landing Country Inn
The de Jonghs rent modern rooms and run an excellent restaurant on 25 oceanfront acres. $$

Liscombe Lodge
The Liscombe River tumbles past cabins and the historic lodge, tucked into a quiet cove. $$

HOPE FOR WILDLIFE

Founded by Hope Swinimer, **Hope for Wildlife** treats 7000 wild animals annually and responds to 40,000 inquiries. The TV series *Hope for Wildlife* is about to film its 10th season and now airs in more than 100 countries. The center operates four wildlife drop-off sites across the province. Opportunities to visit the center in Seaforth are few, but if the timing is right, don't miss it: it's open to visitors noon to 3pm on Saturday, and in July and August from noon to 3pm on Wednesday. Check hopeforwildlife.net for the date of the annual open house fundraiser in August.

KEN MORRIS/SHUTTERSTOCK ©

Lawrencetown Beach

up of dozens of buildings, most of them original. Interpreters working as blacksmiths, carpenters and general-store merchants bring this former shipbuilding and trading town to life. Visitors can dress in period costume and role-play everything from a blacksmith's apprentice to a criminal incarcerated in the jailkeeper's house.

MORE HISTORIC VILLAGES

The **Highland Village** (p97) in Cape Breton Island, another living-history village, recreates the Celtic settler experience. You can relive the French Acadian settler experience at the **Village Historique Acadien de la Nouvelle Ecosse** (p73) in Pubnico.

Surf's Up

Ride those North Atlantic waves

Lawrencetown Beach is the surfing capital of eastern Canada, if not the entire country. Surfers in wetsuits ride the waves here year-round. The cold-water sport is so popular that several surfing schools and a TV show – *Diggstown*, about a surf-loving legal aid lawyer – have sprung up. **East Coast Surf School** provides daily lessons and rents boards and

WHERE TO EAT ON MARINE DRIVE WEST

Memory Lane Cookhouse
The self-serve lumberjack-cookhouse meals at this heritage village are devoured at plank tables. $

Henley House Pub & Restaurant
With Sober Island Brewing next door, Henley pairs generous pub fare with craft beer. $

Uprooted Market & Cafe
Local, organic produce sold at the market goes into fresh sammies and soups. $

suits at the beach. **Halifax Surf School** operates similarly at **Martinique Beach Provincial Park**, another lengthy stretch of fine sand. It's washed by gentle waves and equipped with change rooms and washrooms.

A Village at the City's Edge

Explore Fisherman's Cove

Having been swallowed up by the city – it's technically in urban Halifax – the little fishing port of **Fisherman's Cove** is still the real deal. Marking the beginning of Marine Drive, this 200-year-old settlement has been transformed to welcome visitors while retaining its identity as an authentic, working fishing village. Stroll the row of 20 brightly painted waterfront shanties, each an individual shop. Browse original artwork or jewelry, order up a mess of fish-and-chips, or shop for souvenirs from among the work of more than 100 artisans. It's so close to Halifax's urban area that you can hop on a city bus to get there. Extend your walk into tiny **MacCormacks Beach Provincial Park**, which is within sight of three islands: Lawlor, McNabs and Devils.

Dutch Treats

Shop for cheese and trinkets

In **East Lawrencetown**, the **Atlantic Dutch Shop** faithfully recreates a little piece of Holland in the basement of a Dutch family home. Never fear: there's Gouda cheese, but the shop is stuffed with thousands of other Dutch goods from licorice to cookies to ceramic knickknacks.

Follow Your Nose

Hike headlands, forests and marshes

Just outside Halifax's urban core, the **Salt Marsh Trail** crosses 9km of coastal wetlands and small bridges where birdlife is abundant. It's an easy walk on a former railway bed. For every Eastern Shore beach there's an equally attractive coastal hiking trail. At **Taylor Head Provincial Park**, trail lengths vary from 1.6km to 8km through backcountry forest and along beaches to the tip of the narrow peninsula. Over 19km of trails meander along the **Liscomb River Trail System** through forest, along coastline, over swinging bridges and past waterfalls. The **Chapel Gully Trail** in Canso begins with a very short estuary loop. An interpretive panel then presents options for up to three hours of coastal hiking.

PRIZE SANDCASTLES

Every August for nearly 50 years, up to 10,000 people have watched hundreds of participants sculpt temporary works of art with sand at **Clam Harbour Beach Provincial Park**. Kids with beach pails work alongside teams with shovels, trowels and water spray bottles to vie for awards and cash prizes. The coveted People's Choice Award was recently won by a sand dragon. A fantasy based on *Alice in Wonderland* won the 2022 adult sculpture division, while a kraken destroying a boat and castle won in 2023. Sheldon the Octopus recently placed first in the children's category. Of course, beachgoers don't need to wait for a competition to spend the day sculpting their own creation at the shore.

MARINE DRIVE WEST ACCOMMODATIONS

Salmon River Country Inn
Historic inn with a Bavarian feel in its rooms and restaurant. Ask about Viking Dinners. $$

Webber's Lake Charlotte
Vintage motel on sprawling grounds that's within walking distance of Memory Lane. $

Murphy's Campground
Generations of jovial Murphys have run this seaside campground. Book a mussel-collecting boat tour. $

TOUR THE WILD ISLANDS

When the Nova Scotia Nature Trust created the **100 Wild Islands Coastal Wilderness** the name caught the collective imagination...but the real count is even higher. There are actually 282 islands in this archipelago of protected places, totaling 28 sq km of uninhabited rocky outcrops, forested islets and secluded mini beaches along 32km of coastline. Experienced guiding companies such as **Coastal Adventures** and the **Norse Cove Camping & Kayak Centre** in Tangier rent sea kayaks, provide training and lead tours around the islands. For those who want to get out on the water but prefer not to paddle, **Sober Island Boat Tours** in Sheet Harbour runs sightseeing and lobster-fishing tours.

All Aboard!

Visit Musquodoboit Harbour's vintage station

The restored 1918 flared-roof railway station at the **Musquodoboit Harbour Railway Museum** hosts a visitor-information center and gift shop. Outside, train hobbyists and kids will enjoy wandering among some unusual railcars including a snowplow, a mail crane and a caboose. Check out the on-site beer garden, food truck and ice-cream shop.

Get an Eyeful

See big, bold art

There's absolutely no missing the home and outbuildings belonging to **Barry Colpitts**. The folk artist's simple house beside Rte 7 near East Ship Harbour blazes top to bottom with bright trim, and it's stuck all over with delightfully painted carvings of fish, birds, people and objects. He's happy to receive visitors. Colpitts' works are among the collection at the **Black Sheep Folk Art Gallery**, in a former fish-plant building in **West Jeddore**.

True History & Tall Tales

Explore the Chedabucto Triangle

The Chedabucto Triangle extends east to the tip of mainland Nova Scotia, linking Guysborough, Larrys River and Canso. At the **Courthouse Museum**, which documents the history of **Guysborough**, one full wall is dominated by a Prohibition-era tapestry promoting the 'Guysborough Total Abstinence Society, Instituted 1830.' The museum sells Temperance Society T-shirts. In contrast, the **Authentic Seacoast Distillery & Brewhouse** makes beverages such as Rare Bird Craft Beer, Glynnevan Whisky and Sea Fever Rum. It also operates Guysborough's historic **DesBarres Manor Inn** and 10 new **Yurts in the Vineyard** perched between the ocean and its vineyards and hop yards.

Learn about regional and local Acadian history at **Parc de nos Ancêtres** (Ancestors' Park) in Larrys River and Place Savalette (p91), a nearby National Historic Site overlooking Tor Bay and the Sugar Islands below.

Visitors to **Canso** can hop on a free boat from the Parks Canada visitor center to the **Canso Islands National Historic Site**. A trail leads to the remains of a once thriving fishing and trading community, first of Mi'kmaq and then of French and English settlers.

WHERE TO EAT ON MARINE DRIVE EAST

Beanie's Bistro
Adjacent to Sherbrooke Village, Beanie's makes great Reubens, fishcakes and baked goodies. $

SeaWind Landing Restaurant
The excellent restaurant at SeaWind specializes in local, seasonal seafood. $$

Big G's Pizza & Restaurant
Guysborough's pizzeria makes unexpectedly delicious pita wraps and lobster sandwiches. $

ROBERT BIRD/ALAMY STOCK PHOTO ©

Artist Barry Colpitts' house

After you leave Canso on Rte 16, you'll find the strange **Prince Henry Sinclair Monument** standing at a scenic lookout. A plaque claims that Sinclair sailed 12 ships into Chedabucto Bay in 1398, a century before Christopher Columbus crossed the Atlantic. It's a largely unproven, even dismissed historical theory, but it's fun to ponder the possibility.

COMMUNITY & NATURE IN TOR BAY

Jude Avery's book *The Forgotten Acadians* documents French settlers on the Eastern Shore.

I feel privileged to be a lifelong resident of the Tor Bay area. Our three children never felt denied living here. The smallness of our area allowed us to get involved in community development and take on leadership roles. We are witnessing a great cultural awakening, but we also enjoy daily fun experiences with friends and family: clearing lake ice for a skate or a hockey game, walking along a beach, paddling a river or playing music in someone's house. To watch a sunrise over the bay or a deer prance gingerly to the water's edge teaches us the beauty of nature.

Baddeck & Cape Breton Island

GETTING AROUND

Air Canada and WestJet fly into JA Douglas McCurdy Sydney Airport, where several car-rental companies operate. Car ferries run to and from Newfoundland dock in North Sydney. The only road link to Cape Breton Island is across the Canso Causeway. Unless you're cycling, the only way to get around Cape Breton is by car. Follow signs for the scenic drives: Ceilidh, Cabot, Marconi, Bras d'Or Lake and Fleur-de-lis. There's no public transit, but towns are walkable. Some towns have parking meters, but generally parking is free.

TOP TIP

Plan to spend at least three to five days on Cape Breton Island. It's considered to be among the world's most beautiful islands, partly for the delightfully scenic 300km Cabot Trail. Zipping around the island in a day or two barely scratches the surface of its natural, cultural and historical riches.

At the heart of Cape Breton Island, the pretty village of Baddeck sits on the shores of Canada's largest inland sea, Bras d'Or Lake (pronounced bra-door). It's within convenient reach of most island attractions, such as the Cabot Trail and Fortress Louisbourg, as well as Mi'kmaw, Gaelic and French Acadian regions. At the same time, it's worth lingering in the town itself. The 200-year-old settlement has attracted tourists since the late 1800s. Among the first visitors were inventors Mabel and Alexander Graham Bell, who loved it so much they moved to Baddeck in 1885 and lived there until their deaths in 1922 and 1923. Baddeck has plenty of restaurants and hotels, including a 150-year-old inn. With the relatively new Bell Bay Golf Club, the historic Bras d'Or Yacht Club, and boat rentals of all kinds to explore the Kidston Island Lighthouse and the lakeshore, there's plenty to keep visitors pleasantly occupied.

NATALIA BRATSLAVSKY/SHUTTERSTOCK ©

Bras d'Or Lake

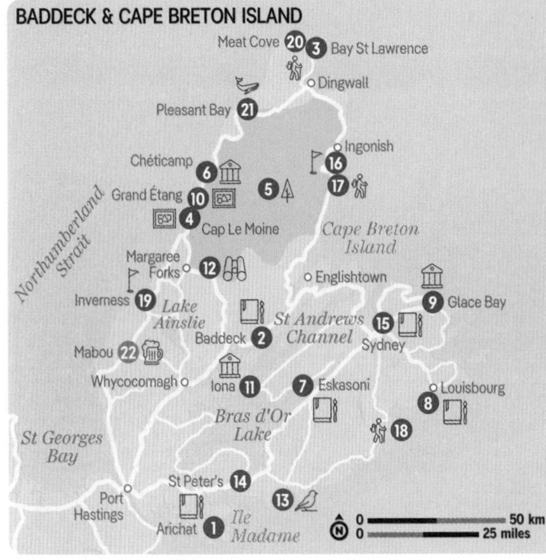

SIGHTS
1 Arichat
2 Baddeck
3 Bay St Lawrence
4 Cap Le Moine
5 Cape Breton Highlands National Park
6 Chéticamp
7 Eskasoni
8 Fortress of Louisbourg National Historic Site
9 Glace Bay
10 Grand Étang
11 Highland Village
12 Margaree Valley
13 Point Michaud Beach Provincial Park
14 St Peter's
15 Sydney

ACTIVITIES, COURSES & TOURS
16 Cape Breton Highlands Links
17 Cape Smokey Provincial Park
18 Gabarus Wilderness Area
19 Inverness
20 Meat Cove
21 Pleasant Bay

DRINKING & NIGHLIFE
22 Mabou

A Hundred Thousand Welcomes

Discover Celtic heritage

Experience *céad míle fáilte* (a hundred thousand welcomes) in Cape Breton's Celtic communities.

On a hilltop with grand views of Bras d'Or Lake's southern shores, the 11 buildings set on 17 stunning hectares at the **Highland Village** living museum are designed to teach and preserve Gaelic heritage and language on the island. In buildings ranging from a replica 18th-century stone hut to a cheery yellow early-20th-century wooden house, costumed interpreters live and work as Gaelic settlers as they were across a span of 200 years. They might be forging a horseshoe, baking cookies, quilting a family heirloom, tending chickens or weeding the garden. A lazy horse might also wander over to the fence next to the church to watch a summer wedding.

At the **Gaelic College** near **Englishtown**, Gaelic language and arts programming are more formalized. Themed sessions, camps and workshops on weaving and kilt making, and events such as storytelling and concerts take place year-round. The **Great Hall of the Clans** museum takes visitors on a worldwide journey to explore the Gaelic diaspora.

Every October when Cape Breton's mountainsides light up with fall colors, the entire island resounds with the **Celtic**

WESTERN COAST ACCOMMODATIONS

Mabou River Inn
It's more motel than inn, but the 11 rooms here are comfortable and central. $

Maison Fiset House
Eight color-themed B&B units in Chéticamp come with glass-wall patios and mammoth breakfasts. $$

Chéticamp Campground
Several trailheads lead from Chéticamp, one of several full-service national-park campgrounds. $

WHAT'S A CEILIDH, ANYWAY?

It seems everywhere you go on Cape Breton you'll hear the word *ceilidh* (pronouned kay lee). *Ceilidh* is Gaelic for a social visit, gathering or party, and Nova Scotia is famous for its impromptu kitchen parties built around traditional music. Fiddlers, guitarists and percussionists jam away the evening while dancers scuff the pattern off the old linoleum flooring – that's a Cape Breton *ceilidh*. When a *ceilidh* is held in a community hall or local pub the dancers have more room, but the spirit of a close-knit community shaking off the cobwebs is the same. Harkening back to their Scottish roots, renowned Cape Breton fiddlers compose their own jigs, reels and strathspeys for just such occasions.

BRESTER IRINA/SHUTTERSTOCK ©

Highland Village (p97)

Colours International Festival. Some 50 concerts are performed by Celtic musicians from around the world at 35 venues ranging from intimate community halls to the island's largest stages.

The 185km **Celtic Shores Coastal Trail** meanders along Cape Breton's southwest coast, through forest and beside Lake Ainslie (Nova Scotia's largest natural lake). It hops from village to village in the most Celtic part of the island. Whether you're hiking or cycling the trail, or driving the parallel Rte 19, be sure to stop at the cozy **Red Shoe Pub** in **Mabou**. The room feels more like a community hall when it hosts Celtic music jams or *ceilidhs* almost every night.

To a Tee

Top-notch golf in Inverness

Once a broken-down coal-mining town, **Inverness** is now midway through a major rejuvenation kickstarted by two

CENTRAL & EASTERN STAYS

Inverary Resort
Cape Breton's leading resort in Baddeck has lodge rooms, cottage suites and water sports. $$

Telegraph House Hotel
A hotel since it was built, this 1861 Baddeck beauty has the excellent Cable Room restaurant. $$

Ceilidh Country Lodge
This Baddeck classic is more motel than lodge, but the views from its hillside perch are unmatched. $

new world-class golf courses. Some fairways run between the beach, where locals like to spend summer afternoons, and the town's main street, which is still lined with duplex company houses from the mining days. Opened in 2011, **Cabot Links** consistently ranks in the world's top 100 courses, as does its sister course, **Cabot Cliffs**, opened in 2015. Fairways reminiscent of those in Scotland, the birthplace of golf, run parallel to sand dunes and clip the edges of bluffs that drop into the sea.

Through the Margaree Valley

Cape Breton's Acadian heart

The drive north from Inverness passes through the Margaree Valley, the most pastorally beautiful part of the island, where once-abundant salmon followed the Margaree, a Canadian Heritage River. When the coastal road reaches Margaree Harbour, it joins the Cabot Trail. One of the most pleasant experiences on the island is gently floating on an inner tube down the Margaree River for a couple of hours with tour company **Live Life in Tents**.

Beyond the Margaree, the culture shifts from Gaelic to French Acadian. In **Cap Le Moine**, look for **La Bella Mona Lisa**, a delightful roadside gallery of whimsical, folksy art. Just a few kilometers further at **Grand Étang**, the **Centre Mi-Careme** is a great introduction to Acadian arts and crafts. The center's name comes from the French for 'mid-Lent,' when Acadians don handmade masks, dress wildly and party to traditional music. Artist-in-residence Diane Bourgeois leads summertime mask and folk-art workshops for all ages.

On the other side of **Chéticamp**, **Les Trois Pignons** museum presents local Acadian history and houses the **Elizabeth LeFort Gallery and Hooked Rug Museum**. Some 300 works are on display, many by the woman who perfected the humble craft and brought it to world attention. LeFort hooked portraits of movie stars, US presidents and other famous people. She even presented some of her works in person to the portrait subjects, including John F. Kennedy, Elizabeth II and Pope Pius XII. As a result, her work is believed to be in collections at the White House, Buckingham Palace and the Vatican.

Drive from Sea to Sky

Highlands National Park and enclaves

From Chéticamp, Rte 30 enters **Cape Breton Highlands National Park**, then rises and falls over coastal headlands before turning inland to plateau on French Mountain. One of the most iconic images of Nova Scotia is the view at the end

THE BELLS OF BADDECK

Mabel and Alexander Graham Bell moved with their family to **Baddeck** in 1885. Nearby, the inventors built a large home they dubbed Beinn Bhreagh, Gaelic for 'beautiful mountain.' The Bells and their assistants experimented here with sound, watercraft and flight. Most famously, Alexander invented the telephone, but he and his team also set watercraft speed records, invented the metal detector and built the *Silver Dart*, an early aircraft that lifted from the sea ice near Baddeck on February 23, 1909, making it the first controlled powered flight in the British Empire. The fine museum at the **Alexander Graham Bell National Historic Site** tells the full story.

Royal Hotel
Among the chain hotels along Sydney's waterfront, this 1895 boutique gem stands out for its history. **$$**

Cranberry Cove Inn
Louisbourg's cranberry-colored Victorian inn has period furnishings and a verandah overlooking the harbor. **$**

Dundee Resort & Golf Club
On Bras d'Or Lake, golfers and water-sports lovers have a choice of rooms and cottages. **$$**

NORTH AMERICA'S FIRST SINGLE MALT

Set among the low, moody mountains of western Cape Breton, between Mabou and Inverness on Rte 19, is a scene right out of rural Scotland. **Glenora Distillery** is North America's first single-malt-whisky distillery, producing 'the water of life' since 1990. The white building set against the green hillside backdrop and built right over its water source, MacLellans Brook, is the realization of a vision by the distillery's late founder, Bruce Jardine, who was assisted by Bowmore Distilleries of Scotland. Tours of the giant copper stills, samples from the aging barrels in the warehouse, dinner set to traditional music at the fine restaurant, and a night in a chalet or inn room tempt visitors to linger.

of the looping, 8km **Skyline Trail**: you look back down the coastal road from the viewing platform. From here, the road descends with equally breathtaking views into the **Pleasant Bay** enclave, where lots of accommodations and adventure options, such as **True North** glamping domes and the **Whale Interpretive Centre**, await.

From the intersection at Cape North, continue on the Cabot Trail or turn north for a drive to what feels like the ends of the Earth at **Bay St Lawrence**, and beyond to **Meat Cove**, where there's camping and hiking. The provincial government recently announced a $6.4-million commitment to build the 50km Seawall Trail from Meat Cove across the most remote part of Cape Breton to Pleasant Bay. The project, including a series of overnight huts, is slated for completion by 2026.

Across Warren Brook from the **Broad Cove Campground**, where there's a small beach, follow the graveled **Mary Ann Falls Road** to the falls, where swimming beneath the cascade is a favorite park activity.

At the edge of the national park, historic **Keltic Lodge** is perched on a narrow peninsula where the **Cape Breton Highlands Links** begins. Designed by golf architect Stanley Thompson and built with shovels and horses, the 1941 course is nicknamed Thompson's 'mountains and oceans course.' It's considered his masterpiece and among the world's finest. The best views of Ingonish, Keltic Lodge and beyond are from the new, year-round gondola at **Ski Cape Smokey**.

On the return route to Baddeck beyond the national park, a short trail awaits at the top of **Cape Smokey Provincial Park** for equally expansive mountaintop views. The road below is dotted with artisan shops. Designer Barbara Longva creates whimsical hats at **Sew Inclined**, and the **Glass Artisans Studio & Gallery** offers glass-blowing classes and handmade works. The Steele sisters sell their paintings and make fine chocolates at **Cabotto Chocolates**.

Continuing south, the Cabot Trail reaches the far end of a long sand spit and a short crossing on the Englishtown cable ferry. On the other side, before returning to Baddeck, drop into the **Giant MacAskill Museum**, dedicated to the 2.36m-tall, 193kg giant who was born here in 1825. The little attraction tells big tales of Guinness world record-setting feats of strength such as lifting a one-ton anchor.

Living Mi'kmaw Culture

A visit to Goat Island

Walking the 2.4km trail on Goat Island in **Eskasoni** is like traveling into a past when only Indigenous people lived here.

WHERE TO EAT IN WESTERN CAPE BRETON

Clove Hitch Bar & Bistro
Unassuming Port Hood place that's indeed a hybrid, with smash burgers and vegetable curries. $$

Woodroad
Experiential dining by chef Daryl MacDonnell in a cliff-edge house built by his brother, Peter. $$$

Freya & Thor Gallery & Cafe
Bright, folksy art makes the baked goodies and espresso drinks here even more enjoyable. $

Cabot Trail

Eskasoni Cultural Journeys animates stops with basketry, dancing, smudging (a cultural ceremony) and cooking sessions. At one stop, interpreters talk about how the Mi'kmaq hunted and how they built their wigwams (cone-shaped structures made of wood and birch bark). At another stop, Mi'kmaw interpreters teach their traditional game, *waltes* (pronounced walt iss), played with a wooden bowl, dice and sticks.

THE CABOT TRAIL

For many, the Cabot Trail *is* Cape Breton Island, and for good reason. The 300km driving route dotted with scenic lookoffs takes in the most dramatic third of the island, following the undulating coast, reaching the tops of the ancient tabletop mountains, and descending into communities of Gaelic, French Acadian and Mi'kmaw origin. **Cape Breton Highlands National Park** (p99), overlapping with a third of the Cabot Trail, offers much to see and do: nature tours, artist studios, new and historic resorts, heritage rivers, spectacular hiking trails, accommodations, restaurants and camping. Set several days aside to make frequent, sometimes lengthy stops. For the best views, drive the trail counterclockwise, departing from and returning to Baddeck.

Mine Shafts & Ghosts

Sydney's industrial, spooky past

Coal mining and steel making once employed tens of thousands of people in and around **Sydney**. Nearly extinct now, these industries are remembered at the **Cape Breton Miners' Museum** in **Glace Bay**. It's more than a collection of artifacts: interpreters descend with visitors into a mine shaft.

WHERE TO EAT ON THE CENTRAL & EASTERN ISLAND

Chanterelle Restaurant, Inn & Cottages
Recommended for its rooms, locavore dining and mushroom-foraging outings. $$

Governor's Pub and Eatery
Chef Ardon Mofford has secured Governor's reputation as the island's best combo pub and fine-dining spot. $$

Glace Bay Chip Wagon
North America's oldest French-fry truck, the blue 1942 landmark chip wagon specializes in fat Belgian fries. $

BEST WHALE- & BIRD-WATCHING TOURS

Love Boat Seaside Whale & Nature Cruises
Small craft with hydrophones seek out whales and seals from Chéticamp.

Capt. Mark's Whale & Seal Cruise
Zodiacs spot pilot, minke and humpback whales, seabirds and seals off Pleasant Bay.

Bird Island Tours
See puffins, razorbills and kittiwakes nesting on rocky pillars.

Donelda's Puffin Boat Tours
Spot puffins, eagles and seals on the cruise from Englishtown to the Bird Islands.

Captain Cox's Whale Watch
From Cape Breton's northern tip, Cox's adds sea caves, waterfalls and shipwrecks to wildlife sightings.

Dixon's Zodiak Seafari
Departs from Neil's Harbour to the open Atlantic to find whales, dolphins, sunfish and seals.

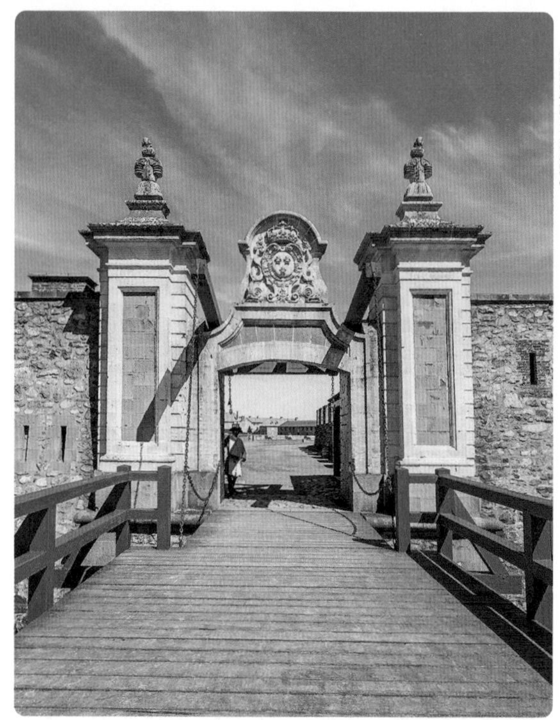

BENEDEK/GETTY IMAGES ©

Fortress of Louisbourg

The best way to get to know Sydney is by taking an **Old Sydney Society Ghost Tour**. A guide in period costume leads tours to the St Patrick's Church Cemetery and creaky old Cossit House, a museum full of creepy stories. It's neither spooky nor historical, but the **18m-high fiddle**, the world's largest, makes a popular selfie background on the waterfront.

A Historic Fortress

Immerse yourself in the 18th century

North America's largest historical-reconstruction site, the **Fortress of Louisbourg** was founded by France in 1713 and is a Canadian tourism landmark. The remote location of the fortified village east of Sydney was highly strategic in the seesaw Anglo-French battle for dominance over the lucrative cod fishery and the entrance to the Gulf of St Lawrence, the main artery into the continent. The British took the fortress

ISLAND CRAFT-BEER TAPROOMS

Route 19 Brewing
Three taproom levels regularly fill with golfers, tourists and locals for pub fare and house beers.

Breton Brewing
Local music, trivia nights and excellent sour beers liven up Breton's taproom in Sydney River.

Big Spruce
On a hillside overlooking Bras d'Or Lake; try Silver Tart, inspired by Alexander Graham Bell's summer raspberry refresher.

in 1745 and 1758, razing it after the second conquest. Two centuries later, beginning in 1961, Louisbourg slowly rose from the ruins. Today, you can imagine the harbor crammed with fishing, naval and merchant ships, and the village filled with sailors, soldiers and civilians. Visitors stroll the streets, pausing to chat with dozens of costumed interpreters who might be patrolling the bridge at the main gate, tending the garden, chasing a gaggle of noisy geese, constructing a wheelbarrow or just gossiping on a bench. A fun if noisy experience at Louisbourg is firing a cannon or a musket. Another favorite is sampling rum grog – each of the five ingredients tells an important chapter in history. For example, lemon prevented scurvy aboard ships that spent months (and sometimes years) at sea. Try role-playing a prisoner shackled in an iron collar, or dining on period-accurate dishes at one of several sites, including the **Hôtel de la Marine** and the **Storehouse Tavern**. Spending the night at the fortress is the most immersive of all the experiences on offer. Choose from an 18th-century canvas tent, the guardhouse, the more comfortable **Lartigue House** or, if you dare, the fortress prison.

The Neglected Coast

Wild ocean and lake shores

Too many tourists skip everything on Cape Breton's east coast except Fortress Louisbourg. Certainly, it's less dramatic and far less populated than the west coast and Sydney areas, but this region known as the Fleur-de-lis Trail has its own rewards. For a totally wild experience, hike into the coastal **Gabarus Wilderness Area**, a coastline that feels as far removed from the human world as it's possible to get. For golfers, the **Lakes at Ben Eoin Golf Club & Resort** is yet another exceptional island course. Built on three plateaus, fairways overlook Bras d'Or Lake and the hills beyond. For families, there's the nearby **Ben Eoin Beach RV Resort** on a spit of sand reaching into the lake. It can get a bit crowded, but the warm, calm waters of this inland sea make for great swimming and paddling. On the much wilder Atlantic side, lonely **Point Michaud Beach Provincial Park** and **Lillie's Stretch Hiking Trail** on either side of a dramatic headland will appeal to those looking for unspoiled coastline and the chance to spot seals and seabirds.

Winding Rte 4 follows the contours of Bras d'Or Lake, reaching its most populated place in the village of **St Peter's**, where a single canal lock (a National Historic Site) separates the saltwater lake from the ocean. It's worth pausing here for a walk along the short trails of **Battery Provincial Park** to **Jerome Point Lighthouse**. At Cape Breton's southeastern tip, a short causeway leads to **Isle Madam** and the 300-year-old Acadian village of **Arichat**, which have always depended on the fishery. Fresh seafood dishes dominate every menu.

THREE UNDERRATED ISLAND HIKES

Michael Haynes, author of *Hiking Trails of Cape Breton*, recommends the best unsung island hikes.

White Point
Hike to a former fishing village for dramatic scenery, the grand sweep of sand beaches at the mouth of Aspy Bay, the stark ridge of the Aspy Fault, like a wall to the north, and grim St Paul's Island, the northernmost outpost of Nova Scotia.

Gull Cove
Once it was larger than Sydney, but nothing remains of this community now but stone foundations. See scenic views of Gabarus Bay toward Fortress Louisbourg. Continue to remote Winging Point with its seals and seabirds.

Cape Mabou Highlands
Be sure to include either Sight Point or Beinn Alasdair Bhain for views high above the Northumberland Strait.

JOSHUA DAVENPORT/SHUTTERSTOCK ©

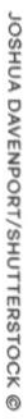

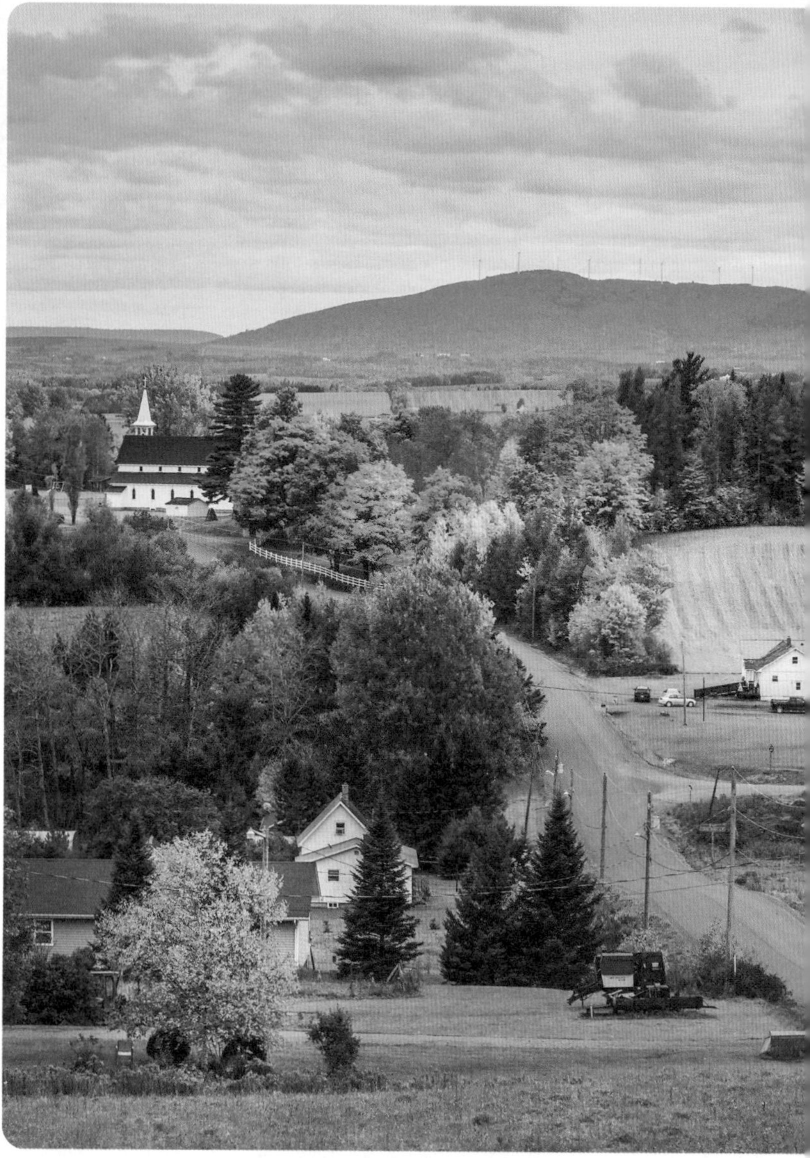

Above: New Brunswick countryside; Right: Saint Andrews (p121)

THE MAIN AREAS

FREDERICTON
Capital region along a picturesque river. p108

MONCTON
Dynamic hub for culture and fun. p113

SAINT JOHN
Lively port city near Fundy. p117

SAINT ANDREWS
Charming town amid coastal wonders. p121

New Brunswick

NATURAL WONDERS AND CULTURAL PRIDE

Vibrant cities, scenic towns and charming villages boast friendly folks, and attractions galore, from mighty tides and majestic forests to dazzling beaches and historical offerings.

Steeped in history and natural beauty, New Brunswick offers a wealth of family fun, outdoor adventure and fresh seafood. Visitors can witness the world's highest tides, play on warm beaches, hike spectacular trails, kayak sea caves, and explore an array of arts and cultural activities.

The province is about 85% forested. In the 19th century lumber and shipbuilding industries bustled, and in the 1920s pulp and paper mills developed. New technologies ended the shipbuilding era, though forestry, pulp and paper remain major economic contributors. Meanwhile, traditional industries of farming and fishing are still key sectors.

Indigenous peoples – the Wolastoqiyik (Maliseet), Mi'kmaq and Passamaquoddy – were the first to live here. In 1604 the French came, settling around the Bay of Fundy (Acadia). A century and a half later, in 1755, British authorities forced the French from their homes in what is known as the Expulsion of the Acadians.

In 1783 British Loyalists arrived, seeking refuge during the American Revolution. To accommodate them, the British government officially established New Brunswick in 1784. The province was one of the first to form in Canada, in 1867.

Acadians began returning to the region in the late 18th century. Their descendants form a significant part of today's population, which totals about 820,000. New Brunswick is Canada's only bilingual province, with French and English the official languages.

EDMUNDSTON
Year-round outdoor adventure. p125

CAMPBELLTON
Border city where nature beckons. p128

BATHURST
Seaside hub of urban experiences. p131

MIRAMICHI
Rich heritage and world-class fishing. p134

Find Your Way

New Brunswick is a sprawling province with tons to do and see. The big decision is when to go and where to stay. Locals are always happy to help steer your course.

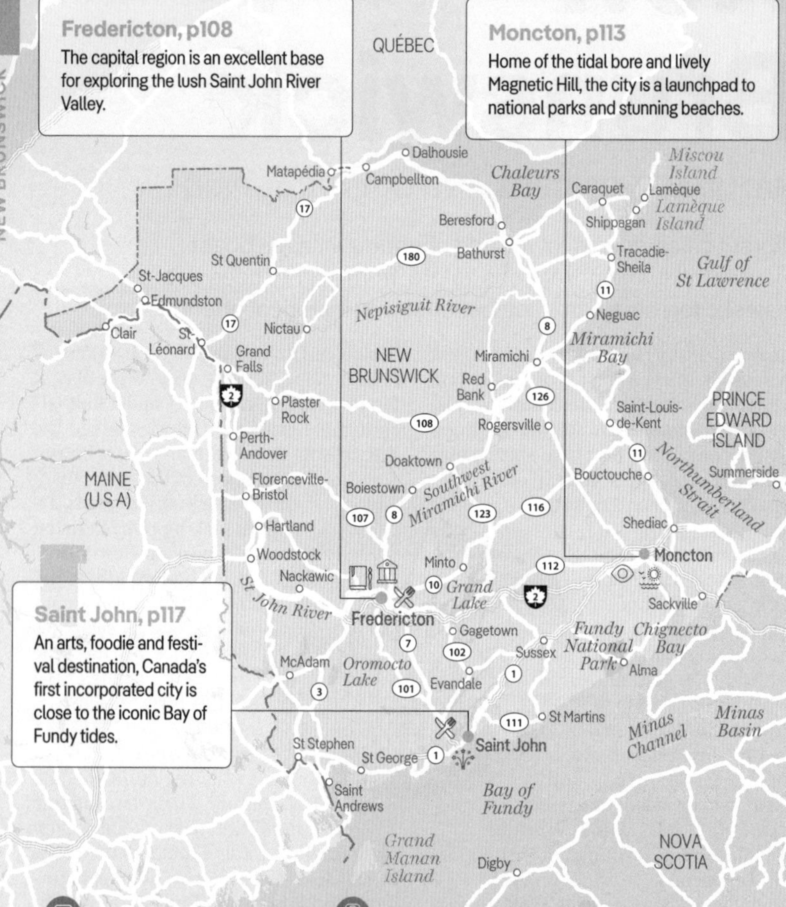

Fredericton, p108
The capital region is an excellent base for exploring the lush Saint John River Valley.

Moncton, p113
Home of the tidal bore and lively Magnetic Hill, the city is a launchpad to national parks and stunning beaches.

Saint John, p117
An arts, foodie and festival destination, Canada's first incorporated city is close to the iconic Bay of Fundy tides.

CAR & MOTORCYCLE

The province's variety of possible road trips makes it essential to have your own vehicle. Enjoy scenic rides on paved highways along rivers and lakes, tranquil journeys on secondary roads or country adventures on unpaved roads.

BUS

Maritime Bus has routes between many New Brunswick communities. Fredericton, Moncton and Saint John have their own bus services.

Bouctouche Dune (p114)

Plan Your Time

Sprawling New Brunswick has many outstanding attractions, so planning is key. Consider the focus of your visit – beaches, culture, the Bay of Fundy, history or wilderness? – and go from there.

Pressed for Time

- Schedule two to three days for the **Bay of Fundy** (p113). Start in **Moncton** (p113), with attractions such as the **tidal bore** (p113). Follow Hwy 114 to the formations at **Hopewell Rocks** (p113) and try zip-lining at **Cape Enrage** (p113). Hike in **Fundy National Park** (p113), then drive the spectacular **Fundy Trail Parkway** (p120) to **Fundy-St Martins** (p120) or on to **Saint John** (p117).

A Week-Long Stay

- Add **Saint Andrews** (p121) or the **Fundy Isles** (p123) to the shorter itinerary. If beaches are your thing, stay around **Moncton** (p114). Alternatively, head up Hwy 11 to the **Irving Eco-Centre/Bouctouche Dune** (p114), **Kouchibouguac National Park** (p114), or **Miscou Island** (p133) on the Acadian Peninsula. For all things outdoors, make **Edmundston** (p125), **Campbellton** (p128), **Bathurst** (p131) or **Miramichi** (p134) your hub.

Seasonal Highlights

SPRING

Visit a maple-sugar camp, hunt for fiddleheads and attend the Frye Festival, the Edmundston Book Fair or Paddlefest.

SUMMER

This is the time for many festivals, outdoor recreation of all kinds and enjoying the sun, sand, sea and serenity.

FALL

See the season's vibrant colors on a leaf-peeping drive or hike, go apple picking at a farm and visit a fall fair.

WINTER

So much snow. So much fun! Enjoy skiing, snowboarding, snowshoeing and more. (Festivals, too!)

Fredericton

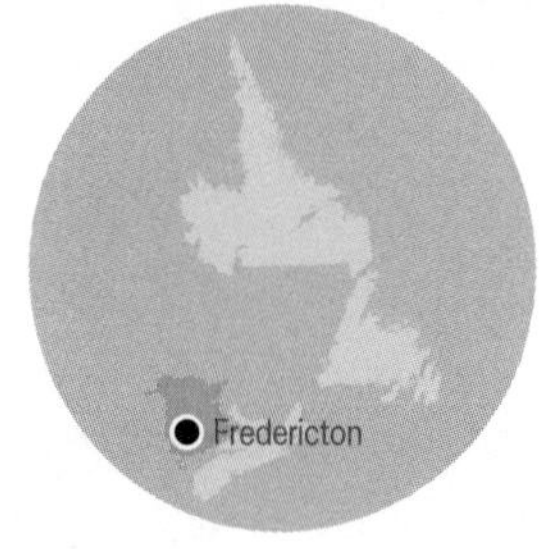

Situated along the beautiful Wolastoq (Saint John River) in the western-central part of New Brunswick, Fredericton serves as the provincial capital.

First inhabited by the Wolastoqiyik (Maliseet), the lands around the Saint John River would see European settlement begin in the late 18th century, including the arrival of Loyalists, which led to the founding of Fredericton in 1785.

Today, the Saint John River remains a key facet of life in the Fredericton capital region, with the waterway forming a lovely backdrop to communities that are now home to descendants of the Wolastoqiyik, French and Loyalists, and a growing international population. The area offers loads of opportunities for outdoor activities and a diverse range of venues to explore local history and culture, from outstanding art galleries and museums to heritage sites and festivals. Meanwhile, superb restaurants and cafes are everywhere, as is a multitude of excellent craft breweries.

GETTING AROUND

Fredericton International Airport (YFC) is the closest airport to the city and offers mostly domestic flights. The Fredericton capital region has a well-connected road network with parking available throughout the downtown area. Head to the Visitor Information Centre at Fredericton's City Hall for a free parking pass. Maritime Bus offers bus service within the province with a stop in Fredericton, and Fredericton Transit operates a bus service that covers the city and surrounding areas.

☑ TOP TIP

Fredericton is known for its pedestrian- and cyclist-friendly infrastructure, including multi-use trails and designated cycling lanes. Walking and biking are great ways to explore the downtown area, parks and riverfront, especially during the warmer months. Didn't bring your bike? The region offers rentals, including cruiser bikes, e-bikes, e-scooters and adaptive bikes.

Wander the Garrison District

Fredericton's historical heart

Check out the **Historic Garrison District**, centered on Queen St between York and Regent Sts. The area includes heritage buildings and landmarks, including the iconic Officers' Square, where you can see the Changing of the Guard in summer. The Garrison District is also home to the Fredericton Region Museum, which offers more information about the city's past.

On summer Thursdays the **Garrison Night Market** features performers of all kinds and more than 100 vendors selling handmade products. At the year-round Fredericton Boyce Farmers Market, held Saturday mornings, more than 200 vendors offer everything from maple syrup to cribbage boards shaped like fish.

Inspire your creativity at the **Beaverbrook Art Gallery**, a cultural masterpiece showcasing an impressive collection of Canadian and international artwork. Art-lovers will find many other exhibit spaces and boutiques in the area. (For more on Atlantic Canada's gallery scene, see p247.)

FREDERICTON

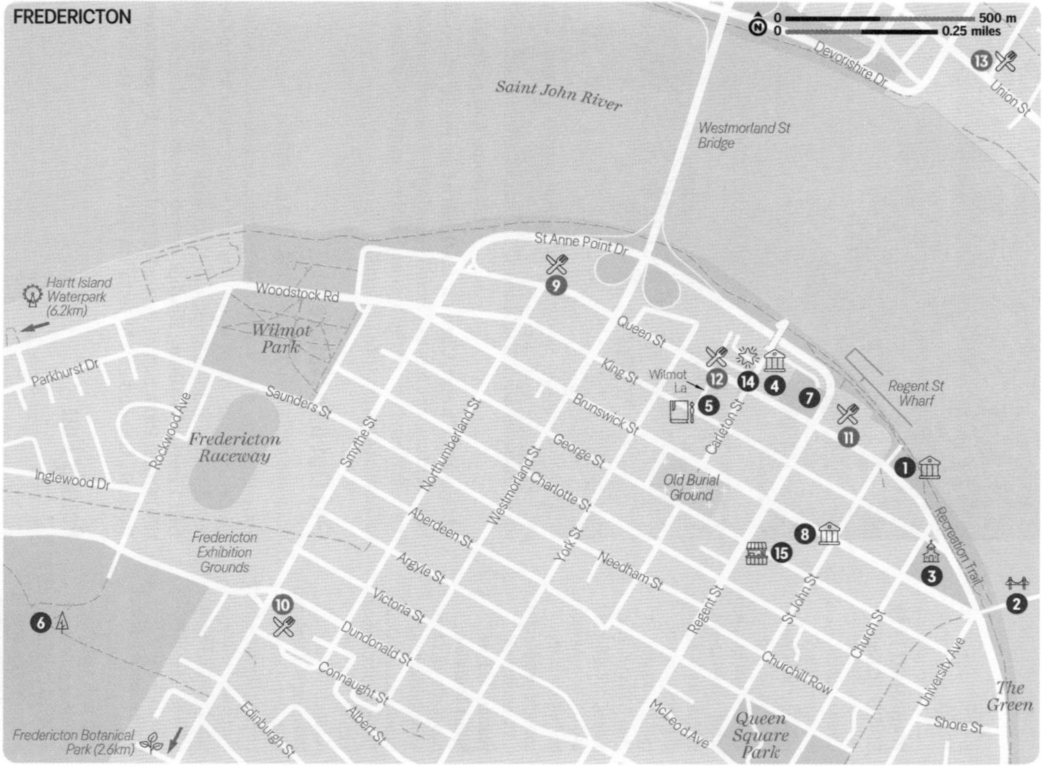

Saint John River
GVICTORIA/SHUTTERSTOCK ©

WABANAKI TREE SPIRIT TOURS

If you stroll in Fredericton's 160-hectare Odell Park, you'll find elements of a typical urban green space, such as trails and playgrounds. But take a walk with St Mary's First Nation elder Cecilia Brooks and her son, Anthony, and you're in for something different.

Through their **Wabanaki Tree Spirit Tours** the duo leads wild-food walks and culinary experiences in Odell. The expedition begins with Cecilia – an elder of Wolastoqey, Mi'kmaw, Mohawk and Korean ancestry – offering lessons about the park's history and significance. The tour highlight, along with the opportunity to learn about medicinal plants and Indigenous culture, is sampling delicious snacks made by Cecilia and Anthony: a balsam-fir tea and cookies made from acorn flour.

ED COREY/SHUTTERSTOCK ©

Bill Thorpe Walking Bridge

Majestic **Christ Church Cathedral** is modeled on a 14th-century church in Norfolk, England. Opened in 1853, it's considered one of the best and earliest examples of Gothic Revival architecture in Canada.

Get Out into Nature

Walk and cycle Fredericton's trails and gardens

Tour the local area on foot, or by bike, e-bike or e-scooter. Fredericton has more than 120km of trails, many along the beautiful Saint John River and Nashwaak River. Head to the **Bill Thorpe Walking Bridge** for city views. Explore beautiful **Odell Park** and its extensive trail system. **Fredericton Botanic Garden** can be found at the park's western end.

Family Fun

Make some memories

Take the crew bowling or laser-tagging at the **Kingswood Entertainment Centre** or splashing around **Hartt Island Waterpark** in Fredericton. **Quilli's Family Fun Factory Aquatic Park** in Upper Kingsclear is another nearby option.

WHERE TO STAY

Delta Hotels by Marriott Fredericton
Waterfront hotel with contemporary rooms, fitness center, indoor and outdoor pools, spa and dining. $$

Quartermain House B&B
Outstanding bed-and-breakfast with personalized service in a beautifully restored Victorian home. $

Crowne Plaza Fredericton-Lord Beaverbrook
Convenient riverside location near Beaverbrook gallery with modern rooms, dining options and great views. $$

Unlock the Past

Prison history at Science East

Up for a little jail time? **Science East**, an interactive, kid-friendly museum in downtown Fredericton, now has guided tours about the York County Jail once located at the site. Opened in 1842, the lockup occupied the entire Brunswick St building until it closed in 1996. The stone structure was repurposed as a museum three years later. Visitors can glimpse vestiges of the building's former use, such as heavy cell doors that frame the public washrooms on the main floor. Sign up for a 30-minute tour to learn about the facility's double-wall structure and hear tales of the jailers – and their families – who, for a time, lived in the same building as the prisoners, albeit in separate areas.

Splish-Splash, Vroom-Vroom!

Paddling, snowmobiling and more beyond Fredericton

Those heading west from Fredericton might trek to **Crabbe Mountain** for outdoor fun or **Mactaquac Provincial Park** to hike, swim, picnic, or rent a canoe or kayak to paddle on Mactaquac Lake. (Houseboats are also available.)

The **Nackawic waterfront** is another popular spot for fishers and boaters in summer, snowmobilers in winter. The town also boasts the **World's Largest Axe**, symbolizing the importance of the forest industry to the region.

In summer, head north of Fredericton to **Nashwaak Tubing & Kayak Rentals** or **Drifters Tubing on the Nashwaak River** and rent tubes for a Nashwaak River float. Or go east and hit the **Minto mountain-biking trails**, passing turquoise ponds as you ride ridges shaped by 400 years of coal-mining history.

Step Back in Time

More history awaits

There's plenty for history enthusiasts in the Fredericton region. Check out the **New Brunswick Military History Museum** in Gagetown or **Kings Landing** living-history museum in Prince William, which showcases life in the 19th century. You can even try your hand at forging a horseshoe.

WHERE TO EAT IN FREDERICTON

Wolastoq Wharf
Enjoy a dreamy lobster roll with truffle aioli on a Parmesan-crusted bun at this excellent northside seafood restaurant. **$$$**

Claudine's Eatery
Welcoming Claudine's has hearty East Coast comfort food such as smoked-salmon eggs Benedict and lobster poutine. **$$**

The Palate
With great food, wine list and service, the Palate also offers a daily blue-plate special at lunch. **$$**

Byblos
Cozy Byblos serves up authentic and delicious Middle Eastern cuisine, such as shawarma, grape leaves and hummus. **$**

Isaac's Way
Casual, colorful Isaac's Way puts the focus on local ingredients and products. **$$**

WHERE TO GRAB A COFFEE

Chess Piece Patisserie & Cafe
Terrific coffees and teas, decadent desserts and other yummy fare in a charming downtown location. **$**

Heaven Inn Devon Cafe
Quaint cafe in a heritage property with a lovely selection of drinks, sandwiches and sweets. **$**

The Landing
Cool riverside spot in Marysville; get a coffee or treat, or even get your bike fixed. **$**

BOTTOMS UP

Feel like a cold one? You've come to the right place! The Fredericton area is considered Atlantic Canada's craft-brew capital.

A unique way to explore the region's brew scene is via the **Taproom Trail**. Use a passport-style map, available at participating locations or Fredericton Tourism, for a self-guided tour. Visit eight of the 11 participating taprooms, collect corresponding stamps and get a 'Fred Tap Trail' shirt.

Craft breweries include Graystone, TrailWay, Picaroons, Grimross and Half Cut. Also worth a stop are Big Axe Brewing in Nackawic and Off Grid Ales in Harvey. Cideries include York County Cider, and you'll find spirits at distilleries such as First Light, Black Galley and Devil's Creek in Fredericton, and Moonshine Creek in Waterville.

VINTAGEPIX/SHUTTERSTOCK ©

Hartland Covered Bridge

You Say Potato

Celebrate the spud

West of Fredericton, take a snack break by touring **Covered Bridge Potato Chip Factory** in Waterville and sampling fresh-off-the-line treats that you can season as you wish. (The company's name refers to the nearby **Hartland Covered Bridge**. At 391m, it's the longest covered bridge in the world.)

Pass rich farmlands as you head north to Florenceville-Bristol, the 'French Fry Capital of the World' and home of McCain Foods, the world's largest manufacturer of frozen potato products. Learn about New Brunswick's agricultural history at **Potato World**, where you can also race a pedal tractor or shoot a potato gun.

Spinning a Yarn

Visit an 1850s woolen mill

Knitters may want to head south from Fredericton to York Mills and visit **Briggs & Little** (p236), Canada's oldest woolen mill, opened in 1857. The company still manufactures pure wool yarns on-site, turning raw wool from Canadian sheep into yarn in a multitude of colors.

Ghosts of Trains Past

Beautiful McAdam station

South of Fredericton, the village of McAdam is home to the **McAdam Railway Station**. While no longer seeing rail traffic, the beautiful building once served as the province's largest passenger station and is now partially used as a museum.

Moncton

Moncton is a survivor. Weathering the collapse of the shipbuilding industry in the 1860s and the closure of the rail yards in the 1980s, it has rebounded as an economic and cultural dynamo. It's New Brunswick's largest city, with about 84,000 residents. The region of Greater Moncton has 152,000 when tri-community neighbors Dieppe and Riverview are added.

The Mi'kmaq first inhabited this area along the Petitcodiac River, famed for its tidal bore. Later came Acadians, who were displaced during the Expulsion. In 1766 Pennsylvanian immigrants established homes in 'Monckton,' named for the British soldier who helped capture Fort Beauséjour. Acadians ultimately returned to the region, with Irish, Scottish and others joining the mix. Today, diversity flourishes as immigration thrives.

Known as the Hub City for its central location within the Maritime provinces, Moncton has excellent accommodation, dining and shopping, as well as arts and entertainment venues. Natural wonders are close by.

GETTING AROUND

Moncton is located along major roads, including the Trans-Canada Hwy, making it easily accessible by car. Moncton and Sackville are stops on the VIA Rail train connecting Halifax and Montréal. Maritime Bus offers service within the province with stops in the Moncton area, and Codiac Transpo runs buses in the tri-communities of Moncton, Riverview and Dieppe. Those municipalities also offer a network of bike lanes and multi-use trails, making it a bike-friendly area.

The Tide Is High

Witness a big, big wave

Launch your visit by learning about the **Bay of Fundy** and its famed high tides (p119). Start at **Bore Park** and witness Moncton's **tidal bore**, which occurs twice daily. During very high tides surfers have even ridden the bore. See tide charts or the digital billboard near Bore Park for bore times. Arrive early.

Forty minutes away at **Hopewell Rocks Provincial Park**, you can walk around giant rock formations at low tide and later watch the tide rise up around them. Go kayaking with **Baymount Outdoor Adventures** to weave around the formations. At **Cape Enrage**, enjoy panoramic Bay of Fundy views and activities such as zip-lining and rappeling. Fifteen minutes from there, **Fundy National Park** is another great spot to see the tidal range, as is the **Fundy Trail Parkway** (p120).

TOP TIP

The Annapolis Valley is known for its apple orchards and, increasingly, its vineyards. Visit in May, when the scent of flowers fills the air during the Apple Blossom Festival, or in fall, when apples are abundant at farm stands.

SIGHTS
1 Acadian Museum
2 Moncton Museum
3 Notre-Dame-de-l'Assomption Cathedral

DRINKING & NIGHTLIFE
4 Tire Shack Brewing Co

ENTERTAINMENT
5 Avenir Centre
6 Capitol Theatre

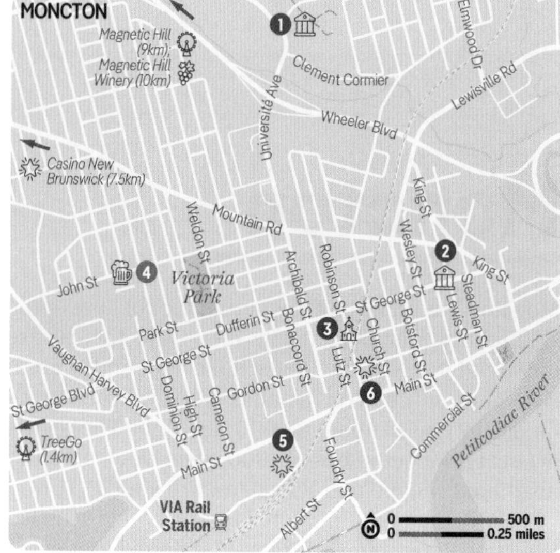

FESTIVAL FEVER

Greater Moncton Highland Games & Scottish Festival
Feel the Celtic spirit at this high-energy event, kicking off the region's festival season in June.

Atlantic Nationals Automotive Extravaganza
Car-lover? Be in Moncton in July.

International Buskers Festival
New in 2023, this event enlivens Moncton's riverfront in July.

Sandpiper Festival
In August, thousands of shorebirds that stop in Dorchester to feed during their annual migration.

Balloon Fiesta
Sussex's September fest is proud to say it's Atlantic Canada's largest free outdoor event for families.

Life's a Beach

Sandy shores and starry skies

The region boasts the country's warmest saltwater beaches. For awesome sandy shores, head to **Parlee Beach Provincial Park** in Shediac, **Aboiteau Beach** in Cap Pele or **Murray Beach Provincial Park** in Little Shemogue.

The **Irving Eco-Centre/Bouctouche Dune**, 40 minutes from Moncton, is another gem. The stretch of golden sand spans 12km and contains interpretive displays as well as a boardwalk with beach access.

Adventure for all ages awaits at two national parks in the region: **Fundy National Park** and **Kouchibouguac National Park**. Kouchibouguac has terrific beaches and scenic spaces for camping, paddling, biking and hiking. Fundy has a similar assortment of recreational offerings as well as a beautiful golf course. Both parks are designated **dark-sky preserves**, making them stellar places to view the night sky.

Lobster for All

Crustacean fans, rejoice!

Be sure to grab a lobster roll or fried clams on your coastal travels. Contact **Shediac Bay Cruises** about its LobsterTales

WHERE TO STAY IN MONCTON

Delta Hotels by Marriott Beausejour
Upscale hotel with luxurious amenities, spacious rooms and a convenient location. $$

Canvas Moncton
A boutique Hilton hotel offering stylish accommodations, an artsy vibe and a central downtown location. $$

Hyatt Place Moncton
Located opposite Moncton's Avenir Centre, this modern, clean, comfortable hotel has an included breakfast. $$

cruise. While in Shediac, sit atop the **World's Largest Lobster** - an enormous concrete-and-steel statue. Stroll to the **Homarus Centre** to learn about lobsters and marine ecosystems. Attend the July **Shediac Lobster Festival** for crustacean-themed fun.

A Magnet for Fun

Moncton's got you covered

Please the young and young-at-heart with a visit to Moncton's iconic Magnetic Hill. Put your car in neutral and feel it roll backwards, seemingly uphill! **TreeGo** in Moncton's Centennial Park has aerial adventure courses for children, teens and adults.

A Beautiful Stay

Discover Acadian history

The **Acadian Coastal Drive** runs from Aulac in the south to Dalhousie in the north, with a spur to the Acadian Peninsula and the Acadian Isles of Lamèque and Miscou. Pick up the route near Moncton to reach picturesque fishing villages and local shops where Acadian flags are flown with pride. In Aulac you can explore **Fort Beauséjour-Fort Cumberland**. In 1750, French authorities ordered the construction of a fort at Pointe-à-Beauséjour, which some believe was so named due to its attractive location. (*Beauséjour* translates to 'beautiful stay.') In 1755 the British captured Fort Beauséjour and renamed it Fort Cumberland.

In Bouctouche, enjoy theater, comedy, music and food at **Pays de la Sagouine**. This immersive cultural village, located on a small island, is entirely based on *La Sagouine* by acclaimed Acadian writer Antonine Maillet.

Just south of Moncton, **Doiron House** in Memramcook provides a glimpse of 18th-century Acadian life. Nearby **Monument-Lefebvre** highlights Acadian history and achievements.

Immersive Heritage

Learn about Mi'kmaq culture

Journey into Mi'kmaq culture with the **Heritage Path Tour** offered at the **Elsipogtog First Nation**, an hour from Moncton. Guides provide knowledge about beliefs and traditions, and offer a safe space to answer visitors' questions. Participants can take part in a smudging ceremony and view an authentic wigwam, longhouse and sweat lodge made by a local elder.

WHERE TO EAT IN MONCTON & THE SOUTHEAST

Gusto Italian Grill & Bar
Italian cuisine with a modern twist in Moncton. Enjoy homemade pastas, wood-fired pizzas and delectable desserts. **$$**

Atelier Tony
Charming Dieppe bistro offering a fusion of French and international flavors and showcasing fresh, innovative dishes. **$$$**

Bistro Le Chat Bleu
Worth the drive to Baie Verte for traditional Acadian cuisine, seafood dishes and hearty comfort food. **$$**

Calactus Restaurant
Popular Moncton spot offering a diverse menu of delicious vegetarian and vegan dishes. **$$**

Pirate De La Mer
A seafood-lover's paradise in Bouctouche serving fresh Maritime dishes including lobster, scallops and more. **$**

WHERE TO GET A COCKTAIL IN MONCTON

Palette Urban Rooftop Bar & Patio
Trendy rooftop bar with a chic ambience, spectacular views and handcrafted cocktails. **$$**

Third Glass
Downtown bar with expertly made cocktails and a large selection of wines by the glass. **$$**

Brix Experience
Participate in a cocktail class and craft your own signature drink. Culinary classes also offered. **$$**

WHY I LOVE MONCTON

Cathy Donaldson, Lonely Planet writer

We didn't plan to settle here permanently when we arrived 25 years ago. But my husband and I were quickly hooked – thrilled to find such a friendly, inclusive community. It's been a wonderful place to raise our kids, who have benefited from the linguistic and cultural diversity. The location is central to friends and family. We love being close to the ocean, so we can build sandcastles and enjoy sunset beach picnics. We've had fun in countless parks and green spaces, especially treasuring our hikes in nearby Fundy. This is indeed a special place. We're here to stay.

MEUNIERD/SHUTTERSTOCK ©

Transportation Discovery Centre

Past Present

Moncton's museums

Eye-catching Resurgo Place is home to the **Moncton Museum**, which recounts the city's story, and the **Transportation Discovery Centre**, with interactive exhibits and hands-on activities.

On the Université de Moncton campus, the **Acadian Museum** holds one of the world's largest collections of Acadian artefacts. The towering sandstone **Notre-Dame-de-l'Assomption Cathedral**, known as the Mother Church of Acadians in New Brunswick, houses **MR21** (the Monument for Recognition in the 21st century), an interpretation center that uses digital technology to immerse visitors in the Acadian experience.

Take in a Show

Live music and cultural entertainment

See what's on at the Avenir Centre, which has hosted everyone from Sting to Def Leppard. Casino New Brunswick hosts free live music at its Hub City Pub. The 1920s Capitol Theatre showcases a variety of musical acts, plus musical theater, dance performances and comedy.

For something delightfully different, **Ballet by the Ocean** (balletbytheocean.ca) features outdoor performances by the Atlantic Ballet. Spectators enjoy pairings of local food and wine.

Taste Local Flavors

Wine, beer or spirits

Moncton's **Magnetic Hill Winery** produces crisp dry whites, rosés and bold reds from estate and local grapes, as well as fruity wines such as cranberry, blueberry and maple. Also in Moncton, **Tire Shack** microbrewery prides itself on a diverse range of artisanal beers from hoppy ales to rich stouts. In nearby Memramcook, sample gin, rum and other small-batch spirits at **Crooked River Distillery**.

Saint John

Old and new meet in Saint John. Walk narrow streets with well-preserved architecture, peruse the City Market, then enjoy boutiques, restaurants and a vibrant arts scene.

The Wolastoqiyik (Maliseet) initially inhabited the area, with Mi'kmaq to the east and Peskotomuhkati (Passamaquoddy) to the west. In 1783 British Loyalists established settlements on either side of the Wolastoq (Saint John River): Parr-town to the east and Carleton to the west. The two settlements were incorporated as Saint John in 1785.

Located in southern New Brunswick where the Saint John River meets the Bay of Fundy, the port city was a key center for shipbuilding, trade and transportation in the 19th century. Fires destroyed part of the city, and economic downturns and industrial decline also caused turmoil. The city has since rebuilt and adapted, in part by diversifying with manufacturing, energy and IT.

Today, Saint John is a major center, and a prominent cruise-ship port.

GETTING AROUND

Your own vehicle is the most flexible way to explore Saint John and the surrounding areas, but Maritime Bus offers service within the province and has a terminal in Saint John. Saint John Transit runs the city bus network. Saint John's city center is pedestrian-friendly, and cyclists can enjoy bike lanes and shared roads. Bike and e-scooter rentals are also available.

Eat, Drink & Be Merry

Explore uptown Saint John

Saint John's downtown is called 'uptown' for its elevated position compared to the waterfront. Stroll charming streets lined with interesting boutiques, excellent restaurants and inspiring art galleries. Visit the iconic Old City Market (open Monday to Saturday year-round) to chat with vendors and score yummy food items and handmade crafts. In summer, check out the **Waterfront Container Village**, a marketplace and entertainment venue. At **Reversing Falls** you can watch the Bay of Fundy tides collide with the Saint John River, creating swirling white water. Grab a Moosehead beer after your travels: **Moosehead Brewery**, based in Saint John, is Canada's oldest independent brewery.

TOP TIP

The Saint John Region encompasses the city of Saint John and communities including Rothesay, Quispamsis, Grand Bay-Westfield and Fundy-St Martins. When planning a visit to Saint John, consider spending time in its Towns by the Bay as well as the majestic Fundy Trail Parkway, the entrance to which is near Fundy-St Martins (p120).

Look Back at Stonehammer

See billion-year-old fossils

Stonehammer Geopark – named for the first geologists who explored the area, Saint John's Steinhammer Club, formed in

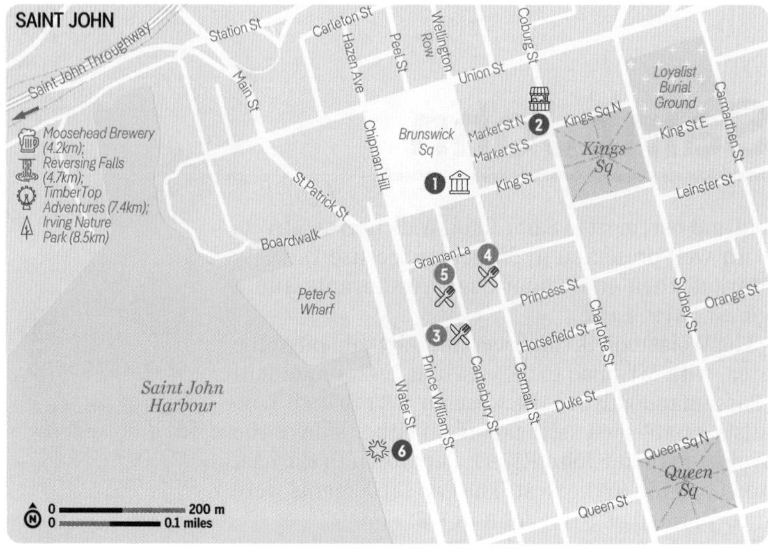

SIGHTS
1 New Brunswick Black History Society
2 Old City Market

EATING
3 Britt's Pub & Eatery
4 Italian by Night
5 Thandi

ENTERTAINMENT
6 Waterfront Container Village

1857 – is a 2500-sq-km region where geologists have uncovered an almost complete fossil record going back a billion years.

With Saint John at its center, the geopark runs from Norton to Fundy-St Martins, along the Fundy coast to Lepreau Falls and across to Grand Bay-Westfield. (Keep in mind that this is a region, not a traditional park with an entry gate.) It includes more than 60 significant geological and fossil locales, such as Saint John's Reversing Falls, where visitors can see evidence of an ancient ocean and the formation of the supercontinent Pangaea.

In 2010 Stonehammer became North America's first Unesco Global Geopark, an international designation that recognizes geologically significant areas that become living, working landscapes where science and local communities cooperate for mutual benefit.

Black History in New Brunswick

Look back to move forward

A visit to the **New Brunswick Black History Society** in Saint John's Brunswick Square shopping center offers a nuanced perspective on an important part of local history.

Discover more about the 3300 Black Loyalists who arrived in 1783 after the American Revolution. Learn about **Beaver Harbour**, settled the same year by Quaker Loyalists and the **first place in North America to ban slavery**. Find out about

WHERE TO STAY AROUND SAINT JOHN

Delta Hotels by Marriott Saint John
Contemporary hotel with excellent amenities in a prime location near uptown attractions. $$

Shadow Lawn Inn, Rothesay
Historical inn with lovely rooms, great service and exceptional dining at The Robertson. $$

Beach Street Inn, Fundy-St Martins
Welcoming spot for a seaside getaway near Fundy Trail Parkway, sea caves and beaches. $$

DOUG MCLEAN/SHUTTERSTOCK ©

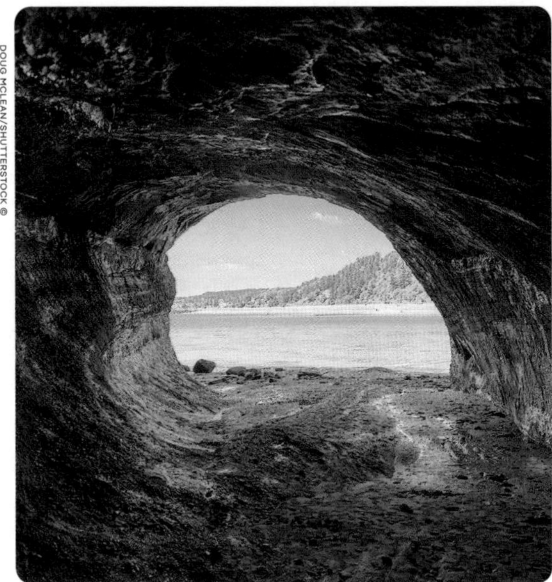

Stonehammer Geopark

the 300 enslaved people who fled here from the eastern United States in 1815 and established a community known as **Willow Grove** near present-day Fundy-St Martins.

Another worthwhile stop is the **Tomlinson Lake Hike to Freedom** in Carlingford, near Perth-Andover. It follows the **northernmost route of the Underground Railway**, which helped to carry many enslaved families to freedom in the mid-1800s.

All About the Bay

World's highest tides

Located between New Brunswick and Nova Scotia, the funnel-shaped **Bay of Fundy** is famous for having the highest tides in the world. There are roughly two high tides and two low tides every 24 hours. During each tide cycle the bay fills and empties of almost 100 billion tonnes of water – famously, that's more than the flow of all the world's rivers combined.

Visitors can see the effect of the massive tidal range at **Hopewell Rocks Provincial Park**, the **Saint John Reversing Falls** and the **tidal bore** (p113) in Moncton.

VISITING STONEHAMMER

Catrina Russell-Dolan, programs and operations manager at Stonehammer, offers tips to get the most from your visit.

Under the bridge (at Saint John's Reversing Falls Rapids) you can see one-billion-year-old light-gray marble from South America on one side and 500-million-year-old dark-gray shales and sandstones from northern Africa on the other.

Amateur fossil hunters can explore **Stonehammer Geopark** using the virtual map (go to stonehammergeopark.com) or through a guided tour, but note that fossils found in New Brunswick are protected by law. If you find a fossil, please leave it in place, note its location, photograph it and send the information to the New Brunswick Museum.

I was inspired to study geology when I learned about all of the amazing things that rocks can tell us about the past. It's like being able to travel through time and space without ever leaving your backyard.

WHERE TO EAT IN SAINT JOHN

Italian by Night
Stylish uptown restaurant with authentic Italian fare, an excellent wine list and great service. $$$

Thandi
Popular family-owned business known for its Indian curries, samosas, pakora, pad thai and more. $$

Britt's Pub & Eatery
Lively pub offering a diverse menu including delicious burgers and top-notch seafood chowder. $$

Fownes Head Lookout

Explore the Fundy Parkway

See Amazing Places

Drive 45 minutes east of Saint John to **Fundy-St Martins**, a starting point of the Unesco-designated **Fundy Biosphere Region**: 440,000 hectares of coastal land from Fundy-St Martins to the Tantramar Marsh near the Nova Scotian border and inland to Moncton. The area is distinctive for its geological formations, diverse terrestrial and marine ecosystems, rich cultural heritage and cross-section of rural communities and urban areas. The Fundy Biosphere Region is the birthplace of the national **Amazing Places** program, which highlights 50 sites of spectacular natural beauty within the region's boundaries and promotes the use of 47 hiking and biking trails to reach them.

Eight of the 50 sites can be found along the **Fundy Trail Parkway**, a 30km scenic drive that hugs the Bay of Fundy. Find the parkway's western entrance near Fundy-St Martins. (Go to fundytrailparkway.com for visitor info.) Minutes from the western entrance, **Fownes Head Lookout** has a fantastic view of rugged, tree-topped cliffs interspersed with stretches of pristine beach.

Among the Amazing Places to check out as you follow the parkway's curves are **Fuller Falls**, **Big Salmon River**, **Long Beach**, **Dragon's Tooth**, **Seely Beach**, **Cradle Brook**, **Eye of the Needle** and **Little Salmon River Gorge**. There are opportunities galore to walk on the ocean floor, hike, bike and beachcomb. Stop at the **Interpretative Centre** at Big Salmon River to learn about the area's past as a flourishing logging, fishing and shipbuilding community.

For a relatively easy 2.3km hike, take the **Walton Glen Gorge Trail**. Park at P15 and follow the wide, crushed-rock path to breathtaking views from the wooden observation deck perched 40m above the massive gorge, nicknamed the **Grand Canyon of New Brunswick**. More advanced hikers (with decent footwear) can do the **Eye of the Needle Trail**, a strenuous 2.4km path that descends into the narrowest part of the valley below. For more of a challenge, try the 64km **Fundy Footpath**, a multiday backpacking trip that starts at the **Big Salmon River suspension bridge** and ends in Fundy National Park.

ACTIVE FAMILY FUN

Want the kids to let off some steam? North of Saint John, **Rockwood Park** has around 9 sq km hectares of beautiful lakes, trails and footpaths where you can hike, bike, swim, skate and more.

Irving Nature Park, a 243-hectare wooded park, is also great for walking, hiking and biking. There are a children's forest, a playground and life-size mazes just outside the main entrance. **TimberTop Adventures** is a high-ropes experience where you can climb, traverse and zip-line tree to tree. For another adventure, take the ferry to the **Kingston Peninsula**, where you can go for a hike and then stop for treats at the **Kingston Farmers Market**.

Saint Andrews

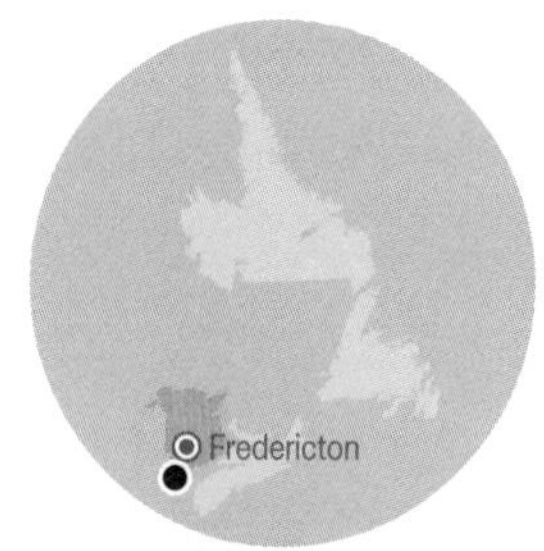

Coastal Saint Andrews – also known as Saint Andrews-by-the-Sea – is a renowned vacation spot. Situated on a peninsula in the Bay of Fundy close to the Canada–United States border, it's long been one of New Brunswick's premier holiday destinations.

The original inhabitants here were the Peskotomuhkati (Passamaquoddy) and Wolastoqiyik (Maliseet). Loyalists arrived in 1783. The town is now a National Historic Site partly because it has retained elements of a British colony, including a grid layout.

Saint Andrews sits between Passamaquoddy Bay and the mouth of the Saint Croix River. Since Passamaquoddy Bay is an inlet of the Bay of Fundy, it experiences the bay's famous tidal variations, with water levels rising 8m or more twice a day. This makes Saint Andrews a super spot to view the watery drama. It's also an ideal hub for travel across Charlotte County, such as to the Fundy Isles of Grand Manan, Deer Island and Campobello Island.

GETTING AROUND

The closest major airport to the region is Saint John Airport, about 125km away. Your own car is recommended for exploring the area, which has good road networks connecting towns and attractions. Parking is readily available in central areas. Multi-use trails offer scenic routes for walking, running and cycling. Bike and e-bike rentals are available in some areas, as are taxi and shuttle services.

Stroll the Coastal Downtown

A picture-perfect setting

Start your journey on **Water Street** in the heart of downtown Saint Andrews. Admire the architecture and view the terrific mural depicting the community's seafaring heritage. Browse the street's boutique shops and galleries, such as **Serendipin' Art** and **Sunbury Shores Arts & Nature Centre**. Recharge with a coffee or tea at Honeybeans. While you're sipping, ponder a **whale-watching cruise** (p122) that day or the next. At Market Wharf, take time to enjoy scenic views of the harbor, which is especially dramatic at sunset. Sip a cold beverage at **Saint Andrews Brewing Company**.

Further down Water St, at Patrick St, you can walk to the **Pendlebury Lighthouse**, which guards the entrance to the harbor. Make your next stop Kingsbrae Garden, a horticultural masterpiece. Explore the lovely grounds, as well as sculptures and walking trails. Stop for refreshments at **Savour in the Garden** or the **Garden Cafe**.

TOP TIP

Keep an eye out for deer that may be wandering through the downtown core. While they may add a touch of natural beauty to your experience, remember to admire them from a respectful distance and avoid feeding or approaching them – for their safety and yours.

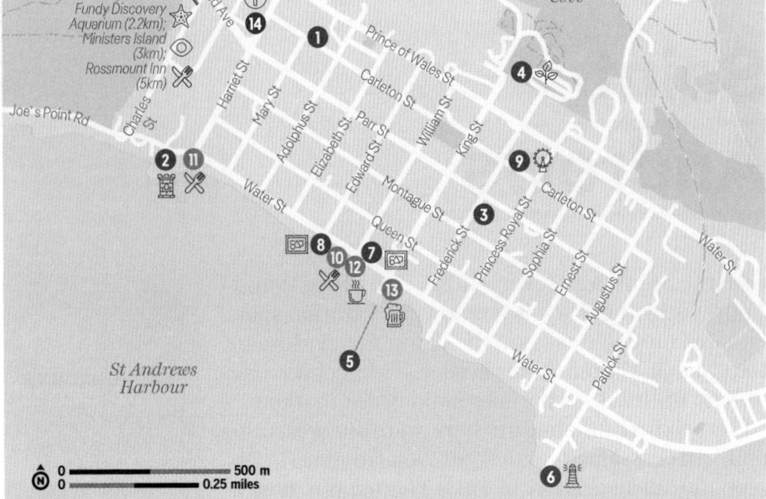

SIGHTS
1 Algonquin Resort
2 Blockhouse
3 Charlotte County Archives
4 Kingsbrae Garden
5 Market Wharf
6 Pendlebury Lighthouse
7 Serendipin' Art
8 Sunbury Shores Arts & Nature Centre

ACTIVITIES, COURSES & TOURS
9 Saint Andrews Community Playground

EATING
10 Gables
11 Niger Reef Tea House

DRINKING & NIGHTLIFE
12 Honeybeans
13 Saint Andrews Brewing Company

INFORMATION
14 Welcome Centre

Whether or not you're staying on the property, drop by theAlgonquin Resort for a peek. Opened in 1889 and once owned by the Canadian Pacific Railway, the stunning Tudor-style complex with a top-rated golf course sprawls atop a hill not far from the downtown core.

Complete your tour with a visit to the Blockhouse, a military fortification that overlooks the town. Take in the panoramic views and learn about the region's military past. History buffs may also be interested in the **Charlotte County Archives**, which offers guided tours of the **County Courthouse** and the **Old County Gaol**, constructed in 1832.

Creatures of the Bay

Go whale watching

Bay of Fundy whale-watching tours operate from Saint Andrews, Grand Manan and Campobello Island. Humpback, minke and pilot whales are commonly sighted, as are dolphins. Whale-watching season runs from June to October, with August the best month to spy whales and other sea life.

In Saint Andrews you can find more info at the **Welcome Centre** or at **Market Wharf**, where various tour operators are situated. Many companies have websites allowing you to book ahead. Note that tours are seasonal and subject to weather conditions.

WHERE TO STAY IN SAINT ANDREWS

Algonquin Resort
Iconic upscale hotel with a multitude of amenities and beautiful views of Passamaquoddy Bay. $$$

Rossmount Inn
Friendly inn with comfortable rooms and an excellent restaurant. $$

Treadwell Inn
Boutique, centrally located waterfront inn with pleasant rooms, most with private balconies. $$

RUSS HEINL/SHUTTERSTOCK ©

Grand Manan

Explore the Fundy Isles

Hop from island to island

Saint Andrews is part of the Charlotte Coastal Region, which includes island and mainland municipalities in southwestern New Brunswick along the Bay of Fundy. Island municipalities include Grand Manan, Campobello Island and Deer Island, which are part of the picturesque **Fundy Isles**.

For a breathtaking coastal journey, go island-hopping. From Saint Andrews drive 40 minutes to Blacks Harbour, timing your arrival to coincide with the ferry departure to **Grand Manan**. (There's no fee for crossing to Grand Manan, but fees are charged on the return trip.)

The 'Queen of the Fundy Isles,' Grand Manan is worth a one- or two-night stay to allow you to explore its fishing villages, beaches, shops, museums and restaurants, and hike island trails to amazing vistas. (Hole in the Wall and Swallowtail Lighthouse trails are standouts.) You can also take a whale-watching tour or go on a cruise to see puffins.

After your Grand Manan sojourn, return by ferry to the mainland or begin the tour known as the **Quoddy Loop**. Depending on the itinerary you choose, the loop might encompass

VISIT MINISTERS ISLAND

Located across from Saint Andrews, **Ministers Island** (open May to October) makes for a novel day out because it is only accessible by car or bicycle or on foot during low-tide hours. Follow Bar Rd to the island and note the sign indicating your safe departure time. (Bar Rd is submerged at high tide.)

Once you've purchased a pass to the 202-hectare island at the ticket booth, follow signs to parking if you've come by car. Begin your outing at Covenhoven, a summer estate built in the 1890s and owned by Sir William Van Horne, president of the Canadian Pacific Railway. From Covenhoven you can walk or bike to other focal points, including Van Horne's circular bathhouse.

WHERE TO EAT IN SAINT ANDREWS

Rossmount Inn
Creative cuisine, locally sourced ingredients and warm hospitality. Consistently outstanding. $$$

Niger Reef Tea House
Fresh, delicious lunch and dinner selections served in a relaxing setting with an awesome view. $$

Gables
Request waterside seating at this casual, cozy eatery loved for its tasty fare and friendly service. $$$

BEST FOR FAMILY FUN

Fundy Discovery Aquarium, Saint Andrews
Learn about the bay's tides and marine animals, and see Delilah, a 13m model of a North Atlantic right whale.

New River Beach
A coastal paradise with sandy shores and crystal-clear waters off Rte 175 near Pocologan.

Whale-watching
Exciting whale-watching tours (p122) are offered through companies in Saint Andrews, Grand Manan and Campobello Island.

Ganong Chocolate, St Stephen
Enjoy a sweet adventure to this museum and store. Ganong is Canada's oldest chocolate and candy company.

Saint Andrews Community Playground
Discover tons of fun at this downtown playground with Tudor-style structures, slides and climbing adventures.

TERRY W RYDER/SHUTTERSTOCK ©

Franklin D. Roosevelt's summer residence, Campobello Island

some or all of the following stops: St Stephen, Saint Andrews, St George, Deer Island and Campobello Island in New Brunswick; and Lubec, Eastport and Calais in Maine. Plan at least one overnight stay for a more relaxing tour.

To begin one version of the Quoddy Loop, leave Saint Andrews and drive 40 minutes to L'Etete. Take a free car ferry across the Bay of Fundy to 45-sq-km **Deer Island**, the smallest inhabited island of the Fundy Isles. Kayak the calm waters around the island, savor local seafood or go for a hike, such as to the Deer Island Point Lighthouse. If you do the latter, look for the **Old Sow**, the largest tidal whirlpool in the western hemisphere and another stunning result of the Bay of Fundy's tidal currents.

To continue the Quoddy Loop, take a ferry from Deer Island to **Campobello Island**, famed for its connection to the Roosevelt family. Visit Roosevelt Campobello International Park, summer residence of the late President Franklin D. Roosevelt. Explore trails, gardens and Roosevelt Cottage. Whale-watching tours are also offered from Campobello.

For a two-nation coastal getaway, cross the Franklin Delano Roosevelt Memorial Bridge from Campobello to **Lubec**, Maine. (Bring your passport.) If you're staying in Canada, backtrack to Herring Cove Provincial Park for an incredible beach and majestic views. Complete the coastal loop by returning via ferry to the mainland.

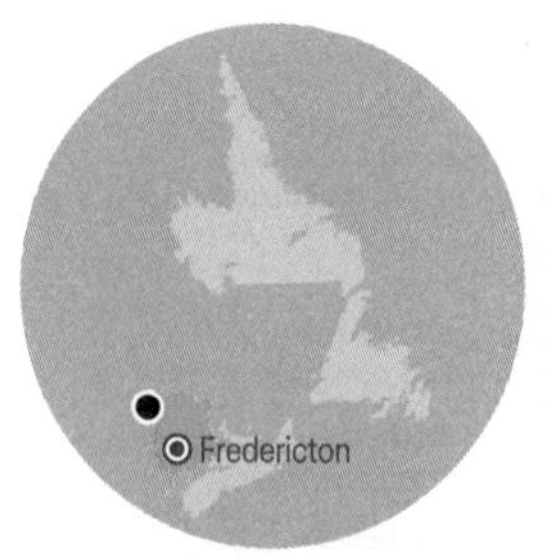

Edmundston

Located in the northwestern part of New Brunswick and bordering Québec and Maine, the Edmundston-Madawaska region is the northwest gateway to the Maritime provinces. It's also an outdoor-recreation hot spot, well situated at the confluence of the Wolastoq (Saint John River) and the Madawaska River, surrounded by the Appalachian Mountains.

The history of the region – which includes Grand Falls, Edmundston and the Upper Madawaska area – is rooted in the traditions and culture of the Wolastoqiyik (Maliseet) and Mi'kmaq peoples. European settlement began in the 19th century when Acadian and Scottish immigrants arrived.

A logging industry developed and, later, mining operations flourished. As the mining industry declined, growth came in the form of industries such as agriculture and hydroelectric power. Today, those sectors remain, complemented by manufacturing, healthcare, education and tourism. The region is a popular destination for nature enthusiasts, who enjoy pursuits such as hiking, cycling, skiing and snowmobiling.

GETTING AROUND

The closest Canadian airport is Fredericton International Airport (YFC). Car travel is the most convenient option for area adventures, with several rental agencies here. Maritime Bus offers service within the province with a stop in Edmundston. The region offers beautiful scenery and opportunities for cyclists. Walking is a great way to explore downtown areas as well as the region's many trails.

Get Outside

Nature tranquil and rugged

Since the Edmundston region has such a concentration of natural attractions, start your area tour at one of its best: the **New Brunswick Botanical Garden**, about 10 minutes from downtown. Nature, culture and art merge in its 12 thematic gardens, spread over 8 hectares along the Madawaska River. Indulge your senses with a peaceful walk along lovely trails adjacent to flowering annuals, perennials, roses and other plant species. Stop for a snack or a meal at Café Flora and enjoy patio views overlooking a pond with a waterfall.

Before leaving the area, go next door to the **République Provincial Park**, a 44-hectare recreational park offering scenic hiking and cycling trails, a playground and picnic sites.

TOP TIP

Take time to exit major highways and immerse yourself in the region's natural beauty. Do some birdwatching in the Madawaska wilderness. Paddle serene lakes. Go geocaching or walk the Prospector's Trail. Hit the beach at Baker Lake. Explore scenic forests by ATV or, in winter, snowmobile. Cycle the Madawaska Trails.

SIGHTS
1 Cathedral of the Immaculate Conception
2 Edmundston Art Centre
3 Madawaska Historical Museum

EATING
4 Moonshin'hers

DRINKING & NIGHTLIFE
5 Ateepic
see 4 Brasseurs du Petit-Sault

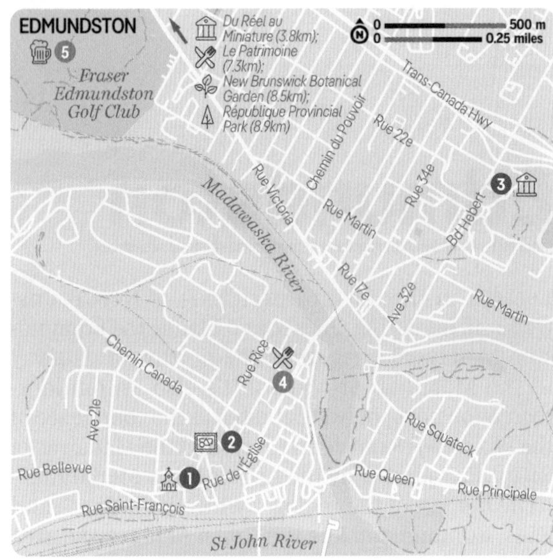

Downtown Edmundston

Visit shops, cathedral and museums

On a leisurely walk along De L'Église St you can admire the architecture and browse shops, boutiques, and the free exhibits at the **Edmundston Art Centre**. Step inside the **Cathedral of the Immaculate Conception**, an impressive stone structure built between 1925 and 1927, to appreciate its stunning stained-glass windows.

Learn more about the history of the region at the **Madawaska Historical Museum**, where displays highlight Acadian heritage and local industries.

For an intriguing look at railroad history in the region, visit **Du Réel au Miniature**, a railroad interpretation center owned and operated by Guy and Geraldine Laforge. Ask Guy for a guided tour of the outdoor exhibits and his indoor collection, which includes a massive model-train operation in the basement.

Enjoy a scenic stroll along the banks of the Madawaska River and across the pedestrian bridge spanning the waterway.

Time for a cold brew? Stop by one of the region's craft breweries: **Ateepic**, in the Fraser Edmundston Golf Club, or downtown at **Brasseurs du Petit-Sault**. (Other breweries in the area include the **Grand Falls Brewing Co** – you guessed it: it's in Grand Falls.)

WHERE TO STAY IN EDMUNDSTON

Best Western Plus
Modern property with impressive foyer, spacious rooms and a good breakfast. $$

Four Points by Sheraton
Downtown hotel with comfy rooms, on-site restaurant, indoor pool, fitness center and friendly staff. $$

Auberge Micky
Lovely property just off the highway with inn rooms and cabins. Great dining at Chantal's. $

SANDI CULLIFER/SHUTTERSTOCK ©

Grand Falls Gorge

La Bagosse

A history of hooch

The Upper Madawaska region is known for producing that alcohol of legend: moonshine. The village of **Saint-Hilaire**, located along the Saint John River close to the US border, was a hub for the illegal alcohol trade during Prohibition and home to the 'Al Capone of Madawaska', Maxime Albert. You can discover the history of *la bagosse* (moonshine) at the village's Maxim Albert House Museum and take part in August's Festival de la Bagosse.

Wintry Thrills

Cruise by snowmobile

The Edmundston region has more than 650km of snowmobile trails. Edmundston and Grand Falls are western anchors for the **Northern Odyssey**, which allows riders to traverse 1500km of trails winding in and out of Edmundston, Campbellton, Bathurst and the Acadian Peninsula.

Adventure to Grand Falls

It's totally gorge-ous

For a roaring good time, drive 45 minutes from Edmundston to **Grand Falls**, home of the awe-inspiring **Grand Falls Gorge**. Watch the powerful Saint John River cascade through the narrow gorge and drop 23m to form the largest waterfall east of Niagara Falls. The **Grand Falls Gorge Trail** winds along the edge of the gorge, offering stunning viewpoints, and adventure playground **Zip Zag Park** has zip lines crossing the chasm. On Saturday mornings from May to October, head to the nearby **Grand Falls Farmers Market** for delicious treats and local music.

BEST EATS

Chantal's Steakhouse, Saint-Jacques
Excellent food and service and a welcoming ambience characterize this popular stop. **$$$**

Le Patrimoine, Edmundston
Delicious fare including wood-fired pizza makes this worth the short drive from downtown. **$$**

Moonshin'hers, Edmundston
Enjoy creative dishes at this casual eatery next to Les Brasseurs du Petit-Sault brewery. **$$$**

Valley View Restaurant, Edmundston
Friendly service and tasty menu options merge at this Grey Rock Casino eatery. **$$**

Café Flora, Edmundston
Fresh, light and flavorful offerings in a tranquil location at the New Brunswick Botanical Garden. **$**

Campbellton

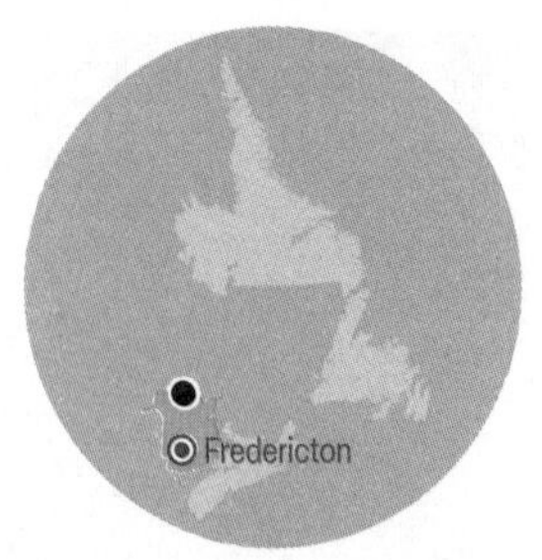

GETTING AROUND

Bathurst Airport services regional carriers, and Greater Moncton Airport hosts domestic and international flights. Maritime Bus provides service within the region with a stop in Campbellton, but your own car gives you maximum flexibility. There are cycling-friendly routes in the area and bike rentals are readily available.

A key gateway to the Maritime provinces, Campbellton is a pretty waterfront city on New Brunswick's northern border with Québec. It has everything you'll need to gear up for adventures in its nearby wilderness areas, from stores for supplies, restaurants and amenities to fill the tanks, and accommodations for a good night's rest. Set amid the Appalachian Mountains, the shores of Chaleur Bay and the mouth of the Restigouche River, Campbellton's beauty is a teaser for what lies ahead. Nature-lovers flock to the region for climbing, mountain biking, camping, hiking, skiing, snowmobiling, ATVing, paddling and fishing. The area's original inhabitants, the Mi'kmaq, were followed by French settlers in the mid-1700s. British colonization came in 1833, and the community was incorporated as a town in 1889 and as a city in 1958. Campbellton's history has been closely tied to fishing and forestry, but today the economy is diverse, with tourism a primary sector.

Go Wild on the Restigouche

Discover the beloved river

Lush forests, rolling hills and a sense of complete tranquility form the backdrop to the crystal-clear Restigouche River. In 1998 a stretch of the Upper Restigouche was designated a Canadian Heritage River. An outstanding Atlantic salmon habitat, the river is one of North America's premier fly-fishing destinations. If you'd like to fish here, research provincial regulations before you arrive.

Campbellton's **Restigouche River Experience Centre** offers visitors a range of information about the river including a touch pool. Salmon fishers will enjoy the center's collection of flies, reels and rods. East along the waterfront, at Salmon Plaza, **Restigouche Sam** is an 8.5m stainless-steel Atlantic salmon perched in jumping form.

Southwest of Campbellton, along the Little Main Restigouche tributary, **Les Chalets Restigouche** has campsites and well-equipped log cabins that blend with the natural environment. Owners Geneviève Trottier and Sébastien Hodgson can offer tips on things to do and see in the area.

TOP TIP

You don't have to go hard-core to enjoy the natural beauty around Campbellton. Take a scenic drive along the Restigouche River, follow peaceful trails, go birdwatching, do a leisurely canoe trip or stop for a swim. The Bay of Chaleur has some of the warmest saltwater beaches north of Virginia.

YINGNA CAI/SHUTTERSTOCK ©

Restigouche Sam

What a Family Tree!

Kedgwick's tribute to the past

In the category of unique attractions in New Brunswick, the Pioneer Tower in Kedgwick has to be a contender. The tower is home to the Restigouche County community's famed **Pioneer Tree**, an 11m artwork that pays tribute to the area's founding families. Completed in 2015, the tree is adorned with 8400 wooden maple leaves embossed with names.

The idea developed as organizers prepared for the 2015 Kedgwick Parish centennial celebrations. Artist Sylvio Dugas came up with the concept and set the project in motion. Entirely handmade by local artisans, the remarkable piece can be viewed from various angles by taking stairs to landings along the tower's perimeter.

Lose Yourself in Nature

Mt Carleton and Sugarloaf parks

A 90-minute drive south of Campbellton, remote **Mt Carleton Provincial Park** has more than 17,000 hectares of Appalachian wilderness to explore. Beautiful **Mt Carleton Lodge & Cafe**, overlooking Lake Nictau, offers visitors a place to relax, grab a snack and get information on available activities.

BEST PLACES TO FUEL UP

Chez Phil's Kitchen, Charlo
Seasonal beachfront spot with amazing fish tacos, wicked fries and a priceless view. **$**

Smoke on the Water, Campbellton
From burgers to pulled-pork sandwiches, this is the place to get your barbecue fix. **$**

Snack Bar Restigouche, Dalhousie
Yummy charcuterie boxes and New Brunswick beer and wine selections set against Chaleur Bay views. **$**

Croissant Delice, Dalhousie
You'll think you're in Paris with this selection of French pastries, including croissants and *macarons*. **$**

Brasserie 1026 Bar & Grill, Campbellton
Good pub fare and drinks in this Quality Hotel and Conference Centre restaurant. **$$**

WHERE TO STAY IN THE REGION

Quality Hotel & Conference Centre, Campbellton
Central, well-appointed hotel with bridge and riverside views, a good restaurant and superior service. **$$**

Les Chalets Restigouche, Kedgwick
Excellent base for adventures, with stellar hosts. Varied accommodations include cozy log cabins. **$**

Old Church Cottages, Flatlands
Lovely options include glamping domes and a church converted into a luxury three-bedroom cottage. **$$$**

WHERE TO GO FOR A SWIM

Inch Aaran Beach, Dalhousie
Lovely saltwater beach with adjacent tennis courts and other amenities. Popular spot for birdwatching.

Charlo Beach
Long sandbar beach with salt water on one side, fresh water on the other. Great amenities, campground and picnic area.

Tide Head
Freshwater swimming area at the confluence of Black Brook and the Restigouche River. Playground and picnic area, too.

Nictau Lake, Mt Carleton Provincial Park
After a summer hike, cool off with a dip at this unsupervised beach, open to park visitors.

Restigouche River
Swimming is possible in several places along this scenic river and its tributaries.

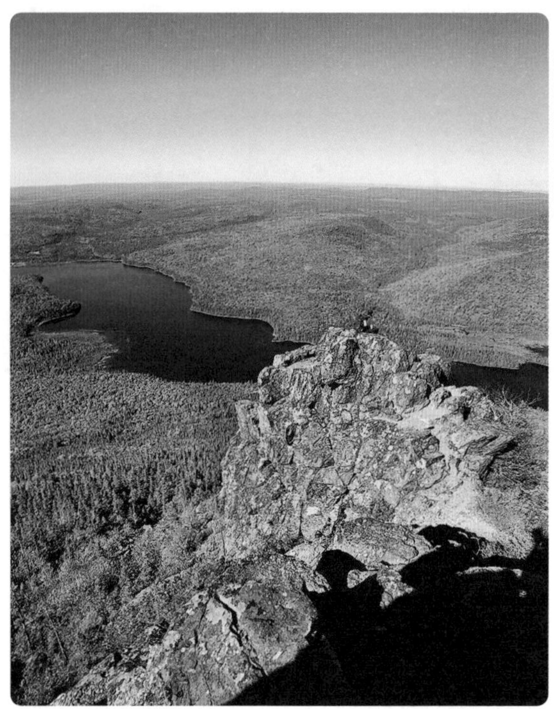

MARC GUITARD/GETTY IMAGES ©

Mt Carleton Provincial Park

At 820m, **Mt Carleton** is the highest summit in the Maritime provinces. If you reach the top on a clear day, you'll be treated to exceptional views of pristine forest below. There are another 10 trails, including a wheelchair-accessible route at Williams Falls, and Mt Sagamook, considered to be the most challenging hike in the park.

Mt Carleton is a great destination for bird-lovers, with 100 species identified, and it's an ideal landscape for spotting black bears, moose, red foxes and white-tailed deer. Stay overnight to admire the skies in this designated **dark-sky preserve**. Consider taking part in the Royal Astronomical Society of Canada's Mt Carleton Star Party. Weather permitting, the park is considered one of the best stargazing sites in Canada.

Just south of Campbellton, on the other side of Rte 11, **Sugarloaf Provincial Park** has a mountain-bike park and more than 25km of hiking and biking trails. It's a superb destination for a family-friendly getaway or an action-packed escape. Hike to the summit of 305m **Sugarloaf Peak** to take in the outstanding views.

In winter, Sugarloaf offers downhill skiing, sliding hills, tube rentals, snowshoeing and skating. As well, there are cross-country skiing trails and unserviced winter camping for the hardy.

Bathurst

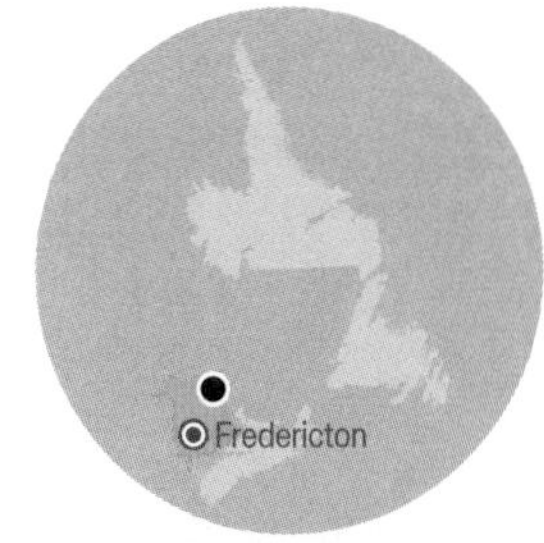

The hub city of northeastern New Brunswick, Bathurst is part of the Chaleur Region. It sits at the southernmost point of Chaleur Bay on Bathurst Harbour, an estuary at the mouth of four rivers: the Nepisiguit River, Middle River, Little River and Tetagouche River.

The first settlers to the region were primarily the Mi'kmaq, who occupied the area for centuries before Europeans arrived. Acadians were among the first European settlers, followed by Scottish and Irish immigrants who were drawn here by the area's natural resources, including timber and fish. Historically a center of shipbuilding, forestry, farming and fishing, Bathurst has evolved to embrace other sectors such as mining, manufacturing, tourism and health care. Pabineau First Nation, a Mi'kmaq community, lies just south of the city.

Bathurst and the Chaleur Region sit along the 750km Acadian Coastal Drive, which winds northward from New Brunswick's southeast and runs along the Acadian Peninsula.

GETTING AROUND

There are flights from Montréal-Pierre Elliott Trudeau International Airport to Bathurst Regional Airport. Another option is to fly to Greater Moncton Roméo LeBlanc International Airport, 230km southeast of Bathurst in Dieppe. Rental vehicles are available at both airports. Province-wide bus service is available through Maritime Bus. Cyclists can follow the scenic Acadian Peninsula Veloroute, a 310km bike path that connects seven municipalities and one rural district.

Wander the Bathurst Waterfront

Cool shops and cold beer

In Bathurst's **Waterfront Village**, picturesque boardwalks allow pedestrians to admire spectacular views of the Bay of Chaleur. Visitors will find a cluster of shops run by seasonal vendors, as well as art, good eats at Nectar restaurant and cool refreshments at **Frostbites** ice-cream shop.

For a tasty beer, see the friendly folks at waterfront **13 Barrels Brewing**. The brewery's Gnarly Light Lager won gold at a 2023 Canadian craft-beer competition, and its Tall Tales won silver at a regional event. Just down the street, **Four Rivers Brewing Co.** also makes impressive craft beers.

Restaurant options abound downtown. Fresco features everything from fresh seafood to delectable Italian cuisine. Local favorite **Pizza 13** serves up pepperoni and veggie choices, as well as unique picks such as the Bayonne, topped with prosciutto, goat cheese and honey.

TOP TIP

Don't worry if you're not fluent in French: locals appreciate efforts to engage with their language and culture. Try using terms such as *bonjour* (hello), *merci* (thank you) and *s'il vous plaît* (please). Too embarrassed to try? Just be polite when you speak English and chances are you'll be understood.

EATING
1 Fresco
2 Frostbites
3 Lucia's Cuisine
4 Nectar
5 Pizza 13

DRINKING & NIGHTLIFE
6 13 Barrels Brewing
7 Four Rivers Brewing Co.
8 Kaffeine Espresso Bar

The Acadian Peninsula

Red, white, blue and yellow

You'll see them as soon as you arrive on this jut of land in northeastern New Brunswick: flags striped with red, white and blue, and punctuated by a yellow star. The Acadian flag catches your eye across the **Acadian Peninsula**, a region steeped in history and culture.

In the 1600s French settlers arrived in this area, establishing thriving communities and developing a unique culture. The Expulsion of the Acadians in 1755 caused widespread displacement and hardship, but over time the Acadians returned and reclaimed their cultural heritage.

Visitors coming from southern New Brunswick can begin their tour of the peninsula in **Neguac**. From **Ile-aux-foins Park**, a causeway runs to a beach and bird sanctuary, and interpretive signs describe local flora and fauna.

Thirty minutes northeast on Rte 11, the **Historical Museum of Tracadie** recounts the history of Hansen's disease (leprosy) in the region from 1844 to 1965. While it's now a rare, treatable illness, the infection had taken seven lives in the area by 1844. To prevent its spread, 37 sufferers were sent unattended to quarantine in wretched conditions on Sheldrake Island. In 1849 the quarantine station was moved to Tracadie, but it wasn't until 1896 that the Hôtel-Dieu de St-Joseph de Tracadie hospital opened with an isolation wing for sufferers of the illness.

Before you leave Tracadie, stock up on craft-brewery products at **Brasseux d'la Côte**.

Continue to **Lamèque**, one of two islands off the northeastern tip of the peninsula. At **Au P'tit Mousse** be sure to order the garlic fingers with a delicious whipped donair sauce.

Village Historique Acadien

Consider staying a night on Lamèque or on **Miscou**, the neighboring island. On Miscou you'll find gorgeous beaches, a historical lighthouse and untouched nature. Boardwalks allow tourists to meander through stark but beautiful terrain. Enjoy scrumptious seafood at **La Terrasse à Steve** after you explore.

Check out the **New Brunswick Aquarium** in **Shippagan** for family fun, then stop in the bustling port of **Caraquet**. Plan to spend a few hours or a full day at the **Village Historique Acadien** in **Bertrand**. This exceptional open-air museum has historical buildings housing an array of characters who portray Acadian life from 1770 to 1949. Before you leave the peninsula, visit **Distillerie Fils du Roy**, the first distillery in Acadie and an award-winning treasure.

BEST SPOTS TO ENJOY NATURE

Pokeshaw Park
View iconic rock formations, home to many seabirds, in Chaleur Bay. There's also great heritage info and a beach.

Daly Point Nature Reserve, Bathurst
Extensive network of trails within 40 hectares of pristine salt marsh where you can spot birds and wildlife.

Nepisiguit Mi'gmaq Trail
Historical hiking trail that follows the Nepisiguit River from Mt Carleton park (p129) to Daly Point.

Youghall Beach
Enjoy stunning views along this sandy beach. Excellent amenities include showers, volleyball courts and a playground.

Birch Bark Adventures, North Tetegouche
Go dogsledding or snowshoeing on forest trails, or do some ice fishing on Chaleur Bay.

WHERE TO STAY

La vieille école de Miscou, Lamèque
An old school now offers spacious rooms, plus a delicious breakfast and genuine service. $$

Cielo – Glamping Maritime, Haut-Shippagan
Combines luxury and nature with beachside glamping domes and exceptional amenities. $$$

Atlantic Host, Bathurst
Central hotel with excellent amenities, including an indoor pool with hot tub and sauna. $$

Miramichi

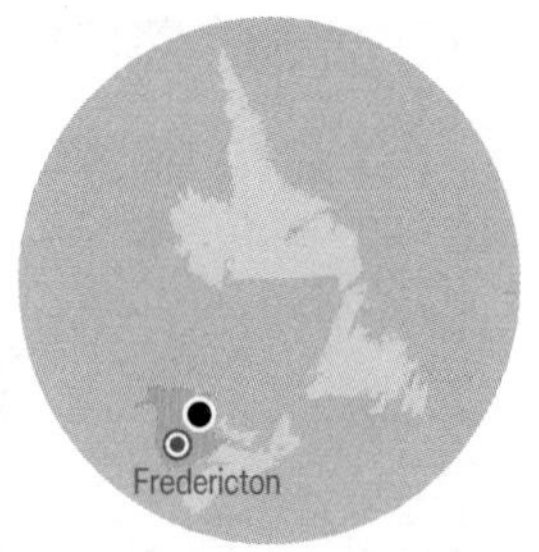

GETTING AROUND

Miramichi is located about 175km northeast of Moncton and about 122km southeast of Bathurst. You can fly into the region via Bathurst Regional Airport, Greater Moncton Roméo LeBlanc International Airport or Fredericton International Airport. Miramichi is on the VIA Rail route connecting Halifax and Montréal. Maritime Bus offers service within the province with a stop in Miramichi. Bike rentals are available in the region, and taxis are for hire within the city of Miramichi.

TOP TIP

Plan your trip around one of the Miramichi Region's festivals, such as the Folksong Festival (August), Irish Festival (July), Scottish Festival (August), Rock n' Roll Festival (July/August) or the Miramichi Striper Cup (May), or join the celebrations at a local Indigenous powwow.

Locals will tell you this is a place rich in history, natural beauty and great hospitality – and they're quite right. The region brims with festivals and is home to diverse cultures and traditions. Locals are resilient people who are deeply connected to the land and the Miramichi River, which is world famous for its salmon fishing.

The Mi'kmaq were the first people to live here, and in the 17th century French settlers arrived, establishing trading posts and a vibrant Acadian community. After the Expulsion of the Acadians, Scottish and Loyalist immigrants came, followed by the Irish. Today, the cultural tapestry is a blend of Mi'kmaq, Acadian, Scottish, Irish and English influences. The region is home to three Indigenous communities: Esgenoôpetitj (Burnt Church), Metepenagiag (Red Bank) and Natoaganeg (Eel Ground).

The city of Miramichi, formed by the amalgamation of several communities in 1995, is the largest city in northeastern New Brunswick.

Exploring Miramichi

Breweries, tubing and historic sites

Begin in the city of Miramichi, where **New Maritime Beer**, **Timber Ship Brewing**, **Carroll's Distillery** and the **Three Dog Distilling Company** aim to please. For a handcrafted cocktail, local beer or glass of vino, try **Apero Lounge**. Head to **O'Donaghue's Irish Pub** for fish and chips.

Get to know the majestic 250km Miramichi River with **Miramichi River Boat Tours**, which depart from Ritchie Wharf. Another fun option is **tubing the Miramichi** with a local tour company such as Gallan's Miramichi River Tubing, Vickers River Tubing or McCormack's Outdoor Adventures. Wear a bathing suit and sunscreen, plus a hat and sunglasses.

Spend the night at the scenic **Rodd Miramichi River**, which offers access to the river and recreational trails. Start the next day at **Beaubears Island**, home to two important

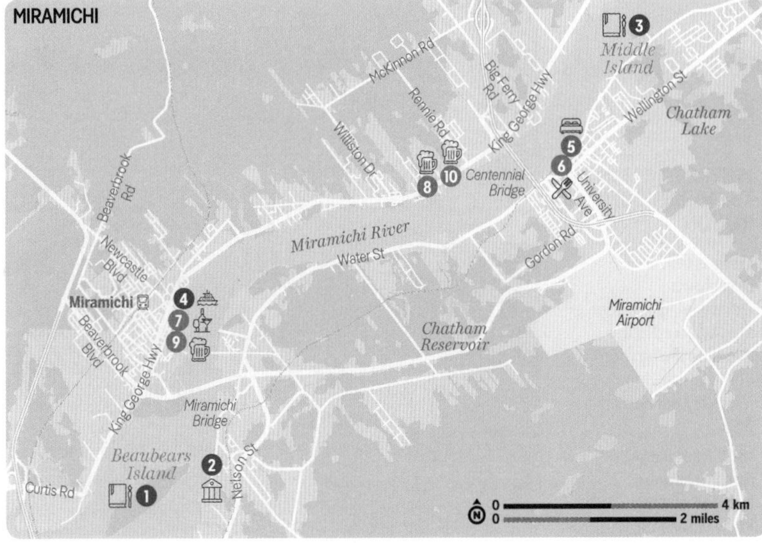

sites: the **Boishébert National Historic Site**, where visitors can learn how the island acted as a refuge for Acadians after the 1755 Expulsion; and the **Beaubears Island Shipbuilding National Historic Site**, which details the golden age of Miramichi shipbuilding in the 1850s. Access to the island is available in summer by boat from **Beaubears Island Interpretive Centre** in Miramichi.

For more fascinating history, stop at the **Middle Island Irish Historical Park**. Located in the Miramichi River, Middle Island was a quarantine station in the 19th century for Irish immigrants fleeing the great famine.

SIGHTS
1 Beaubears Island
2 Beaubears Island Interpretive Centre
3 Middle Island Irish Historical Park

ACTIVITIES, COURSES & TOURS
see 4 Miramichi River Boat Tours
4 Ritchie Wharf

SLEEPING
5 Rodd Miramichi River

EATING
6 O'Donaghue's Irish Pub

DRINKING & NIGHTLIFE
7 Apéro
8 Carroll's Distillery
9 New Maritime Beer
10 Timber Ship Brewing

Angling for a Good Time

Settle in for some fishing

Stay at the beautiful **Red Bank Lodge** or at one of the other fishing lodges that dot the riverbanks, such as in or near Sunny Corner, Blackville, Doaktown or Boiestown. Most offer guided fishing packages for anglers of all levels. Popular outfitter options include Upper Oxbow Adventures & MROC Lodges, Country Haven Lodge and Cottages, Wilson's Sporting Camps and Four Nature Resort. At **Ledges Inn** you can combine fishing with gourmet dining.

Local Insights

Museums in Boiestown and Doaktown

Get a taste of lumberjack life at the **Central New Brunswick Woodsmen's Museum** in Boiestown or stop at the **Atlantic Salmon Museum** in Doaktown to learn more about salmon fishing on the Miramichi. Don't miss walking the

WHERE TO EAT IN THE MIRAMICHI REGION

Ledges Inn, Doaktown
Outstanding gourmet meals served in the riverside dining room of the Ledges Inn. Excellent service. **$$$**

1809 Restaurant & Bar, Miramichi
Located on the Rodd Miramichi River, this eatery has exceptional riverside views and delish offerings. **$$**

O'Donaghue's Irish Pub, Miramichi
Lively spot serving super fish and chips, other pub fare and, of course, Guinness. **$$**

Namaste Bistro, Miramichi
A gem for its flavorful curries to crispy pekoras, handcrafted cocktails, wine and draft beer. **$**

Lower Ledge Gastropub, Doaktown
Quality pub food at reasonable prices with good selection of beer and cocktails. **$**

WIRESTOCK, INC./ALAMY STOCK PHOTO ©

McNamee/Priceville Footbridge

McNamee/Priceville Footbridge just west of Doaktown in McNamee. At 200m, it's the longest suspension footbridge in New Brunswick and provides picturesque views of the Southwest Miramichi.

Step Back in Time at Metepenagiag

Experience longstanding Indigenous culture

Immerse yourself in history and nature – and sample delicious food – with **A Taste of Metepenagiag 'Ookdotaan'**, an experience offered at **Metepenagiag Heritage Park** in the Metepenagiag First Nation. Tour beautiful exhibits and learn about the lives of the Mi'kmaq here. Walk local trails and hear Metepenagiag stories before enjoying seasonal fish or game with wild rice, hot bannock and, if you're lucky, fresh fiddleheads. Later, you can learn about two national historic sites: the Augustine Mound, a ceremonial burial mound created 2500 years ago, and the Oxbow Site, which provides archaeological evidence of a campsite and proves this Mi'kmaq community has endured here for more than 3000 years. You can't visit the sites because of their cultural importance, but you can see them as you paddle past in a kayak with a guide.

WHERE TO STAY

Rodd Miramichi River, Miramichi
Comfortable accommodations, scenic river views and great dining at a popular downtown Miramichi property. $$

Ledges Inn, Doaktown
Beautiful lodge fronting the Southwest Miramichi with terrific options for dining, outdoor activities and relaxation. $

Red Bank Lodge, Metepenagiag First Nation
Lovely cedar lodge with stunning views a short walk from fascinating Metepenagiag Heritage Park. $$

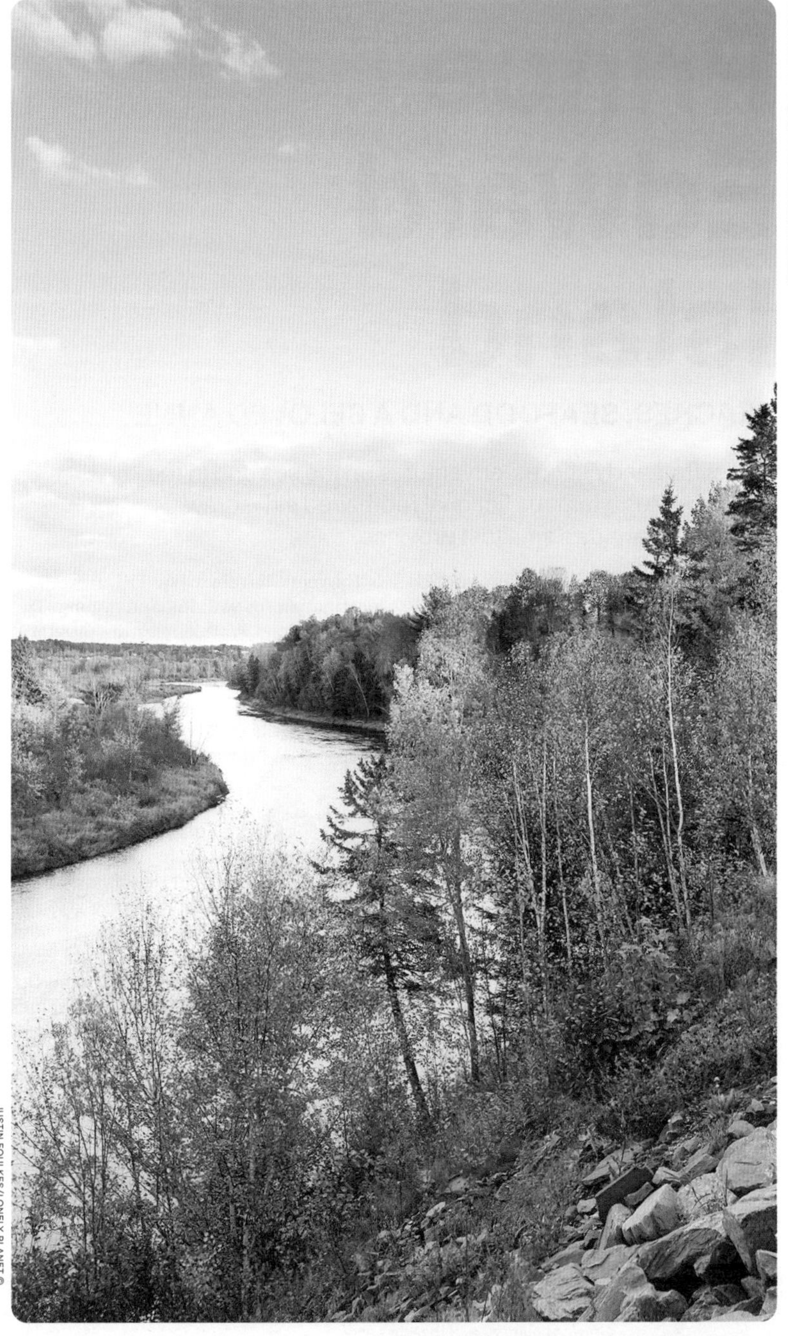

JUSTIN FOULKES/LONELY PLANET ©

Miramichi River, Metepenagiag Heritage Park

Prince Edward Island

BEACHES, SEAFOOD AND A BELOVED ANNE

Red cliffs, sandy shores, adventures on the sea and in the kitchen – plus a famous fictional red-haired girl – draw visitors to Canada's smallest province.

Most visitors to Prince Edward Island (PEI) come for the dozens of beaches, from quiet coves to broad dune-backed expanses of sand. But there's more to the island than fun in the sun. PEI remains a largely rural region of rolling green hills, where many of its 160,000 residents earn their living from the land or the sea. The ocean supplies lobsters, oysters, mussels and more, while in the red earth, potatoes, corn and many types of berries thrive. In farmers markets, cooking classes, craft breweries and waterfront restaurants, and from the capital city of Charlottetown to the many small towns, you can sample the bounty of 'Canada's Food Island.'

The gentle terrain makes PEI an excellent destination for walking and cycling. The 700km Island Walk circles the province, while the Confederation Trail, a former rail line, stretches 273km from tip to tip. However you get around, you can learn about PEI's varied histories, with cultural experiences in local Indigenous communities and sites illustrating the island's role in Canada's birth.

Yet it's Lucy Maud Montgomery's *Anne of Green Gables* novels, written in the early 1900s and set around the author's Cavendish hometown, that put Prince Edward Island on the tourist map. Montgomery's books take you back to a more bucolic era that, even in present-day PEI, never seems far away.

THE MAIN AREAS

ELENATHEWISE/GETTY IMAGES ©

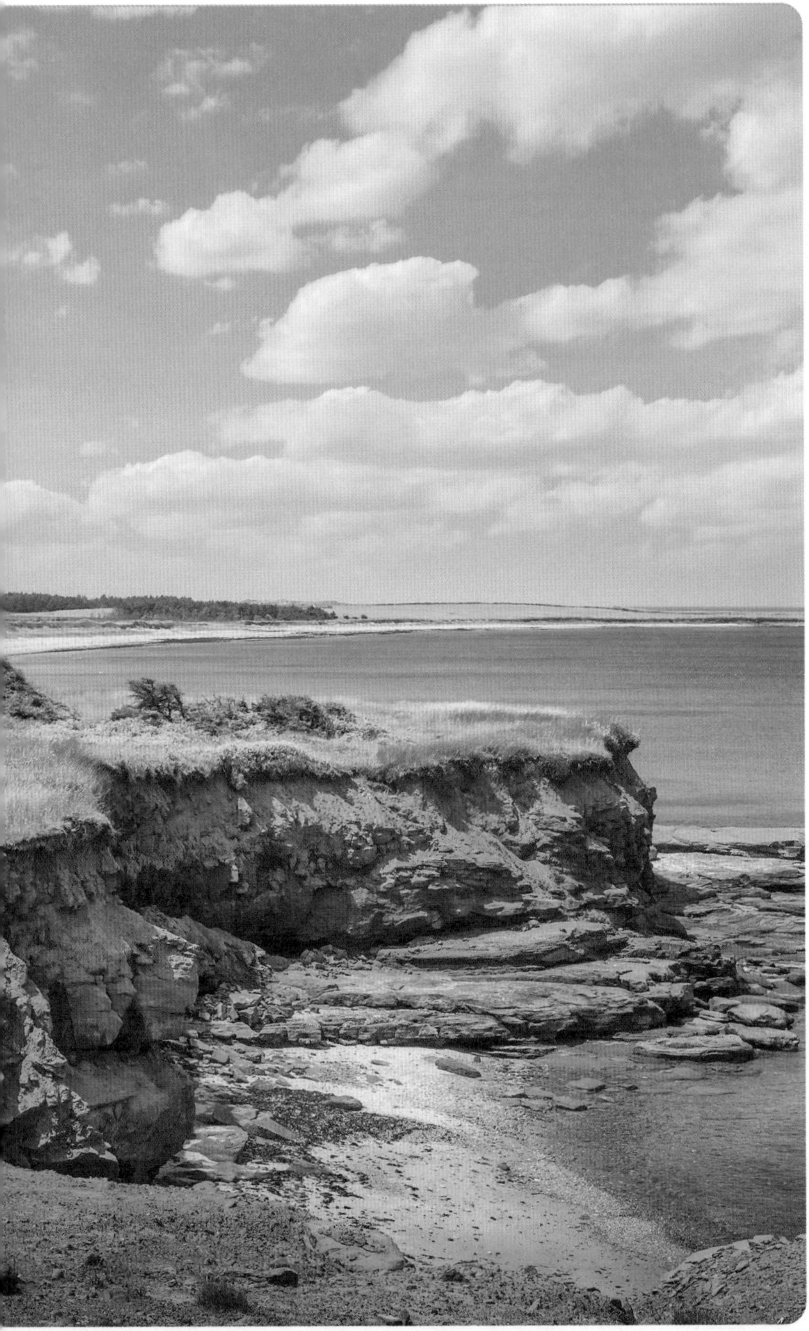

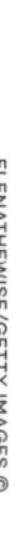

Left: Mussels; Above: Red cliffs at East Point, Prince Edward Island

BY CAR
Exploring PEI is easiest by car. The 12.9km **Confederation Bridge** connects the island to mainland Canada. You pay the hefty bridge toll only when you leave, and it's most economical to enter the island by ferry from Nova Scotia and exit over the bridge.

BY FERRY
From Wood Islands in eastern PEI, 75-minute ferries travel to/from Nova Scotia. From Souris, ferries make the five-hour trip to Québec's Îles de la Madeleine.

Find Your Way

You could drive straight across PEI in less than four hours, but slow down and take time to explore. Much of the region's beauty is found along its meandering coasts.

Cavendish & North-Central PEI, p148
Learn about Lucy Maud Montgomery's life and her *Anne of Green Gables* novels in the author's hometown, which is also convenient to the beaches of PEI National Park.

Charlottetown, p142
Start in the province's waterfront capital for an introduction to the region's history, to enjoy music, art and theater, and to tap into PEI's food scene.

Souris & Eastern PEI, p155
Set sail with a lobster fisher, learn to tong for oysters, and meander through the small communities along PEI's eastern shores.

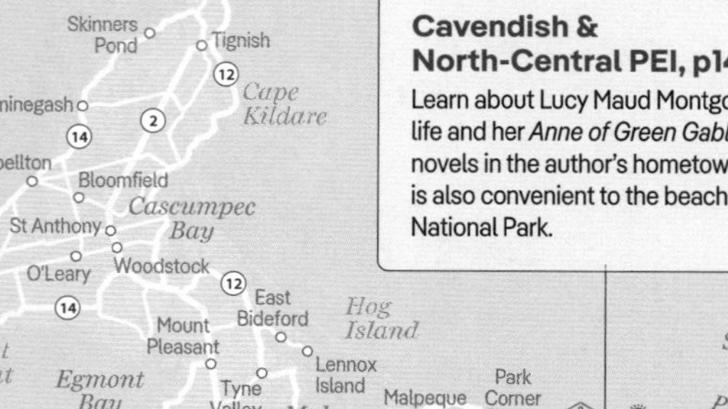

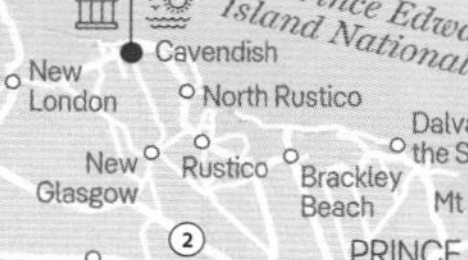

Victoria Row, Charlottetown (p142)

Plan Your Time

You can take in the highlights of compact PEI in a couple of days, but allowing time for unique island experiences will make your stay more special.

A Long Weekend

- Stroll around the historic streets and harbor in **Charlottetown** (p142), or get oriented with a walking tour. Head north to **Cavendish** (p148) to see the *Anne of Green Gables* sites and enjoy the beaches in **Prince Edward Island National Park** (p152). Take a kayak excursion, go on an oyster crawl or enjoy a traditional lobster supper, ending your night with music in a local pub.

A One-Week Road Trip

- After exploring Charlottetown and Cavendish, hike between scenic **Greenwich Dunes** (p153) in the national park, then have dinner at historic Dalvay-by-the-Sea. Continue east for a lobster cruise from **Souris** (p155) or a stay in the floating wine barrels at **Nellie's Landing** (p157). Walk or cycle along the **Confederation Trail** (p158) before coming back to Charlottetown for a cooking class or food tour.

Seasonal Highlights

SPRING

PEI's lobster season begins in May. In June, PEI celebrates **Indigenous Peoples' Day**. The **Festival of Small Halls** schedules concerts island-wide.

SUMMER

Book ahead! Summer brings the **Cavendish Beach Music Festival**, the **Tyne Valley Oyster Fest** and **Pride PEI**.

FALL

Autumn is a favorite for fall colors and food events, including the **Fall Flavours Festival** and the **International Shellfish Festival.**

WINTER

From mid-October into May, PEI stays quiet and often snowy, with many attractions, lodgings and restaurants closed.

Charlottetown

GETTING AROUND

Charlottetown's compact downtown core is easy to explore on foot. The local bus system, T3 Transit, operates routes around the city and from Charlottetown to destinations across the island. Rural buses run infrequently, though, so check schedules in advance.

Both geographically and economically, Charlottetown is Prince Edward Island's heart, central to attractions, transportation and services. Victorian-era homes and low-rise heritage buildings line the downtown streets, and walkways along the harbor and through city parks draw both residents and visitors for regular strolls. Like many North American cities, PEI's provincial capital sprawls out from the center with shopping malls and big box stores. Yet only a short distance beyond, you're in the island's countryside.

Charlottetown is known as the birthplace of Confederation, where plans for the union that became the country of Canada were laid, and several sites can tell you about this heritage. PEI's largest city is its food and entertainment hub, too, with more restaurants, culinary experiences (anchored by the Culinary Institute of Canada), music clubs and theaters than you might expect in a city of fewer than 50,000 souls.

TOP TIP

Have a question about your PEI trip? Ask an Islander. Tourism PEI, the provincial tourism organization, has recruited friendly residents to answer visitor inquiries. Search for 'Ask an Islander' on its website (tourismpei.com) to submit your query.

Birthplace of Confederation

Exploring Canada's early days

In 1864 Charlottetown hosted a meeting to discuss the possible union of Britain's North American colonies. Held in Province House, a stone manor that has housed PEI's Legislative Assembly since 1847, the Charlottetown Conference laid the foundation for the Canadian Confederation, established in 1867 with four provinces: Nova Scotia, New Brunswick, Québec and Ontario. PEI joined the new country in 1873.

Province House National Historic Site normally shares the story of Charlottetown's role in the country of Canada's birth. While it undergoes a multiyear renovation, you can visit the **Confederation Chamber replica** inside the Confederation Centre of the Arts. Watch a film about the historic confab and, around a replica of the conference table, talk with the interpreters about the 23 attendees and the issues Canada's creation raised, especially for Indigenous communities.

NAME/CREDIT ©

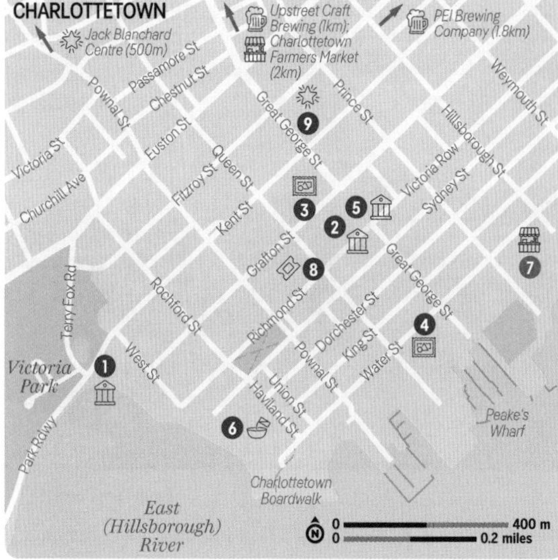

SIGHTS
1 Beaconsfield Historic House
2 Confederation Centre of the Arts
3 Indigenous PEI Store
4 PEI Crafts Council Gallery
5 Province House National Historic Site

ACTIVITIES, COURSES & TOURS
6 Culinary Institute of Canada

EATING
7 Founders Food Hall

ENTERTAINMENT
8 Guild
9 Trailside Music Hall

Costumed actors lead you through Charlottetown's heritage on the entertaining **Confederation Players Walking Tours**. Book online or in person at the Confederation Centre of the Arts.

The one-hour **Secrets of Charlottetown Walking Tours** offer a different take on island history. Guides share tales of bootleggers, kidnappings, duels and ghost ships as you walk, learning about heritage buildings, local characters and unsolved mysteries. It's great fun.

For more history, tour Beaconsfield Historic House, built in 1877 for shipbuilder James Peake and his wife, Edith, and furnished in elegant period style. The guides' stories transport you to PEI in the Victorian era.

To see Charlottetown from the water, take a sightseeing cruise with **Ride Solar** on a solar-powered electric boat.

Food & Drink Experiences

Tasty tidbits and trails

Start your Charlottetown food adventures at **Founders Food Hall** near the waterfront, where vendors range from French-Caribbean **Datcha** (try the cod bokit on a house-made bun) to **Dal's Potato Bar**, which tops PEI spuds with Turkish-style condiments, to **Oh Fudge!**, which crafts tasty

LOCAL EATS

Farmacy + Fermentary
Salads, bowls and sandwiches brim with fermented veggies and produce from the owners' farm. $

Leonhard's Café & Restaurant
Fab baked goods and all-day breakfasts. Creative lunches range from schnitzel to roasted-beet tarts. $

Gallant's Seafood
Casual shop-cafe specializing in crab cakes, fried oysters and anything fresh from the sea. $

CANADA'S FOOD ISLAND

Crystal MacGregor is Director of Communications & Marketing for the Food Island Partnership, a PEI-based nonprofit economic-development organization. Here she shares her tips for sampling local products. @canadasfoodisland

Book a Food Experience
See how it all happens: go **oyster tonging** (p43) or **clam digging** (p146), set sail with a **lobster fisher** (p155), or spend the afternoon with a **potato farmer** (p162).

Know Your Bivalves
How do you choose among the dozens of PEI oyster varieties? Check out thesocialshell.com, which maps the island's oyster regions and tells you about their tastes and variations.

Whet Your Appetite
The Canada's Food Island website (canadasfoodisland.ca) features a month-by-month guide to local foods.

Founders Food Hall

sweets from island potatoes. The food hall hosts live music some evenings.

To see what's in season, join city residents at the **Charlottetown Farmers Market**, where 60-plus stalls are stocked with local produce and prepared foods on Saturdays year-round and on Wednesdays between late June and early October. The market is north of downtown, on T3 Transit's Rte 1. From July into September, the **Downtown Farmers' & Artisans' Market** sets up Sundays in the city center.

The **Culinary Institute of Canada** trains many of the country's emerging chefs, but you don't have to be a pro to attend a **Culinary Boot Camp**. These informative yet relaxed half- or full-day courses for home cooks might include Savor the Season, highlighting local seafood and produce, or Island Flavours, where you shop at markets before preparing a PEI feast.

If you want a guide for your gastronomic wanderings, sign up for **Experience PEI's Taste the Town Food + Fact Tour**. On this 3½-hour walking tour you'll stop for food and drink while learning about the city's heritage and culinary culture.

As in many locations, craft beer is having a moment on PEI. In Charlottetown, find local suds at **Upstreet Brewing** and **PEI Brewing Company**. Besides serving pizza and beer, Upstreet works to benefit the community as PEI's first B-Corp certified company.

If you have a car (and a designated driver), follow the **5-15 Fermentation Trail**, five rural beverage producers that are each only a 15-minute drive from Charlottetown. Sample the

GO GLAMPING

Meridian 63
Tiny off-the-grid camping cabins with sleeping lofts bring style to Strathgartney Park. $$

Treetop Haven
Wake up in the forest in your TreePOD, a geodesic dome with a deck. $$

Nature Space Resort
Sleep in a yurt, paddle the lagoon and stretch into yoga at this peaceful retreat. $$

wares at Island Honey Wines, Deep Roots Distillery, Barnone Brewing, Matos Winery and Riverdale Orchard Cidery, and be back in the city by suppertime.

Charlottetown's Arty Side

Galleries, theaters and toe-tapping music

The **Confederation Centre of the Arts** is the city's central art and music space. Throughout the year the centre's **Art Gallery** mounts changing exhibitions by Canadian visual artists, and its theaters host plays, concerts and other arts events. Look for performances by the **Mi'kmaq Heritage Actors**, an island-based Indigenous theater company. The center presented *Anne of Green Gables – The Musical* for more than 50 years (1965 through 2019); this popular production will be back on stage beginning in 2024.

The Guild is another downtown performance space with a small art gallery. In the Arts Hotel, **Trailside Music Hall** programs regular concerts by local and regional musicians. You can hear free live music outdoors on Victoria Row, presented by **Always on Stage** in July and August, and more music near the harbor as part of the **Sounds of the Waterfront** summer series. **Ceilidh In the City** presents traditional foot-stomping island music at the Jack Blanchard Centre from June into the fall.

For local crafts, visit the **PEI Crafts Council Gallery**, which exhibits and sells jewelry, textiles and other works by island artists. Check its website for details about craft workshops, such as a basket-making class with a Mi'kmaq weaver. If you're specifically interested in Indigenous art, visit the **Indigenous PEI Store**, which opened downtown in 2023.

The Island Walk

Circumnavigate PEI

Modeled after Spain's Camino de Santiago, the Island Walk is a 700km walking and cycling route that circles Prince Edward Island. Starting and ending in Charlottetown, and passing PEI's sandy beaches, above its red cliffs, and through its forests, the walk is divided into 32 segments of 20km to 25km that you can tackle individually or as an extended loop.

Most of the terrain is relatively gentle, following PEI's flat shorelines and gradually rolling hills. Part of the route follows the Confederation Trail along a former rail line, while other sections take you on dirt roads and (mostly) secondary roadways. The route is designed to be walked clockwise, with signs marking turns as well as segment start and endpoints.

PLANNING YOUR ISLAND WALK

The Island Walk website (theislandwalk.ca) and Facebook group (facebook.com/groups/486034768677776) are the best places to start planning your adventure.

Outfitters including **Go for a Walk: Island Walk Coordination Service** (goforawalkpei.com) and **Outer Limit Sports** (walk.ols.ca) can help you organize your trip. **MacQueen's Bike Shop** (macqueens.com) provides planning services for cyclists.

The Island Walk doesn't have **accommodations** or other services at each segment's end. You'll need to plan for where you'll eat and sleep. Whether you camp or stay in B&Bs, it's often easier to stay in one location for several days and use buses, taxis and transportation that innkeepers provide to get to and from the trail. A growing number of accommodations are welcoming Island Walkers.

TAKE A COFFEE BREAK

Receiver Coffee
Caters to coffee connoisseurs at several locations, including the 1876 sandstone Brass Shop.

Kettle Black
A cozy downtown coffeehouse where you can work, chat or relax with your caffeine.

The Shed
Specializes in Vietnamese-style coffee, served black, with condensed milk or with frothy egg.

Beyond Charlottetown

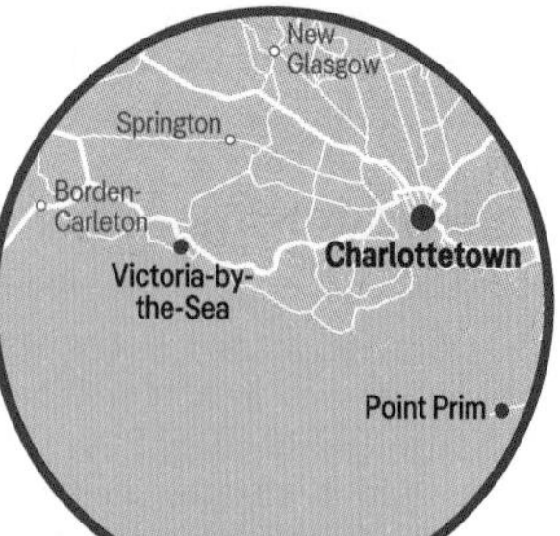

Climb to the top of PEI's oldest lightstation, explore the island's history and stop for seafood by the sea.

GETTING AROUND

The Victoria, Orwell and Point Prim areas aren't easily accessible without a car. If you're walking the **Island Walk** (p145), the route takes you into Victoria; otherwise, buses on T3 Transit's Borden-Charlottetown route can take you as far as Crapaud, 3km north of Victoria.

Whether you travel east or west from Charlottetown, you can day-trip to seaside villages and unique historic attractions.

A popular excursion to the southwest takes you to Victoria-by-the-Sea. Founded in 1819, this fishing village became a significant seaport in the late 1800s, though today it's known more for its seafood restaurants than for its ships.

East of Charlottetown, two heritage sites explore PEI's agrarian past and a narrow peninsula leads to Point Prim Lighthouse, the island's oldest coastal beacon. Nearby, you can take a unique tour through PEI's geologic history. There may not be dinosaurs, but along this route you can hunt for fossils on the beach, stop for tea, and imagine what it would be like to guide ships along the rocky shores.

Victoria-by-the-Sea

Supping by the shore

TIME FROM CHARLOTTETOWN: **30 MINS**

'Seas the day. Order the lobster roll,' advises the neon sign over the bar at the Lobster Barn, an eatery on the docks in **Victoria-by-the-Sea**. And perhaps that's the best reason to day trip to this cute seaside village, 35km southwest of Charlottetown: to sample the local seafood. Whether you're craving freshly shucked oysters, fish and chips, or lobster rolls, **Landmark Oyster House**, **The Lobster Barn** and **Richard's** all have their fans among seafood savants.

Besides the restaurants, Victoria has several art galleries and craft shops to browse. You can stop in at **Island Chocolate**, a family-run chocolatier and dessert cafe, to watch the chocolate makers at work. The rich aromas are sure to entice you to sample a hot chocolate or leave with a box of bonbons. To explore further afield, rent a bicycle, kayak or paddleboard from **By-the-Sea Kayaking** on Victoria's waterfront. It offers half- and full-day kayak tours, as well as a **kayaking & clam**

SNACK STOPS

Island Chocolate, Victoria-by-the-Sea
The handmade bonbons and Sunday-only chocolate waffles are mouth-watering motives for a South Shore day trip. $

Point Prim Chowder House
Chowder, steamed clams and lobster rolls overlooking the ocean near Point Prim Lighthouse. $$

Bar Vela Pizzeria
A shipping container surrounded by picnic tables on Point Prim Rd turns out creative pizzas. $

Orwell Corner Historic Village

digging experience. Continuing east from Victoria, you can swim or catch some sun at **Argyle Shore Provincial Park** or **Canoe Cove Beach**.

Point Prim

A lookout across the sea TIME FROM CHARLOTTETOWN: **45 MINS**

PEI's oldest lighthouse sits at the tip of a narrow finger of land east of Charlottetown and makes the focal point of an enjoyable scenic drive. At **Point Prim Lighthouse**, built in 1845, you can climb the steep ladder-like stairs to the lookout for views of both sides of the point and out at the seemingly endless sea. A small exhibit area tells you about the structure's history and design – it's one of only three round brick lighthouses in Canada – and about the lighthouse keepers who kept watch here over the years.

On your way to or from Point Prim, you can go back in time at two historic sites. At **Orwell Corner Historic Village**, a living history site that takes you to rural PEI in the 1800s and early 1900s, start in the agricultural museum that details the lives of settler-farmers, with quotes about how they picked berries, grew potatoes and oats, or sold milk and cheese from their own cows. In the village itself, staffed by interpreters in period costumes, you can wander through the school, a general store, a blacksmith shop and other buildings; in summer, a tea shop in the community hall serves pastries, coffee, tea and lemonade. The village also raises horses, goats, chickens and other animals using traditional 1895 farming methods.

Down the road, at the **Sir Andrew MacPhail Homestead**, the 1850s center-gabled house that belonged to an island doctor-writer, you can get another view of rural island life as you tour the home. Take a break with soup or a sandwich in the tearoom.

TOP TIP

Black-and-white bovine mascots lure ice-cream lovers into **COWS Creamery** shops island wide, but visit the company's flagship outside Charlottetown for free self-guided tours.

PREHISTORIC ISLAND TOURS

Geologist Laura MacNeil shares tales of geologic wonders on her fascinating **Prehistoric Island Tours**, 90-minute narrated beach walks through one of the island's most significant fossil sites. She'll show you how to identify different fossils and take you through PEI's geological evolution with straightforward explanations that appeal to both kids and adults. Her witty visual aids, from fossilized footprints to images of creatures such as *Dimetrodon borealis* (which predated the dinosaurs), help bring this history to life.

The tours depart from a secluded beach near Vernon Bridge, about a 30-minute drive east of Charlottetown. MacNeil sends detailed directions when you register for a tour.

Cavendish & North-Central PEI

GETTING AROUND

Convenient for day-trippers if you can accommodate the limited schedule, T3 Transit buses can take you between Charlottetown and Cavendish or North Rustico. A seasonal Summerside–Cavendish route operates as well. You can walk or cycle between sites and restaurants within Cavendish or North Rustico, though the towns themselves are 7km apart; it's 12km from Cavendish to Rustico.

TOP TIP

For a more peaceful stay than in well-trafficked Cavendish, consider lodgings in nearby communities such as North Rustico or Kensington. You can also day trip to the Anne sites from Charlottetown or Summerside, both 37km away.

Canada's most famous fictional character may be a high-spirited red-haired girl from Prince Edward Island whom author Lucy Maud Montgomery created in her *Anne of Green Gables* novels. Montgomery grew up in Cavendish, and several sites around the town highlight the novels' landmarks and places important in the writer's life.

East of Cavendish, North Rustico has a sandy beach, a scenic boardwalk and a cluster of seafood restaurants, while in Rustico, PEI's oldest Acadian community, you can learn more about this heritage. To the west, you can road trip around a scenic peninsula in search of quiet shores, lively music and local oysters. But in Cavendish, amid the waterparks, minigolf courses, souvenir shops and other touristy tat, it's all about spunky Anne and her literary legacy.

Anne of Green Gables

Time-travel into history and fiction

The legacy of *Anne of Green Gables* takes you into both history and fiction, as you visit sites that were important in Lucy Maud Montgomery's life and learn about the people, places and belongings that she incorporated into her novels.

At Parks Canada–operated **Green Gables Heritage Place**, well-designed displays trace the author's life and times. Then as you enter the adjacent farmhouse known as Green Gables, you walk into the fictional world. The author based her fictional setting on this real home, which belonged to Montgomery's cousins, the Macneills. Curators furnished the house as it was described in the novels, and costumed interpreters bring you into Anne's daily life. Book a behind-the-scenes experience called Ropes Down, which lets you examine artifacts in more detail. A Cordial Visit allows you to join 'Anne' for a chat and a sip of raspberry cordial (definitely not currant wine).

Outside, walk the trails along Lovers Lane or through the Haunted Woods, locations that figured in Montgomery's books, or to **Lucy Maud Montgomery's Cavendish**

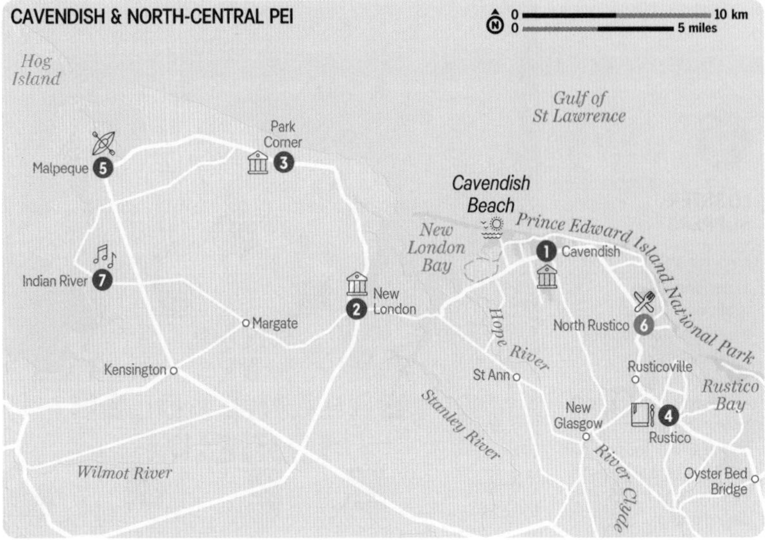

SIGHTS
1 Cavendish
2 New London
3 Park Corner
4 Rustico

ACTIVITIES, COURSES & TOURS
5 Malpeque

EATING
6 North Rustico

ENTERTAINMENT
7 Indian River

Homestead, where Maud lived from 1876 to 1911 and wrote *Anne of Green Gables*, *Anne of Avonlea* and other novels and stories. Though only the house's foundation remains, staff introduce the author's life here, including how her grandmother and then she herself ran the town post office from their kitchen.

In New London, 11km west of Cavendish, you can visit the **Lucy Maud Montgomery Birthplace**, the house where Maud was born. The author's scrapbooks and letters are among the artifacts on display.

Rustico & North Rustico

Nature, seafood and Acadian culture

In the 1760s, the first Acadians settled in these towns east of Cavendish, and many residents trace their roots to this era. Visiting **Farmers Bank of Rustico** (now a museum) and **Doucet House National Historic Site** can tell you more about this heritage.

In the 1860s, led by Reverend Georges-Antoine Belcourt, local families contributed an average of $10 each, raising nearly $4000 to launch Canada's first 'people's bank.' Operating from 1864 to 1894, Farmers

MORE ANNE

For still more *Anne of Green Gables* attractions, visit the **Anne of Green Gables Museum** (p151) in Park Corner and the **Bideford Parsonage Museum** (p162) in the Tyne Valley.

WHERE TO STAY

North Rustico Motel & Cottages
Unfancy but well-located family-owned rooms and cabins. $$

Kindred Spirits Inn & Cottages, Cavendish
On this 2.5-hectare property, guest rooms are traditional and larger cottages are modern. $$

Barachois Inn, Rustico
Two houses – one Victorian elegant, one more contemporary – make up this high-end inn. $$$

LOBSTER SUPPERS

A classic PEI experience is a traditional lobster supper, pairing local crustaceans with chowder, mussels, salads, pies and more. Your price depends on the size of lobster you choose, but note that this isn't a budget dining option.

Launched in the 1950s, **New Glasgow Lobster Suppers** are still going strong. In the river-view dining room, your server brings your choice of soups, mussels, salads and sweets, and offers you a lobster bib before you attack your shellfish.

In North Rustico, **Fisherman's Wharf Lobster Supper** features an 18m-long buffet table where you can choose all the salads, soups, mussels, rolls, fruit and desserts that you want. You almost don't need the lobster (but don't miss it).

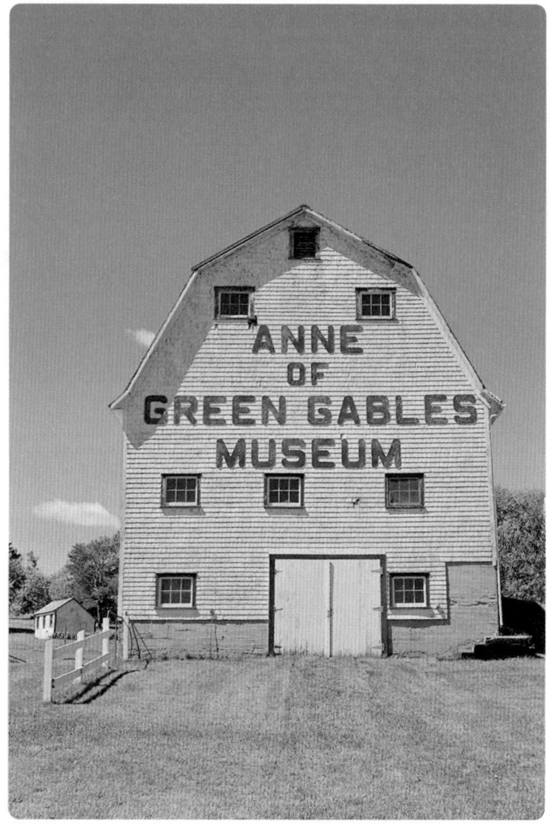

Anne of Green Gables Museum

Bank provided small loans – and self-sufficiency – to these Acadian farmers.

A log structure dating to 1772, **Doucet House** is the oldest house on PEI. Moved from its original location at Grand-Père Point (Cymbria), the restored home is outfitted with period furnishings. An entertaining – and appetizing – way to spend a summer evening is with a **Traditional Acadian Meal**, offered in the Doucet House kitchen. You'll help prepare bannock to bake in an outdoor oven, butter and ice cream, before supping on chicken *fricot* (a hearty soup), *rapûre* (a baked shredded potato dish) and meat pie served with mustard pickles.

NORTH RUSTICO FOOD

Olde Village Bakery
Visit this old-school bakeshop for top-notch muffins, breads and pastries. $

On the Dock
This harborside seafooder serves awesome lobster biscuits, plus lobster rolls and other ocean fare. $$

Blue Mussel Café
It's worth a special trip to this airy waterfront cafe for excellent fresh seafood. $$$

For fresh seafood, visit the restaurants on **North Rustico harbor**, where **Outside Expeditions** also offers several kayaking tours, from a family-friendly beginner excursion to a six-hour exploration of Prince Edward Island National Park from the water. Back on land, you can lounge on the pinkish sands of **North Rustico Beach** (part of PEI National Park), cycle the **Gulf Shore Way West** above the beaches between North Rustico and Cavendish, or stroll North Rustico **boardwalk** with views across the water.

Route 20 Loop

Ocean, oysters and more Anne

A scenic drive along Rte 20 west of Cavendish takes you to another *Anne* site, a pretty ocean beach, and one of the island's best-known oyster-producing areas.

LM Montgomery's aunt and uncle, Annie and John Campbell, lived in the Park Corner homestead that's now the **Anne of Green Gables Museum**. The author was married in this 1872 home, where artifacts include the organ played at her wedding and 'Anne's Enchanted Bookcase,' which featured in the novel. Also on display is a collection of Montgomery's books translated into languages from Slovakian to Hebrew to Korean.

Detour off Rte 20 at Malpeque for **Cabot Beach Provincial Park**, where red cliffs back the sandy beach. Inside the park, which also has a campground, **Malpeque Bay Kayak Tours** rents kayaks and paddleboards and offers guided paddling excursions. Several nearby restaurants serve **fresh local oysters**.

To end your day with something more special, book a spot at **The Table Culinary Studio**, which prepares elaborate seven-course meals highlighting locally grown and sourced ingredients in a former New London church. Another idea? Attend a concert at **Under the Spire**, a summer music series in the French Gothic St Mary's Church, constructed in Indian River in 1902.

ISLAND OYSTERS

Malpeque Bay Oyster Barn
Sate your mollusk cravings at this seasonal family-run seafood spot near Cabot Beach Provincial Park, where you can pair your local raw or pan-fried oysters with island-made craft beer. **$$**

Carr's Oyster Bar
Another destination for freshly shucked Malpeques, this seafood restaurant overlooks the water in Stanley Bridge. They host regular live music events, too. **$$**

Sou'West
On a sunny afternoon, nab a seat on the waterview patio at this seafood-centric bar and grill, and dig into seafood chowder, steamed mussels, lobster rolls – and oysters, of course – facing New London's wharf. **$$$**

Prince Edward Island National Park

Charlottetown

GETTING AROUND

You can reach the Cavendish-North Rustico area of the national park on the T3 Transit bus from Charlottetown. Within the park, cycling the Gulf Shore Way can take you through the park's Cavendish or Brackley-Dalvay sections. Otherwise, you'll need a car to get to or around the park.

With more than 65km of shorefront along the island's northern coast, Prince Edward Island National Park is all about the beach. The park is divided into three sections: Cavendish-North Rustico, Brackley-Dalvay and Greenwich.

Close to the *Anne of Green Gables* attractions, Cavendish-North Rustico draws plenty of visitors to its sandy beaches and to its 200-site Cavendish Campground, the park's largest place to camp.

Beaches line the shores of Brackley-Dalvay at the park's center, where campers can stay in the 100-site Stanhope Campground. Both park camping areas accommodate tents and RVs, or you can choose oTENTiks (platform tents) or Bunkies (tiny cabins).

While most of the park was established in 1937, Greenwich, its easternmost section, was added in 1998, primarily to protect its fragile coastal dunes. Visit Greenwich Interpretation Centre to learn about the unique parabolic dune structure, the region's Indigenous roots and its eco-systems.

Beach Days

Choose your favorite sands

You'll find one sandy beach after another throughout PEI National Park. Cavendish Beach at the park's western end tends to be the most crowded, but if you walk away from the parking lots and entry points, you can often find quieter sands. Immediately east of Cavendish Beach, **Oceanview Lookoff** has a picnic area and a lookout where you can gaze across the sea. Continuing east along Gulf Shore Way West, the scenic parkway above the shore, which also has a paved walking/cycling trail, takes you to several more beaches (most with fewer services than Cavendish) until you reach North Rustico Beach, just outside that town.

At the western end of the Brackley-Dalvay section, large, sandy Brackley Beach is another popular strand. As in the Cavendish area, you can follow the parkway – here, it's called

TOP TIP

Parks Canada offers interpretive programs throughout the summer in the national park, from Indigenous storytelling to nature talks to a meditative sunset walk on the beach. Check the park website to see what's happening when.

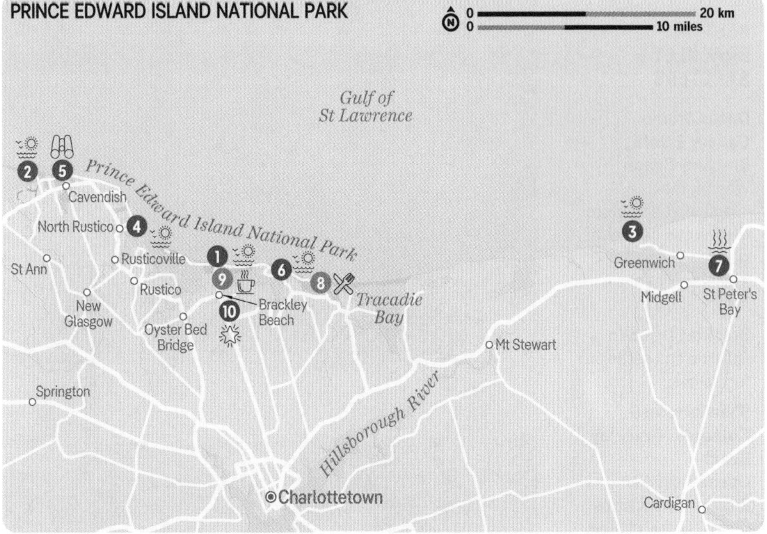

Gulf Shore Way East – through this section of the park by car or bike, or on foot. **Ross Lane Beach** and Stanhope Beach are closest to Stanhope Campground.

Greenwich Beach at the park's eastern end is normally quietest, although all the beaches are busy throughout July and August. June and September are good alternatives, but if you plan to camp, confirm campground opening dates (normally mid-June through mid-September).

In 2022, Hurricane Flora swept across PEI, uprooting trees, washing out beaches and damaging some of the island's iconic red cliffs. While most of the national park has reopened, repairs from the storm are ongoing. Check the park website or visitor centers for the most current information on areas that may still be affected.

SIGHTS
1 Brackley Beach
2 Cavendish Beach
3 Greenwich Beach
4 North Rustico Beach
5 Oceanview Lookoff
6 Ross Lane Beach
see 6 Stanhope Beach

ACTIVITIES, COURSES & TOURS
7 Mysa Nordic Spa & Resort

EATING
8 Dalvay by the Sea
9 Dunes Studio Gallery & Cafe

ENTERTAINMENT
10 Brackley Drive-In
see 9 Shaw's Hotel & Cottages

Out on the Trails

Park hiking and cycling

Most of the 50km of walking paths in PEI National Park are rated easy or moderate. There are no mountains here! If you can only hike one park trail, follow the moderate 4.8km **Greenwich Dunes trail** that leads you across a floating boardwalk and between the park's landmark dunes to the coast.

QUICK BITES

Richard's
Pick up fish and chips or lobster rolls in Covehead, convenient to the Brackley-Dalvay beaches. $$

Seafood Shack
Love lobster? Choose from lobster rolls, lobster chowder, lobster grilled cheese and more in Morell. $$

Black & White Cafe & Bistro
Espresso drinks, all-day breakfast and sandwiches at St Peters Landing near Greenwich. $

BEST OF BRACKLEY & ST PETERS

Dunes Studio Gallery & Cafe, Brackley Beach
Wander the imaginative sculpture garden and gallery, or sit down to *banh mi* or a summery beet salad in the cafe. **$$**

Brackley Drive-In
Drive up and settle in for a movie.

Shaw's Hotel & Cottages, Brackley Beach
Opened in 1860, Shaw's now includes rooms, suites, chalets and cottages. The bistro has live music throughout summer. **$$**

Mysa Nordic Spa & Resort, St Peters Bay
Nordic-style spa with thermal baths and cold-water plunges. Come for the spa, stay in an upscale cottage or suite, or dine in the farm-to-table restaurant. **$$$**

LUCIE KUSOVA/SHUTTERSTOCK ©

Cavendish Dunelands trail

Another pretty walk is the gentle **Cavendish Dunelands trail**, which winds behind the grassy dunes east of the Oceanview Lookoff. The trail is 2.3km each way.

You can walk or (better still) cycle along the mostly flat **Gulf Shore Way**, which crosses the park's Cavendish-North Rustico and Brackley-Dalvey sections. While it's unshaded, it can take you from beach to beach, with many scenic viewpoints. Note that these sections aren't contiguous; to cycle between these two park areas, you'll need to go out to the road.

The park doesn't offer bike rentals, but private operators do, including **Outside Expeditions**, whose North Rustico location is convenient to the park. Charlottetown-based **MacQueen's Bike Shop** rents bikes and offers shuttle services for cyclists. Also in Charlottetown, **Outer Limit Sports** offers rentals and can plan cycling tours around the island.

Whether you're hiking or cycling, remember these essentials: water, snacks, sunscreen and insect repellent.

MORE COOL SLEEPS
Two other distinctive accommodations near the national park's Greenwich area are **Nature Space Resort & Retreat** (p156) and **45 Steps, the Culinary Beachside Inn** (p158).

Souris & Eastern PEI

Whether you want to fish for your supper, climb a lighthouse, escape into nature or indulge in a fine island feast, you can find these experiences in eastern PEI. The town of Souris makes a good base for exploring, convenient to adventures, historic attractions and many of the island's 61 lighthouses. Stroll the boardwalk backing Souris' scenic red-sand beach, and on the town's main street look for Oh Fudge!, which crafts fudge in many flavors using PEI potatoes. It's a must-try.

The Inn at Bay Fortune, near Souris, is PEI's most renowned culinary destination, and from Souris, you're close enough to day trip into PEI National Park, especially to explore the Greenwich dunes. Montague is another eastern community with more services – and two craft breweries. Further south at Nellie's Landing in Murray Harbour, you can stay in PEI's most unusual accommodations, where you sleep on the water in a floating wine barrel.

GETTING AROUND

T3 Transit's eastern routes connect Charlottetown with Souris, St Peters and Montague/ Georgetown. There's also a bus that travels between Souris, Georgetown and Montague, and a 'tip-to-tip' bus that can take you across the island between Souris and Tignish. While service is infrequent, bus travel is extremely economical if it works with your schedule. You'll have a lot more flexibility to explore, though, if you have your own vehicle.

Ocean Adventures

How to catch your dinner

Julie Chaisson says that many people's PEI bucket list includes getting out in a boat, sampling fresh seafood and meeting an islander. She and her husband, JJ, a musician and lobster fisher, help you do all three on excursions with their business, **The Fiddling Fisherman**. After setting out from Souris Harbour on their family fishing boat, *Chaisson a Dream*, you'll drop a lobster trap and 'catch' your dinner to enjoy on board to the tunes of Chaisson's fiddle.

Another PEI experience is to 'tong' for oysters (gather shellfish using long tongs). **Along the Edge Experiences** organizes **Oyster Tong & Shuck**, where you'll learn to collect and shuck oysters, then eat what you've harvested.

On **clam-digging tours** with Georgetown-based **Tranquility Cove Adventures**, you'll cruise to deserted Boughton Island, dig for giant bar clams, then steam and eat your haul. The company can also take you **mackerel fishing**.

TOP TIP

Traveling to or from PEI by boat? The island's two passenger-ferry ports are in eastern PEI. From Wood Islands, 75-minute ferries connect PEI with Nova Scotia. From Souris, ferries make the five-hour trip to Québec's Îles de la Madeleine (Magdalen Islands).

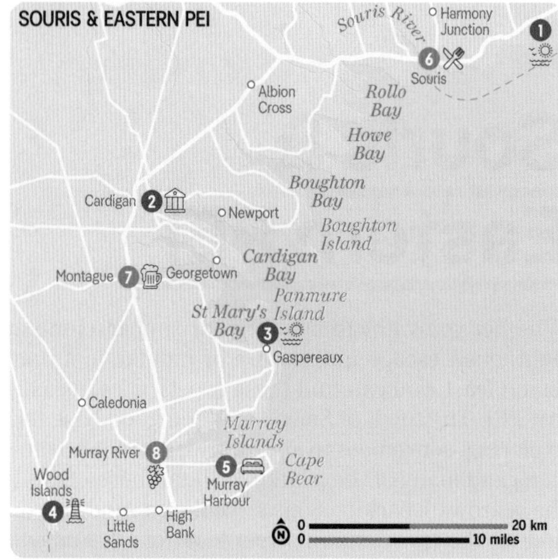

In addition to renting glamping yurts where you stay in the forest, **Nature Space Resort & Retreat Centre** has developed several outdoor experiences. It's partnered with an oyster farm for an **Oyster Lovers Kayak Experience**, where you go for a paddle, float through an oyster lease and learn all about oyster farming (yes, there are samples). It also offers **Paddles & Pints**, combining kayaking and craft-beer tasting; a **Sunset SUP** tour; a **yoga/SUP adventure**; and **kayak tours** of the peaceful lagoon adjacent to its property.

Experience PEI sets up local experiences around the island, from a **Mussel & Lobster Boil** to a **private sandcastle-building lesson** with a professional sand sculptor. Check its website for more ideas, locations and schedules.

Seafaring History

Lighthouses, museums and more

The beach in **Basin Head Provincial Park** east of Souris is known for its 'singing sands' that make a singing sound as you walk. Also in the park, **Basin Head Fisheries Museum** documents the island's fishing heritage with quotes from fishers past and present, historic photos and exhibits about everything seagoing, from lighthouses to fishing boats to ship-to-shore radio. Stop at **Basin Head Interpretive Park**, where

MONTAGUE-AREA MUNCHIES

Lucky Bean Coffee
Hang out over coffee, breakfast or a sandwich in this laid-back Montague cafe. $

Maroon Pig Sweet Shop
Pick up a butter-tart square and browse the art at this Georgetown bakery-gallery. $

Bogside Brewing
Pair beer with barbecue or smoked meats in this Montague brewer's rustic tasting room. $$

BRYTTA/GETTY IMAGES ©

East Point Lighthouse

outdoor panels discuss how Indigenous people used various plants and fish. While it doesn't provide a lot of information, this roadside park adds an Indigenous perspective currently lacking in the fisheries museum.

East Point Lighthouse stands guard over the island's easternmost shores, with exhibits about shipwrecks and profiles of its lighthouse keepers, a job only five long-serving men held from 1867, when the lighthouse opened, until 1989, when automation eliminated the need for a human lightkeeper.

Need a book? A gray shingled hut by the river in Cardigan houses **Canada's smallest library**.

PEI's first museum, set in Montague's 1888 former post office and customs house, **Garden of the Gulf Museum** tells you about the community's history.

Drive up the peninsula bounded by the Cardigan, Brudenell and Montague Rivers to **Panmure Island Lighthouse**. Constructed with an uncommon octagonal tower, the four-story, wood-shingled lighthouse was completed in 1853. After browsing the museum, climb the ladder to the lookout, where on a clear day views extend along the coast and across the sea to Nova Scotia. South of the lighthouse, you can walk the sandy beach in **Panmure Island Provincial Park**, with views back to the lightstation.

WHERE TO STAY

Shanty Stay
Ten simple 'shanties' behind Souris' main street channel the island's seagoing past with rustic wood walls and a beachy vibe. **$**

Sirens Beach Motel
At this funky and fun motel above the water at the island's east end, the owners are especially welcoming to Island Walkers. **$$**

Nellie's Landing
PEI's most distinctive accommodations may be these floating wine barrels docked in Murray Harbour, with modern washrooms and an outdoor kitchen nearby. **$$**

Georgetown Historic Inn
Built in 1840, this harbor-view inn has eight rooms with country quilts and nautical decor. The homey dining room serves breakfast and dinner. **$$**

Johnson Shore Inn
Comfortable 12-room inn overlooking the Gulf of St Lawrence on the island's north shore. **$$**

MORE LIGHTHOUSES

Wood Islands
Exhibits in this 1876 lighthouse feature rum running, sea glass and a mysterious burning ship.

Cape Bear
This lighthouse's telegraph station received the first distress signal in Canada from the sinking *Titanic*.

Souris East
The light atop this tapered tower guides ferries traveling between PEI and the Îles de la Madeleine.

SOUTHEASTERN FAVORITES

Jen Smith and Cal Fraser own Nellie's Landing, with accommodations, a marina and e-bike rentals in Murray Harbour, a quiet community that they describe as 'a village lost in time.' Fraser is also a lobster fisher. They shared some favorite things to do in southeastern PEI:

Guernsey Cove
This secluded sandy spot has cliffs on both sides.

Panting's Shore
Another quiet beach, Panting's Shore is near Northumberland Provincial Park.

Confederation Trail
You can cycle or e-bike to the village of Murray River, then loop south to Rossignol Estate Winery and east to Cape Bear Lightstation, or alternatively pedal up to Double Hill Cidery.

Historical Tours of Murray Harbour
For something totally different, take a ghost walk with this tour company.

CHASE CLAUSEN/SHUTTERSTOCK ©

Rossignol Estate Winery

Tasting Tour

Culinary and cocktail experiences

The island's most celebrated dining destination is the **Inn at Bay Fortune**, a luxury lodging where chef Michael Smith and his team prepare **The FireWorks Feast**, a farm-to-table extravaganza that begins with a tour of the on-site farm, followed by an 'oyster hour' and an elaborate multicourse repast. The inn is a short drive west of Souris.

At **45 Steps, the Culinary Beachside Inn**, a contemporary inn on the north shore, guests can join the 'Kitchen Club,' for private dinners, cooking classes or other culinary events.

Eastern PEI has several craft breweries, including **Bogside Brewing** and **Copper Bottom Brewing Company** in Montague. **Myriad View Distillery**, just west of Souris, makes 'moonshine' and other spirits (and yes, its property has an amazing ocean view). Near Murray Harbour, **Double Hill Cidery** has an outdoor tasting room high on a hill with expansive vistas over the fields to the water. It crafts some of its ciders from wild island apples and offers cider on tap, tasting flights and cider cocktails. Prefer wine tasting? Stop into **Newman Estate Winery** in Murray River or **Rossignol Estate Winery** east of Wood Islands.

Summerside & Western PEI

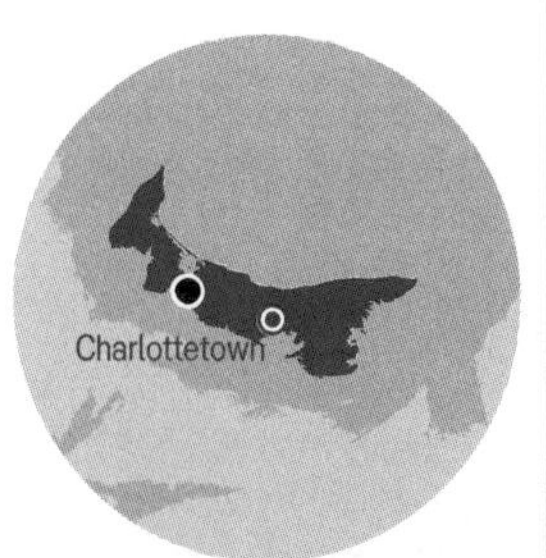

PEI's second-largest city, Summerside is the gateway to the tranquil, rural western end of the island. Sixty kilometers west of Charlottetown, the city sprawls from its waterfront, and heritage homes – many converted into small inns or museums – line its central streets. From Summerside you can head west or instead go north for your *Anne of Green Gables* fix; Cavendish is less than 40 minutes' drive away.

Lennox Island Mi'kmaq First Nation occupies a spur of land 45km northwest of Summerside where you can book a cultural experience to learn about their heritage and current-day life. Acadian communities also call western PEI home, with a museum and music center showcasing this culture. The west has more eclectic experiences as well, whether you want to understand the island's fox-farming history, its potatoes or the influence of the ever-present wind. And what's more 'island' than sleeping in a lighthouse?

GETTING AROUND

Several T3 Transit buses run weekdays between Summerside and Charlottetown. You can also travel by bus west from Summerside to Miscouche, Wellington, O'Leary and Tignish. A 'tip-to-tip' bus crosses the island between Tignish and Souris, with stops in Summerside, Charlottetown and several other communities. As in other parts of the island, though, it can be challenging to get around without your own vehicle, since service is infrequent.

Summerside History

From heritage homes to fox farms

Summerside's most unusual attraction may be the **International Fox Museum**, which documents how, in the early 1900s, PEI became the first place to successfully raise foxes in captivity. With stories of fox-breeding entrepreneurs and their effect on the island economy, the museum's multimedia exhibits detail the industry's rise and fall, from its early-20th-century peak when fur became increasingly fashionable until WWII closed European markets and mid-century attitudes toward fur garments began to change. The museum is on the 2nd floor of the former Armoury building, which has additional area history exhibits on the first level.

Wyatt Historic House Museum offers a different look at the community's heritage. Wanda Lefurgey Wyatt and her sister, Dorothy, grew up in this home, which was built in 1867, the year of Canadian Confederation. Wanda lived here from

TOP TIP

The North Cape Coastal Drive circles western PEI to its 'North Cape' tip. En route, you can sample the spuds at the Canadian Potato Museum, stop for toe-tapping tunes at the Stompin' Tom Centre and learn how the island harnesses the wind. A useful road trip planning resource is northcapedrive.ca.

SIGHTS
1 Cap-Egmont
2 Lennox Island
3 Miscouche
4 O'Leary
5 Summerside
6 Tyne Valley
7 Wellington

SLEEPING
8 Tignish

ENTERTAINMENT
9 Abram-Village
10 Skinners Pond

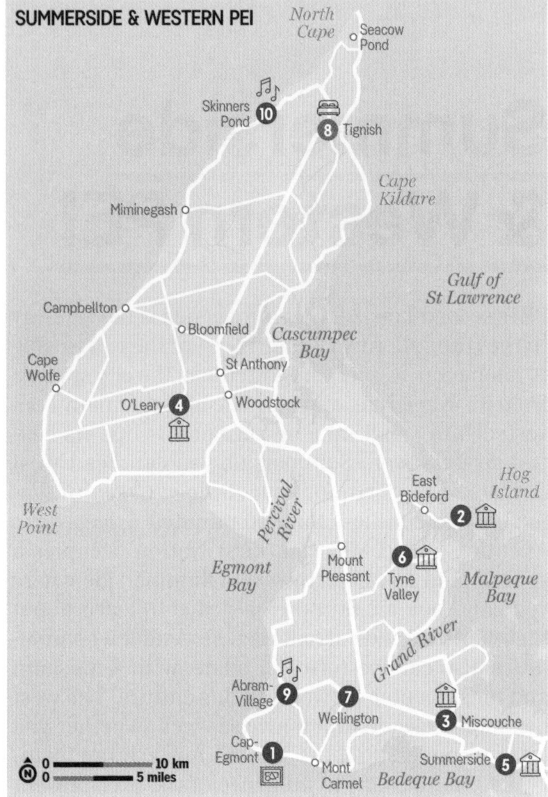

1895, when she was born, until 1998, when she died at age 102. Guided tours of Wyatt House tell you more about the Wyatt family and life in Summerside during this era. Buy tour tickets at **Lefurgey Cultural Centre** nearby, where you can also browse a small art gallery.

As you're walking around Summerside, **Eptek Art & Culture Centre** is worth a look for its changing displays of work by local artists. The gift shop sells island-made crafts.

Lennox Island

Indigenous cultural experiences

Roughly 450 members of the Lennox Island Mi'kmaq First Nation live on **Lennox Island**, where a short bridge and cause-

STAYS AROUND SUMMERSIDE

Warm House Inn
With welcoming proprietors, hearty breakfasts and cozy rooms, this Summerside B&B deserves its name. $$

Summerside Inn B&B
This Queen Anne Revival home offers traditionally furnished guest rooms and ample morning meals. $$

Home Place Inn
The friendly owners of this Victorian-era Kensington B&B are quick with tips for nearby adventures. $$

Mi'kmaw dancers, Lennox Island

way over Malpeque Bay connect this community to the rest of PEI. Community members have developed several cultural experiences, where you can learn about their heritage and daily life through food, art and music.

Book **Bannock & Clams in the Sand**, and you'll grill local mollusks and prepare this biscuit-like bread in a firepit, buried under the sand, using a traditional cooking technique. Other workshops include **Quill Work on Birch Bark**, where you're introduced to this craft, and **The Beat of the Drum**, where you make your own moose-hide drum and learn about its importance in Mi'kmaw culture.

Whether you book a cultural experience or not, visitors can explore **Lennox Island Cultural Centre**, where exhibits detail the nation's legends, heritage and cultural practices. Staff are usually around to give you a free tour. The community also welcomes visitors for special events, including celebrations of **Indigenous Peoples Day** (June) and the nation's annual **Mawi'omi** (powwow; August). Book cultural experiences and get event details on the **Experience Lennox Island** website (experiencelennoxisland.com).

EATING AROUND SUMMERSIDE

Samuel's Coffee House
Serves all-day breakfast, pastries, smoothies and sandwiches, plus a long list of coffee drinks. **$**

South Central Kitchen & Provisions
Creative sandwiches, soups and sweets lure the lunch crowd to this casual Summerside eatery. **$**

Evermore Brewing Co
Summerside brewpub offering craft beer, live music and an upscale pub menu. **$$**

Holman's Ice Cream
Many locals swear by Holman's premium housemade ice creams and sorbets that rotate through a long list of flavors. **$**

Island Stone Pub
Burgers, seafood and steak are the draws at this friendly local pub inside Kensington's former rail depot north of Summerside. **$$**

TYNE VALLEY EATING

Tyne Valley Teas
Stop for a cuppa in this cute tearoom, also serving light meals and afternoon tea. $

Backwoods Burger
Known for clam poutine and overflowing burgers, with several branches across western PEI. $

Valley Pearl Oysters
Oysters, raw or fried, headline the pubby menu at this local hangout. $

THE TYNE VALLEY

In 1894–95, Lucy Maud Montgomery taught school in the rural Tyne Valley, boarding with a minister's family in the restored home that's now **Bideford Parsonage Museum**. Tour guides tell you how her time here influenced her writing.

The **PEI Shipbuilding Museum** recounts how, in the early 1800s, the island's old-growth forests became wood for sailing ships. On the same property, you can tour **Historic Yeo House**, the 1865 home of shipbuilding magnate James Yeo and his family.

The old-school **PEI Shellfish Museum** on the Bideford waterfront is packed with details about island oysters, scallops, lobsters and more. More lively, perhaps, is the **Tyne Valley Oyster Festival**, an August music and mollusk fest.

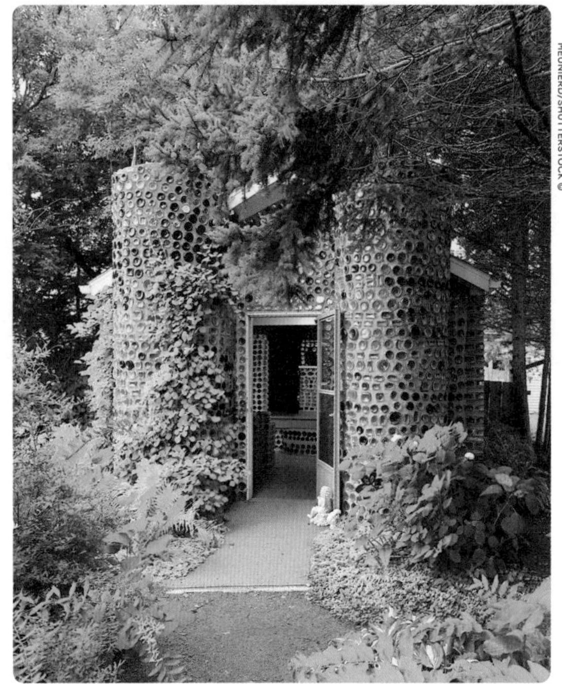

MEUNIERD/SHUTTERSTOCK ©

Maisons de Bouteilles

Acadian Culture

***Bonjour* to heritage and music**

PEI's Acadian population may be small, but these French-speaking peoples, who began arriving on the island in the early 1700s, continue to influence local culture. As you drive PEI's back roads, particularly west of Summerside in the area known as the Évangéline region, you'll notice many houses, mailboxes, and fences painted the red, white and blue – with a gold star – of the Acadian flag.

At the **Acadian Museum** in Miscouche, less than 15 minutes' drive west of Summerside, a short film introduces the history of PEI's French-speaking communities. The exhibits expand on this heritage and illustrate traditional foods, language and other aspects of daily life.

In Abram-Village, Acadian musicians take to the stage on summer weekends at the **Village musical acadien**; come before the show for a classic Acadian meal. Also at the Village,

MORE ISLAND EXPERIENCES

Oyster School
Cascumpec Bay Oyster Co. teaches you about oyster history, farming, shucking and sampling.

Potato Farming
From the Canadian Potato Museum, chat with a farmer while touring a spud farm.

Fun with Falcons
Meet a falconer and his birds on his Cornwall property; book through Experience PEI.

La Galette Blanche Bakery (named for an Acadian white biscuit) sells meat pies, *rapûre* and baked goods to go.

This region has another quirkier cultural attraction: the **Maisons de Bouteilles** (Bottle Houses). The late Édouard Arsenault constructed three buildings on his Cap-Egmont property entirely from reclaimed glass bottles. Arsenault used more than 25,000 bottles, set in cement, to craft two houses and a chapel, located in a garden near the sea southwest of Wellington. The result is weirdly beautiful, especially when the shining sun illuminates the multicolored glass.

Out West

Circling the island's quiet side

Sample locally grown potatoes, learn about the wind and sleep in a lighthouse along PEI's **North Cape Coastal Drive**, which circles the island's western end. While Rte 2 speeds through the center of the island, following the coastal roads leads you through smaller towns and along the sea.

In O'Leary, a giant spud marks the entrance to the **Canadian Potato Museum**, which is crammed with trivia about PEI's major crop – its varieties, its uses around the world, its diseases, even its legends. The on-site **PEI Potato Country Kitchen** serves potatoes, of course, from baked potatoes loaded with cheese, chili or other toppings – with a side of homemade potato chips – to poutine, French fries, potato soup... you get the idea. For dessert, try the seaweed pie (angel food cake layered with Irish moss).

Stompin' Tom Centre in the coastal hamlet of Skinners Pond is a music hall and museum inspired by the life of Canadian country-music icon Stompin' Tom Connors. Born in New Brunswick in 1936, Connors was sent to live with a Skinners Pond family when his mother could no longer care for him, and PEI has claimed the musician, who went on to write more than 300 songs, as its own. The center, which has a small cafe, hosts spirited free midday concerts in summer, as well as other music events.

As you approach the North Cape, you'll see whirring wind turbines along the shore. Blow into the **North Cape Wind Energy Interpretive Centre** for exhibits that are part local history and part promotion for wind-based energy. You'll learn about wind folklore, too. Nearby, have a look at **North Cape Lighthouse** or follow the 5.5km **Black Marsh Nature Trail**, a boardwalk across a bog and above the ocean, with views for miles.

If you decide to stay out west, consider the welcoming 16-room **Tignish Heritage Inn** in the town of the same name. Surrounded by gardens, this brick structure once served as a school and convent, affiliated with **St Simon & St Jude Roman Catholic Church** next door. Peek into this 1860 High Gothic church that's still in use today. Stop across the street at **MJ's Bakery & Caboose Cafe** for pastries or a sandwich, or sit down at **Our Family Traditions** for fish and chips or another hearty homestyle meal.

BEACH GOATS

Can goats go paddle-boarding? On PEI they can. At **Beach Goats**, a small beachside farm near Wellington, you can SUP in the shallow sea with a goat onboard. In addition to these **Seas the Day Paddleboarding** sessions, owner Devon Saila offers several experiences with her herd of curious goats, including a Drop-in Sampler that introduces you to the animals.

Other options include private **Come and Play** sessions, where you're encouraged to do whatever activities the goats choose; **Dirty Feet Shirts**, where baby goats will imprint your T-shirt with their red-sand footprints; and **goat yoga** on the beach, where the animals might join you in a downward dog. Check beachgoats.ca for schedules and booking details.

ELENA ELISSEEVA/SHUTTERSTOCK ©

Above: St John's (p170); Right: Moose

THE MAIN AREAS

Newfoundland & Labrador

ICEBERGS, PUFFINS AND GEOLOGICAL WONDERS

Atlantic Canada's largest province is a friendly and fun-loving land of storytellers, musicians and unparalleled natural beauty.

Don't be surprised when strangers call you m'love and m'darlin' in Canada's most idiosyncratic and most affectionate province. When the Dominion of Newfoundland reluctantly joined the rest of the country in 1949, it brought its own time zone (half an hour ahead of Atlantic Time, except in most of Labrador) and colorful sayings such as 'whadda ya at' (what are you doing) and 'yes b'y' (you can't be serious).

The province is really two provinces in one. The island of Newfoundland is almost as big as the other three Atlantic provinces combined. Mainland Labrador is nearly triple the size of Newfoundland. People are admittedly still finding their way after the 1992 cod moratorium wiped out a longstanding way of life for fishing families. But they're now celebrating a trifecta of natural riches – icebergs, puffins and whales. Nature can't be controlled, but you might luck into seeing all three in one trip. And then there are Unesco-backed geological wonders in places such as Gros Morne National Park, the world-renowned home to the Tablelands, where you can walk on an alien orange exposed section of the Earth's mantle. From the music-drenched capital of St John's to the vibrant outport communities, this unfailingly friendly province warmly embraces everyone it meets. When you return – and you will – people are sure to say 'welcome home.'

TWILLINGATE
Iceberg Alley. **p192**

GROS MORNE NATIONAL PARK
Geology and hiking. **p196**

L'ANSE AUX MEADOWS NATIONAL HISTORIC SITE
Viking hot spot. **p204**

LABRADOR
The last frontier. **p207**

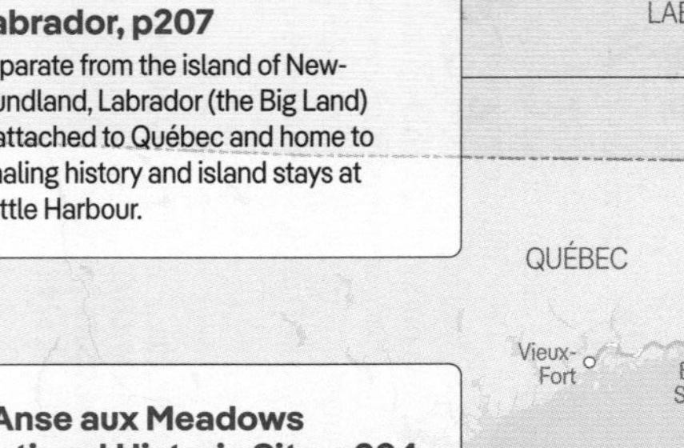

Labrador, p207

Separate from the island of Newfoundland, Labrador (the Big Land) is attached to Québec and home to whaling history and island stays at Battle Harbour.

L'Anse aux Meadows National Historic Site, p204

Lovers of Norse history gravitate to the only authenticated Viking site in North America to follow in the footsteps of explorer Leifur Eiríksson.

Gros Morne National Park, p196

Take a rare walk on an exposed area of the Earth's mantle, cruise down a land-locked fjord and hike up mountains and through forests.

Twillingate, p192

Positioned at the heart of Iceberg Alley, this busy northern town's protected harbor is ideal for sea kayaking and whale watching.

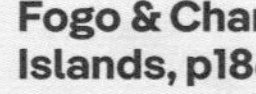

Fogo & Change Islands, p186

Fogo is an art-infused island that's home to so much more than its world-famous inn, and where you can day-trip over to Change Islands.

CAR & MOTORCYCLE

A road trip is the best way to explore this sprawling province, giving you the freedom to forge your own route through cities, historic towns, outport communities and national parks.

FERRY

Ferries connect North Sydney in Nova Scotia to either Argentia (16 hours) or Port Aux Basques (seven hours). Ferries to Labrador and St-Pierre and Miquelon must be booked, while those to smaller islands can't be reserved.

PLANE

Most people fly into St John's, but airports in Deer Lake and Gander cut down driving time to central and western Newfoundland. Air Saint-Pierre flies to the French territory of St-Pierre and Miquelon.

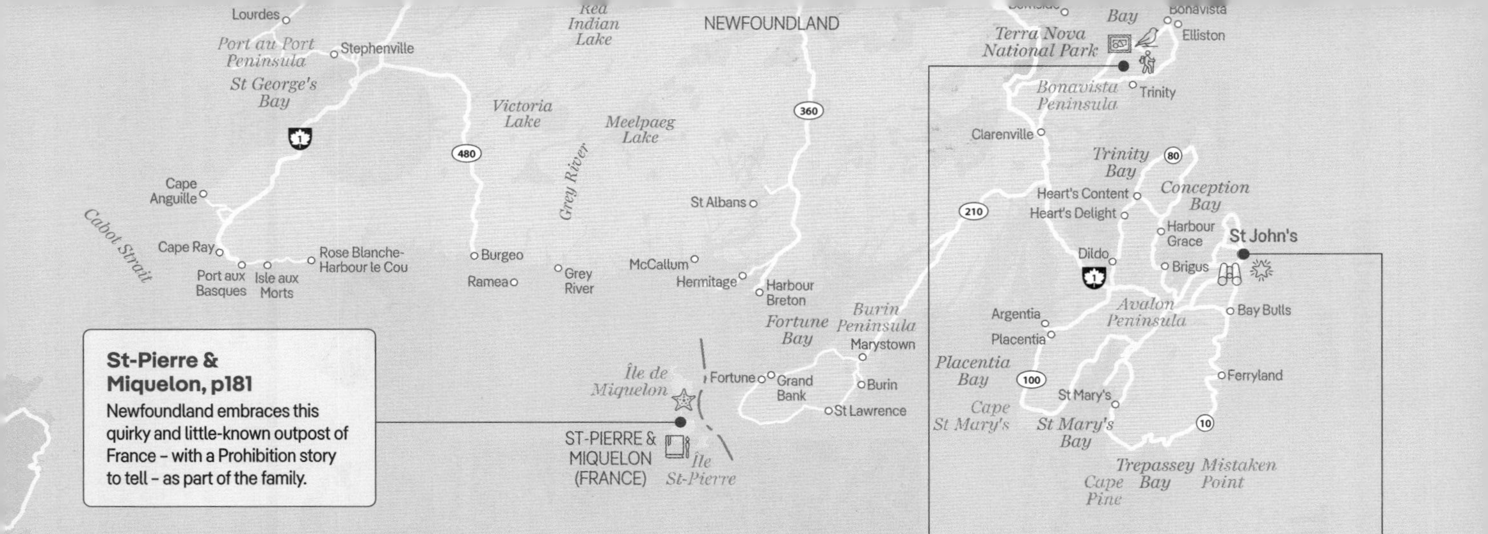

Find Your Way

You'll rack up thousands of kilometers just driving across the island of Newfoundland – more if you make it to Labrador. Ferries will transport you to smaller islands, Labrador and a French territory off the south coast.

St-Pierre & Miquelon, p181

Newfoundland embraces this quirky and little-known outpost of France – with a Prohibition story to tell – as part of the family.

Bonavista Peninsula, p178

Artists, makers and creators infuse historic communities with a new vibrancy, while a puffin colony and Unesco-backed natural and geological wonders keep visitors busy.

St John's, p170

The capital boasts colorful row houses, nightly live music and places to be the first to see the sun rise in North America.

Plan Your Time

Newfoundland and Labrador is so much bigger than people realize. It's a place to slow down and embrace nature and geology, and then swap stories over a pint with locals.

ALL CANADA PHOTOS/ALAMY STOCK PHOTO ©

L'Anse aux Meadows National Historic Site (p204)

Pressed for Time

● St John's can be covered in a whirlwind day. Start with a **walking tour** (p170), then head to **Signal Hill** (p172) for a coastal hike and **Cape Spear** (p173) for whale watching. Enjoy lunch at **Mallard Cottage** (p172), while exploring Quidi Vidi Village, and then have dinner at **Terre** (p173) before heading out for **live music** (p172).

● The next day, drive the Irish Loop to Bay Bulls for a boat tour to the **Witless Bay Ecological Reserve** (p176) to see a puffin colony, seabirds and perhaps whales. If it's iceberg season, take a **boat tour** from St John's (p172) instead.

Seasonal Highlights

To get the most out of your visit, stick to the May-to-September window, when most places are open and plenty is happening. Winter is tough unless you snowmobile.

MAY

Icebergs, while a natural phenomenon and never guaranteed, typically start arriving from Greenland and the Canadian Arctic and last a month or two.

JUNE

Atlantic puffins arrive for the summer to breed in colonies on isolated islands. They fly back to sea by August.

JULY

Bastille Day celebrations take over St-Pierre and Miquelon on July 14 with games, meals, fireworks and a ball.

MEUNIERD/SHUTTERSTOCK ©, GREG AND JAN RITCHIE/SHUTTERSTOCK ©, ERI KAY/SHUTTERSTOCK ©,

Four Days to Explore

● After a day in St John's, hit the road for the Bonavista Peninsula. Take a whale-watching tour in **Trinity** (p180), visit the **Random Passage Site** and finish with a show at the marvellous **Rising Tide Theatre** (p179). Sleep and dine at **Fishers' Loft Inn** (p179) and do the **Skerwink Trail** (p180) before bed.

● Then it's on to **Elliston** (p178) to see puffins from land and look for root cellars. Dive into Bonavista's history by learning about John Cabot at **Ye Matthew Legacy** (p180), and then check out the artisans and eateries along **Church St** (p180).

If You Have More Time

● Fly into Deer Lake and spend a night at **Upper Humber Settlement** (p202) before driving to **Gros Morne National Park** (p196). From one or more of the park's communities, intersperse **hikes** (p196) with explorations of the fabled **Tablelands** (p196) and a **freshwater fjord** (p198).

● Viking enthusiasts will head north to **L'Anse aux Meadows** (p204), but everyone else should drive east to hop a ferry to **Fogo Island** (p186). See historic saltbox houses juxtaposed with modern architecture, go for a hike, visit museums and buy arts and crafts. Visit **Growlers Ice Cream Shop** (p187) after dinner at **Bangbelly Bistro** (p187).

AUGUST

It's prime time to see migrating whales, including the world's largest population of feeding humpbacks, from land, boat or sea kayak.

SEPTEMBER

Roots, Rants and Roars runs in Elliston, with a feast, cod wars and a hike to dine at the ocean's edge.

OCTOBER

Fogo Island Arts Week's open studios, workshops, tours and exhibition openings overlap with the **Fogo Island Partridgeberry Harvest Festival**.

DECEMBER

The **Mummers Festival** culminates in a parade honoring a Christmas tradition of visiting homes in costume to perform for food and drink.

St John's

GETTING AROUND

Downtown St John's is walkable and there's Metrobus, taxis and the car-sharing app Turo. The St John's Hop On Hop Off bus has 10 stops on a two-hour loop between downtown and Cape Spear. Once you leave the city, beware of moose (there are an estimated 110,000 of them) and don't drive when it's dark – you can be killed if you hit one of these huge animals.

In local slang, a 'townie' is someone from St John's and a 'bayman' is, well, pretty much everybody else living a rural life. By Newfoundland standards, St John's is huge, with 112,000 people. It's the place where most visitors touch down first, ready for live music, seafood and pub banter. Snap your photos of the iconic 'Jellybean Row' houses, climb Signal Hill to gape at the North Atlantic, and look for whales off Cape Spear. Almost everything you need to do is in the walkable downtown core – except for Quidi Vidi Village, a fishing village-turned-neighborhood in a sheltered inlet a few minutes' drive away. Eat at Mallard Cottage, drink Quidi Vidi Brewery's Iceberg Beer (brewed with water harvested from icebergs), shop at the Quidi Vidi Village artisans studios and check out events at the wharf. St John's is also the launch point for the East Coast Trail's 26 hikes.

TOP TIP

Locals mostly cringe at the screech-in ceremony that makes Come From Aways into honorary Newfoundlanders by kissing a cod, drinking screech rum, eating flambéed bologna and reciting a creed to get a certificate. But Christian's Bar, the oldest pub on George St, has embraced the fun.

Downtown Walking Tour

Wander the provincial capital

Start at **Jellybean Row**, the nickname used for those iconic colorful row houses. Thing is, there isn't such a place. Instead, it's a series of houses on streets such as Kimberly Row, Prescott St and Gower St. Next, stop for coffee on Duckworth St at **Toslow**. A couple of blocks away is **Crafted Treasures** for souvenirs, **Fred's Records** for Newfoundland and Irish traditional music, and **Mandy Lee Dawe Clothing** and **Posie Row** for more clothes, jewelry and gifts. Then it's a short, uphill hike to the **Rooms**, the province's largest public cultural space and home to a museum, archives and a cafe with sweeping harbor views.

Head back downhill to Water St. Here's where you'll find **NONIA**, a not-for-profit cottage industry that employs 175 knitters and weavers across the province to make mitts, hats and sweaters. The **Craft Council Shop & Pantry** carries the work of more than 150 local artists. Stop in at **Andersons Butcher & Takeaway**, **Johnny Ruth** (an indie fashion and

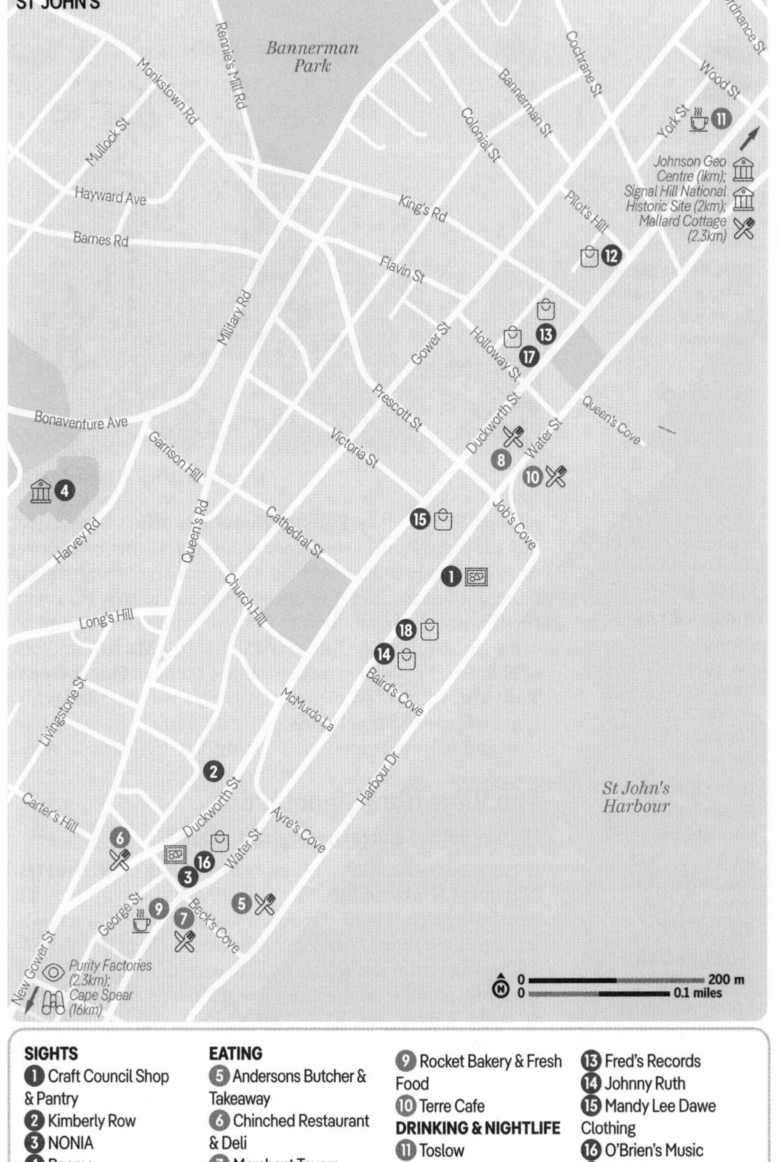
ST JOHN'S
Bannerman Park
Rennie's Mill Rd
Monkstown Rd
Mullock St
Hayward Ave
Barnes Rd
Military Rd
Bonaventure Ave
Garrison Hill
Harvey Rd
Queen's Rd
Long's Hill
Livingstone St
Carter's Hill
New Gower St
George St
Beck's Cove
Water St
Duckworth St
Ayre's Cove
McMurdo La
Church Hill
Cathedral St
Victoria St
Prescott St
Gower St
Holloway St
Flavin St
King's Rd
Colonial St
Bannerman St
Cochrane St
Pilot's Hill
Queen's Cove
Job's Cove
Baird's Cove
Harbour Dr
York St
Wood St
Ordnance St
Johnson Geo Centre (1km); Signal Hill National Historic Site (2km); Mallard Cottage (2.3km)
Purity Factories (2.3km); Cape Spear (16km)
St John's Harbour
0 200 m
0 0.1 miles
SIGHTS
1 Craft Council Shop & Pantry
2 Kimberly Row
3 NONIA
4 Rooms
EATING
5 Andersons Butcher & Takeaway
6 Chinched Restaurant & Deli
7 Merchant Tavern
8 Portage
9 Rocket Bakery & Fresh Food
10 Terre Cafe
DRINKING & NIGHTLIFE
11 Toslow
SHOPPING
12 Crafted Treasures
13 Fred's Records
14 Johnny Ruth
15 Mandy Lee Dawe Clothing
16 O'Brien's Music
17 Posie Row
18 Twisted Sisters Boutik

WHERE TO HEAR MUSIC IN ST JOHN'S

Musician Jordan Harnum, who runs **Olde House Shows** with partner Joelle Sunshine, shares his recommendations for live music in St John's.

Bannerman Brewing Co.
For original music, songwriters and launch parties.

Shamrock City Pub
For nightly music by local groups such as the Navigators.

Broderick's on George
For nightly live music by artists like D'Arcy Broderick, Ronnie Power and Kevin Evans.

Green Sleeves Pub & Eatery
For nightly live music, alt-rock and four-hour sets by Nick Earle and other acts from across the province.

O'Reilly's Irish Newfoundland Pub
For nightly live music and the long-running open-mic Tuesdays.

VALLEYBOI63/SHUTTERSTOCK ©

Signal Hill National Historic Site

gift boutique) and the **Twisted Sisters Boutik**, where you can buy the irreverent 'Jesus, Mary & Joseph' T-shirt by Crooked Arse Creations that references Mary Brown of fried-chicken fame and Joseph (Joey) Smallwood, the politician who brought the Dominion of Canada into Confederation in 1949 and became its first premier. Check out **O'Brien's Music** and Rocket Bakery & Fresh Food before joining **Iceberg Quest Ocean Tours** in search of whales, seabirds and icebergs. End with a pint on **George Street** and ponder its claim to have the most bars and pubs per square foot of any North American street.

The View from Signal Hill

Military battles and technological triumphs

Setting aside the military history for a moment, **Signal Hill National Historic Site** has the city's best urban hike. The North Head Trail is 1.7 strenuous kilometers that starts with a steep climb down stairs, over rocks and along the Narrows – a passage from the North Atlantic Ocean to the harbor. It's the most popular of the site's five trails and sees more than 35,000 hikers a year. Best of all, you wind up in the eclectic **Battery** neighborhood and can recuperate at the Battery Cafe.

This site once protected St John's from military attack as England and France fought for control of lucrative fishing grounds, and it's where Italian inventor Guglielmo Marconi received the world's first transatlantic wireless signal in 1901.

WHERE TO STAY

JAG Hotel
A rock-and-roll-themed boutique hotel where moose is served at Exile restaurant. $$

Alt Hotel St John's
Stylish hotel with flexible check-out times when you book direct and yoga mats on request. $$

Inn by Mallard Cottage
Seven king suites and one common area spread over two Quidi Vidi Village houses. $$$

Cabot Tower opened in 1900 to honor Queen Victoria's 60 years on the throne and commemorate the 400th anniversary of the European 'discovery' of Newfoundland by Italian navigator-explorer John Cabot. It houses a gift shop and an exhibit about Marconi and wireless communications. A flagpole on the tower's roof symbolizes how flags were once raised here to signal the impending arrival of ships.

Parks Canada animates Signal Hill with guided tours, rifled musket demonstrations and a ceremonial Noon Day Gun, but plenty of people just come for the unparalleled view and the chance to spot whales and icebergs. In the visitor center, the **Newfoundland Chocolate Company** cafe serves chocolate-covered oatcakes. It's a five-minute walk down Signal Hill Rd to the Johnson Geo Centre, a science center that tells how the *Titanic* met its tragic demise off the coast of Newfoundland.

The Edge of Canada

Military history, lighthouses and nature

At **Cape Spear**, the most easterly point of land in Canada, people start arriving at dawn to be the first in North America to see the sun rise. They stand on the viewing platform and craggy, dangerous cliffs yearning to see icebergs or migrating whales such as humpbacks, fins or minkes. **Cape Spear Lighthouse National Historic Site** is a 20-minute drive from downtown St John's and yes, it rents out binoculars. Northern gannets and Atlantic puffins might make appearances – hire **Bird the Rock** for custom bird and nature tours here and further afield.

On top of these natural wonders, Cape Spear has the remains of a WWII coastal defence battery and the province's oldest surviving lighthouse. During WWII, this place was on a direct convoy route from Europe to North America and became home to a battery equipped with two 10ft guns to protect the entrance to St John's Harbour from the threat of German U-boats. Gun emplacements were built at the tip of the cape and connected by underground passages to magazine and equipment rooms. The barracks, mess halls and canteens are gone, but concrete bunkers and two guns remain. 'Disappearing guns' hide behind a wall so enemy ships can't see them, and lift up when fired.

There's an active 1957 lighthouse and the privately run **Cape Spear Art Gallery** in the assistant lightkeeper's home. **Cape Spear Lighthouse** dates back to 1836 and has been refurbished as a lightkeeper's residence from that era. You can access the **East Coast Trail**'s Cape Spear Path from here.

BEST EATS IN ST JOHN'S

Mallard Cottage
A Quidi Vidi Village spot with a cake table, a menu that changes daily and weekend brunch. **$$**

Terre Cafe
Elevated dining in the Alt Hotel with a 'Let the kitchen cook for you' option. **$$$**

Chinched Restaurant & Deli
Home to nose-to-tail dining and a deli. The signature dish is crispy buffalo pig ears. **$$**

Merchant Tavern
Smash burgers, a raw bar and homemade pasta that can be gluten free or vegan. **$$$**

Portage
Head to this upscale-casual spot, opened in 2022, for artfully plated, family-style dinners. **$$**

WHERE TO EAT FISH & CHIPS

Chafe's Landing
Anthony Bourdain had fish, chips and beer at this Petty Harbour spot for *Parts Unknown*. $

Ches's Famous Fish & Chips
Started in 1951, this institution believes fish 'is a staple worthy of the best treatment possible.' $

Duke of Duckworth
Accessed through McMurdo's Lane, this iconic spot boasts a large draught-beer selection. $

Beyond St John's

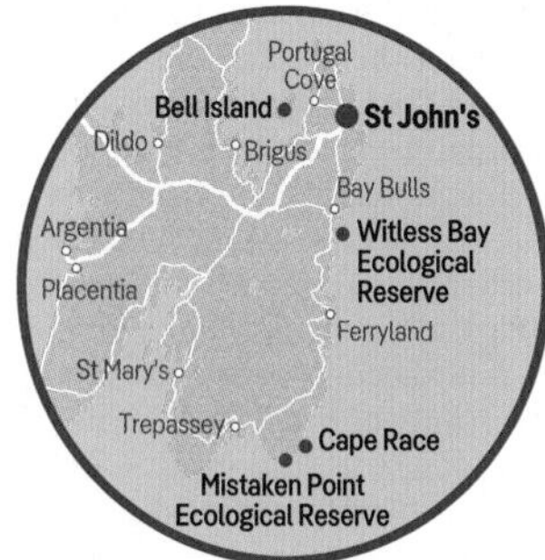

Bell Island and the Irish Loop deliver fascinating mining history, geology and birding.

Places

Bell Island doesn't boast the name recognition of its friendly rival Fogo Island, but it does have an unusual iron-ore-mining history and remarkable geology, with cathedral cliffs, sea caves and sea stacks. Ocean Quest Adventures offers sea-cave kayaking plus boat-dive opportunities to WWII shipwrecks off the island. The ferry is just minutes from downtown St John's.

The Irish Loop, south of the capital, is a 312km road trip for coastal vistas and unparalleled birding and geology-related opportunities. More than half a million Atlantic puffins (not to mention whales and sometimes icebergs) summer in the Witless Bay Ecological Reserve. The Unesco-protected barrens of Mistaken Point Ecological Reserve hold the world's oldest fossils.

GETTING AROUND

The Bell Island–Portugal Cove ferry goes multiple times a day, making the 5km passing in 20 minutes. The ferry is about eight minutes from St John's International Airport in the town of Portugal Cove-St Philip's. The Irish Loop is 312km, but a detour to Cape St Mary's Ecological Reserve gets you to one of North America's most accessible breeding seabird colonies, home to thousands of northern gannets, black-legged kittiwakes, common murres and more.

Bell Island

TIME FROM ST JOHN'S: **20 MINS** (car) + **20 MINS** (ferry)

Go underground and back in time

Some 2200 people call Bell Island home now, but that number swelled past 12,000 during its heyday as an iron-ore-mining community. The **#2 Mine Tour & Museum** has become the island's anchor attraction since it opened in 1998. Most of the staff, including executive director Teresita (Teddy) McCarthy, are descendants of the miners.

Six Wabana mines – two surface and four below the sea in Conception Bay – operated here from 1895 to 1966. During two attacks on Bell Island in 1942 to disrupt the supply of ore to steel mills assisting the war effort, U-boat torpedo strikes sank four anchored ore boats, killing 69 sailors and destroying a pier. The order, signed by Adolf Hitler, was given to the museum by the daughter of U-boat Captain Fritz Rolf Rüggeberg as an expression of grief. Artifacts and historical photos (some by renowned photographer Yousuf Karsh) paint a picture of how tough life was for the miners.

Don a hard hat and descend into the cold, damp tunnels on an hour-long guided tour for a more visceral understanding of the miners who strapped candles to cotton hats in

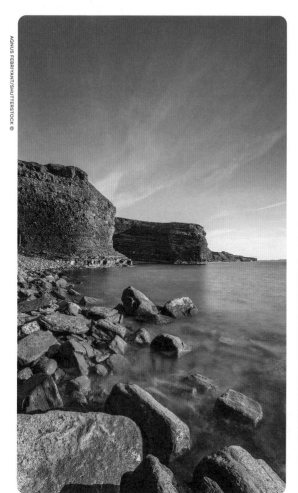

Bell Island

a dangerous bid to see during long shifts, and of the conditions that led to the deaths of 106 men. At recreated stables, learn how horses pulled ore carts. One flooded area is set aside for commercial diving tours. After the war, things improved somewhat until the mine closed abruptly in 1966, devastating the community and sending most people off-island for work.

TOP TIP

Provocatively named Dildo boasts a giant, Hollywood-style sign, a roadside 'Welcome to Dildo' sign and a statue of mascot Captain Dildo.

BELL ISLAND'S HIDDEN GEMS

Alfred Hynes, who runs the Rose Castle Inn and Gracie Joe's cafe, shares recommendations for the island's best experiences.

Grebe's Nest
See sea stacks and a tunnel cut by fishermen through a cliff to a beach where you can picnic and collect rocks.

Bell Meadow
Sit and watch whales, have a picnic, fly a kite, pick berries and see wildflowers and birds.

Seamen's Memorial
A memorial to the 69 men killed when a German U-boat attacked two iron-ore carriers anchored offshore in 1942.

Theatre of the Mine
Community theater plays in the mine shaft every summer.

Bell Island Lighthouse
People just love lighthouses.

WHERE TO EAT NEAR ST JOHN'S

Grounds Cafe
Farm-to-fork meals in Murray's Garden Centre in Portugal Cove near the Bell Island ferry. $

Dicks' Fish & Chips
By the Bell Island ferry terminal; add dressing and gravy to your fish and chips. $

Irish Loop Coffee House
All-day breakfasts, fish cakes, oatcakes and a wraparound deck with ocean views in Witless Bay. $

WHERE TO STOP ON THE IRISH LOOP

Myrick Wireless Interpretation Centre
This replica of the Marconi Wireless Station in Cape Race tells the story of receiving the first distress call from the *Titanic*.

Cape Race Lighthouse
Still operational and a national historic site; the lantern houses a rare hyper-radial Fresnel lens.

Tony's Tours
Local interpreter-storyteller Tony Power leads hikes from Trespassey that touch on flora, fauna (such as caribou), history and even ghosts.

Running the Goats Books & Broadsides
A micro-press in Tors Cove that celebrates provincial and regional life and culture.

Ferryland Lighthouse
Take a 25-minute hike to an 1870 lighthouse and pre-order lunch from Lighthouse Picnics.

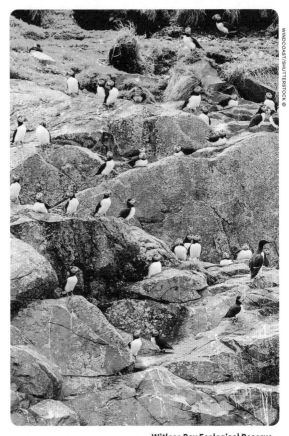

Witless Bay Ecological Reserve

Witless Bay Ecological Reserve

TIME FROM ST JOHN'S: **35 MINS**

Seabird central

From St John's it's a quick half-hour trip south on Irish Loop Dr to the **Witless Bay Ecological Reserve** in search of migrating humpback whales, North America's largest Atlantic puffin colony and other breeding seabirds such as Leach's storm-petrels, common murres, razorbills, black guillemots, black-legged kittiwakes and gulls. Gatherall's Puffin & Whale Watch, O'Brien's Whale & Bird Tours, Molly Bawn Whale &

WHERE TO STAY IN THE IRISH LOOP

Edge of the Avalon Inn
A Trespassey hotel-restaurant where the innkeeper has deep community connections and will provide insider tips. $

Keeper's Kitchen B&B
A St Shott's home away from home with foraging feasts and a 'shipwreck heroes' experience. $

Cliffs Edge Retreat $$
Stylish rooms (some with private hot tubs) and a full-service RV park in Tors Cove. $$

Puffin Tours and Captain Wayne's Marine Excursions run narrated boat tours that sometimes luck into icebergs. The reserve's four islands – Gull, Green, Great and Pee Pee – lie just a few kilometres off the Avalon Peninsula between Bay Bulls and Bauline East.

Witless Bay is also the base for the popular **Puffin & Petrel Patrol**. Created by Juergen and Elfie Schau in 2004 and now run by the Canadian Parks and Wilderness Society's Newfoundland and Labrador Chapter (CPAWS), it enlists volunteers in August and September to help rescue young birds that are drawn to shore by light pollution and face getting run over or killed by wildlife and pets. Volunteers armed with nets and pet crates go out at night in search of the land-stranded, vulnerable seabirds. The birds are released to great fanfare the next morning at the beach and sometimes on boat tours. Young puffins are called pufflings – but it should be pointed out that they don't have the famous striped beaks that mating adults temporarily produce. You must pre-register to secure a spot on the patrol.

Mistaken Point Ecological Reserve

TIME FROM ST JOHN'S: **2 HOURS**

Life before the dinosaurs

In the **Edge of the Avalon Interpretive Centre**, they rather poetically say that walking on bedding planes filled with fossils at the **Mistaken Point Ecological Reserve** is like snorkelling over a 565-million-year-old-sea floor. *Ediacara biota* were soft-bodied creatures that lived at the bottom of a deep, dark ocean millions of years ago – 300 million years before the dinosaurs – when all life was in the sea. They were buried under volcanic ash and dust in what's called an Ediacaran 'Pompeii' and nearly forgotten. Locals called them 'flowers in the rocks,' but it wasn't until a Memorial University of Newfoundland grad student and field assistant mapping Precambrian rocks along the coast spotted them in 1967 that anybody realized their significance. As news spread and fossils were stolen, locals began lobbying for the site to be protected from erosion and humans.

To properly see this Unesco World Heritage Site that protects the world's oldest and largest collection of biologically complex marine-life fossils, you'll have to pay to join a guided tour. The reserve has catalogued more than 6000 fossils representing about 30 species. It extends along 17km of coastline between Portugal Cove South and Cape Race on the Irish Loop. Tours start at the interpretive center, last up to four hours and include driving your own vehicle to the trailhead parking lot before hiking. The center is worth a visit. You can also take the Rookery Trail to soaring cliffs to look for seabird colonies and whales, or the Freshwater Trails across the eastern hyper-oceanic barrens – a distinct eco-region – to the water's edge.

A STOP IN DILDO

Dildo is far better known for its name than its actual physical beauty, which is a shame, because the phallic headlands the town is (supposedly) named for are quite gorgeous. This is a small settlement and there's not a heap to do besides snap some nice sunset photos of the bay, but it's well worth stopping to sink a beer at the excellent **Dildo Brewing Company** (dildobrewingco.com), which has combined a strong range of craft beers and a savvy awareness that you can sell anything if you brand it with the name 'Dildo.'

Bonavista Peninsula

GETTING AROUND

Clarenville is the last major center before the peninsula, so fuel up at Bare Mountain Coffee House. It's an hour's drive from there to Trinity, and another 45 minutes to Bonavista. The peninsula is much larger than you might expect, so factor in driving times between communities.

The Bonavista Peninsula is slowly being transformed by young creatives eager to embrace and revitalize rural life. It takes several hours to drive across the peninsula, through two dozen communities. At the southern end, Trinity draws theater-goers and those in search of whales, icebergs and seabirds. It's next door to Port Rexton and the gateway to the popular Skerwink Trail. Passing through Port Union, the town that unions built, you'll continue north to Elliston, the Root Cellar Capital of the World, where people come to see a puffin colony from land instead of from boat tours. Bonavista, the largest center, is the furthest north. It's home to a full-size replica of the *Matthew*, the ship that Italian explorer John Cabot sailed from Bristol in England to Newfoundland in 1497. To tie the region's natural, geological and cultural heritage spots together, get the Discovery Unesco Global Geopark adventure map.

TOP TIP

Port Union, the only union-built town in Canada, tells the story of activist William Coaker, the Fishermen's Protective Union and why they built this community starting in 1916 as their headquarters. Tour restored factory buildings and stroll the historical district reading interpretive panels at what's now a national historic site.

Puffins & Root Cellars

Elliston's distinctive attractions

Tiny Elliston has three lures: puffins, root cellars and sealing history. The **Elliston Puffin Viewing Site** offers one of North America's closest views of the charismatic seabird from land. From May to September, breeding puffins are drawn to a rocky outcrop that offers protection from land-based predators. They ignore the throngs that watch them from shore just a few meters away. The puffin site is free to visit, but consider a donation. It's just past the municipal park that hosts the **Roots, Rants & Roars** food festival every September. Elliston started calling itself the Root Cellar Capital of the World after restoring and documenting 133 of the subterranean outdoor structures where people once stored their garden harvest over the winter. Eat traditional fare at **Nanny's Root Cellar Kitchen** before doing a self-guided root-cellar tour. The **Home From the Sea/John C. Crosbie Sealers Interpretation Centre** is a museum and art gallery that

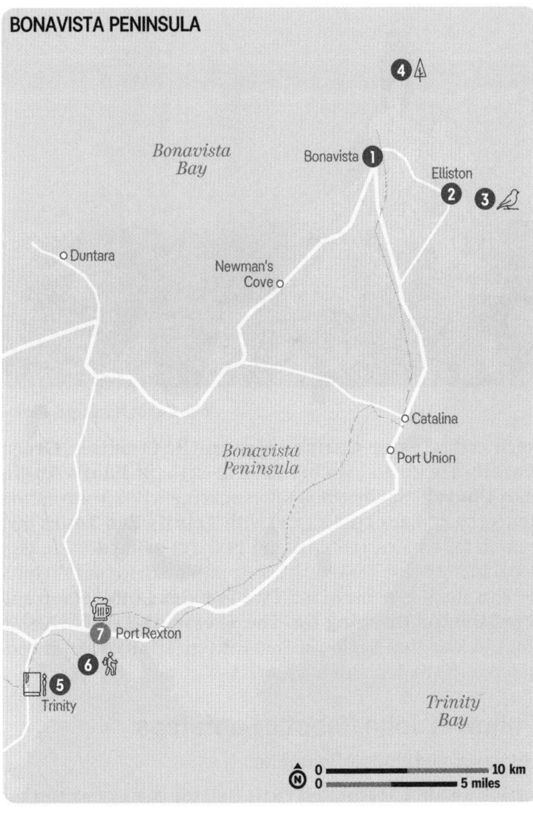

SIGHTS
1 Bonavista
2 Elliston
3 Elliston Puffin Viewing Site
4 John Cabot Municipal Park
5 Trinity

ACTIVITIES, COURSES & TOURS
6 Skerwink Trail

DRINKING & NIGHTLIFE
7 Port Rexton

humanizes the story of sealers and the sealing industry that sustained Newfoundland's early settlers. A seaside memorial statue and monument honor men who lost their lives sealing.

Visit Historic Trinity

Theater, ocean adventures and coastal hikes

Every summer Trinity's **Rising Tide Theatre** comes to life as artistic director Donna Butt brings in up to 50 artists to perform a pageant, dinner theater and plays. The quaint town is considered one of the province's best-preserved historic centers – the *Trinity Historic Sites Map* from the visitor center will help you find a dozen buildings to marvel at,

WHERE TO STAY

Fishers' Loft Inn, Port Rexton
Community-minded, arts-focused inn on a hillside with dining. **$$**

Artisan Inn & Vacation Homes, Trinity
The inn's Twine Loft serves three-course dinners. **$$**

Harbour Quarters Inn, Bonavista
Restored heritage inn with a harbor-view restaurant and locally made furniture. **$$**

BEST IN BONAVISTA

Bonavista Mayor **John Norman**, CEO and co-owner of Bonavista Living and Bonavista Creative, shares recommendations for what to see in the area.

Discovery Unesco Global Geopark
A network of 13 sites that includes hikes, coastal views, geologic wonders and fossils.

Filming Sites
Several movies and TV shows film here every year. *Peter Pan & Wendy* filmed at the Tickle Cove Sea Arch and Cape Bonavista's Dungeon (a collapsed sea cave).

Garrick Theatre
The province's oldest theatre has been developed into a complex hosting shows, music, movies and a martini bar.

Boreal Diner
Casual fine-dining spot with gluten-friendly options and vegetarian and vegan dishes.

Bonavista's Church Street
One of the last intact main streets in rural Newfoundland boasts artisanal shops.

John Cabot Municipal Park

such as the **Lester-Garland Mercantile Premises**, **Green Family Forge** and Gothic Revival–style **St Paul's Anglican Church**. Skipper Bob offers marine wildlife adventure tours (by Zodiac or sea kayak) with **Trinity Eco-Tours** that search for whales, seabirds and icebergs while delving into local history and geology. It's a 10-minute drive past Trinity to Port Rexton, home of the **Two Whales Coffee Shop** and **Port Rexton Brewing Co.** The **Skerwink Trail**, a 5.3km coastal loop that begins in Port Rexton/Trinity East, is considered the region's hiking jewel.

Follow in John Cabot's Footsteps

Historical and modern Bonavista

In **John Cabot Municipal Park**, a statue commemorates the Italian explorer who mistakenly made landfall in here in 1497 while sailing the *Matthew* from Bristol, England. Legend has it he said *'O buono vista'* (Oh happy sight) and thus Bonavista was born. Cabot was seeking a western passage to Asia but instead helped lay Britain's later claim to Canada. The story continues at **Ye Matthew Legacy**, an interpretive center (with a fabulous gift and craft shop) that houses a 92ft-long, full-scale replica of the wooden ship that was made to mark the 500th anniversary of Cabot's voyage.

Jumping ahead to 1843, the **Cape Bonavista Lighthouse** is one of the few in the world where you can climb the stone tower to see the historic oil-fueled light. The **Mockbeggar Plantation** recreates the time in 1948 when debate swirled about whether Newfoundland should join Canada. On the harbor, the restored heritage buildings that make up **Ryan Premises National Historic Site** convey the outport's rich fishing and sealing heritage.

For modern Bonavista, there's **East Coast Glow**, with iceberg-infused, wild-crafted skincare products, the **Newfoundland Salt Co.** and **Bonnabooch Kombucha**. The **Bonavista Biennale** is a free contemporary art event that spreads out at 20 sites along a 165km route for a month every two years.

St-Pierre & Miquelon

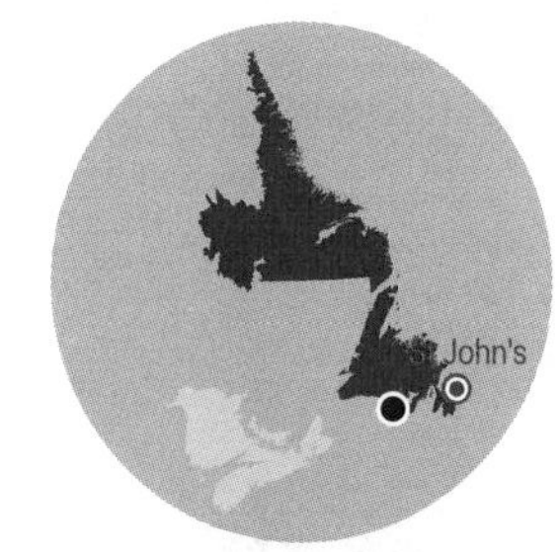

One of the quirkiest things Newfoundland has going for it is that it's just 20km from France. Yes, really: St-Pierre and Miquelon is a self-governing territorial collectivity of France and home to 6600 people who speak French, spend euros, drive Peugeots and celebrate Bastille Day. Phones bounce between cell towers in the two countries, and while the rocky landscape may look like the rest of Canada, the people, architecture, way of life and vibe are unmistakably European.

Most people live on St-Pierre, the 'culture island,' while larger Miquelon-Langlade is the 'nature island' and boasts a seal colony and free-ranging horses. Then there's the US Prohibition connection. St-Pierre once legally filled warehouses with Canadian and global booze and sold it to bootleggers who smuggled it into the US. The tiny but fascinating archipelago even has its own time zone, which is half an hour ahead of the time zone in Newfoundland.

GETTING AROUND

There are two ways to get to St-Pierre and Miquelon: by plane or by boat. It's a quick flight from St John's on Air Saint-Pierre, which also flies from Halifax, Montréal and the Magdalen Islands in Québec. SPM Ferries makes daily 90-minute crossings between Fortune (Newfoundland) and St-Pierre. Once you're in the country, you can explore most places on foot, but you may need to hire a taxi or book a tour.

Exploring St-Pierre

The capital's colorful downtown

From St-Pierre's ferry terminal, explore the capital on foot. Dive right into the *macarons* and pastries at the **Boulangerie Pâtisserie David Girardin**, an anchor of the waterfront since 1987. Once you're fortified, wander narrow streets (**rue Amiral Muselier** is a favorite) and take in homes with vividly painted clapboard siding and window trim. Look for tambours, a distinctive style of small, enclosed front porches.

Head to **Fronton Zazpiak-Bat**, a walled court where a Basque handball game called *pelota* is played. Continue to the **Cathédrale de St-Pierre**. Opened in 1690 and destroyed by a 1902 fire, it was rebuilt in the style of Basque churches, and newer stained-glass windows were a gift from Charles de Gaulle. Near the harbor, **Square Joffre**'s wrought-iron entrances lead to a sombre memorial to sailors lost at sea. The **Pointe aux Canons Lighthouse** is by fishing shacks called

TOP TIP

The lunch break is sacrosanct and so everything grinds to a halt between noon and 2pm. Reservations are essential for both lunch and dinner, which starts fashionably late. Canadians can enter with government-issued photo ID, but everyone else needs a passport. Electrical sockets are round and 220V.

SIGHTS
1 Grand Barachois
2 Île-aux-Marins
see 3 Maison de la nature et de l'environnement
3 Miquelon
4 St-Pierre

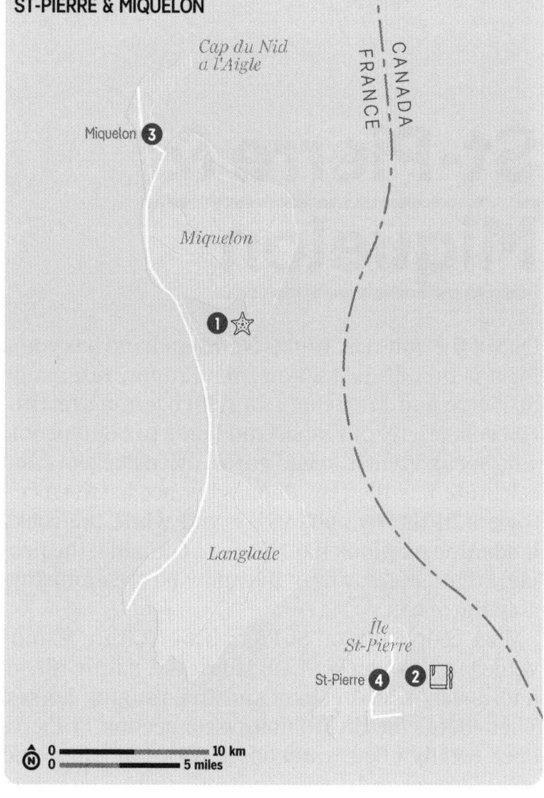

BEST PLACES TO EAT IN ST-PIERRE

Le Roc Cafe
End a meal of crêpes, *gaufres salées* (waffles) and galettes with homemade ice cream and espresso. **$$**

Le Bar à Quai
A constantly changing menu showcases everything local, from lobster and seafood to root vegetables. **$$$**

Le Feu de Braise
Perched over lively rue Albert Briand, this restaurant offers traditional French cuisine and more than a dozen flavors of pizza. **$$**

Le Select
A traditional brasserie with escargots, house charcuterie and burger specials that serves Sunday brunch. **$$$**

L'Îlot
A sun-splashed hotel restaurant with harbor views, Saturday buffets and Sunday brunch. **$$$**

Les Salines, where a friendly group called **Les Zigotos** offers dory tours in traditional wooden boats. Take a photo with the giant stylized ampersand created by tourism officials.

Learn more about the early days of fishing, religion, medical care and schooling at **Musée Heritage**, which also showcases Prohibition-era memorabilia. Stock up on French wine at the **C.I.A.** (which stands for Comptoir d'Importation des Alcools) or **Chez Julien**, a corner grocery store. The **Arche Musée et Archives** houses a French guillotine once used to behead a murderous fisherman, and offers various themed walking tours back outside. The atmospheric **St-Pierre Cemetery** has more than 1000 tombs and monuments. To see more, book a guided hike with **Escapade Insulaire** or a van tour of the entire island with **Le Caillou Blanc**.

WHERE TO STAY IN ST-PIERRE

Les Terrasses du Port SPM
The capital's newest hotel complex features a spa, a restaurant and modern design. **$$**

Hôtel Robert
Just a three-minute walk from the ferry, the hotel counts Al Capone as a former guest. **$$**

Auberge Quatre Temps
Make yourself at home with a free shuttle and a restaurant that serves dinner only to guests. **$$**

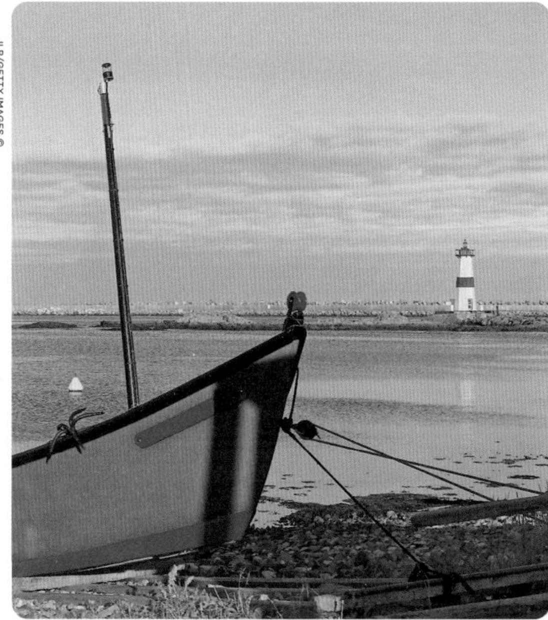

Pointe aux Canons Lighthouse (p181)

Meet Dory Lovers

A passion for wooden boats

In a country named for the patron saint of fishermen, **Les Zigotos** are passionate about the archipelago's fishing history and the wooden dories once used in the small-scale fishery. With 125-odd members, this nonprofit association has built and restored 11 traditional flat-bottomed fishing boats. Members work in a warehouse at one end of the harbor, and then hang out at the other end in *les salines* (colorful waterfront sheds once used to store salt, salted fish and fishing gear). Wander down to shed 20 around 6pm and you'll likely find them gathering for a crab boil and *petite soupe* (rum and Coke). From mid-June to mid-September, Les Zigotos host dory tours that pass Île aux Marins and may go cod fishing or out to Grand Colombier, a rocky and uninhabited island where puffins and other seabirds summer. Getting a translation for the word *zigotos* from this free-spirited group is nearly impossible. All they'll say is 'it's a funny name, but when we do something, we do it seriously.'

A PROHIBITION LOOPHOLE

The colorful story of how this French outpost became North America's alcohol warehouse during Prohibition unfolds quietly inside the **Musée Heritage**. Vintage rum, whisky, wine and Champagne bottles are preserved alongside wooden barrels and crates, and the straw and burlap bags once used as packing material. One photo shows a booze-packed schooner along a pier full of men and horses pulling carts. When the US banned booze between 1920 and 1933, no such rules existed here. Waterfront warehouses legally stockpiled liquor and American bootleggers did the dirty work sailing it south. Opinions are divided on whether Al Capone visited. No photos exist, but author Jean-Pierre Andrieux swears the gangster left behind a hat.

WHERE TO EAT BAKED GOODS

Boulangerie-Pâtisserie des Graves
Find quiche, salads and pizza alongside all your favorite French bakery staples. $

Boulangerie Beck
An extensive bread list complements classics such as *pains au chocolat* in this atmospheric shop. $

Super U
Outpost of a French supermarket chain selling cakes and treats from Guillard Gourmandises. $

A NATURE DESTINATION

The mandate of **Maison de la nature et de l'environnement** is to create environmental awareness among locals and turn visitors on to nature, and so the modern interpretation center, made of now-weathered wood, stays open year-round. History panels give a crash course in how this archipelago came to be French, before themed rooms detail its marine, forest, coastal/dune and bog/freshwater ecosystems and the measures in place to protect them. Most, but not all, signage is bilingual and there's a short film. Ask about guided eco-walks, check out the hiking trail poster and look for *Nature Guide: Discover 15 Hiking Trails in Saint-Pierre et Miquelon* in the gift shop.

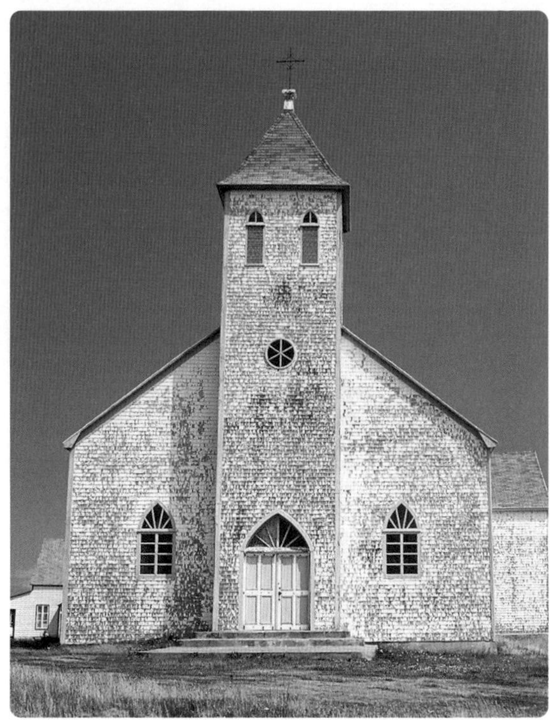

MICHAEL DWYER/ALAMY STOCK PHOTO ©

Notre-Dame-des-Marins church, Île aux Marins

Work with Fish-Skin Leather

Embrace your inner artist

It's a challenge to source fish-skin leather these days, but it was once common in fishing communities around the world. Artist Erika Simon brings it in from France or Iceland to **Chez Rika Simon**, her St-Pierre studio-boutique where she sells jewelry and leathercraft. She also offers short workshops, teaching people to make luggage tags or keychains shaped like whale tails using fish or cow leather in just 90 minutes.

A Day on Miquelon-Langlade

Explore the nature island

From St-Pierre, take the ferry to wild and windswept **Miquelon** for a day of nature explorations. Miquelon-Langlade, two islands joined by a 12km sandy isthmus called La Dune, may

WHERE TO EAT IN MIQUELON

Snack-bar à Choix
After steak *frîtes* with Roquefort butter, save room for crêpes topped by bakeapple (cloudberry) sauce. $$

Restaurant L'Auberge de L'Ile
Galettes de sarrasin (buckwheat pancakes) stuffed with ham, cheese and eggs are a specialty. $

Domane SAS
Grocer that sells local pâté, charcuterie, foie gras, terrines and Miqu'ale craft beer. $

only be home to 600 people, but they're big and you'll want a guide with a vehicle. The highlight is the **Grand Barachois**, a natural lagoon that is the summertime home of a colony of harbor seals. Zodiac tours go when the tide is right. The isthmus is bordered by sand dunes where you can have beach time and see semi-wild horses that belong to the Miquelonnais and roam freely every summer.

Homes and businesses are clustered in the village of Miquelon, where a **grand dérangement monument** speaks to the deportation of 10,000 Acadian people by the British beginning in 1755 (some were sent here from what's now Atlantic Canada). The wooden **Notre Dame des Ardilliers** church dates to 1865, and the **Miquelon Culture Patrimoine** is a small community museum in a house. After a photo stop at the **Cap Blanc lighthouse**, continue to the **Cap de Miquelon**, where you can see Newfoundland and where a sign points to Paris, 4253km away. Set aside several hours to hike the cape, through bogs and boreal forest, past carnivorous plants and white-tailed deer, to ocean views.

Langlade, where Dunefest is held every July, is a cottage community with more hiking. **Chez Janot** is a beloved seasonal hot spot for a drink and local music. Watch for marine mammals and seabirds as you sail back to St-Pierre or, better yet, spend a night in a B&B.

Journey Back in Time

Visiting Île aux Marins

In a word, cod lured fishermen from Normandy and Brittany to this area hundreds of years ago. Take a 10-minute water taxi on Le P'tit Gravier from St-Pierre to Île-aux-Marins. Nicknamed Pioneers Island, and home to 683 people in its heyday in 1892, this tiny, car-free island is now a living museum that celebrates fishing heritage.

The highlight is *les graves*, large areas of pebbles and stones once used to dry cod. A series of original buildings help paint a picture of days gone by. There's a washhouse and a town hall, while a former school houses the **Musée Archipélitude** and more than 3000 heritage objects. The people who once lived here were nicknamed *pieds rouge* (red feet) for the color their feet turned when they were bait fishing. They were all Catholic, and so there is the **Notre-Dame-des-Marins church**, a grotto and an old seaside cemetery to explore. Interpretive plaques do a good job of conveying the history, but the **guided tours** with l'Arche Musée et Archives are wonderful. The last permanent residents left in 1965 and now there are just a few summer homes, including two that can be rented through Sauvegarde de Patrimoine de l'Archipel. **La Maison SPA** holds 16 people, while **La Maison Marie-Ange** holds 20.

Bring a picnic or eat by the wharf at **La Maison Jézéquel**. It's not well marked, but you can walk to the western end of the island to find a playground and what's left of the **Transpacific**, a cargo ship that met its demise on treacherous shoals in 1971.

WHERE TO PICNIC

Maïté Legasse, a chef who runs Au P'tit Kakawi, a bed-and-breakfast in her home in Miquelon, shares recommendations for simple ways to enjoy French gastronomy.

La Pointe aux Canons
In St-Pierre, watch the port activity while enjoying oysters from Pêcheries Paturel and Champagne from Le Tire Bouchon. Bring an oyster knife.

Étang de Mirande
In Miquelon, watch the sunset here with foie gras from La Ferme de l'Ouest SARL and white wine from SAS Simon Detcheverry. Bring a corkscrew.

Île aux Marins
Enjoy the beautiful, historic island with a bottle of red wine plus a baguette, *saucisson*, salted butter and La Ferme du Grand Large's goat cheese.

Fogo & Change Islands

GETTING AROUND

There's no public transportation on Fogo, although Fogo Island Bus Tour offers custom tours. You can't book the ferry from Farewell to Fogo. Instead, motorists line up 30 to 120 minutes in advance and wait to see if they get on. Check online to see if the ferry is on a one- or two-vessel schedule. Crossings take 45 to 75 minutes, sometimes stopping in Change Islands. If you day-trip to Change Islands from Fogo, be prepared to pay cash for your return fare.

TOP TIP

If you can access a kitchen, the Fogo island Fish Co-operative sells seafood weekdays from three processing facilities. The Joe Batt's Arm branch handles live lobster, cod and other fish. The one in Seldom has shrimp. The Fogo outlet has raw and cooked crab, sea cucumber, herring, mackerel and squid.

Fogo Island is Newfoundland and Labrador in miniature. A spirited fishing outport that's home to 10 communities and traditional saltbox houses, it drew global attention when the Fogo Island Inn launched a decade ago in a minimalist white building designed by Todd Saunders and perched on stilts on the Atlantic coast. It takes a half hour to drive across the island from end to end, a day if you want to follow all the roads, and a week if you want to do everything. If that's not quite remote enough for you, take Fogo Island Boat Tours to Little Fogo Islands to see the puffins, or hop a ferry to Change Islands to see endangered ponies. On the main island, you can hike the bogs, barrens and forests, swim at Sandy Cove Beach, and climb rocky Brimstone Head to what's cheekily called one of the four corners of the flat earth.

Walk with Purpose

Admire Fogo's architecture and art

At the end of **Joe Batt's Point Trail** (aka the Great Auk Trail) stands a magnificent bronze sculpture of a **Great Auk** facing wistfully out to sea. The flightless seabird that once bred on nearby Funk Island was hunted to extinction for the European feather trade. It's part of American artist Todd McGrain's *Lost Bird Project* and faces a similar statue in Iceland, where fishermen shot the last confirmed mating pair of auks in 1844. Fogo Island has a dozen hikes – along the coast and through bogs and forests – although maps don't always list them all. To see Shorefast's four off-grid artist-in-residence studios, take the Great Auk Trail past Long Studio, Deep Bay Trail to **Bridge Studio**, Turpin's Trail East past Squish Studio, and a boardwalk off Rte 334 near Shoal Bay to **Tower Studio**. Al Dwyer runs **Al's Walking Tour of Tilting & Oliver's Cove** to immerse you in Tilting's history, culture and nature. In Fogo, the challenging **Fogo Head Trail** goes from the battery at Garrison Point to the island's highest lookout, while the popular Brimstone Head Trail is a short,

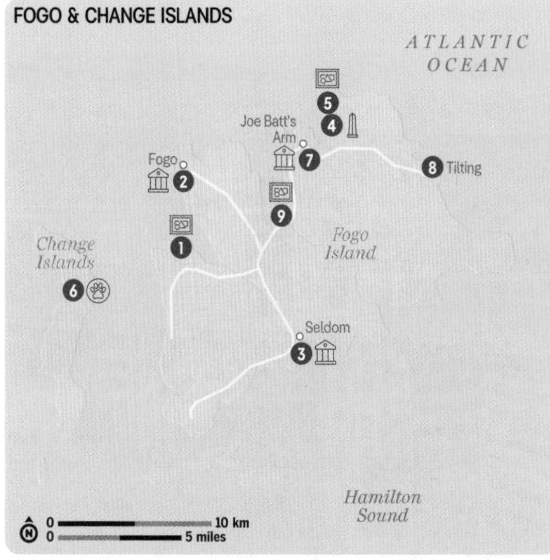

SIGHTS
see 7 Brett House Museum
1 Bridge Studio
see 8 Dwyer Premises
2 Experience Fogo
3 Fogo Island Marine Interpretation Centre
4 Great Auk
5 Long Studio
6 Newfoundland Pony Sanctuary
7 Punt Premises
see 8 Squish Studio
8 Tilting
9 Tower Studio

ACTIVITIES, COURSES & TOURS
see 2 Brimstone Head Trail

steep climb to a viewing platform and that playful sign about the four corners of the flat earth.

Tilting's Culture

More Irish than Ireland

The tight-knit Irish-Catholic community of **Tilting** is a National Historic Site because its landscape illustrates how Irish settlers adapted to the fishing-outport lifestyle beginning in the 1730s: subdividing land lots for extended-family neighbourhood clusters around the harbor; tending to fenced gardens; and enclosing fields for livestock. **Féile Tilting** celebrates Irish Newfoundland culture every September. The **Tilting Heritage Centre** is a hub.

Life in a Fishing Community

Visit heritage structures

It's a mouthful to say the **Fogo Island Marine Interpretation Centre**, but since the museum is housed in the restored Fishermen's Union Trading Co store in Seldom, it's easier to slyly say you're going to the F.U. What was once a cooperative store where fishermen could barter their catch

WHERE TO EAT ON FOGO ISLAND

Growlers Ice Cream Shop
Hand-crafted ice cream in Joe Batt's Arm; partridgeberry jam tart is the signature flavor. $

Bangbelly Bistro & Punch Buggy Pizza & Coffee Co.
The bistro has Fogo's best food, and the sister company has a fun walk-up window. $

Cod Jigger Diner
This central spot revolves around cod, so try the fish cakes or the cod bites. $

WHY I LOVE FOGO ISLAND

Jennifer Bain, Lonely Planet writer

I got lost the first time I came to Fogo Island. I thought this place was just a famous inn on a barren island and didn't expect so many forks in the road and so many communities. The second time I came to this island off an island, I impulsively bought a house between the ocean and a rocky pond. And then I took a boat ride and saw my first Atlantic puffins. A colony returns to Little Fogo Islands every summer to breed, just like I return each year with my family to the one place in the world where I can slow down and breathe (and talk, eat, hike and fish for cod).

EYESTRAVELLING/SHUTTERSTOCK ©

Punt Premises, Joe Batt's Arm

for provisions is now the island's showpiece museum. Learn about 'the Fogo Process,' where residents faced with declining cod stocks in the 1960s were famously advised to resettle, drift and perish, or develop. They stayed and launched a producers' cooperative that still processes fish and seafood. Smaller buildings house a cod-liver-oil factory and a birding

WHERE TO STAY ON FOGO ISLAND

Peg's Place
A longstanding spot in Fogo with six en-suite rooms and a homemade breakfast. $

Old Salt Box Co.
Three of this company's eight restored and contemporary saltbox vacation homes are on Fogo. $$

Brimstone Head RV Park
Run by the Lions Club, this park has 27 RV sites plus more sites for tent camping. $

exhibit about the nearby Funk Island Ecological Reserve and the extinct great auk. Fogo's newest museum is Shorefast's **Punt Premises** in Joe Batt's Arm. Named for a traditional rowboat, this restored heritage home with a fishing stage celebrates and preserves the history of the inshore fishery. It's near **Brett House Museum**, where you can see a root cellar. In Tilting, don't miss the **Old Post Office** and the **Dwyer Premises**, one of the last spots in the province to see a full range of buildings (a house, store/shed, flakes and stage) associated with the family-based inshore fishery. The community of Fogo has **Bleak House Museum** (once home to an influential fish-trade merchant), the **Old Schoolhouse** (dating from 1888) and the **Marconi Wireless Relay & Interpretation Centre**, which was built in 1911 as a communication link for mariners and fishermen. Relive the everyday life of Fogo settlers at **Experience Fogo**.

Hardy Island Ponies

Change Islands' beloved breed

Change Islands is home to 150 or so people and an abundance of photogenic fishing stages, but it's best known for the critically endangered breed of pony that calls the Newfoundland Pony Sanctuary home. It's here that you'll find Netta LeDrew, who has been championing these gentle but hard-working creatures since 2005, scrounging up volunteers and cobbling together donations and sponsorships for hay and special grains.

The province recognizes the pony as a heritage animal, and the **Newfoundland Pony Society** preserves, protects and promotes it. The breed evolved for the harsh demands of outport life from ponies that settlers brought with them from the British Isles in the 1600s. They have hooded eyes, low-set tails, and small, furry ears to ward off frostbite and bugs. They were used for things such as ploughing fields and hauling wood. Most are short and stocky. There were about 12,000 of them on Newfoundland in the 1960s, but that number dropped to under 100 by the 1980s, when many ponies were shipped away and auctioned for meat. Their numbers have since rebounded slightly.

At her not-for-profit refuge, LeDrew knows the names, birthdates and lineage of all nine of her ponies. St George's Princess, born in 1981, is the eldest. Kate of the Cove was christened by the governor general's wife and is an escape artist. Lily of the Cove was the first of 10 foals born at the sanctuary – ponies are no longer bred here because nobody is buying them. In summer LeDrew opens the sanctuary for self-guided tours and pony rides for children.

BEST THINGS TO DO ON CHANGE ISLANDS

Change Islands Interpretation Centre
Full of quilts and knitted goods, this craft shop doubles as a geology-interpretation center.

Olde Shoppe Museum
Pete Porter's jukebox plays the 1928 song 'Squid Jiggin' Ground' that Arthur Scammell wrote about these islands.

Squid Jiggers Trail
Follow the volcanic coastline past coves, viewpoints and a glacial erratic called White Rock.

Shoreline Trail
Pack a picnic to follow this trail along the western coast in search of geological formations.

Seven Oakes Island Inn & Cottages
Pioneering innkeeper Beulah Oake, now in her 80s, will provide home-cooked meals.

Beyond Fogo & Change Islands

The gateway to Fogo, Gander has a rich aviation history and played a pivotal role during September 11.

GETTING AROUND

Most streets are named for famous aviators. Alcock Cres and Brown Cres honor John Alcock and Arthur Brown, who in 1919 were the first to fly nonstop across the Atlantic. Charles Lindbergh, who in 1927 made the first nonstop flight from New York to Paris, lives on at Lindbergh Rd. Earhart St commemorates Amelia Earhart. A map of the town also reveals that the head of a gander (male goose) is formed by Memorial Dr, Edinburgh Ave and Elizabeth Dr.

Thanks to the hit Broadway musical *Come From Away*, everybody knows that Gander is the town that 'welcomed the world' when North American airspace was closed after the September 11 terrorist attacks and 38 planes were diverted here. Some 10,000 Ganderites, along with neighbors in seven unsung communities, rose to the challenge of feeding and comforting about 6600 'plane people' from 95 countries, plus 17 dogs and cats and two Bonobo apes, for up to five days. Now Gander International Airport is a gateway for those driving one hour north to the Fogo Island ferry in Farewell or 90 minutes to Twillingate, and this commercial center is a good place to stock up on groceries and other essentials.

Gander

TIME FROM ST JOHN'S: **45 TO 75 MINS** + **1 HOUR**

The airport's modernist time capsule

For years, the mid-century modern international lounge at **Gander International Airport** was usually closed unless you knew to ask the security guard for a private tour. Then, after the *Come From Away* musical had boosted tourism, the airport reimagined it in 2022. Now the lounge is a public space before security. The glamorous terrazzo floor with geometric motifs is intact. So is the vintage yellow, orange and navy furniture, such as modular couches by German designer Klaus Nienkamper, moulded acrylic armchairs by Americans Charles and Ray Eames, and benches from Canada's Robin Bush. The mezzanine has exhibits and artifacts, including one of the town's three World Trade Center beams.

YQX welcomed its first plane in 1938 and helped with WWII efforts before hitting its stride during the Jet Age of the 1950s and 1960s, when most flights between Europe and North America stopped here to refuel. Locals swung by to spot movie stars such as Marilyn Monroe, presidents including Fidel Castro and celebrities such as Muhammad Ali and Soviet defectors. A stylish new terminal, with the international lounge and the province's first escalator, was opened in 1959 by Queen Elizabeth II, who freshened up from an Eames swivel chair in the ladies' powder room. For good luck, rub the heads of the seven stylized birds in Arthur Price's *Birds of Welcome* sculpture. Study the 23m *Flight and its Allegories* mural by Canadian artist Kenneth Lockhead to ponder the feelings we experience related to flying. Stop in at **Union East & Drinks** and **Gander Goods** for locally made art and handcrafted items.

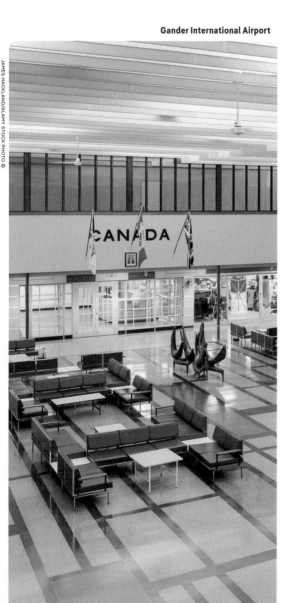

Gander International Airport

JAMES HACKLAND/ALAMY STOCK PHOTO ©

TOP TIP

The All-New Rosie's Restaurant & Bakery dishes up comfort food like cod *au gratin* and sells dough for toutons to pan-fry at home.

BEST PLACES FOR THE SEPTEMBER 11 STORY

North Atlantic Aviation Museum
The corner devoted to September 11 has a binder of thank-you letters.

Gander Town Hall
A World Trade Center beam is mounted outside on a boulder in the Compassion Monument.

Gander & Area Chamber of Commerce
An official *Come From Away* photo sign explains that the chamber helps organize reunions.

Gander Collegiate
A *Come From Away* site that housed 404 passengers from Lufthansa Flight LH400 and turned its cafeteria into a kitchen.

Royal Canadian Legion Branch 8
This *Come From Away* site housed Aer Lingus passengers and 'was a place for merrymaking' and countless screech-in ceremonies.

Twillingate

GETTING AROUND

The town of Twillingate spreads out over a north and south island connected by bridges to each other and Newfoundland. It includes communities such as Cow Head and Durrell, and a walkable 'historic district' along Main St. Driving the long, forested stretch of the south island is called 'coming across the island.'

If Newfoundland and Labrador is where icebergs come to die, then Twillingate is one of the most popular places to see these glacial giants off in the spring and summer. An easy drive from Gander International Airport, the town that calls itself the Iceberg Capital of the World is famously part of 'Iceberg Alley,' which stretches from the coast of Labrador to the southeastern coast of the island of Newfoundland. Originally called Toulinquet because it reminded the French of islands near Brest, and renamed Twillingate by English settlers, it's actually two islands joined by a bridge and a causeway to shore. When the icebergs are gone you can whale watch, kayak, hike, climb the Long Point Lighthouse and explore museums. There's even a winery, a brewery and an Artisan Market full of things made by people from across the province. This community of 2200 punches way above its weight.

TOP TIP

Riff's department stores, started by James Riff in the 1930s, are part of the fabric of rural life, and locals do the 'Riff's challenge' to see how many they can shop at each summer. Everything is always on sale and Twillingate's branch is in a garish red-and-white building.

Glacial Giants

Hunt icebergs and whales

Talking about icebergs makes Diane Davis choke up. The retired teacher from Gander has such a profound love for them that she created a Facebook group called **Newfoundland Iceberg Reports**, where she encourages locals and visitors to post photos and share sightings. Mindful that up to 90% of an iceberg can be underwater, she warns people to only go out with licensed tour-boat operators that keep a respectful distance. Remember that an iceberg sank the *Titanic* off the coast of Newfoundland.

Icebergs are large chunks of ice that break off from glaciers, and these ones come from western Greenland and the Canadian Arctic. It takes them about three years to float this far south, arriving in April or May in mesmerizing shapes and sizes, in shades of white and aquamarine. Some years they leave early, or don't come at all. Occasionally they bring dangerous stowaways – polar bears that use them as a platform to hunt seals but don't get off in time.

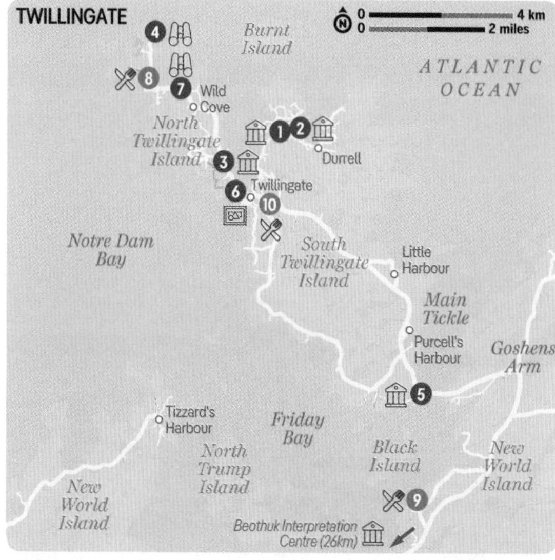

SIGHTS
1 Auk Island Winery
2 Durrell Museum
3 Isles Wooden Boat Museum
4 Long Point Lighthouse
5 Prime Berth
6 Scot's Pencil Art Studio
see 4 Twillingate Lighthouse Heritage Museum
see 3 Twillingate Museum
7 Wild Cove

EATING
see 3 Blue Barrel Gallery Cafe
8 Crow's Nest Café
9 Doyle Sansome & Sons
10 Mary Brown's Chicken
see 6 Split Rock Brewing Co.

ENTERTAINMENT
see 6 Olde House Shows

People gravitate to Twillingate because icebergs can often be seen from land, from the viewing platform at Long Point Lighthouse, the beach at **Wild Cove** and the cliffs at **Spencer's Park**. **Twillingate Adventure Tours** offers iceberg-hunting and whale-watching trips in a rigid-hull Zodiac, but even if you don't luck into seeing either there could be seabirds, seals and rock formations (like Middle Finger Rock) to gape at. Guides regale you with local history and iceberg factoids. At the end of the trip, they just might open a cooler and let you take home a bag of bergy bits for your drinks.

Coastal Hiking

Take in cliffs, birds and sea stacks

As **Rockcut Twillingate Trails** (rockcuttrails.ca) puts it, these connected island communities have 'a coastline that begs to be explored.' People walking to abandoned or resettled communities, berry pickers, wood cutters and grazing animals, plus 'fishermen, sealers and older folks walking to look out over the sea' have forged countless informal trails here over the years. Since 2020, passionate volunteers have secured government funding to enhance and expand trails to Spiller's Cove, French Beach, Codjacks Cove, Lower Little

WHERE TO STAY IN TWILLINGATE

Twillingate & Beyond
Has a five-room inn, a jacuzzi suite, a house, or a hostel with dorm or private rooms. $$

Hodge Premises Inn
Seven seaside rooms in a heritage building run by the owners of the Anchor Inn. $$$

Iceberg Alley Bed & Breakfast
Be treated like family, and get tips on local attractions, at this friendly B&B. $$

BEST MUSEUMS IN TWILLINGATE

Durrell Museum
Famously home to a mounted polar bear and 11 concrete replicas of extinct great auks.

Isles Wooden Boat Museum
Do a deep dive into local boat-building history, and see boats in the upstairs workshop.

Twillingate Museum
Learn about Twillingate-born opera singer Georgina Ann Stirling, who used the stage name Marie Toulinquet.

Twillingate Lighthouse Heritage Museum
Inside a baby-bottle-shaped brick lighthouse, exhibits showcase provincial lighthouses and the cod-fishery collapse.

Prime Berth
An eclectic fishing heritage center with memorabilia-packed seaside buildings and a whale skeleton.

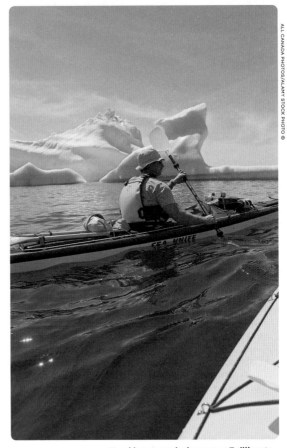

Kayaking among icebergs near Twillingate

Harbour and Purcell's Harbour, with plans to slowly expand each year. Rockcut's free color map (available online and at most local businesses) details the trails it has upgraded and added signs to, along with other popular point-to-point or looped options, noting the distance, difficulty and features of each. Enjoy sea stacks, sea caves, osprey nests, ponds, beaches, lookouts and – above all – rugged coastlines. Fees for backcountry campsites go toward maintaining and expanding the trails.

WHERE TO ENJOY THE ARTS

Olde House Shows
Jordan Harnum and Joelle Sunshine perform songs and share stories from their living room.

Wild Island Kitchen
Crystal Anstey takes people from sea to plate with outdoor culinary experiences.

Scot's Pencil Art Studio
Scot Lewis creates pencil art and has a giant, photogenic lobster trap outside his studio.

Go for a Paddle

Experience sea kayaking

Bobby Gorman and his wife, Marie Magnin, gave up corporate Toronto to build a life around ecotourism here on 'the Rock.' Now she's the town clerk and manager, and he's the owner and head guide at sea-kayaking tour company **Rock Adventures**. For kayaking, there are guided morning, afternoon and sunset options on Twillingate Harbour and Notre Dame Bay, depending on the weather. Most tours include two hours on the water in double kayaks plus time to gear up with wetsuits, paddling mitts and tops, and safety gear. Sometimes you'll luck into eagles, icebergs and whales. Gorman also runs the Rockcut Ultra trail-running race, with options for 50km and 19km.

Fruit Wine & Extinct Seabirds

A winery tour with a difference

The Auk Island Winery tour shares a surprisingly dark backstory while cheerfully showcasing how berries, fruits and flowers are transformed into wines. When Grant Young, president of Downhome Publishing, took over Notre Dame Winery in 2007 he renamed the business and its wines to honor the province's culture. The great auk was a flightless black-and-white seabird originally mistaken for a penguin whose eggs, meat, oil and feathers helped sustain the region's early Beothuk people. But the auks were hunted to extinction by Europeans for food, bait, down and private collections. Auks bred nearby on barren Funk Island, and the last breeding pair was killed in 1844 off Iceland (although one was reportedly seen off Newfoundland's Grand Banks in 1852). Young wanted people to remember how humans caused the auk's extinction and think carefully about our role in preserving the ecosystem.

The tour celebrates other seabirds in the auk family, such as the murre (turr) that is still hunted and the beloved Atlantic puffin that is the province's official bird. The orange-and-blue winery is a nod to the colors that puffin bills turn during mating season.

On the wine front, Auk Island works with blueberries, partridgeberries (lingonberries), bakeapples (cloudberries) and crowberries (Newfoundland blackberries) hand-picked by locals and frozen for year-round production. Raspberries and strawberries come from local farms. Dandelions were added in 2017, and Kiss Me Arse, a dandelion-blueberry wine, is the top seller. A few specialty dessert wines are made using water harvested from icebergs. The winery has a tasting counter, gift shop, vacation rental suite and restaurant.

BEST PLACES TO EAT IN TWILLINGATE

Blue Barrel Gallery Cafe
A small lunch menu and patio round out this airy coffeeshop that makes 'Twilly sodas.' **$**

Crow's Nest Café
This tiny and perpetually busy Crow Head spot makes pea soup, chili and paninis. **$**

Split Rock Brewing Co.
Drink small-batch ale, listen to music and eat burgers in the brewery's Stage Head Pub. **$**

Mary Brown's Chicken
An iconic chain that started in St John's and uses Canadian chicken and potatoes. **$**

Doyle Sansome & Sons
In nearby Hillgrade, this seafood spot with a seaside deck has a massive lobster pool. **$$$**

Gros Morne National Park

GETTING AROUND

Gros Morne is huge and it takes an hour just to drive from Rocky Harbour to Woody Point, but a water taxi across Bonne Bay out of Norris Point cuts the journey to 15 minutes. BonTours runs the seasonal shuttle four times a day. Cars are not allowed, but cyclists can pay an extra fee to transport their bikes. Mountain bikes and e-bikes can be rented from several operators, including Explore Gros Morne.

TOP TIP

Plan your tip around the **Writers at Woody Point** literary festival in August. The six-day event centers on sold-out readings and conversations between authors at the Woody Point Heritage Theatre, but it rounds things out with comedy, film screenings, concerts, hikes and parties.

Gros Morne is among those rare places that live up to the hype. Fjords give way to ancient mountains and dense forests, and then move on to barrens, cliffs and coastlines. People gravitate to this Unesco World Heritage Site to walk the alien orange Tablelands on an exposed slab of the Earth's upper mantle. They hike flat-topped Gros Morne Mountain, the second-highest peak on the island of Newfoundland, and boat down Western Brook Pond past waterfalls cascading from atop billion-year-old cliffs.

The sprawling park – about a quarter the size of Prince Edward Island – turned 50 in 2023. It takes almost 2½ hours to drive end to end, weaving through eight communities that are technically outside the park's boundaries. French fishermen named this place by combining the words for 'big' and 'small rounded mountain that stands alone.' *Morne* can also mean dreary. But even gloomy fog can't dim this mountain park's remarkable beauty.

Walking the Earth's Inner Soul

Ancient, iron-rich rock

The barren landscape is an otherwordly shade of orange that stands in sharp contrast to the rest of lushly forested Gros Morne. A sign urges you to pick up (but not keep) a rusty rock. This heavy igneous rock is full of things such as iron that are poisonous to plants, hence the minimal greenery here at the Tablelands, the park's largest and most prominent geological feature. These orange rocks formed in the Earth's upper mantle beneath an ancient ocean until they were pushed onto the Earth's surface as land masses collided half a billion years ago, building the Appalachian Mountains and assembling a supercontinent called Pangea.

The Tablelands is one of the few places in the world where a sample of the Earth's mantle is well exposed, preserved and accessible. It's rare to be able to walk on the Earth's inner

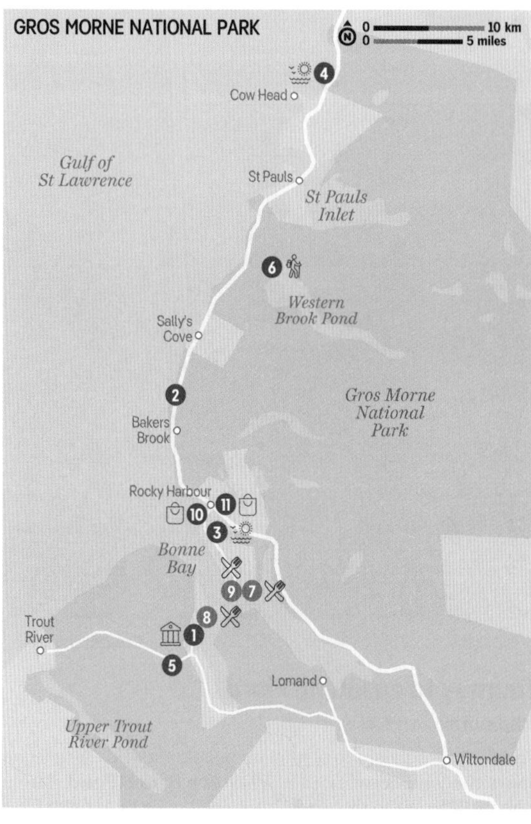

SIGHTS
1 Discovery Centre
2 Green Point Geological Site
3 Rocky Harbour Pond Beach
4 Shallow Bay Beach
5 Tablelands

ACTIVITIES, COURSES & TOURS
6 Western Brook Pond

EATING
7 Black Spruce Restaurant
see 11 Buoy & Arrow
see 11 Java Jack's
8 Old Loft Restaurant
9 Old Store Cafe

ENTERTAINMENT
see 11 Ocean View Hotel

SHOPPING
see 8 Galliott Studios
10 Glass Station
11 Gros Morne Wildlife Museum

soul on something that's normally found far below the crust. There's a gentle 4km trail (with an option for the shorter Serpentine Loop) along an old roadbed at the base of the mountain to a viewing platform in Winter House Brook Canyon. Walk it alone or on a two-hour guided hike that delves into plant life as well as geology. Experienced hikers with navigation skills can ask at the **Discovery Centre** for the *Off Trail Hiking in the Tablelands* map and climb the mountain. Motorists can view the Tablelands along Rte 431 between Woody Point and Trout River. As for the alien hue on these serpentine barrens, the iron in the rock turns rusty as it weathers.

WHERE TO STAY

Stay in Gros Morne
Fifty cottages, suites and hotel-style rooms for all budgets in Rocky Harbour. $$

Gros Morne Inn
Boutique hotel with a sustainability mandate and hot tubs in Shoal Brook near the Tablelands. $$$

Old Cottage Hostel
Two hostel apartments with three or five private rooms in a hospital turned community center. $$

BEST HIKING TRAILS

Gros Morne Trail
This challenging route can be divided into the Approach and Summit trails, or hiked to the first bridge.

Mattie Mitchell Trail
A short interpretive trail that tells the story of a renowned Mi'kmaw hunter, guide and prospector.

Lobster Cove Lighthouse Trails
One trail leads to a driftwood shelter on the beach where you can sign the weathered wood.

Bakers Brook Falls Trail
Take a detour to the moose 'exclosure' that protects a patch of forest from overbrowsing animals.

Green Gardens Trail
A challenging hike meanders from the barrens through boreal forest to the volcanic sea coast.

Gros Morne Trail

Journey to an Inland Fjord

Wild and wonderful

There's an iconic photo of jubilant people standing on a ledge above the landlocked fjord at **Western Brook Pond**. Those who want to get to that exact spot need to be fit enough for a day-long guided hike. The fallback plan is almost as breathtaking and infinitely easier. It begins with the 3km Western Brook Pond Trail hike from the parking lot across a bog and caribou/moose country to the dock. (Parks Canada has all-terrain wheelchairs to loan.) The 'pond' – a Newfoundland term for lake – is in the Long Range Mountains, which are the most northern section of the Appalachian Mountains. Surrounded by deep rock walls, it's 16.5km long, almost 2km wide at the mouth of the gorge and 165m (50 storeys) deep. This fjord was carved out by glaciers during an ice age 25,000 to 10,000 years ago. Once connected to the sea, the pond is now filled with fresh water and so it's no longer a true fjord.

The history of Gros Morne National Park began right here when a provincial geologist visited and started lobbying the

BEST PLACES TO SHOP

Glass Station
Urve Manuel's glasswork, and the work of other artists, can be found at this gallery-studio.

Galliott Studios
An espresso bar, pottery studio and craft shop housed in a restored fishing shed.

Gros Morne Wildlife Museum
The museum showcases the province's wildlife, while the gift shop has antler and bone carvings.

premier to get federal protection for this land. BonTours now runs boat tours here from mid-May to early October using vessels that have a special certification required by Parks Canada and minimal environmental impact. You'll get two lively hours of interpretation about geology and history while floating between towering 1.25-billion-year-old rock cliffs that feature several high waterfalls. This ultra-oligotrophic lake has limited nutrients to support plants and animals, but it's also one of the purest lakes in the world.

Indigenous Education

A path to reconciliation

The province is home to three Indigenous groups: the Inuit, Innu and Mi'kmaq. To look at Gros Morne through the eyes of the Indigenous peoples who lived here for 5000 years before European settlers arrived, Keith Payne teams up with **Discover Gros Morne** (owned by his daughter and son-in-law) to whisk people by Zodiac to an isolated Bonne Bay cove. 'Pretend we're the first people ever to come here and we've got to decide if we're going to stay,' says Payne, a member of the Qalipu First Nation. 'What do you need to survive and can you find it here?' In search of fire, food, shelter and water, guests follow a game trail learning about the plants, berries, seabirds, and land and marine mammals that once sustained life. Payne invites people to try to start a fire (thanks to a special Parks Canada permit) with stone tools, before serving bannock, moose and smoked mackerel. He wraps up by showing off a collection of pelts, sealskin boots and birchbark baskets. The tour out of Norris Point is called **Discover Mekapisk**, using the Mi'kmaw name for the Long Range Mountains. Mindful of the genocide of the coastal Beothuk people, the goal is to look at the First Peoples with the respect they deserve. Over in Woody Point at the park's Discovery Centre, *Miawpukek: The Middle River Exhibit* details the life and traditions of the Miawpukek First Nation of Conne River, who are the Mi'kmaq people of central Newfoundland.

Where the Rocks Tell Time

Get a geological guide

A semi-obscured and aging interpretive sign at **Green Point Geological Site** (near Green Point Campground) makes a valiant attempt at relaying the site's global importance. So does a plaque bound to a boulder that lauds how the 'global stratotype for the boundary between the Cambrian and Ordovician systems' was designated here after being discovered in

BEST PLACES TO EAT IN GROS MORNE

Black Spruce Restaurant
Elevated dining in Norris Point's Neddies Harbour Inn. Reservations recommended. **$$$**

Old Store Cafe
A Norris Point hot spot with a coffeeshop on one side and a gift shop and ice-cream bar on the other. **$**

Old Loft Restaurant
A seaside Woody Point spot that serves Newfoundland fare such as cod, halibut and capelin. **$$**

Buoy & Arrow
Rocky Harbour's go-to eatery for lobster rolls and moose (and sometimes bear) burgers. **$$**

Java Jack's
Meals with vegetarian options are served at this two-level Rocky Harbour restaurant, gallery and coffeeshop. **$$$**

BEST PLACES TO SWIM

Shallow Bay Beach
Cow Head's famed beach boasts a long stretch of fine sand and warm, shallow water.

Rocky Harbour Recreation Complex
Set in the woods, this rec center has an indoor pool/whirlpool for open swims and laps.

Rocky Harbour Pond Beach
Unmarked swimming area off Pond Rd with a sandy beach and picnic area.

FOR THE LOVE OF COD

There's nothing locals look forward to more than news of the recreational food fishery dates. The season typically runs Saturday, Sunday and Monday from early July until early October, with a partial break in September. Locals and visitors can catch five groundfish (including cod) a day. Boats of three or more can catch 15. **BonTours** takes people cod jigging from Norris Point. You'll learn how jigging is the action you do with your rod to entice the fish, and how to set the hook and reel in your fish. Donate your catch to the community or get it cleaned and take it home for a meal. Stop in at the **Bonne Bay Aquarium & Research Station** to see more fish.

RAYMOND GEHMAN/GETTY IMAGES ©

Green Point Geological Site

a bed of shale and limestone exposed in the cliff. Unless this makes perfect sense, you'd be wise to take one of Parks Canada's free summer hikes.

The tour starts with a short walk to the shoreline to see a seasonal fish-staging area. You'll learn that the Canadian government wisely decided not to expropriate land from traditional communities when it established the park. Then you'll walk on billion-year-old rocks, learn the difference between igneous, sedimentary and metamorphic rocks, and identify some of the more intriguing specimens. You might even come to understand plate tectonics, a scientific theory about how old oceans closed and mountains were formed.

Your guide will help you admire this world-renowned sequence of layered rocks and hidden fossils. Almost 500 million years ago, you see, these rocks formed on the bottom of an ancient ocean and it was here that geologists discovered fossils that define the boundary between the Cambrian and Ordovician periods. Green Point is part of five geological zones in Gros Morne. Together they tell the story of the Earth's transformation. Before the 90-minute tour ends, you'll be reminded that it's illegal to pocket any rocks.

Beyond Gros Morne National Park

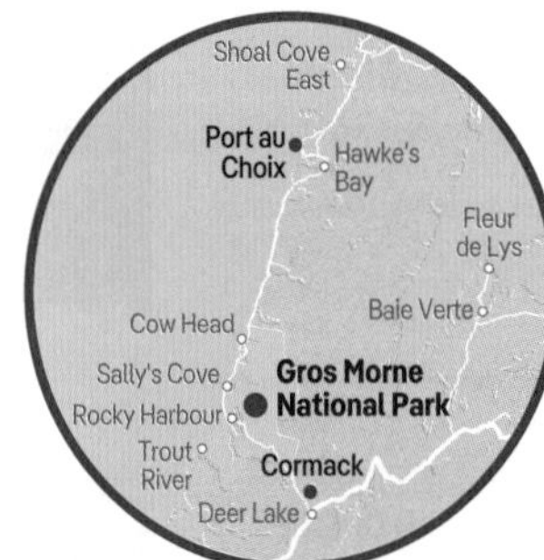

There are worthy stops on your drive to the national park, and beyond its northern end.

In their mad scramble to get to Gros Morne National Park, visitors tend to fly into Deer Lake International Airport and then drive straight north to the park, bypassing some worthy things to do in town or on the way. Likewise, there's so much to do in the park itself that many visitors never give themselves enough time to drive 90 minutes beyond the northernmost community, Cow Head, to an underrated national historic site in Port au Choix, where there's a resident herd of caribou and otherworldly limestone barrens. If possible, factor in a little extra time in your trip. If there's one thing Newfoundland forces you to do, it's slow down and enjoy simple pleasures.

Caribou

Places

Cormack p202
Port au Choix p203

GETTING AROUND

If you hear Newfoundlanders and Labradorians speak about 'RDF,' they're talking about rain, drizzle and fog. This western region gets plenty of all three, so factor the elements into your daily driving times – while watching for moose and caribou along the road. And given the popularity of Gros Morne, be sure to secure your car rental well in advance.

TOP TIP

Daredevils love Marble Zip Tours in Steady Brook, alongside Marble Mountain Ski Resort, for the Spider Challenge high ropes and obstacle course.

BEST STOPS IN PORT AU CHOIX

Ben's Studio
Ben Ploughman makes 3D wooden pictures and gives guided tours ($5) of his studio to explain his unique style of folk art, combining recycled lobster-trap laths, hand-carved characters and other sculpted pieces.

French Rooms Cultural Center
A local-history museum that delves into the French fishery, the resettlement era and Point Riche Lighthouse.

French Bread Oven
At a satellite location of the cultural center, staff in period costume bake buns in a reconstructed outdoor oven like the kind once used here by French fishermen. They serve them inside at communal tables with local jams (partridgeberry, squashberry and blueberry) and tea.

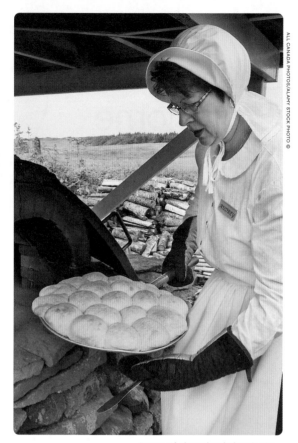

Port au Choix National Historic Site

Cormack

TIME FROM GROS MORNE NATIONAL PARK: **45 MINS**

A farm stay with Indigenous storytelling

In the woods of the historic farming community of Cormack, just outside Deer Lake, Lauralee and Mark Ledrew run a bed-and-breakfast farm stay called **Upper Humber Settlement**. What's unique about their sustainable farm is that it offers agricultural and cultural experiences to overnight guests and curious visitors who just have a few minutes or hours to spare.

There are culinary experiences, Indigenous fire-circle meditations, farm and forage tours, and farm-to-table storytelling.

BEST PLACES TO EAT AROUND DEER LAKE

Crooked Feeder Brewing Co.
This family-friendly Cormack brewery-taproom has frozen cocktails and pub grub including Texas barbecue. $

Humber Café
Unpretentious spot for cod, burgers and fries with dressing and gravy inside the Deer Lake Motel. $

Deer Lake Big Stop Restaurant
Eat fish cakes at the Irving gas station after taking a photo of the giant moose statue out front. $

You can pick strawberries and make jam, walk the land looking for moose and caribou (or maybe just moose poop and black flies), or simply take a half-hour guided tour of the permaculture farm. The Ledrews bought the 2.5 hectares of land in 2012, and launched the four-room B&B in 2020 to help finance their dreams. The farm has expanded under their care and they now raise pigs, ducks and egg-laying chickens using regenerative agriculture techniques such as no-dig gardening, while growing food naturally without pesticides or herbicides.

Lauralee, who has started exploring her Mi'kmaw heritage and is part of the Qalipu First Nation, leads an Indigenous medicine-wheel- and fire-wheel-circle meditation that teaches participants about themselves and the world around them, and culminates in roasting bannock on a stick over the fire. She's been making bannock, a quick bread brought here by early settlers and fur traders and embraced by Indigenous groups, since she was a girl helping care for her siblings. With foodie flair, she gets guests to forage for fresh spruce tips and then mashes them with sugar to sprinkle over buttered bannock.

Port au Choix

TIME FROM GROS MORNE NATIONAL PARK: 1½ **HOURS**

Honoring the First Peoples

In a magical coastal area where Indigenous groups fished and harvested seals for 6000 years, a resident herd of rare woodland caribou delights visitors. **Port au Choix National Historic Site** hands out information cards warning people to give the at-risk species space by staying at least 30m away and not feeding them.

The visitor center tells the story of the first peoples to live and bury their dead here – the Maritime Archaic. It details how the Groswater and Dorset peoples, and the more recent Indigenous peoples who were ancestors of the Beothuk, came next and lived here until the Europeans arrived. There's a reconstructed domed Dorset dwelling and plenty of artifacts, but those excavated by archaeologists from a Maritime Archaic burial site in the 1960s have now been concealed from public view in the spirit of reconciliation.

Outside, take two hiking trails across the Point Riche Peninsula and its rare limestone barrens looking for endangered flowers such as Barrens willow, Fernald's braya and Long's braya. Find the metal sculpture of an Indigenous mother and child near Point Riche Lighthouse, and two more of seal hunters and a kayaker near Phillip's Garden. In Port au Chohix, the fishing capital of western Newfoundland, a small sacred burial ground is a protected space called the Gathering Circle. Ask Parks Canada staff about the Seal for All Seasons program to learn how the tradition of harvesting seals for food and clothing continues, a story you can explore at **Great Northern Peninsula (GNP) Crafts Producers**, an Economusée run by a cooperative in Shoal Cove East.

BEST PLACES FOR KIDS

Newfoundland Insectarium
A Reidville nature museum that boasts live and mounted insects, arachnids and arthropods from around the world, plus a butterfly pavilion. Owners Lloyd and Sandy Hollett even have adorable axolotls (amphibian salamanders) at this seasonal spot.

Cormack Bee Co.
This sustainable honey-based business sells pure Newfoundland honey and bee-inspired earrings and knickknacks. Make time for one of the two apiary tours: the 'NewBee' and 'fully interactive beekeeper' experiences.

Deer Lake Beach
This sandy urban beach with shallow water is a local hot spot. There's a kiosk, washrooms, foot-rinsing stations, and Mobi-mats for those who use wheelchairs and strollers.

L'Anse aux Meadows National Historic Site

GETTING AROUND

For iceberg viewing and whale watching, park at Fishing Point Municipal Day Use Park in St Anthony. Iceberg Alley Trail is an accessible boardwalk that takes you past a lighthouse to a viewing platform overlooking the Atlantic. There are other town trails, including one to a waterfowl sanctuary at Bottom Brook Park with endangered harlequin ducks and other species.

TOP TIP

The St Anthony area, along the northern coast, boasts the province's longest iceberg and whale season, with opportunities to see both from late spring through summer. The 10-day Iceberg Festival in early June revolves around guided walking and boat tours plus musicians, chefs, craft suppliers and storytellers.

It's all about the Vikings if you drive about four hours northeast of Gros Morne National Park along Rte 430/Viking Trail to L'Anse aux Meadows National Historic Site. This Unesco World Heritage Site is the only authenticated Viking site in North America and it's also the earliest evidence of Europeans on this continent. Parks Canada preserves and presents the seaside site, while a nonprofit organization runs the nearby Norstead: A Viking Village & Port of Trade, a replica port of trade that includes a wooden boat that was sailed here from Greenland. It's fascinating to see the Norse story presented two different ways. This is also prime iceberg and whale-watching territory. Many visitors to the area choose to base themselves in the town of St Anthony, where the story of medical missionary Sir Wilfred Grenfell comes to life thanks to the work of the Grenfell Historical Society.

Voyage of the Vikings

Norse foothold

One thousand years ago, Norse explorer Leifur Eiríksson left Greenland to find new territory and landed here where wood was plentiful. This 'Viking' expedition (the term should really just be used for men when they were raiding) built a winter base camp while searching for a place with wild grapes they called Vinland. For centuries the story was part of oral history and then the written Vinland Sagas, but its exact location was a mystery. Then, in 1960, Norwegian explorer and writer Helge Ingstad and his archeologist wife, Anne Stine, traced the legend to the village of L'Anse aux Meadows, where fisherman George Decker led them to what was believed to be an old Indigenous camp. Excavations yielded a spindle whirl and an iron boat nail that proved the Norse were the first known Europeans to set foot in North America. They abandoned this

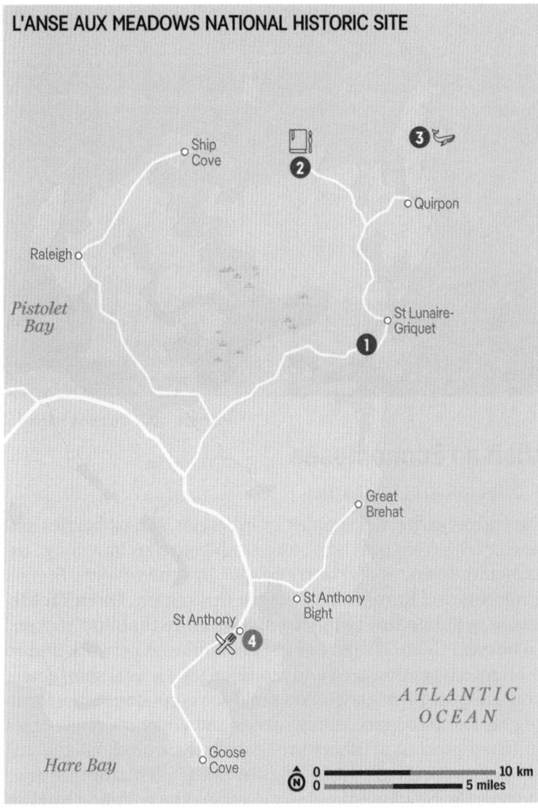

SIGHTS
1 Dark Tickle
2 L'Anse aux Meadows National Historic Site
see 2 Norstead: A Viking Village & Port of Trade

ACTIVITIES, COURSES & TOURS
3 Quirpon Island

EATING
see 2 Norseman
4 RagnaRöck Northern Brewing Co
see 4 Old Store Cafe

site and burned the buildings within a decade, possibly when relations with early Indigenous peoples soured.

Parks Canada finished the excavation and created L'Anse aux Meadows National Historic Site. Unesco gave it World Heritage Site status for being the only verified Viking site in the New World and for what it reveals about global migration. Start outside the visitor center by the Stine and Ingstad bust, and then go in for a film and interpretive displays. Guided tours pass the *Meeting of Two Worlds* sculpture and delve into the archaeological history before leaving you with costumed interpreters in the Viking Encampment's reconstructed sod huts. Save time for the Birchy Nuddick Trail along the coast, bogs and barrens.

NORSE CULTURE

Norstead: A Viking Village & Port of Trade offers a tactile spin on the Norse story. Run by a nonprofit, Norstead replicates a Norse port of trade from the Viking era (790 to 1066 CE), with dimly lit buildings made with wood-panelled walls and earthen floors. Costumed interpreters hang out in a chieftain's hall, church and blacksmith shop, encouraging you to finger trade beads, examine hand-dyed yarn, don helmets and brandish swords. The boathouse showcases a 54ft replica Viking *knarr* (cargo ship) called the *Snorri*, which was built in Maine and then sailed here from Greenland by nine men to recreate Leifur Eiríksson's voyage.

WHERE TO EAT AROUND L'ANSE AUX MEADOWS

Norseman
Fresh and creative meals, with a nod to vegetarians and allergies, in L'Anse aux Meadows. **$$$**

RagnaRöck Northern Brewing Co
Eat wings in a spot named for the Norse apocalypse (Ragnarök) and Newfoundland's nickname (the rock). **$**

Rebel Coffeehouse
This St Anthony coffeeshop doubles as a craft store and sells oatcakes with bakeapple butter. **$**

A BELOVED DOCTOR

Why is the name Dr Wilfred Grenfell still spoken with reverence? This medical missionary from England joined the Royal National Mission to Deep Sea Fishermen to help isolated coastal communities. He built his first hospital at Battle Harbour in 1893 and made St Anthony the Grenfell Mission headquarters in 1900. He established schools and orphanages, was once famously stranded on an ice floe and was knighted in 1927. Grenfell Historic Properties tells this story at the Grenfell Interpretation Centre/ Grenfell Handicrafts (which has a statue and tearoom), and in the local hospital rotunda with the ceramic Jordi Bonet Murals. Behind Grenfell House Museum, Tea House Hill Trail leads to the spot where Grenfell's ashes rest.

BARBARA VALLANCE/GETTY IMAGES ©

Iceberg near Quirpon Island

Visit an Economusée

A celebration of five berries

Partridgeberries, bakeapples, crowberries, squashberries and blueberries from peat bogs, forests and barrens have long sustained Indigenous and Norse people, Basque whalers, French explorers and European settlers in this region. **Dark Tickle**, based in St Lunaire-Griquet, employs more than 100 'pickers' to harvest them. It's part of the Economusée network and so it offers a reception area and boutique plus a workshop where you can peer through windows and see employees transforming berries into jams, jellies, sauces and vinegars. A few cases of berry-picking artifacts are scattered throughout the gift shop. Interpretive panels line the walls, explaining things such as the Newfoundland name versus the common English name of each berry. Partridgeberries, for example, are also called lingonberries. Berries are delivered, packaged, labelled and frozen until needed, so production runs year-round. Berries are thawed, cleaned, washed, cooked in a steam kettle with sugar and sometimes natural pectin, and bottled and labeled. Upstairs, the charming **Café Nymphe** works Dark Tickle products into the menu. Outside, take a short boardwalk through a berry-filled landscape.

Boating Around Quirpon Island

Scenic sea voyage

From the dock in the tiny community of Quirpon (pronounced car-poon), Linkum Tours whisks people out in Zodiacs in search of whales, dolphins, icebergs, seals and seabirds. You'll also see the company's Quirpon Lighthouse Inn, dramatically perched at the edge of **Quirpon Island**. The island reportedly has unique currents that draw the capelin and herring that hungry whales feed on. The water stays deep right up the rocky island, so it's a favorite spot for humpbacks chasing their next meal. Guests at the 10-room inn can hike for miles and whale watch from shore, sometimes peering down from the cliffs practically right into the mouths of the whales.

Labrador

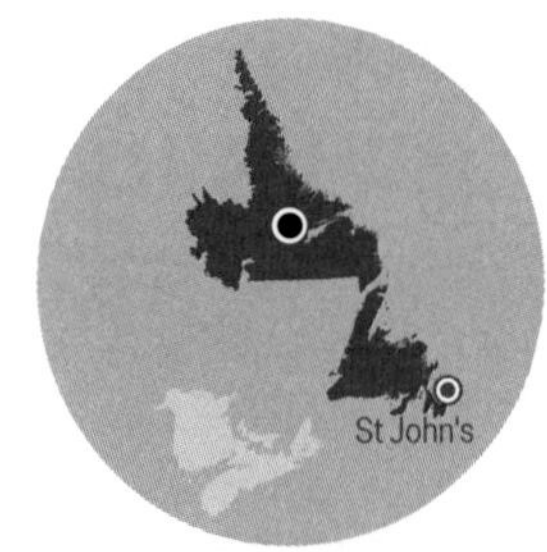

Labrador is the mainland portion of the province – the unsung behemoth known as 'the Big Land' that brushes up against Québec. You can road-trip the 1149 isolated kilometers of the Trans-Labrador Hwy, but you're more likely to take the ferry over from Newfoundland to the Québec–Labrador border and explore the two-hour stretch of coastline up to Mary's Harbour. This will get you to Red Bay National Historic Site, where Basque whalers once produced the oil that lit the lamps of Europe, and on to Battle Harbour, a tiny island run by a historic trust that lets you overnight in a national historic site and learn the story of the Labrador cod fishery's heyday and collapse. True to its name, the Big Land is full of vast, empty stretches where it's just you, the moose and perhaps icebergs and whales passing by just offshore.

Sleep in a Living Museum

Telling fish tales

The gem of Labrador is Battle Harbour, an achingly charming restored 19th-century fishing village on a wee island that's run by a historic trust. Once the salt-fish capital of the world, **Battle Harbour** is now a national historic site and national historic district that tells the story of the cod fishery's heyday and demise.

From Mary's Harbour it's a 75-minute private ferry ride to the remote island, where you'll get an orientation and lunch before a guided walk through restored mercantile buildings. You'll learn how John Slade and Co. from England set up fishing premises here around 1775, how salt cod is created and how an outport community sprang up around the cod, seal and salmon fishery. When the government announced the cod moratorium in 1992, wiping out more than 30,000 jobs and a way of life, the Battle Harbour Historic Trust took over, turned fishermen into restoration carpenters and began revitalization work.

Battle Harbour opened to overnight guests in 1996 and is always evolving. Guests settle into the Battle Harbour Inn, the

GETTING AROUND

Driving distances are huge in Labrador. Polar bears and the fact that many spots are only accessible by plane or boat make it a challenge to explore. Adventure Canada runs small-ship voyages. Its Greenland and Wild Labrador route explores Torngat Mountains National Park and Hebron and Nain in northern Labrador. Torngat Mountains Base Camp and Research Station flies in people from Happy Valley-Goose Bay for three-, four- and seven-day packages.

TOP TIP

It's essential to plan trips around Labrador Marine's ferry between St-Barbe in Newfoundland and Blanc-Sablon in Québec. Double bookings aren't tolerated. Check into the ferry terminal at least one hour before the crossing or lose your spot. The ferry stays on Newfoundland time and takes one hour and 45 minutes.

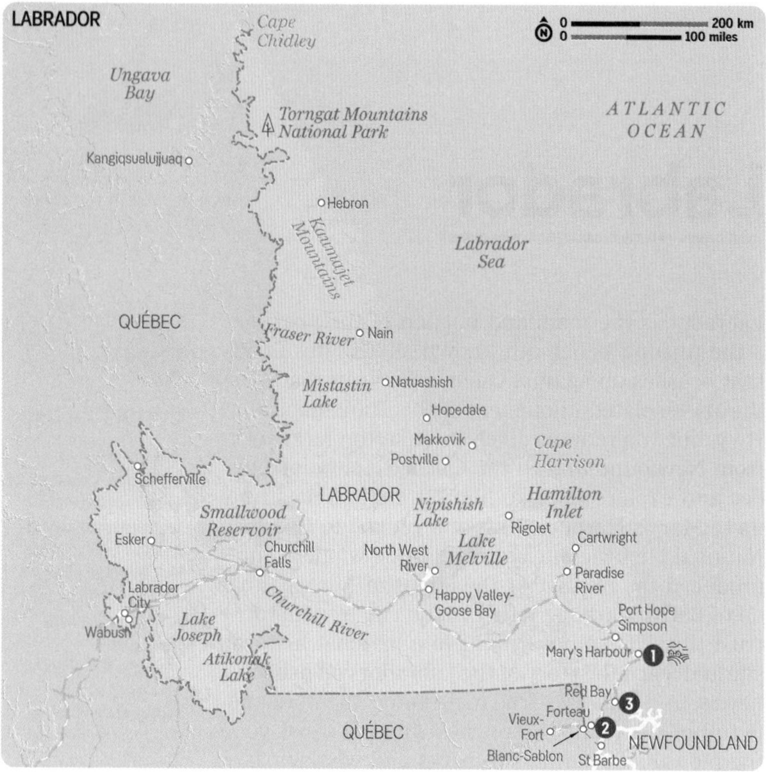

LABRADOR

Cape Chidley
Ungava Bay
Torngat Mountains National Park
ATLANTIC OCEAN
Kangiqsualujjuaq
Hebron
Kaumajet Mountains
Labrador Sea
QUÉBEC
Fraser River
Nain
Mistastin Lake
Natuashish
Hopedale
Makkovik
Postville
Cape Harrison
Schefferville
LABRADOR
Smallwood Reservoir
Nipishish Lake
Hamilton Inlet
Rigolet
Esker
Churchill Falls
North West River
Lake Melville
Cartwright
Paradise River
Labrador City
Wabush
Lake Joseph
Churchill River
Happy Valley-Goose Bay
Port Hope Simpson
Atikonak Lake
Mary's Harbour
Red Bay
Forteau
Vieux-Fort
QUÉBEC
Blanc-Sablon
St Barbe
NEWFOUNDLAND
0 200 km
0 100 miles

SIGHTS
1 Battle Harbour
2 L'Anse Amour National Historic Site
3 Red Bay National Historic Site
see 3 Selma Barkham Town Centre

ACTIVITIES, COURSES & TOURS
see 3 Boney Shore Trail

SLEEPING
see 2 Florian Hotel
see 2 Forteau Bay Cottages
see 3 Whaler's Station

Merchant Building or small cottages – heated by wood stoves – and gather in the dining room for traditional meals. Wi-fi only works above the general store in the Loft bar-lounge.

You might take the island's trail past two cemeteries, a small plane crash site and 1904 Marconi wireless station, go cod fishing, berry picking or hiking, or chat with locals at their summer homes. Heavenly white buns are served at most meals and you can even learn Daphne Smith's secret recipe before you reluctantly go.

WHERE TO STAY IN SOUTHERN LABRADOR

Forteau Bay Cottages
Cook for yourself in cozy cabins near a short path to a beach in Forteau. **$**

Florian Hotel
This 21-room boutique hotel in Forteau boasts ocean views and a restaurant. **$$**

Whaler's Station
This Red Bay hot spot has places to stay and a popular fish-and-chips restaurant. **$**

Red Bay National Historic Site

Basque Whaling

Stations on the Labrador coast

The story begins around 1530, when whalers from the Basque region of northeastern Spain and southwestern France crossed the Atlantic Ocean in search of whale oil. They set up a dozen seasonal whaling stations along Labrador's south coast, hunted bowhead and right whales and processed whale oils to sell to Europe as lamp fuel and lubricant for about 70 years.

The largest station was in Red Bay's harbor. Lured by mysterious red 'pebbles' along the coast that turned out to be terracotta roofing tiles the Basque used as part of their ships' ballast, archaeologists discovered the long-forgotten station in 1977. It's now **Red Bay National Historic Site** and a Unesco World Heritage Site.

The site is spread out over two locations. On shore, the Parks Canada interpretive center details the region's whaling history and has artifacts such as a Basque chalupa (a wooden boat used to hunt and kill whales). On Saddle Island, a short boat ride away (and included with admission), an interpretive trail passes by what were once rendering ovens, cooperages, wharves, temporary living quarters and a cemetery. Several wrecks, including the *San Juan* whaling galleon, are in the harbor.

While you're here, go to the **Selma Barkham Town Centre** (named for the woman who discovered evidence of Labrador's Basque whaling history) for the *Red Bay Right Whale Exhibit*. It showcases the ancient skeleton of a bowhead whale and explains how Greenland right whales (bowheads) and North Atlantic right whales were almost wiped out and are now protected. Whale bones still litter the shoreline along the town's **Boney Shore Trail**.

EVIDENCE OF THE EARLIEST PEOPLES

About 9000 years ago, hunter-gatherers arrived from the Maritimes in search of seals, fish and walruses. Part of the Maritime Archaic tradition, these earliest peoples left behind only a few stone tools and campsites. In 1973 archaeologists discovered an elaborate burial mound at L'Anse Amour containing a child's skeleton and artifacts such as a toggling harpoon.

L'Anse Amour National Historic Site is the oldest funeral monument in North America. A platform overlooks the mound of stones. A plaque reveals the child's body was covered in red ochre, wrapped in animal skins or birch bark, and placed in a pit with spearheads, a walrus tusk, a harpoon head, painted stones and a bone whistle.

TOOLKIT

The chapters in this section cover the most important topics you'll need to know about in Atlantic Canada. They're full of nuts-and-bolts information and valuable insights to help you understand and navigate Atlantic Canada and get the most out of your trip.

Brier Island (p78), Bay of Fundy

DAVE REEDE/DESIGN PICS/GETTY IMAGES ©

Arriving

While some visitors may arrive here by car, many fly to Halifax, Nova Scotia. Halifax Stanfield International Airport is 35km from downtown Halifax. The airport is a single terminal handling domestic and international flights. Rental-car counters are on the lower level of the airport parkade. Taxis, buses and shuttle service to downtown are also available.

Visas

Visas are not currently required for US citizens traveling to Canada. Requirements for non-Americans differ by country. International travelers must carry acceptable identification.

SIM Cards

TIf your device can be unlocked from its home network, you can use a foreign SIM card and purchase that card in Canada. Wi-fi and bluetooth can be enabled without a SIM card.

Border Crossings

Anyone crossing the border to Canada by air or land must carry proof of identity and citizenship. Entry is determined by the Canada Border Services Agency (CBSA).

Wi-fi

High-speed wi-fi is free in the Halifax international airport. The airport's wi-fi connection page also gives travelers links to information about airport amenities, such as dining and shopping.

Public Transport from Airport to City Centre

Halifax

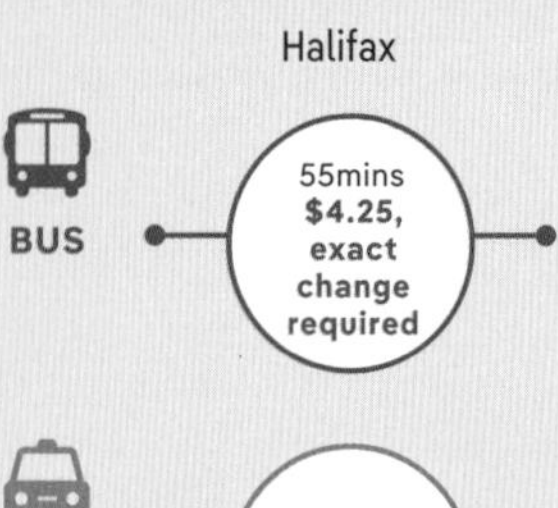

BUS — 55mins **$4.25, exact change required**

TAXI — 30-40min **$65-80**

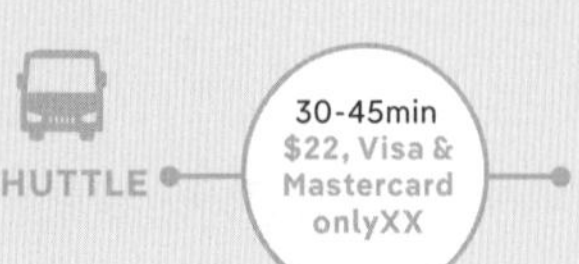

SHUTTLE — 30-45min **$22, Visa & Mastercard onlyXX**

CUSTOMS DECLARATION

Familiarize yourself with Canadian customs regulations and be prepared to complete a customs declaration form. You will be required to declare any items you are bringing into the country, including currency, food and certain goods. If you need Canadian currency, you can exchange it at the airport or withdraw from ATMs.

CLOCKWISE FROM TOP: FUSE/GETTY IMAGES ©; NIYAZZ/SHUTTERSTOCK ©; GAGODESIGN/SHUTTERSTOCK ©
FAR RIGHT: MAKS_PH/SHUTTERSTOCK ©

Getting Around

Nothing beats the freedom of having your own car in Atlantic Canada, especially if you're planning to explore the region's rural villages, tucked-away beaches and scenic back roads.

TRAVEL COSTS

Rental
From $100/day

Gas
About $1.80/litre

EV charging
From $1.80/hour

Bicycle rental
From $60/day

Renting a Car

Book a rental vehicle well ahead of your travel, as high demand often results in limited supply. Also note that the supply issue has caused prices to spike. Consider bringing your own vehicle if you're within driving distance of your destination.

Road Conditions

Driving in and around Halifax is fairly easy, with road congestion rare except at rush hour. When crossing either of Halifax's two bridges, you can pay by cash or an electronic tolling device. Most vehicles are $1.25, with cash lanes accepting quarters, $1 coins and $2 coins.

TIP

Before leaving on a road trip, check for closures or detours, such as via provincial transportation websites or navigation apps.

BREAKING THE ICE

In areas where bodies of water freeze in winter, such as between Nova Scotia and Newfoundland and Labrador, icebreaking ships are used to maintain year-round transportation links. The Canadian Coast Guard icebreaking program ensures that marine traffic moves safely through or around ice-covered waters. From December to May, icebreakers and hovercraft operate along the East Coast from Newfoundland to Montréal and in the Great Lakes. From June to November, icebreakers provide services in the Arctic.

Bus & Train

Maritime Bus serves Nova Scotia, New Brunswick and Prince Edward Island (PEI); DRL Coach Lines serves Newfoundland. VIA Rail's Montréal–Halifax route is offered three times weekly, with stops in several communities in Nova Scotia and New Brunswick. There's no rail service in PEI or Newfoundland and Labrador.

Train Tickets

Traveling by rail with kids? VIA Rail offers 50% off economy-class tickets for children between two and 11. Other discounts are available for those who book ahead or who travel on Tuesdays, those 60 and over, Canadian military personnel, members of Indigenous communities, and groups of 10 or more.

Plane

Several airlines provide service within Atlantic Canada, including Air Canada, WestJet, Porter, PAL Airlines, Air Saint-Pierre and Air Borealis. The availability and frequency of flights may vary depending on demand, seasonality and other factors. Delays are common.

DRIVING ESSENTIALS

Drive on the right

Speed limit is 50km/h in urban areas, 80km/h on most secondary roads and 100km/h or 110km/h on most highways.

.08

Blood-alcohol limit is 0.08, or 80mg of alcohol in 100mL of blood, for fully licensed drivers

Money

CURRENCY: **CANADIAN DOLLAR ($)**

Credit Cards

Credit and debit cards are widely accepted in Atlantic Canada, especially in urban areas and tourist destinations. Visa and MasterCard are the most commonly accepted. American Express and Discover may have more limited acceptance. Inform your card issuer about your travels prior to departure to avoid issues.

Taxes

Each province and territory in Canada charges GST, a 5% tax on goods and services. Most provinces charge an additional 5% to 10% provincial sales tax (PST). Nova Scotia, New Brunswick, PEI and Newfoundland and Labrador charge a blended GST and PST, called a Harmonized Sales Tax (HST), totaling 15%.

Tipping

Gratuities are rarely included in Canadian restaurant bills. Tip about 15% of the total bill before tax for wait staff. The same applies for taxi drivers. Tip porters and doormen $2 to $4 per bag. For maid service, tip $2 to $3 per day, $5 per day at luxury properties.

HOW MUCH FOR...

Local museum entry
$5 to $20

Entry to a national park
from $7.25

A municipal bus fare
from $2.50

A lobster roll
from $18

HOW TO... Save Money

Atlantic Canada has parks and attractions well worth their admission. If you're on a budget, there are also fantastic provincial and municipal parks as well as other public spaces that don't cost a dime. Stroll Halifax's Public Gardens or Fredericton's Riverfront Trail. Relax on the white sands of Basin Head Provincial Park in PEI. Free parks and attractions are a great way to stretch the vacation dollar.

LOCAL TIP

Many cities offer year-round farmers markets, which are great places to stock up on fresh food. (Rural communities may offer markets seasonally.) Grab a homemade meal, dessert or local fruit.

LOONIES & TWOONIES

Canadian currency shares similarities with other dollar-based currencies. However, it has distinct features. For example, Canada does not have a $1 bill. Instead, Canadians use a $1 coin, called a 'loonie' because it features an image of a loon. There is also a $2 coin, known (of course) as a 'twoonie,' which has an inner ring of a different color to distinguish it from the loonie. Another interesting feature: both English and French are present on banknotes and coins, reflecting Canada's status as a bilingual country.

Accommodations

Go Luxe

While Atlantic Canada may have fewer options then larger centers when it comes to luxury accommodations, there are many exceptional properties waiting to wow visitors. Head to Fox Harb'r Resort in Nova Scotia or Newfoundland's Fogo Island Inn. Among other winning options are the Algonquin Resort in New Brunswick and The Inn at Bay Fortune in PEI.

Find a B&B

Choosing a bed and breakfast for a stay is a great idea on many fronts. These charmers offer cozy rooms, homemade breakfasts and personalized experiences. Their warm hosts can provide insider knowledge about the area, share local stories and create a welcoming atmosphere that immerses visitors in the rich culture and hospitality of Atlantic Canada.

Try Glamping

One of the reasons visitors flock here is to explore nature's bounty. Many seek eco-friendly accommodations, from yurts to off-grid cabins. For those who want to be close to nature but still enjoy a bit of luxury, geodesic domes are a popular option. These 'glamping' structures, found in all four provinces, feature amenities such as real bedding, pillows and hot showers.

Budget Sleeps

For budget accommodations, consider options such as motels, hostels and university dorms. Motels offer affordable rates and basic amenities. Hostels provide budget-friendly shared accommodations and communal spaces for socializing. Some universities offer dormitories as accommodations during non-academic periods. Check online booking platforms and university websites or contact local tourism offices for options.

HOW MUCH FOR A NIGHT...

B&B room
$100-400

Average hotel room
$200-300

University dorm room
$75

Camp Out

From basic campsites to larger spaces for recreational vehicles, campground choices vary in the region. Use free services such as Camping Select to find the option that suits you. Consider taking advantage of your surroundings by picking a property near a picturesque ocean beach or riverside vista. Keep in mind that campgrounds may be crowded in summer months.

THE AIRBNB DEBATE

Websites such as Airbnb are a source of debate in Atlantic Canada and across the country. With a national crisis due to a lack of housing, there is concern about the impact of those buying homes and apartments only to list them year-round as short-term rentals. Other issues such as noise and parking have added to the backlash in some communities. If you go the Airbnb route for accommodations, be respectful of the neighborhood. And watch for steep added fees that might make a hotel or other option just as affordable.

Family Travel

Atlantic Canada is excellent for family travel. Play in the ocean surf or build sandcastles along stunning coastlines. Go whale watching, river tubing or mountain biking. Discover history at national parks, museums and unique sites. Have a lobster cookout, dance at a fiddle show, decipher constellations under a sky full of stars. The possibilities are endless and memories are guaranteed.

Save More

A little planning can mean a lot of savings when it comes to family travel here. Consider organizing your trip around a free summer festival where entertainment and activities abound. Contact the tourism association where you'll be staying for info on other free or low-cost activities that may be happening. Ask about coupons for local restaurants and attractions, too.

Facilities

- Changing facilities are commonly available in gas station and restaurant washrooms as well as various attractions.
- Breastfeeding spaces or family washrooms with a chair are sometimes provided in public places. You can legally nurse your baby in public.
- Many hotels offer cots, cribs and playpens for an additional fee.

Eating Out

Children's menus are available at most family-friendly restaurants; some also provide crayons and coloring sheets to entertain kids while they wait for their meals.

While many restaurants have high chairs, there's no guarantee. Consider bringing a portable high chair.

Getting Around

Many services (ie VIA Rail, Marine Atlantic, Bay Ferries) offer discounts for children. Some offer free travel for kids of certain ages.

Children must use car seats or appropriate restraints while traveling in a vehicle. Review regulations for your destination.

KID-FRIENDLY PICKS

Prince Edward Island National Park (p000)

Build sandcastles, play in the surf, bike seaside trails and camp amid the stars.

Fortress of Louisbourg (p000)

Kids have fun doing the 'Rookie Tour' and exploring how different childhood was 300 years ago.

Witless Bay Ecological Reserve (p000)

Search for whales and puffins on a boat trip just south of Newfoundland.

Hopewell Rocks (p000)

Witness the world's highest tides and, later, walk the (muddy) ocean floor.

BE NATURAL

Hands-on activities and up-close experiences can make the best memories on family travels. At historical sites such as the Fortress of Louisbourg in Nova Scotia, kids can feed livestock and help with gardening as they learn about 18th-century life. Whale-watching excursions off the coasts of New Brunswick, Nova Scotia and Newfoundland provide thrilling encounters with majestic marine creatures. Budding scientists can search for fossils along the Bay of Fundy. Little adventurers can hunt for icebergs, fish for lobster or hear stories from Indigenous peoples as they follow trails created thousands of years ago. Let nature and history be your guides.

Health & Safe Travel

INSURANCE

In general, visitors are not required to have travel insurance upon entry to Canada. However, since Canada does not cover hospital or medical services for visitors, it is recommended to purchase health insurance prior to travel here to ensure you don't face a hefty bill for medical costs that may arise. Canadians are covered when traveling within Canada.

Beach Hazards

While there's been an increase in shark sightings in recent years, attacks are rare. Avoid swimming in areas with seals or other creatures that may be prey for sharks. Watch for rip currents. Jellyfish are common in Atlantic waters, but most stings aren't deadly. Remove tentacles from stings with tweezers, and soak skin in hot water for 20 to 45 minutes.

Cannabis

The recreational use of cannabis (marijuana) is legal in Canada, subject to provincial or territorial restrictions. The legal age to purchase, possess or consume cannabis is 19 across Atlantic Canada. Check the province you plan to visit to learn the laws governing where cannabis can be purchased and consumed. Cannabis use in a vehicle (moving or not) is generally prohibited.

SOLO TRAVEL

Women traveling alone in Canada report few serious problems. They should take the same precautions as they would anywhere else.

WILDLIFE WARNING SIGNS

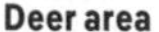

Deer area

Moose area

Caribou area

Bear area

Hurricanes

Hurricane season runs from June to November. While they're uncommon, hurricanes may occur when the waters of the Atlantic Ocean are warm enough to cause a tropical cyclone, which then develops into a hurricane. Communities closest to the Atlantic Ocean are at the highest risk. Stay up to date on storm warnings and risks of hurricanes through Environment Canada.

TICK SAFETY

Black-legged ticks (deer ticks) can transmit Lyme disease and have been found in Atlantic Canada. To protect against tick bites, wear long sleeves and pants in areas they like, such as woods, long grass and parks. Use insect repellents containing DEET and check for ticks after outdoor activities. Promptly remove any attached ticks. Seek medical attention if necessary.

Eating, Drinking & Going Out

When to Eat

Breakfast (6am-10am) can be coffee or tea and cereal, toast or a bagel, or a light meal of eggs, bacon, sausage, pancakes, waffles, oatmeal, fresh fruit, yogurt, fish cakes or beans.

Lunch (noon-2pm) is lighter than dinner, with soup, salad, sandwiches and burgers.

Dinner (5pm-7pm) features more elaborate dishes, including those with seafood, fish or meat and potato, rice or pasta.

Where to Eat

Atlantic Canada has an array of eateries. Food trucks offer quick and tasty options. Cafes provide cozy settings for coffee, tea and light bites. Pubs offer a warm atmosphere, serving classic pub fare and local beers. Diners offer comfort food. Family restaurants provide a welcoming environment with selections for all ages. Seafood restaurants serve fresh catches such as lobster, fish and mussels. Fine-dining establishments showcase upscale dishes with a focus on fresh ingredients.

MENU DECODER

Appetizer Starter

Caesar Cocktail with vodka, Clamato juice and spices, garnished with celery

Charcuterie Cured meats and cheeses

Donair Wrap featuring spiced meat, lettuce, tomatoes, onions and a sweet sauce

Double-double Coffee with two creams and two sugars; ordered at Tim Hortons

Entrée or main course Main dish

Fiddleheads Edible ferns served sautéed or boiled

Flipper pie Newfoundland and Labrador dish made with seal flippers

Fricot Acadian chicken stew

Hodge podge Hearty soup of seasonal vegetables and cream

Jiggs dinner/boiled dinner Ample meal of boiled meat and vegetables

Ployes Acadian buckwheat-flour pancake

Rappie pie Acadian dish made with grated potatoes

Screech Dark rum associated with Newfoundland and Labrador

Timbit Doughnut hole

Toutons Crispy fried dough popular in Newfoundland and Labrador.

Two-four Case of 24 beers

What to Get at a Seafood Restaurant

When ordering at a seafood restaurant in this region, diners may have the choice of how their fish or seafood is cooked, such as pan-fried or deep-fried. Fish and chips are usually deep-fried. The fish used is typically haddock or cod. Customers ordering fish and chips can usually select the number of fish pieces, ranging from one to three, accompanied by a generous serving of French fries and coleslaw. To try a variety of local seafood at once, order a seafood platter, which includes fish fillets, scallops, clams and sometimes lobster or crab. Looking for something lighter? Try a cup or bowl of steaming seafood chowder, a creamy soup made of haddock or cod with chunks of potato and seafood, such as clams, scallops, shrimp, mussels or lobster. Of course, anything with lobster is popular.

HOW MUCH FOR...

A cup of regular coffee at a cafe
$2-4

A cappuccino
$5-7

Diner breakfast
$10-20

Lunch at a seaside restaurant
$15-25

Dinner at a pub
$20-30

Dinner at an upscale restaurant
$50-75

A draft (draught) beer at a pub
$6-8

A glass of wine
$8-12

HOW TO... Buy & Order Lobster

Lobster is available year-round across the region. If you plan to cook your own, you can purchase the live crustaceans from a fish market, lobster pound or grocery store, or seasonally at fishing wharves. Sizes vary from 1lb to 2lb; 1.5lb is optimal for tenderness and meatiness. Prices are per pound (yes, even in metric Canada) and vary from year to year. When you're ordering lobster at a restaurant (see p000), consider the popular lobster roll, which usually features lobster meat lightly dressed in mayo and served on a roll such as a hot-dog bun. Lobster rolls may be served as a platter, with a side of French fries and coleslaw, or as an individual item. Lobster platters feature a cooked 1lb to 1.5lb lobster, which may come partly cracked for ease of eating. Sides may include corn on the cob, potato salad or another potato variation, coleslaw, and fresh bread or rolls. There is also a side of melted butter for dipping, which enhances the flavor and texture of the lobster meat. (Plastic bibs can be worn over clothing, since the meal can be messy.) Lobster chowder is another delicious option. This thick soup combines tender lobster chunks with potatoes, vegetables and a flavorful broth, often enriched with cream. It is often served with fresh bread or biscuits.

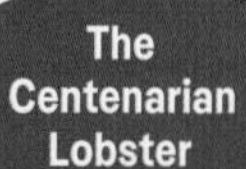

The Centenarian Lobster

On February 11, 1977, a 44lb 6oz lobster was caught off the coast of Nova Scotia. It was estimated to be about 100 years old. The crustacean was eventually sold to a restaurant.

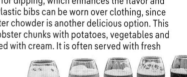

GOING OUT

A night out in Atlantic Canada could be catching a movie at a local theater or attending a concert, dance, play or sporting event. It might also be playing pool, singing karaoke, bowling with a team, taking a harbor cruise, sampling drinks at a wine or cocktail bar, or grabbing a beer at a craft brewery. Some might head to a ceilidh (p000) at the local community center, to listen and dance to live Gaelic music. Others might go to a 'kitchen party' to mingle with pals and maybe step dance when a few in the crowd take to their fiddles.

In urban centers, many start a night out with drinks or dinner with friends at home or at a restaurant. That could be followed by a trip to a downtown club at 10pm or later to hear a live band or DJ and dance.

Visitors to Halifax can find many bars and clubs in and around Argyle St. In St John's, check out George St, known for having the most bars per square foot in North America. In Fredericton, King and Queen Sts are popular areas. In Charlottetown, Victoria Row and the surrounding downtown area are hot spots.

Expect cover charges of $5 to $20 at popular clubs, depending on the venue and event. Dress codes are generally casual, though some clubs may enforce a dressier look. Most bars and clubs close by 2am, with some late-night establishments open until 3:30am.

Responsible Travel

Climate Change & Travel

It's impossible to ignore the impact we have when travelling, and the importance of making changes where we can. Lonely Planet urges all travellers to engage with their travel carbon footprint. There are many carbon calculators online that allow travellers to estimate the carbon emissions generated by their journey; try resurgence.org/resources/carbon-calculator.html. Many airlines and booking sites off er travellers the option of off setting the impact of greenhouse gas emissions by contributing to climate-friendly initiatives around the world. We continue to off set the carbon footprint of all Lonely Planet staff travel, while recognising this is a mitigation more than a solution.

Arts & Crafts

Buy artwork at craft studios such as Village Pottery (PEI), the Newfoundland Weavery, New Brunswick's the Starving Artist or the Cape Breton Centre for Craft & Design, where artisans create on-site.

Go Fair Trade

Grab a cup of joe somewhere like Just Us! (Nova Scotia) or Down East Coffee Roasters (New Brunswick). Purchasing from fair-trade, organic vendors who source their beans from small-scale farmers worldwide supports sustainable farming.

To Market, to Market

Try dulse and fresh corn or buy a handcrafted bowl at one of Atlantic Canada's many farmers markets. Buying directly from farmers and artisans is a great way to learn about local culture and history.

Rent a bike at a local outfitter such as La Bikery in Moncton (New Brunswick) or Outside Expeditions in North Rustico (PEI). Ride coastal trails or scenic paths, get closer to nature and cut fuel costs.

Do a kayak tour with an eco-friendly outfitter. East Coast Outfitters of Lower Prospect, Nova Scotia, offers sea-kayaking tours, giving visitors a chance to learn about natural and cultural history as they paddle.

GET COOKING

Take a farm-to-fork tour at Three Mile Ridge, a family farm in Lethbridge, Newfoundland. Join a group to pick vegetables in the fields and then clean, cook and enjoy them.

CLOCKWISE FROM TOP: SULIT.PHOTOS/SHUTTERSTOCK ©; NEW AFRICA/SHUTTERSTOCK ©; NEW AFRICA/SHUTTERSTOCK ©

INDIGENOUS LEARNINGS

Sign up for a walk with the First Nations Storytellers in Saint John to learn the history of the Wolastoq (Saint John River) and the Mi'kmaq. Enjoy events that celebrate the region's Indigenous communities.

Stargazing

Stargaze in national parks such as Kejimkujik (Nova Scotia), Kouchibouguac and Fundy (New Brunswick) and Terra Nova (Newfoundland), all designated dark-sky preserves. They're committed to preserving the night and reducing or eliminating light pollution.

Get Educated

Visit the Irving Eco-Centre/Bouctouche Dune in New Brunswick to learn about efforts to protect and restore one of the great sand dunes of the region. Learn about local flora and fauna at national-park kiosks.

Enterprising Buys

Get goodies at a social-enterprise bakery, which provides employment opportunities that enrich the lives of staff. Two examples: Baker's Choice Fine Foods in New Minas (Nova Scotia) and Crust Craft Bakery in St John's (Newfoundland).

Promote Local

In social-media posts, highlight regional delicacies, such as a lobster feast at New Glasgow Lobster Suppers, PEI. If you buy local art, tag the artist in a photo.

Go apple picking at a family-owned orchard, such as Belliveau Orchard in Memramcook, New Brunswick.

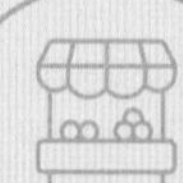

Halifax's Syriana Market employs newcomers to help them learn English and connect with their community.

Joggins Fossil Cliffs

Joggins Fossil Cliffs in Nova Scotia is a leader in sustainable tourism through its eco-friendly guided tours, educational programs on geology and paleontology, support of local communities and efforts to conserve the fossil-rich environment.

RESOURCES

sierraclub.ca/chapters/atlantic
Information on environmental issues.

ecologyaction.ca
Information on environmental issues.

natureconservancy.ca
Information on conservation efforts in the region.

LGBTIQ+ Travelers

Atlantic Canadians are generally a friendly lot to everyone. The region continues to make strides in advancing LGBTIQ+ rights, promoting acceptance and fostering safe spaces. Annual pride events reflect a commitment to diversity and supporting equal rights for all. Visitors will find a host of activities, organizations and supports in place for the LGBTIQ+ traveler.

All About Pride

Up for a party? Visit during summer's Pride festivals. Some of the most popular include Nova Scotia's Halifax Pride, an 11-day celebration with parades and other events. Pride Week in St John's, Newfoundland, is a week of festivities with a parade, concerts and more. New Brunswick's Fredericton Pride has lots on tap, including a parade and activities organized by Monarch, a safe space for youth and adults by day, an adult club by night. At PEI Pride, there's a Queers on Gears bike ride, a Queer AF standup show and more.

INCLUSIVE INFO

Check out Wayves.ca, an independent online publication. It carries information about issues, events and activities that are likely to be of interest to lesbians, gay men, bisexuals and transgender people in Atlantic Canada. The Halifax Rainbow Encyclopedia (gay.hfxns.org) is a rich resource of information for the 2SLGBTQ+/Queer/Q community in Halifax, Nova Scotia.

NOVA SCOTIA & PEI RESOURCES

- For info about LGBTIQ+ offerings in Halifax, Nova Scotia, search discoverhalifaxns.com/plan/lgbthalifaxresources.
- Search 'Rainbow Registered' on the Nova Scotia tourism website (novascotia.com) for tourism operators with national accreditation as 2SLGBTQI+ friendly businesses and organizations.
- For PEI resources, search '2slgbtq-travellers' at tourismpei.com.

NEW BRUNSWICK, NEWFOUNDLAND & LABRADOR RESOURCES

For rainbow-registered businesses in New Brunswick and Newfoundland and Labrador, visit rainbowregistered.ca. Registered accommodations in New Brunswick include Delta Fredericton by Marriott; Sunset View Campground, Nackawic; La Belle Cabane, Kingston; and Creekside RNR, Cocagne. In Newfoundland there's Twillingate & Beyond in Twilllingate.

Getting Started

Atlantic Canada has a rich LGBTIQ+ history. One of Canada's first gay rights organizations, the Gay Alliance for Equality (GAE), formed in 1973. The group's efforts led to the first gay pride parade in 1988. It was actually a pride march protesting a lack of legal protection from discrimination and the threat of homophobic violence. The event would become the annual Halifax Pride.

Accessible Travel

Improvements have been made in Atlantic Canada, but there is still work to be done to make the region barrier free and accessible to all.

Accessible Beaches

Many popular beaches – such as Inverness in Nova Scotia and Parlee in New Brunswick – have accessibility mats. Some also offer floating wheelchairs and beach wheelchairs.

Airport

Airports in Atlantic Canada have accessibility features, from curbside assistance for passengers with a disability and/or reduced mobility to Braille washroom signage. Check airport websites for details.

Accommodation

Urban centers offer more options for accessible places to stay. **Access Advisor** (accessadvisor.weebly.com) has a search tab for accessible accommodations in each of the region's four provinces. **Parks Canada** (parks.canada.ca/voyage-travel/experiences/accessibilite-accessibility/hebergement-accommodation) has information on park accommodations.

WORK UNDER WAY

Nova Scotia's government launched legislation in 2017 aimed at making the province inclusive and barrier-free by 2030. Tourism Nova Scotia and the Tourism Industry Association of Nova Scotia are working to support operators in identifying, preventing and eliminating accessibility barriers.

Transportation

Airlines, VIA Rail Canada, Maritime Bus, Marine Atlantic and Bay Ferries have accessible travel options. Advise representatives of the services you require when you book.

Public Transit

Accessible public transit is available in larger cities – for example, Saint John Transit's low-entry buses can drop to the curb and extend a ramp. However, many small towns and rural communities lack accessible transit.

Iconic Attractions

Peggy's Cove Lighthouse, near Halifax (Nova Scotia), has an accessible deck with views of the iconic lighthouse, waves and rocks. **Cape Spear**, near St John's (Newfoundland), has accessible parking, an accessible visitor centre and wheelchair-accessible bathrooms.

RESOURCES

Parks Canada (parks.canada.ca/voyage-travel/experiences/accessibilite-accessibility/activites-activities#atl) has info on accessibility features at national parks.

AllTrails (alltrails.com/canada/) lists accessible trails in New Brunswick, Nova Scotia, Newfoundland and Labrador and PEI.

Sport Nova Scotia (parasportns.com/accessible-outdoor-recreation-sites) has a list of accessible outdoor-recreation sites.

Spinal Cord Injury PEI (sci-pei.ca/explore-pei) lists everything from accessible restaurants to indoor (and outdoor) recreation sites with accessibility.

Festivals

Many regional festivals have made efforts to improve accessibility. Rated fully accessible by Access Advisor, PEI's Cavendish Beach Music Festival has an accessible parking lot and washrooms, and allows attendees to bring service animals.

Nuts & Bolts

OPENING HOURS

Opening hours vary throughout the year. The following times are typical for high season.

Banks 9:30am to 5pm Monday to Friday.

Cafes 7:30am to 6pm (but highly variable)

Restaurants and pubs 11:30am to 10pm. Some restaurants may open earlier to serve breakfast.

Nightclubs and bars Late afternoon or early evening to between 1am and 3:30am. Some may only be open on certain days, such as Thursday to Saturday.

Shopping malls 10am to 9pm Monday to Friday, 10am to between 6pm and 9pm Saturday, 11am or noon to 5pm or 6pm Sunday.

Shops 9am to 6pm

Weights & Measures

Canada uses the metric system. Imperial units are still used in certain contexts or informally.

Smoking

Smoking is banned throughout Canada in indoor public spaces, public-transit facilities and workplaces (including restaurants, bars and casinos).

GOOD TO KNOW

Time zone
Atlantic Standard Time (GMT -4), Newfoundland Time (GMT -3:30)

Country code
+1

Emergency number
911

Population
2.5 million

Electricity
120V/60Hz

PUBLIC HOLIDAYS

Canada has several public holidays that are celebrated nationwide. On these days some businesses and non-essential services may be closed. Each province or territory may have additional holidays.

New Year's Day
January 1

Good Friday March/April

Easter Monday
Monday after Easter Sunday

Victoria Day Monday before May 25

Canada Day July 1

Labour Day First Monday in September

National Day for Truth and Reconciliation
September 30

Thanksgiving Day
Second Monday in October

Remembrance Day
November 11

Christmas Day
December 25

Boxing Day
December 26

Language

English and French are the official languages of Canada. You'll see both on highway signs, maps, tourist brochures, packaging etc.

You'll find that the French spoken in Canada is essentially the same as in France, and locals will have no problem understanding more formal French.

Basics

Hello. Bonjour. *bon·zhoor*
Goodbye. Au revoir. *o·rer·vwa*
Yes. Oui. *wee*
No. Non. *non*
Please. S'il vous plaît. *seel voo play*
Thank you. Merci. *mair·see*
Excuse me. Excusez-moi. *ek·skew·zay·mwa*
Sorry. Pardon. *par·don*
What's your name? Comment vous appelez-vous? *ko·mon voo·za·play voo*
My name is ... Je m'appelle ... *zher ma·pel ...*
Do you speak English? Parlez-vous anglais? *par·lay·voo ong·glay*
I don't understand. Je ne comprends pas. *zher ner kom·pron pa*

Directions

Where's ...?
Où est ...? *oo ay ...*
What's the address?
Quelle est l'adresse? *kel ay la·dres*
Could you write the address, please? Est-ce que vous pourriez écrire l'adresse, s'il vous plaît? *es·ker voo poo·ryay ay·kreer la·dres seel voo play*
Can you show me (on the map)?
Pouvez-vous m'indiquer (sur la carte)? *poo·vay·voo mun·dee·kay (sewr la kart)*

Signs

Entrée Entrance
Fermé Closed
Ouvert Open
Sortie Exit
Toilettes/WC Toilets

Time

What time is it? Quelle heure est-il? *kel er ay til*
It's (8) o'clock. Il est (huit) heures. *il ay (weet) er*
Half past (10). Il est (dix) heures et demie. *il ay (deez) er ay day·mee*
morning matin. *ma·tun*
afternoon après-midi. *a·pray·mee·dee*
evening soir. *swar*
yesterday hier. *yair*
today aujourd'hui. *o·zhoor·dwee*
tomorrow demain. *der·mun*

Emergencies

Help! Au secours! *o skoor*
Leave me alone! Fichez-moi la paix! *fee·shay·mwa la pay*
I'm ill. Je suis malade. *zher swee ma·lad*
Call ... Appelez... *a·play*
a doctor un médecin. *un mayd·sun*
the police la police. *la po·lees*

Eating & drinking

What would you recommend?
Qu'est-ce que vous conseillez? *kes·ker voo kon·say·yay*
Cheers! Santé! *son·tay*
That was delicious.
C'était délicieux! *say·tay day·lee·syer*

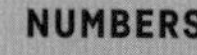

NUMBERS

1 **un** *un*
2 **deux** *der*
3 **trois** *trwa*
4 **quatre** *ka·trer*
5 **cinq** *sungk*
6 **six** *sees*
7 **sept** *set*
8 **huit** *weet*
9 **neuf** *nerf*
10 **dix** *dees*

DISTINCTIVE SOUNDS

Throaty r, silent h, nasal vowels (pronounced as if you're trying to force the sound 'through the nose').

Street Talk

What's up? Quoi de neuf?
Drop it/nevermind! Laisse-tomber!
I can't be bothered/am feeling lazy J'ai la flemme
Enjoy your meal! Bon app!
No way! C'est pas vrai!
Let's go/do it! C'est parti!
Perfect! It's good! Nickel
Oh god! La vache! (literally 'the cow')
Good luck/break a leg Merde
There you go/there you have it Et voilà

And if you want to swear French-style (or express your joy at a gobsmackingly gorgeous view, amazement or disbelief at something... the word is used in many different ways), simply say *Putain!*

DONATIONS TO ENGLISH

Numerous – thanks to the Norman invasion of England in the 11th century, some estimate that three-fifths of everyday English vocabulary arrived via French. You may recognise *café, déjà vu, bon vivant, cliché...*

Language Family

Romance (developed from the Latin spoken by the Romans during their conquest of the 1st century BCE). Close relatives include Italian, Spanish, Portuguese and Romanian.

Must-Know Grammar

French has a formal and informal word for 'you' (*vous* and *tu* respectively); it distinguishes between masculine and feminine forms of words, eg *beau/belle* (beautiful).

False Friends

Warning: many French words look like English words but have a different meaning altogether, eg *menu* is a set lunch, not a menu (which is *carte* in French).

WHO SPEAKS FRENCH?

French is an official language of 29 countries, including France, Belgium, Canada, Democratic Republic of the Congo and Vanuatu.

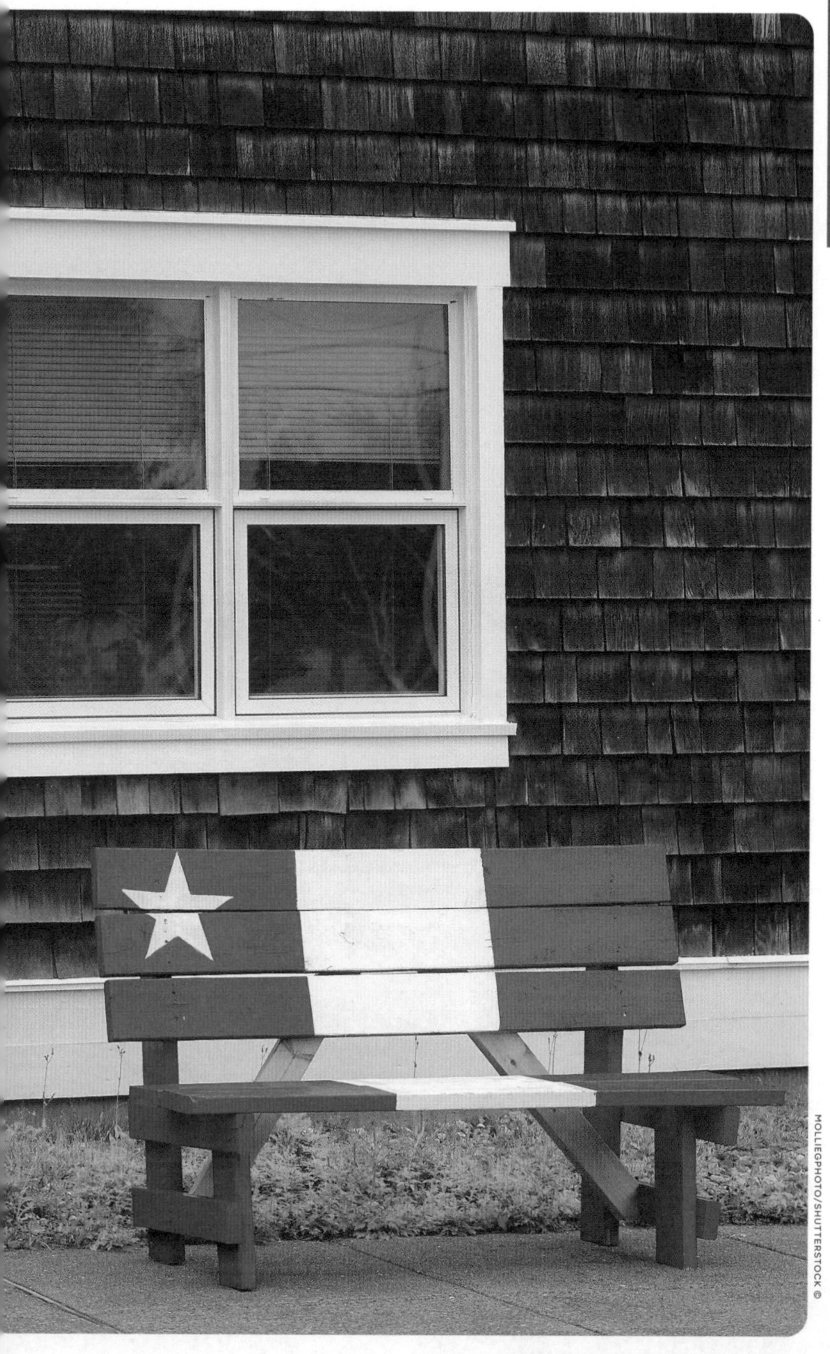
MOLLIEGPHOTO/SHUTTERSTOCK ©

Bench painted with the flag of Acadia (p162)

THE ATLANTIC CANADA

STORYBOOK

Our writers delve deep into different aspects of Atlantic Canadian life

A History of Atlantic Canada in 15 Places

The history of Atlantic Canada is the history of diverse peoples, from the Indigenous communities who have lived here for centuries to those who came afterwards.

Carolyn B. Heller

p230

Atlantic Canada's Diverse Cultures

From its original Indigenous inhabitants to the varied populations that arrived over the centuries, Atlantic Canada has developed a unique mix of cultures that continues to diversify today.

Carolyn B. Heller

p234

Wool Report

A renewed love for handmade mittens (and socks and hats) is helping to keep knitting culture alive.

Jennifer Bain

p236

Atlantic Canada's Music Scene

With influences from varied cultures, music across the Atlantic provinces can provide a toe-tapping, hand-clapping backdrop to your travels.

Carolyn B. Heller

p240

Wild Kingdom

How to be a friend to wildlife when birding, whale watching and driving in Atlantic Canada.

Jennifer Bain

p244

Atlantic Canada's Gallery Scene

Experience vibrant spaces where art communicates culture, history and contemporary expression.

Cathy Donaldson

p247

Whale-watching, Bay of Fundy (p122)

A HISTORY OF ATLANTIC CANADA IN 15 PLACES

The history of Atlantic Canada is the history of diverse peoples, from the Indigenous communities who have lived here for centuries to the Norse, English, Acadian, Irish, Black and other settlers who came afterwards – some who sought to conquer, others seeking their own form of freedom on these 'New World' shores. By Carolyn B. Heller

THE REGION'S EARLIEST Indigenous peoples include the Mi'kmaq and Maliseet, whose territories primarily encompassed what are now the Maritime provinces, and the Beothuk, who are considered Newfoundland's First Peoples. Europeans began arriving around 1000, when Viking seafarers came ashore in Newfoundland, and colonists from Spain, France and Britain turned up over the ensuing centuries. While some established peaceful relations with the Indigenous peoples whose lands they were occupying, far more brought disease, displacement and strife.

Conflict between the French and British dominated the 1700s and 1800s across much of North America, including the Atlantic region. Beginning in 1755, the British ordered the mass deportation of the region's French-Acadian people. The trauma of this Grand Dérangement left its scars, even though many Acadians were eventually able to return, and their descendants still influence the region's language and culture.

In 1864 Prince Edward Island hosted the Charlottetown Conference to discuss the potential union of Britain's North American colonies. That conference eventually led to the Canadian Confederation, established in 1867 with four provinces: Nova Scotia, New Brunswick, Québec and Ontario. PEI joined the country in 1873 as its seventh province (following Manitoba, the Northwest Territories and British Columbia). Newfoundland and Labrador did not join the confederation until 1949.

1. PEI's Fossil Beaches

ANCIENT REPTILES, FOSSILIZED TREES

Before humans walked the Atlantic shores, geologic changes shaped the region's landscape, creating the red cliffs, rocky coasts and lands we see today. On PEI, geologist Laura MacNeil takes visitors back to prehuman times on 90-minute **Prehistoric Island Tours**, narrated beach walks through one of the island's most significant fossil sites. She'll show you how to identify different fossils and take you through PEI's geological evolution with straightforward explanations that appeal to both kids and adults. Her witty visual aids, from fossilized footprints to images of creatures such as *Dimetrodon borealis* (a reptile that predated the dinosaurs), help bring this history to life.

Read more about the tours on page 147

2. Beothuk Interpretation Centre

NEWFOUNDLAND'S FIRST PEOPLES

Newfoundland's **Beothuk Interpretation Centre** tells you about the region's earliest Indigenous peoples through exhibits exploring both archaeological information and Beothuk culture. Archaeological excavations revealed a large Beothuk village dating to 1650–1720 in the Boyd's Cove area, where the interpretation center is now located, and provided details about Beothuk daily life, diet, tools and spirituality. The exhibits also explain how European settlers pushed these Indigenous hunting and fishing people inland and destroyed their traditional culture. You can follow a walking trail to the archeological site and to a bronze statue, *The Spirit of the Beothuk*, honoring the memory of the Beothuk people.

Read more about the Beothul history on page 37

3. Metepenagiag Heritage Park

MI'KMAW CULTURE AND HERITAGE

At **Metepenagiag Heritage Park** on the Metepenagiag (Red Bank) First Nation in New Brunswick, you can learn about the Mi'kmaq people who have lived on these lands for more than 3000 years. The Taste of Metepenagiag 'Ookdotaan' experience gives you the chance to hear Metepenagiag stories as you walk local trails and join in a meal of fish or game with wild rice and hot bannock (plus fiddlehead greens if you're lucky enough to be there at the right time). Another option? Book a glamping-style tipi retreat where you can sleep in a tipi after stories and activities around the campfire.

Read more about the park on page 136

4. L'Anse aux Meadows National Historic Site

WHEN THE VIKINGS ARRIVED

Located at Newfoundland's northeastern tip, this Unesco World Heritage Site is the only authenticated Viking site in North America (though strictly speaking the term 'Viking' should really just be used for men when they were raiding), and it's the earliest evidence of Europeans on this continent. At **L'Anse aux Meadows National Historic Site**, costumed interpreters re-enact life in the encampment that Norse explorers established after arriving from Greenland more than 1000 years ago. Archaeological tours, storytelling events and other experiences help you understand this history and glimpse life here during that long-ago era.

Read more about L'Anse aux Meadows on page 204

L'Anse aux Meadows National Historic Site (p204)

5. Red Bay National Historic Site

THE HISTORY OF BASQUE WHALING

Whalers from the Basque region of northeastern Spain and southwestern France arrived in Labrador around 1530, searching for whale oil. They hunted bowhead and right whales and set up stations to process their oils, which they sold to European markets as lamp fuel and a lubricant. The largest of these stations, at Red Bay's harbor, is now a National Historic Site and Unesco World Heritage Site where you can learn more about these early settlements, and how archeologists identified the site from distinctive red 'pebbles' along the coast that turned out to be terracotta-tile ballast from Basque ships.

Read more about Red Bay on page 209

6. Port-Royal National Historic Site

CANADA'S FIRST PERMANENT EUROPEAN SETTLEMENT

Across the river from the Nova Scotia community of Annapolis Royal, French colonist Samuel de Champlain built **Port-Royal**, a small fortification, in 1605. It was the first permanent settlement in what would become Canada. As you tour the reconstructed community, you can talk with costumed interpreters about life for these French colonists and their relationship with the Mi'qmaq people. In nearby Annapolis Royal, you can visit **Fort Anne National Historic Site**, where 70 Scottish settlers built the first fortifications in 1629. Nova Scotia's name, flag and coat of arms evolved from this short-lived Scottish settlement.

Read more about Port-Royal on page 77

7. Fortress of Louisbourg

WHERE ENGLAND AND FRANCE FOUGHT FOR DOMINANCE

Founded by France in 1713, the **Fortress of Louisbourg** was a strategic site in the seesaw battle between the British and French for control over the lucrative cod fishery and the entrance to the Gulf of St Lawrence. Today, the fort's location east of Sydney, Nova Scotia, is North America's largest historical-reconstruction site, where you can chat with costumed interpreters who go about their day as they might have done when fishing, naval and merchant ships crowded the harbor, and sailors, soldiers and civilians settled the site. You can even spend the night in the fortress's guardhouse or prison.

Read more about the Fortress of Louisbourg on page 102

8. Grand-Pré National Historic Site

ACADIAN SETTLEMENT AND THE GREAT EXPULSION

Nova Scotia's **Grand-Pré National Historic Site** recounts the history of early French settlement and Le Grand Dérangement (Great Expulsion), when the British, beginning in 1755, deported 14,000 Acadians from their homes across the region after they refused to sign oaths of allegiance to the British crown. Many Acadians returned to France, while others traveled to the Louisiana territory, where their descendants became the Cajuns of the American South. Some were eventually able to return to settlements across the Maritime provinces, where their families remain today. Tours of the site help illuminate this history.

Read more about Grand-Pré on page 81

9. Farmers Bank of Rustico

BUILDING ACADIAN SELF-SUFFICIENCY

In the 1760s the first Acadians settled in PEI's Rustico area. Dating to 1772, log-built **Doucet House** is the oldest house on the island, furnished as it would have been during the early days of Acadian settlement. Led by Reverend Georges-Antoine Belcourt, local Acadian families raised nearly $4000 to launch Canada's first 'people's bank,' the **Farmers Bank of Rustico**. Though it operated for only 30 years (1864 to 1894), the Farmers Bank provided small loans – and self-sufficiency – to these Acadian farmers. Both the bank and nearby Doucet House are now historic sites that can tell you more about this heritage.

Read more about these historic sites on page 149

10. Black Loyalist Heritage Centre

BLACK SETTLERS' SEARCH FOR FREEDOM

Following the American Revolution in the late 1700s, more than 10,000 settlers loyal to the British Crown came to Nova Scotia's southern shores. Among them were hundreds of Black Loyalists, freed or escaped from enslavement. Though the British had offered them refuge and land, these Black settlers faced racism and violence, and many chose to leave again, migrating to the new settlement of Freetown in Sierra Leone. Writer Lawrence Hill immortalized this migration in his novel *The Book of Negroes*. You can learn more about this heritage at the **Black Loyalist Heritage Centre** in Birchtown.

Read more about the center on page 71

11. Beaubears Island

ACADIAN REFUGE, SHIPBUILDING HERITAGE

Located in New Brunswick's Miramichi River, Beaubears Island illustrates two different historical periods. At the **Boishébert National Historic Site** you can learn how the island became a refuge for Acadians fleeing the Great Expulsion in 1755; the site takes its name from Charles Deschamps de Boishébert, a French Canadian officer who brought several groups of Acadians to the Miramichi area. The **Beaubears Island Shipbuilding National Historic Site** takes you to the 1850s, the heyday of shipbuilding in the Miramichi region. You can reach the island – and both sites – by boat from the Beaubears Island Interpretive Centre in Miramichi.

Read more about Beaubears Island on page 232

12. Middle Island Irish Historical Park

AFTER FAMINE, ISLAND QUARANTINE

In the 19th century, the failure of Ireland's potato crop triggered widespread famine and a wave of migration to North America. For some Irish immigrants, their first stop in the 'New World' was an isolated island in New Brunswick's Miramichi River. The *Looshtauk*, bound for Québec with 462 passengers on board, docked on Middle Island in 1847 after typhus and scarlet

Province House National Historic Site (p142), Charlottetown

fever swept through the ship; 146 people perished on board, and another 96 died on the island. The New Brunswick government subsequently quarantined other new arrivals here, on the isle that now marks these tragedies at the **Middle Island Irish Historical Park**.

Read more about Middle Island on page 135

13. Province House National Historic Site

BIRTHPLACE OF CANADIAN CONFEDERATION

In 1864, Charlottetown's Province House was the setting for a meeting to discuss the possible union of Britain's North American colonies. This Charlottetown Conference laid the foundation for what became the country of Canada, established in 1867 with four provinces: Nova Scotia, New Brunswick, Québec and Ontario. While **Province House National Historic Site**, which normally recounts Charlottetown's role in Canadian Confederation, undergoes a multiyear renovation, you can visit the **Confederation Chamber replica** inside the Confederation Centre of the Arts. Around a replica of the conference table, you can talk with interpreters about the issues Canada's creation raised, especially for Indigenous communities.

Read more about Province House on page 142

14. International Fox Museum

HOW PEI GOT FOXY

The most unusual attraction in Summerside, PEI, may be the **International Fox Museum**. The small, quirky institution documents how, in the early 1900s, the island became the first place to successfully raise foxes in captivity. Encompassing stories of fox-breeding entrepreneurs, how they became known for the distinctive silver black fox with its highly prized fur, and their effect on the island economy, the museum's multimedia exhibits detail the industry's rise and fall, from its early-20th-century peak, when fur became increasingly fashionable, through WWII's closure of European markets, to the mid-20th century, when attitudes toward fur garments began to change.

Read more about the fox museum on page 159

15. Canadian Museum of Immigration at Pier 21

THE GATEWAY TO CANADA

Often compared to New York's Ellis Island, where migrants arrived in the United States, Halifax's Pier 21 was the first point of entry for 1.5 million immigrants to Canada between 1928 and 1971. This waterfront site is now the **Canadian Museum of Immigration at Pier 21**, which shares many of these settlers' stories through oral histories, photographs and a variety of artifacts, many of which were donated by the people who passed through this immigration station themselves. In addition to permanent exhibits about 20th-century arrivals, temporary exhibitions highlight more contemporary issues related to refugees, resettlement and immigration.

For more on the museum, see page 59

ATLANTIC CANADA'S DIVERSE CULTURES

Indigenous, Black and European peoples all contribute to Atlantic Canada's diversity. By Carolyn B. Heller

MUCH OF ATLANTIC Canada, including present-day Nova Scotia, New Brunswick, Prince Edward Island and parts of Newfoundland, lies on the traditional territory of the Mi'kmaq people. Two other Indigenous groups – the Inuit and the Innu – make their homes in Labrador.

Before European colonizers arrived, the Mi'kmaq migrated between the coasts, where they fished and harvested shellfish, and the inland regions, hunting and harvesting resources from the land. The Inuit and Innu were migratory people as well. Today, most live in permanent communities, incorporating both traditional practices and modern culture into their daily lives.

The first Black person known to have arrived in Canada was Mathieu Da Costa, who came to Nova Scotia in the early 1600s as an interpreter for the French colonizers Samuel de Champlain and Pierre Du Gua De Monts. With the advent of the American Revolution in the mid-1700s, the British government offered Blacks from the United States land and freedom if they chose to settle in the emerging colony of Canada. While the British didn't

Traditionally dressed Mi'kmaw person

necessarily live up to these promises, these Black Loyalists, as they were known, established settlements in Atlantic Canada, particularly across southern Nova Scotia. Many of these Black settlers' lives were recorded in a ledger known as The Book of Negroes, which inspired the 2007 novel of the same name by Canadian author Lawrence Hill, and the subsequent movie.

Halifax also had a significant Black population in that city's east end. Established in the 1840s, the community known as Africville thrived for more than 150 years. Sadly, the Halifax government relocated the residents and destroyed their homes in a misguided 'urban renewal' movement in the 1960s.

THERE ARE NUMEROUS WAYS TO LEARN MORE ABOUT ATLANTIC CANADA'S DIVERSE CULTURES.

As you explore Atlantic Canada, you'll see red, white and blue Acadian flags flying from many homes, and gold Acadian stars decorating houses and fenceposts. These French-speaking settlers began establishing communities throughout Atlantic Canada in the 1600s. Though the British deported most of Canada's Acadians in the 1750s, either to Louisiana (where they established the region's Cajun communities) or to France, in a purge known as Le Grand Derangement (The Great Expulsion), some were able to return. Acadian culture continues to influence the Atlantic provinces in language, music, cultural festivals and foods, such as *fricot* (a chicken stew), meat pies and *rapûre* (a potato casserole), which you'll find across the region and in parts of Québec.

Scandinavian explorers came to what is now Canada as early as the year 1000, establishing settlements in Newfoundland, though few of these early colonists stayed long-term. Spaniards, Italians, French and other Europeans followed, some of whom attempted to co-exist peacefully with the region's Indigenous people, while many others did not. New waves of migrants arrived in the 1800s and 1900s, including Irish and Scottish settlers, who brought traditions such as *ceilidh* (lively music and dance parties) that continue around the region today.

There are numerous ways to learn more about Atlantic Canada's diverse cultures.

Sites such as Nova Scotia's Black Loyalist Heritage Centre and Birchtown Historic Site (p71) in Birchtown and the Africville Museum (p61) in Halifax illuminate the region's Black heritage.

Acadian culture is showcased at such museums as PEI's Acadian Museum (p162) and Farmers Bank of Rustico (p149), the Village Historique Acadien de la Nouvelle Ecosse (p73) and Musée des Acadiens des Pubnicos (p73) in Nova Scotia, the Acadian Museum in Moncton (p116) and the Village Historique Acadien (p133) on New Brunswick's Acadian Peninsula, where you can also follow the 750km Acadian Coastal Drive.

In Halifax, Pier 21 was the gateway to Canada for more than a million immigrants in the 20th century. Visit the Canadian Museum of Immigration at Pier 21 (p59) to hear some of their stories.

Acadian flag lighthouse, Chéticamp (p99)

LEFT: PAUL MCKINNON/SHUTTERSTOCK ©; FAR LEFT: COLSTRAVEL/ALAMY STOCK PHOTO ©

CINDY MILLER HOPKINS/DANITA DELIMONT/ALAMY STOCK PHOTO ©

WOOL REPORT

A renewed love for handmade mittens (and socks and hats) is helping to keep knitting culture alive. By Jennifer Bain

BUNDLES OF RAW sheep's wool, still matted with dirt, twigs and hay, are neatly piled in a rural New Brunswick mill waiting to be transformed into soft knitting yarn. The wool will be fed through machines to be washed, dried, dusted, sorted, blended, carded and spun before it's hand-twisted into butterfly skeins. Most of it will be dyed colors called hunter orange, magenta, mulberry, evergreen, sea foam, brown heather, sheep's gray and rag.

Knitting culture is enjoying a resurgence in Atlantic Canada, and unassuming Briggs & Little Woolen Mills, in York Mills, New Brunswick, is the undisputed epicentre of East Coast knitting. Yarn is shipped to hundreds of retail locations across the country, where people buy it and lovingly transform it into mittens, socks and hats. Some of these creations, in turn, find their way to shops and then into the hands of locals and visitors.

Like baking sourdough bread, knitting is a hobby many people turned to during the pandemic when they were isolating at home. And then came January 2021, and the image of Vermont senator Bernie Sanders watching President Joe Biden's inauguration while wearing a face mask and oversized, patterned mittens. The photo went viral and sparked an internet meme and mitten craze.

A Knitting Revival

In Canada, much credit for the renewed interest in knitting is lavished on Newfoundlanders Christine LeGrow, of Spindrift Handknits, and Shirley A. Scott, authors of *Saltwater Mittens from the Island of Newfoundland: More than 20 Heritage Designs to Knit*. The 2018 book took off during the pandemic and launched a series that so far also includes *Saltwater Classics*, *Saltwater Gifts* and *Saltwater Socks*. (The word 'saltwater' in the titles is a nod to all those who work on – or by – the North Atlantic Ocean.) 'Good warm clothing has always been an essential barrier between us and extinction,' wrote the long-time friends, who studied and collected mittens for decades before recreating heritage patterns for today's knitters.

'Warm woollen mittens were the worker's friend, and the warmer the better,' they explain in their book. 'To hammer a nail, gut a fish, draw and haul water. To split birch for the stove. To hang clothes on a line. To shoot a seabird or snare a rabbit for the pot. Social life, too, required the finest mittens and gloves. For church, for ceremony, and for courting. For much of the year in our quirky climate of freeze, thaw, blow, and drizzle, good mittens made all tasks easier. This continues today. Our winter ensembles are serious business.'

LeGrow and Scott swear by Briggs & Little products because they resemble the homespun yarn used in Newfoundland for centuries and because they come in so many fabulous colors that keep spirits up during dreary weather. The women also admire the fact that the hard-working and hard-wearing yarn is affordable. Wool may be itchy, but it's touted as a planet-friendly and animal-friendly natural fiber. Since it does attract moths and mice, it should be stored in airtight containers and maybe even treated with a eucalyptus-scented wool wash.

Briggs & Little officially counts its start date as 1916, but it existed under two other names dating back to 1857. On a factory tour, Leah Little said the Saltwater books helped the family business reach beyond the knitting world into the fiber world – where people weave, felt, punch, hook, spin and crochet – and kept them so busy during the pandemic they had to temporarily stop accepting new customers.

'You don't have to be a grandmother to knit,' Little stressed. 'Most people that create are versatile in many different mediums.'

Making something well – even a humble mitten – has long been a badge of honor. For years, knitwear just circulated within families. But now mittens, socks and hats are popular and affordable souvenirs. Even so, they don't command the prices they deserve.

'The knitters have gotten a rotten deal over the years,' LeGrow mused in a coffeeshop in St John's, Newfoundland. 'They don't realize their own value.' Woolen mittens typically fetch $50 (less if they're acrylic), but they would cost at least $150 if you paid minimum wage for the time that went into making them.

Rescuing the Trigger Mitt

For their books, LeGrow and Scott came up with colorful names for mittens. Fogo Island Nine Patch Classic Mittens speak to the wild and barren island that has captured international attention in recent years. Blowin' a Gale Trigger Mitts reference the province's legendary winds and choppy seas. Mummers Classic Mitts are a nod to the ancient custom still practiced in the province of putting on a disguise in December and wandering to neighboring homes to swap a song and dance for food and drink.

The authors have also been credited with rescuing trigger mitts from oblivion. A combination mitten-glove, with a separate thumb and index finger, and a 'hand' for the other three fingers, trigger mitts were first favored by hunters, who needed their thumbs and index fingers free but wanted to keep their hand as warm as possible. The mitts were used for hunting, fishing, hanging laundry and berry picking, but you don't need to do any of those things now to just love and wear them.

A downtown St John's shop called NONIA (the Newfoundland Outport Nursing and Industrial Association) has long been the go-to spot to buy trigger mitts, calling them iconic Newfoundland and Labrador outdoor gear. NONIA was founded in 1920 and incorporated as a nonprofit business in 1924 to help outport communities access health services by selling hand-knitted garments to pay for public-health nurses. The government took over that task, but NONIA still employs about 175 knitters and weavers to make sweaters, socks, hats and mitts as well as woven items.

Woollen socks

DON JOHNSTON_PE/ALAMY STOCK PHOTO ©

Valuing Mittens as Folk Art

The Saltwater authors believe the lack of public recognition of knitting as a true folk art can be blamed, in part, on the fact that mittens tend to be 'worn to shreds' and therefore couldn't be donated to museums as quilts and hooked rugs have been.

There aren't any mitten museums in Canada, but the DoubleTree by Hilton St John's Harbourview does have a subtle mitten theme, with a mitten installation in its lobby and framed photos of mittens in some of its rooms.

You don't have to search for mittens in Newfoundland – they're in all the souvenir shops, but they also turn up for sale in gas stations, restaurants, craft shops, farmers markets and thrift shops. On a smaller scale, they're sold across Atlantic Canada, along with hats, socks, sweaters and scarves.

DARRYL BROOKS/ALAMY STOCK PHOTO ©

Cape Breton Centre for Craft & Design

MAKING SOMETHING WELL – EVEN A HUMBLE MITTEN – HAS LONG BEEN A BADGE OF HONOR.

In Sydney, Nova Scotia, the Cape Breton Curiosity Shop sells colorful striped woolen socks hand-knitted in Chéticamp, and sometimes has a basket full of mittens knitted by a local woman for the scores of cruise-ship passengers who show up unprepared for the weather. A block away, the Cape Breton Centre for Craft & Design has a gallery-shop that showcases the work of 100-plus artists. At any time, the work of 10 knitters might be for sale.

In Bonavista, Newfoundland, the Matthew Legacy (a museum that houses a replica of the ship John Cabot sailed to the New World in 1497) has a gift shop filled with woolen mittens, some featuring puffins and mummers. Others, with hearts and swirls, are in a custom Briggs & Little color called bergy blue that's only sold to the Cast On! Cast Off! wool shop in Triton (which has a fun bakeapple-jam color and another evocatively named RDF – local shorthand for rain, drizzle and fog).

Not to be left out, Prince Edward Island punches above its weight on the fiber-artist front. Linda Noble of Belfast Mini Mills started the PEI Fibre Trail years ago and has a pamphlet that now features 20 artisans and producers of local fibers and yarns.

Just down the road, Kim Doherty-Smith runs Fleece & Harmony on her sheep farm. The mill specializes in untreated or 'rustic' yarns that are hand-dyed. Doherty-Smith is also chair of the PEI Fibre Festival. She traces the current knitting boom to 2010, when she distinctly remembers people embracing 'sustainable everything' and starting to put how-to-knit videos on YouTube to reach a younger generation. Fleece & Harmony's YouTube channel now has more than 13,000 subscribers.

A New Generation of Knitters

Knitting seems to have skipped a generation, so many of today's older knitters learned from their grandmothers, while the younger ones learned from YouTube. But knitting remains a compelling pastime where you can make something that you can actually wear, and that something can be as complicated as a sweater or as simple as mittens.

On top of all that, people have now taken to praising the mental-health benefits of knitting. It's relaxing. It keeps you sharp because math and manual dexterity are involved. Doherty-Smith said it's definitely a stress reliever. 'You're doing something with your hands and your mind and it's creative – so it checks all the boxes.'

Mi'kmaw dancer at Mawio'mi Powwow, Halifax

SHAUNL/GETTY IMAGES ©

ATLANTIC CANADA'S MUSIC SCENE

With influences from varied cultures, music across the Atlantic provinces can provide a toe-tapping, hand-clapping backdrop to your travels. By Carolyn B. Heller

MUSIC IN ATLANTIC Canada draws from Indigenous traditions, from the many immigrant groups who have settled here and from all sorts of contemporary inspirations. As you travel the Atlantic provinces, you can hear local tunes in pubs and at powwows, at *ceilidhs* and in concert halls, and everywhere in between. The region has a robust calendar of festivals celebrating classic Celtic music, lively Acadian melodies, folk, jazz and more, and showcasing performers from across the region and from further afield. But the signature music experience here may be the *ceilidh* (kitchen party), which can be held in a bar, in a theater or in an actual kitchen – it's a spirited mix of song, dance, storytelling and foot stomping that may have you singing or humming long after you've returned home.

Indigenous Music

Drumming, singing and dancing have long been part of Indigenous culture across the Atlantic region, which you can still experience at powwows and other cultural celebrations. Respectful visitors are welcome at these events, including the annual **Lennox Island Mawi'omi** on PEI; the **Eskasoni Mawio'mi Powwow**, which takes place in the Eskasoni First Nation, Cape Breton Island; the **Mawita'jik Powwow** in Dartmouth, Nova Scotia; and the **Bay St George Powwow** in western Newfoundland.

Cape Breton's Celtic Music

When a place boasts the world's largest fiddle – the 18m landmark in Sydney, Nova Scotia – you know that music must be an important part of its culture. Claiming more fiddlers per capita than anywhere else on the globe, Cape Breton Island is the region's hub for lively fiddle-dominated Celtic music, which originated with the Gaelic-speaking immigrants from Scotland and Ireland who settled here. To get acquainted with this musical tradition, visit the **Celtic Music Interpretive Centre**, where you can learn more about this musical heritage and enjoy regular concerts.

Fiddlers including **Natalie MacMaster** and **Ashley MacIsaac** may have taken this music beyond Cape Breton, but the Celtic musical tradition carries on in the pubs, festivals and *ceilidhs* that are a regular part of local life. The June **KitchenFest!** (Féis a' Chidsin) is an island-wide kitchen party, and with performers from the region and around the world, the autumn **Celtic Colours International Festival** includes dozens of concerts and other

events that celebrate Celtic music, dance and good cheer.

Acadian Music Past & Present

Just as the Scottish and Irish brought their musical culture to Atlantic Canada, so, too, did the Acadians who've made their homes across the region. With its spirited fiddling and dynamic dancing, Acadian music has similarities to Celtic traditions, though the lyrics, of course, are in French or in the Acadian patois known as *chiac*.

Édith Butler was one of the first Acadian musicians to popularize Acadian music beyond its Maritime roots. Born in New Brunswick in 1942, she began performing on CBC-TV's *Singalong Jubilee* in the early 1960s, and her appearances brought Acadian songs to a nationwide audience. Often called the 'Godmother of Acadian music,' Butler went on to release 27 albums over her decades-long career.

Other influential Acadian musical groups include **Barachois** from Prince Edward Island, which performed in the 1990s and early 2000s, and **1755**, named for the year of the Grand Dérangement (the British-mandated expulsion of the Acadians from the Maritime region). The latter group was established in Moncton in 1975. Its members continued their careers in other successful musical ventures after the group officially disbanded, although they have continued to reunite for periodic performances.

Present-day Acadian musicians no longer stick solely to traditional styles. There are Acadian hip hoppers, rockers, electronic musicians and more. One place to hear a variety of contemporary Acadian performers is at the **Acadie Rock Festival**, held each summer in Moncton.

For lovers of Acadian tunes, the biggest event on Atlantic Canada's Francophone music calendar is the annual **Festival Acadien** (August), which is two weeks of fiddling, crooning and more in Caraquet on New Brunswick's Acadian coast. You'll also find plenty of Acadian performers at Nova Scotia's **Festival acadien de Clare** (July/August), considered the oldest Acadian festival in the world, and at the **Festival de la Mi-Carême** (March). On PEI, you can hear Acadian musicians perform on summer weekends at the **Village musical acadien**.

Atlantic Music Legends

Multiple Grammy and Juno award-winner **Sarah McLachlan** was born in Halifax in 1968, though these days she's more likely to be touring internationally or based in Vancouver, where she founded the Sarah McLachlan School of Music.

Descended from Black Loyalists who settled in Nova Scotia, **Portia White** (1911–1968) grew up singing in her church choir and eventually became a contralto classical vocalist – she's considered the first Black Canadian to become internationally recognized for her performing talent.

Most popular in the 1950s, Nova Scotia-born country legend **Hank Snow** (1914–1999) recorded more than 140 albums over his lengthy career. Another Nova Scotian, **Anne Murray**, who was born in 1945, became the first Canadian female solo singer to reach No 1 on the US charts. Though she retired from performing in 2008, her pop, country and adult contemporary albums have sold more than 55 million copies.

Sarah McLachlan

LEFT: ART BABYCH/SHUTTERSTOCK ©; RIGHT: DAVE G. HOUSER/ALAMY STOCK PHOTO ©

Known for country classics such as 'Bud the Spud' and 'The Hockey Song,' Canadian country icon **'Stompin' Tom' Connors** (1936–2013) grew up in Skinners Pond, PEI, where the Stompin' Tom Centre now includes a small museum about his life. The center hosts spirited free midday concerts in summer, along with other music events.

His family's Maritime roots had a deep influence on folk singer-songwriter **Stan Rogers** (1949–1983). Though he died in an airplane fire when he was only 33, his legacy lives on in the **Stan Rogers Folk Festival**, held every summer in Canso, Nova Scotia.

Acadian folk musician, Pays de la Sagouine (p115)

WITH ITS SPIRITED FIDDLING AND DYNAMIC DANCING, ACADIAN MUSIC HAS SIMILARITIES TO CELTIC TRADITIONS.

Other Music Events

For a sampling of local and regional music, see what's on the schedule at PEI's annual **Festival of Small Halls** (June), with performances at pubs, churches and other venues across the island. Both during this festival and throughout the year, **Trailside Music Hall** in Charlottetown's Arts Hotel is a popular destination for local musicians, as is the **Under the Spire music series**, held in the summer in the 1902 St Mary's Church near Kensington. Also on PEI, the **Cavendish Beach Music Festival** (July) is Atlantic Canada's largest outdoor concert.

Since the 1980s, folk-music fans have made the **Lunenburg Folk Harbour Festival** (August) part of their summer itineraries in Nova Scotia, while jazz lovers head for the annual **Halifax Jazz Festival** (July). There are more music fests in New Brunswick, including the **Miramichi Rock n' Roll Festival** (July/August), the **Miramichi Folksong Festival** (August) and Fredericton's **Harvest Music Festival** (September).

Newfoundland's annual **George Street Festival** (July/August) takes over George St in St John's, transforming it into an outdoor concert venue. Also in St John's, the **Newfoundland and Labrador Folk Festival** (July) features both traditional and up-and-coming folk musicians.

Pubs & More

In Halifax, Nova Scotia, hear local singer-songwriters at **The Carlton**, listen to the blues at **Bearly's**, join the party at **Lower Deck Downtown** or take in a concert at the Marquee Ballroom.

Newfoundland has a lively music scene, especially in St John's. You'll find regular performances in pubs around town, including **Shamrock City Pub**, **Broderick's on George**, **Green Sleeves Pub & Eatery**, the **Ship Pub & Kitchen** and **O'Reilly's Irish Newfoundland Pub**, among others.

For local music in Charlottetown, PEI, head for **Baba's Lounge**, the **Olde Dublin Pub**, **Hunter's Ale House** or **The Local Pub & Oyster Bar**. There's live music some evenings at **Founders Food Hall** near the waterfront, too.

In New Brunswick, Moncton's pubs hosting local bands include the **Old Triangle Irish Alehouse**, the **Tide & Boar Gastropub** and **St James' Gate**.

Tune in at Home

MCBC (the Canadian Broadcasting Corporation; cbc.ca) has compiled a lengthy set of music playlists highlighting performers from across the country. It has created specific 'Sounds of...' playlists for Nova Scotia, New Brunswick, PEI, and Newfoundland and Labrador, each with a mix of traditional and contemporary music. Several other playlists highlight Indigenous musicians. Celtic music, francophone singers and many other collections can introduce you to Canadian performers before your trip and remind you of the tunes you heard on your travels.

Puffins

JACQUESVANDINTEREN/GETTY IMAGES ©

WILD KINGDOM

How to be a friend to wildlife when birding, whale watching and driving in Atlantic Canada. By Jennifer Bain

TRAVELERS TO ATLANTIC Canada often have their hearts set on seeing the 'clowns of the sea' and the 'singers of the sea' – puffins and humpback whales. With viewing this glorious wildlife, though, comes responsibility. For instance, tour boats must keep a certain distance from whales.

There are traveler responsibilities even away from wildlife tours. Signs across Atlantic Canada warn motorists to slow down and watch for moose. If hit, these massive and majestic beasts can crash through windshields and flip onto vehicle roofs, causing injury and death for all concerned. Most accidents happen between dusk and dawn.

Seeing Puffins

Puffins pop up across Atlantic Canada, but the largest colony in North America is found at the Witless Bay Ecological Reserve, just south of St John's in Newfoundland. More than 260,000 breeding pairs return to these islands each year to nest and then prepare their offspring to follow the moon and stars to the North Atlantic Ocean.

How to explain the allure of the puffin, beloved provincial bird of Newfoundland and Labrador? Perhaps it's the comical way they fly just above the sea, like winged cannonballs shooting through the air. Or maybe it's that those orange, yellow and blue-black striped beaks, outrageous orange feet and clown-like faces really do scream circus.

Atlantic puffins spend most of their lives at sea, but between May and September these small creatures with big personalities come to isolated rocky islands and grassy sea cliffs to establish burrows. Puffins typically mate for life and return to the same spot each year to breed.

Tour operators transport people by giant catamarans, Zodiacs and other vessels to see (but not step on) the protected islands. Tours are carefully regulated and respectful of the birds they've come to see.

Puffins aren't endangered, but Nature Conservancy Canada notes that populations declined drastically in the early 1900s, when puffins were hunted for meat, feathers and eggs. They still face threats from climate change, warming oceans and changes to the number and distribution of the fish they eat.

Visitors gravitate to boat tours that combine puffins, seabirds, whales and – early in the season – icebergs. These tours happen across Newfoundland and St Pierre and Miquelon, and, to a lesser degree, in Nova Scotia (Cape Breton and Peggy's Cove)

and New Brunswick (Machias Seal Island and Grand Manan Island). Prince Edward Island has endangered piping plovers but alas no puffins.

The Newfoundland town of Elliston offers the closest views of puffins from land in North America when several thousand nesting pairs take over the end of a rocky outcrop. Puffins prefer solitude but seem to tolerate the camera-toting crowds at the Elliston site. It's free to visit, but donations are gratefully accepted.

The Puffin & Petrel Patrol

Some pufflings (puffin chicks) get confused by light pollution. They mistakenly fly or swim to shore at night, drawn by the artificial lights in homes and businesses, and awkwardly waddle around until they're hit by motorists or killed by pets and predators.

That's where the Puffin and Petrel Patrol steps in.

Volunteers with the Canadian Parks and Wilderness Society have rescued and released thousands of Atlantic puffin and Leach's storm-petrel chicks (though the latter bird garners far less attention). The program started in 2004 when two Germans, Juergen and Elsie Schau, were visiting their holiday home, spotted dead pufflings along the road and took grassroots action.

Now volunteers sign up to search the communities near Witless Bay at night (usually in August) for pufflings, capture them with butterfly nets, transfer them to pet carriers and bring them to a seaside meeting spot. The birds are released to great fanfare the next day, either from a beach or from one of the lucky sightseeing boats.

To manage expectations, it should be said that these birds are too young to have colorful beaks and feet and so they look a little drab. It's also illegal under the Canadian Wildlife Act to handle migratory seabirds without a permit, so don't mount rescues if you're not part of the patrol.

Saving young bird lives is the patrol's priority, but it also aims to teach people about light pollution and encourage everyone to dim their lights.

Whale Watching

Whales can be seen in all four Atlantic provinces, especially in the Bay of Fundy and all around Newfoundland. There are two dozen species in these waters, but the main ones are humpback, fin, minke, orca and Atlantic right whales. Porpoises, the occasional beluga, harbour seals and gray seals (aka horseheads) round things out.

Under federal rules, whale-watching boats must stay at least 100m away from most whales, dolphins and porpoises, since approaching them too quickly, coming too close or making too much noise can disturb, stress and harm them.

Binoculars are a responsible whale-watcher's friend. Move away if a whale approaches. Never feed them, or swim, dive or interact with them. Tour boats aren't allowed to encircle whales, entice them to move, park boats in their path or approach when they're resting. Reputable captains communicate with each other to make sure viewings are staggered.

'Interactions are entirely up to the whales,' is how Gatherall's Puffin & Whale Watch out of Bay Bulls, Newfoundland, frames it. 'We're just there to observe in a respectful manner.'

Wildlife sightings are never guaranteed. You might only see distant black outlines or blasts from blowholes. Or migrating humpbacks could perform a beautiful ballet of fin slaps, breaches, dives and vocalizations.

Here's an insider tip. Capelin (small silver fish) 'roll' with the waves onto the beaches of Newfoundland to spawn by the tens of thousands around mid-June or July. People follow the Twitter hashtag #CapelinRoll20XX to places such as Middle Cove and St Vincent's Beach to take buckets of fish home to eat. Hungry humpbacks also follow the capelin, feeding and diving close to shore in a spectacle that nobody lucky enough to witness it will ever forget.

ATLANTIC CANADA'S GALLERY SCENE

Experience vibrant spaces where art communicates culture, history and contemporary expression. By Cathy Donaldson

IT MAY SEEM surprising that art could ever blossom here.

History chronicles Canada's East Coast as a place where Indigenous populations were subjected to colonization, where Acadians were brutally forced from their homes to other regions, where countless economic storms have been weathered and where Mother Nature has not always been kind.

It's a testament to the resilience and creativity of its people that artistic expression did find fertile ground in Atlantic Canada, with the earliest known artworks being small, portable carvings fashioned by the Dorset people of present-day Newfoundland and Labrador, as well as the works of the Beothuk, Innu, Inuit, Mi'kmaq, Maliseet, Passamaquoddy and other early inhabitants of the region.

Today, artistic endeavors of all kinds flourish here, as visitors can witness at the wealth of outstanding galleries.

'We have a really strong, exciting visual arts scene,' says John Leroux, art historian and Manager of Collections and Exhibitions at the Beaverbrook Art Gallery in Fredericton, New Brunswick. 'The tradition of landscape and portraiture continues, but there is also a strong contemporary presence now. There's abstraction. There's photography. There's sculpture. There's incredible First Nations work. Visitors can prepare to be inspired.

Nova Scotia

The Art Gallery of Nova Scotia (AGNS), now with locations in Halifax and Yarmouth, houses works by prominent Canadian artists such as Alex Colville and Tom Forrestall. Temporary exhibitions highlight regional and national work.

'As in the past, artists working throughout the province today are actively negotiating the roles that they and the things they make play in shaping the story of this place,' says David Diviney, Acting Chief Curator of the AGNS. 'From painters, sculptors, weavers, printmakers, and beyond, Nova Scotia is home to some of the country's finest artists.'

'The gallery contributes to a forum for discussion around art and culture that includes input from across the region and the country, one that reaches as many potential audiences as possible,' says Diviney.

'The aim here is to insert an Atlantic Canadian accent into the larger discourse of art and culture,' he says.

One of the most popular offerings at the Halifax location of the AGNS is an exhibition of paintings by Nova Scotia folk artist Maud Lewis. Also available for a peek is her 'Painted House,' the actual one-room dwelling that served as both living and working space for Lewis and her husband, Everett. After Lewis died in 1970, the province bought the colorful house, restored it and moved it from its Digby County location to the gallery, where it remains on permanent display.

PAINTINGS
FOR SALE.

Work by an ever-growing community of dynamic Indigenous artists can also be seen at the AGNS. That includes pieces by Alan Syliboy, a Mi'kmaw artist from Millbrook, Nova Scotia. Drawing inspiration from Mi'kmaw rock drawings and quill-weaving traditions, Syliboy's colored images, crafted in acrylic and mixed media, explore themes of family, spirituality, struggle and strength. Ursula Johnson, a multidisciplinary Mi'kmaw artist based in Halifax, practices a unique fusion of traditional basket weaving and sculpture, installation and performance art.

Beaverbrook Art Gallery (p108), Fredericton

EMERGING ARTISTS FROM ATLANTIC CANADA CONTINUE TO MAKE THEIR MARK.

Halifax has many other exhibit spaces, from galleries at universities to commercial enterprises, such as the new Blue Building Gallery. More spaces are scattered throughout the province, from the Lunenburg Art Gallery and Ross Creek Centre for the Arts in Canning to the Cape Breton Centre for Craft and Design in Sydney.

New Brunswick

The stunning Beaverbrook is the crown jewel of New Brunswick's galleries. A Fredericton landmark, it features impressive exhibitions and an international collection that includes Salvador Dalí's masterpiece *Santiago El Grande*. It also holds an excellent regional collection, with works by Acadian and Indigenous creators as well as pieces by four iconic Saint John artists: Miller Brittain, Jack Humphrey, Ted Campbell and Fred Ross.

'Emerging artists from Atlantic Canada continue to make their mark in media such as painting, sculpture, ceramics and photography,' says Leroux.

'It's interesting that across the region, even in blue-collar communities such as Saint John, people have recognized for more than a century and a half that the creation of art is important,' he says. 'And it's not just the painters. Take the late Erica and Kjeld Deichmann of Saint John. They were the pioneers of modern ceramic art in Canada and are still revered today. This region has always had great pride in its artists.'

Moncton is home to the Galerie d'art Louise-et-Reuben-Cohen, the Apple Art Gallery and the Aberdeen Cultural Centre. The Owens Gallery, on the campus of Mount Allison University in Sackville, is Canada's oldest university gallery, established in 1895. Throughout the province, visitors can find a treasure trove of gallery gems, such as the Andrew and Laura McCain Art Gallery in Florenceville, and Serendipin' Art in Saint Andrews. The cities of Saint John and Fredericton both hold 'gallery hops' to highlight their wealth of visual arts establishments.

Prince Edward Island

Located in Charlottetown, Confederation Centre Art Gallery is the pride of Prince Edward Island's art community and another gem in the region.

The gallery is one of four pavilions in Confederation Centre of the Arts, a cultural complex opened in 1964. Built in Brutalist style, the complex also houses the memorial to the Charlottetown Conference, a series of meetings held in 1864 that ultimately led to the union of Canada.

'With a national mandate to develop an appreciation and understanding of Canadian visual arts, Confederation Centre Art Gallery focuses on contemporary art and an ambitious exhibition program, while also displaying historical and Indigenous art,' says gallery curator Pan Wendt.

'When visitors arrive, they will see a mix of traditional art forms such as painting, drawing, printmaking, photography and sculpture, as well as digital works, installations using various technologies, and contemporary interdisciplinary works,' says Wendt.

Maud Lewis' 'Painted House', Art Gallery of Nova Scotia (p60)

Within the gallery's historical holdings is a collection of works by Charlottetown-raised artist Robert Harris, as well as archives and objects related to the prominent artist.

'We also hold the Lucy Maud Montgomery archive, including the original manuscript of *Anne of Green Gables*,' says Wendt. 'There are also major works in the permanent collection by Jean-Paul Lemieux, Robert Houle, Edward Poitras, Teresa Marshall, Marion Wagschal and David Askevold, among many others, as well as sizeable holdings of work by PEI artists, such as Brian Burke and Erica Rutherford.'

For a good selection of works by local artists, Wendt recommends a visit to the PEI Crafts Council on Water St in Charlottetown. Meanwhile, quality crafts can be found at venues throughout the province, including at the Island Traditions Store in Richmond.

Among the province's emerging artists is Melissa Peter-Paul, a Mi'kmaw quill artist who does 'gorgeous, inventive pieces,' says Wendt.

Top-notch art-education centers combined with superb galleries have helped to cultivate the region's many talented artists. These facilities include the Nova Scotia College of Art and Design, Mount Allison University, Université de Moncton, the New Brunswick College of Craft and Design and the Grenfell Campus of Memorial University.

Rooms cultural space (p170) overlooking St John's

ONE PONY/SHUTTERSTOCK ©

Newfoundland & Labrador

The Rooms Art Gallery in St John's is the star of Newfoundland and Labrador's gallery scene. Previously known as the Art Gallery of Newfoundland and Labrador and located at the St John's Arts and Culture Centre, the gallery became part of the provincially owned Rooms in 2005. The striking facility is perched on a hill overlooking the city and also houses the Provincial Archives and Provincial Museum.

'The gallery has two floors and over 10,000 square feet of space for permanent collections and traveling exhibits,' says Mireille Eagan, contemporary art curator at The Rooms. 'As a result, we can tell stories in ways that bring the very best artists from the province and throughout the world.'

'Within the gallery's permanent collections are more than 10,000 works, primarily post-1960s pieces but also historical works,' says Eagan. Art with connections to Newfoundland and Labrador is a special focus, with major holdings of work by Christopher and Mary Pratt, Gerald Squires, David Blackwood, Reginald and Helen Parsons Shepherd, Don Wright and Anne Meredith Barry. Recently, the collecting emphasis has shifted to remedy several gaps, focusing on female, emerging, Indigenous and gender-diverse artists.

Contemporary artists of note from the province include Jordan Bennett, Jerry Evans, Billy Gauthier, Glenn Gear, Will Gill, Bushra Junaid, Mark Igloliorte, Mike Massie, Shirley Moorhouse, Meagan Musseau, Ned Pratt and Jessica Winters. New Canadians continue to enrich the cultural landscape, with artists such as Ksenia Korniewska, Nasim Makaremi Nia and Vessela Brakalova making waves with their work.

'The role of The Rooms is to support artists and to ask questions that help visitors see art – and the cultures of the province – in new ways,' says Eagan.

'We view ourselves as a place of research and learning, bringing in high-quality exhibitions and sharing our artists across the province and country,' she says. 'We also host residencies with the national parks in this province and work alongside Fogo Island Arts, the Bonavista Biennale, Gros Morne Creative, Eastern Edge Gallery and many other arts organizations that are key partners in supporting a vibrant arts community.'

INDEX

Map Pages **000**

Map Pages **000**

"With more than 65km of shorefront along the island's northern coast, Prince Edward Island National Park (p152) is all about the beach."

CAROLYN HELLER

"Nova Scotia's South Shore begins in Peggy's Cove (p65), where the red-capped lighthouse is Nova Scotia's best-known landmark."

DARCY RHYNO

Mapping data sources:
© Lonely Planet
© OpenStreetMap http://openstreetmap.org/copyright

THIS BOOK

Destination Editor
Caroline Trefler

Production Editor
Joel Cotterell

Book Designer
Hannah Blackie

Cartographer
Corey Hutchison

Assisting Editors
Sarah Bailey, Soo Hamilton, Jenna Myers, Charlotte Orr

Assisting Book Designer
Mazzy Prinsep

Cover Researcher
Lauren Egan

Thanks Ronan Abayawickrema, Imogen Banniste Anne Mason, Dar O'Connell

Paper in this book is certified against the Forest Stewardship Council™ standards. FSC™ promotes environmentally responsible, socially beneficial and economically viable management of the world's forests.

Published by Lonely Planet

7th edi
ISBN
© Lonely Planet 2024 Photographs